The
Complete Guide
to Cabins and Lodges
in America's State and
National Parks

The
Complete Guide
to Cabins and Lodges
in America's State and
National Parks

By
George Zimmermann

Illustrated by Keith Knore

LITTLE, BROWN AND COMPANY · BOSTON · TORONTO

FIRST EDITION

LIBRARY OF CONGRESS CATALOGING IN PUBLICATION DATA

Zimmermann, George, 1952-
   The complete guide to cabins and lodges in
America's state and national parks.

   Includes index.
   1. Hotels, taverns, etc.—United States—Directories.
2. National parks and reserves—United States—Direc-
tories.   3. Parks—United States—Directories.
I. Title.
TX907.Z56   1985   647′:947301   84-25065
ISBN 0-316-98808-1 (hc)
ISBN 0-316-98837-5 (pbk)

BP

Designed by Dede Cummings

Published simultaneously in Canada
by Little, Brown & Company (Canada) Limited

PRINTED IN THE UNITED STATES OF AMERICA

To Susan,
for her patience, courage, and love

CONTENTS

ILLUSTRATIONS

MAPS

DRAWINGS

ACKNOWLEDGMENTS

MY SINCERE THANKS go to the National Park Service and the parks departments of each of the fifty states for their assistance. In particular, I would like to thank the rangers and superintendents at the more than three hundred parks described in this book for their time and energy. Working with them was an absolute pleasure, and this book would not have been possible without their knowledge, guidance, and cooperation. These individuals labor so that we may relax and enjoy our natural bounty, and they deserve our gratitude and admiration.

As I learned about the history of the many parks presented in this book, I was amazed to discover how many of them — both state and national parks — have benefited from the efforts of the Civilian Conservation Corps. So, belatedly perhaps, I wish to publicly commend the thousands of young men who, during those trying Depression days of the 1930s, toiled to clear roads and trails, to build cabins, recreation buildings, and lodges, and otherwise to carve from the wilderness the parks we enjoy today. Their contribution to our park systems cannot be overstated.

INTRODUCTION

THE BLOOM OF DOGWOOD, the crash of white water surging downstream, the solitary silence of a deep evergreen forest, the fragrance of burning cedar — our parks overwhelm the senses with their beauty, power, and dignity. In a nation of largely homogeneous cities and suburbs, our state and national parks retain the diversity of mountaintop retreats in Maine and desert oases in California's Death Valley, and much more. From the famed geysers at Yellowstone to an isolated Florida peninsula jutting into the Gulf of Mexico, these parks represent endless variations of the North American landscape. Some line shimmering lakes, others trace the banks of gurgling freshwater streams. Some encompass great mountain ranges and glaciers, while still others occupy the verdant lowlands of coastal plains. Each offers its own special concoction of scenic splendor, activities, and attractions, and all await your appreciation.

The Complete Guide to Cabins and Lodges in America's State and National Parks presents more than three hundred state and national parks dispersed throughout the United States. In fact, this book contains information on each and every state and national park in America that offers overnight accommodations in either cabins or a lodge.

The goal of this book is to provide you with all of the information you need to enjoy an overnight, weekend, or week-long stay at any of these state and national parks. Turn to the section for any state that interests you, and you'll discover a description of each park's terrain, its natural highlights, and its amenities. For each location, prominent topographical features, such as waterfalls, beaches, caves, and gorges, are described and predominant flora and fauna are listed. Also included in the descriptions are activities popular at each park, which can range from swimming, boating, and fishing to hiking, golf, hang gliding, and horseshoes.

Apart from being unfamiliar with parks at any distance from home, there is another gap that keeps us from enjoying the splendor of American parks: all too often, we fail to consider cabins and lodges as alternatives to bland motels and hotels when we travel cross-country. Yet our parks stand ready to accommodate travelers in rustic log cabins, contemporary chalets, and impressive stone-and-timber lodges. These facilities run the gamut in the sophistication of their appointments, from primitive to elegant. Most are priced competitively with far less scenic accommodations; some are positively bargains.

In this book, you'll find precise information on each park's lodging, right down to its plumbing and construction materials. Using *The Complete Guide to Cabins and Lodges in America's State and National Parks*, you can select accommodations that suit your taste, budget, and itinerary.

The vast majority of these parks also serve campers. For camping information, please contact the park offices, whose addresses and phone numbers are given at the beginning of each park's description.

While every effort has been made to ensure the accuracy and completeness of each park's description, I recommend that you confirm all details by letter or telephone, particularly such items as price and seasonal availability, which may change. Many of the lodgings listed require advance reservations; they are always a good idea, even if not required. Bearing these tips in mind, you will find this guidebook a handy, up-to-date reference for hundreds of splendid destinations. I hope you will use it often.

George Zimmermann

The

Complete Guide
to Cabins and Lodges
in America's State and
National Parks

The
UNITED STATES

Northeast

Midwest

Midsouth

Southeast

$\mathcal{T}he$

NORTHEAST

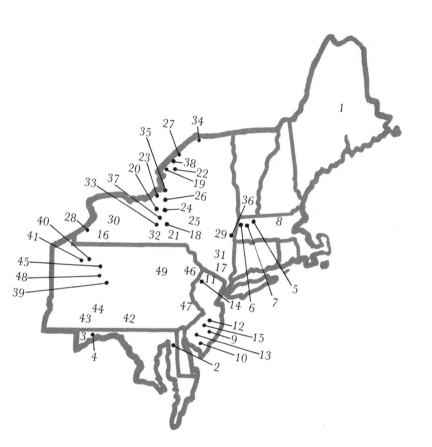

PENNSYLVANIA

39. Black Moshannon State Park
40. Clear Creek State Park
41. Cook Forest State Park
42. Cowans Gap State Park
43. Kooser State Park
44. Linn Run State Park

45. Parker Dam State Park
46. Promised Land State Park
47. Ralph Stover State Park
48. S. B. Elliott State Park
49. Worlds End State Park

Maine

STATE PARK INFORMATION:
MAINE DEPARTMENT OF CONSERVATION
BUREAU OF PARKS AND RECREATION
STATE HOUSE STATION 22
AUGUSTA, ME 04333
(207) 289-3821

TOURISM INFORMATION:
MAINE STATE DEVELOPMENT OFFICE
193 STATE STREET, STATION 59
AUGUSTA, ME 04333
(207) 289-2656

STATE BIRD: *Chickadee*
STATE MAMMAL: *Moose*
STATE TREE: *Eastern White Pine*
STATE FLOWER: *White Pine Cone and Tassel*
STATE FISH: *Landlocked Salmon*

BAXTER STATE PARK
64 BALSAM DRIVE
MILLINOCKET, ME 04462
(207) 723-5140

Former Governor Percival P. Baxter donated this vast wilderness area of two hundred thousand acres to the state of Maine. He made his first land purchase here in 1930, which included Katahdin, at 5267 feet the highest mountain in the state. In 1933, the Maine legislature designated this land as Baxter State Park and named Katahdin's summit Baxter Peak.

Forty-six mountain peaks and ridges define the park's landscape, eighteen of which exceed three thousand feet in elevation. More than 140 miles of trails traverse the park; in fact, Baxter Peak serves as the northern terminus of the famed Appalachian Trail, which stretches south for two thousand miles to Georgia.

Two distinct vegetation zones exist within Baxter State Park: the forest zone, which covers most of the acreage, and the alpine zone on the upper slopes and tableland of Mount Katahdin. Black spruce and balsam firs blanket much of the park, extending from the valleys up to the timberline. The forest floor sustains an almost continuous carpet of mosses, liverworts, and lichens.

Few places offer a better chance than does Baxter to observe and photograph its most popular animal, the moose. Though they are no longer abundant throughout Maine, considerable numbers of moose still inhabit this enormous preserve. White-tailed deer, black bear, mink, weasels, and snowshoe hares also abound.

Baxter's eleven cabins line the shore of Daicey Pond on the west side of the mountain. These eighty-year-old cabins offer wilderness-type accommodations: beds with mattresses, gas lanterns, firewood, and a table and chairs. Lodging is also available in Baxter's bunkhouses.

Canoes can be rented at Daicey Pond and at several other ponds sprinkled throughout the park. Fishing for brook trout in Baxter's clear, cold waters pleases anglers, while other visitors prefer rock climbing, backpacking, and bicycling.

Baxter State Park is eighteen miles north of Millinocket, Maine. Cabins and bunkhouses available mid-May to mid-October. Rates: cabins, $15 to $25 per night; bunkhouses, $4 per night per person. Cash and checks accepted. Reservations taken starting in January for the coming year.

Maryland

STATE PARK INFORMATION:
MARYLAND FOREST, PARK, AND WILDLIFE SERVICE
TAWES STATE OFFICE BUILDING
580 TAYLOR AVENUE
ANNAPOLIS, MD 21401
(301) 269-3771

TOURISM INFORMATION:
MARYLAND OFFICE OF TOURIST DEVELOPMENT
DEPARTMENT OF ECONOMIC AND COMMUNITY
  DEVELOPMENT
45 CALVERT STREET
ANNAPOLIS, MD 21401
(301) 269-3517

STATE BIRD: *Baltimore Oriole*
STATE TREE: *White Oak*
STATE FLOWER: *Blackeyed Susan*
STATE FISH: *Striped Bass*

ELK NECK STATE PARK
4395 TURKEY POINT ROAD
NORTH EAST, MD 21901
(301) 287-5333

Once inhabited by Susquehannock Indians, this park at the head of Chesapeake Bay received its first white visitor in 1608: none other than John Smith. (His expedition had left Jamestown and proceeded north, exploring the Elk, Northeast, Susquehanna, and Sassafras rivers.) In 1824, construction began on the Chesapeake and Delaware Canal, the waterway that would link the upper Chesapeake and Delaware bays. In 1910, the Army Corps of Engineers enlarged the canal and removed several locks, making it a free-flowing watercourse. Today, Elk Neck's visitors delight at the constant passing of oceangoing vessels.

Located astride a narrow peninsula between the Elk and Northeast rivers, this park comprises 1765 acres. Its topography ranges from sandy beaches to heavily wooded bluffs. Water and marsh plants in great variety thrive in swamps only a short distance from upland forests of oak, beech, maple, tulip, poplar, and evergreen. White-tailed deer and songbirds dwell here in great numbers. Elk Neck's extensive water areas are havens for seabirds; each spring and autumn, thousands of gulls, terns, and herons pass over and through the park.

Lifeguards oversee an expansive beach on the Northeast River, while boating enthusiasts take advantage of launching ramps and rental boats on the Elk River. Fishermen try their luck in both rivers, and crabbing is a favorite on the Susquehanna flats.

The Civilian Conservation Corps constructed nine cabins on a hilltop at Elk Neck State Park, each of which sleeps up to four people in two bedrooms. Each has a kitchen, a living room, and a screened porch, and a central washhouse provides hot and cold running water, toilets, and showers.

Elk River State Park is ten miles south of North East, Maryland, on Rte. 272. Cabins available late May to mid-October. Rates: $21 per night, $79 per week. Cash and checks accepted. For summer rentals, a lottery-type draw-

ing is held in mid-January at the Maryland Forest, Park, and Wildlife Service, Tawes State Office Building, Annapolis, Maryland 21401. (301) 269-3771. Spring and fall reservations made through Elk Neck State Park. Cabins rented only for full weeks in summer; two-night minimum the rest of the season.

HERRINGTON MANOR STATE PARK
RFD 5, Box 122
OAKLAND, MD 21550
(301) 334-9180

In 1906, John and Robert Garrett, two brothers from Baltimore, granted two thousand acres of land to their state, stipulating that a forest service be initiated for the protection of woodlands and advancement of forestry. That same year, the Maryland General Assembly established a Board of Forestry to manage the acreage. Herrington Manor State Park occupies 427 acres within Garrett State Forest in western Maryland's Appalachian region.

Recreation opportunities at Herrington Manor multiplied in the 1930s, when the Civilian Conservation Corps dammed Herrington Creek, creating a fifty-three-acre lake. CCC workers also constructed a bathhouse at the beach and ten log cabins on a wooded knoll above the lake. Since then, ten additional log cabins have been built. These twenty units sleep up to six people apiece, and have fireplaces, kitchens, baths with showers, and outdoor picnic tables and barbecue grills.

Canoes, rowboats, and paddleboats can be rented at Herrington Lake, which is stocked with game and panfish. Herrington's ten miles of trails lead hikers past forest plantations of conifers and around the lake. Another popular trail destination is soothing Swallow Falls.

Herrington Manor State Park is five miles northwest of Oakland, Maryland, on Rte. 20. Cabins available year-round. Rates: $32 to $63 per night, $137 to $315 per week. Cash and checks accepted. For summer rentals, a lottery-type drawing is held in mid-January at the Maryland Forest, Park, and Wildlife Service, Tawes State Office Building, Annapolis, Maryland 21401. (301) 269-3771.

Reservations for the rest of the year made through Herr-ington Manor State Park. Cabins rented only for full weeks in summer; two-night minimum the rest of the year.

New Germany State Park
Route 2
Grantsville, MD 21536
(301) 895-5453

New Germany's eleven log cabins, built in the early 1930s by the Civilian Conservation Corps, rest in a lush stand of pines and hemlocks, a setting reminiscent of New England. These charming accommodations sleep up to six people apiece and have kitchens, fireplaces, and baths with showers. Adjacent to each cabin are a picnic table and barbecue grill.

Western Maryland's New Germany State Park marks the location of a once-prosperous commercial center, noted for its numerous sawmills and a gristmill. A thirteen-acre lake, formed by a log dam, provided water pressure to operate the mills. Swauger's Mill Dam bears the name of John Swauger, who built a sawmill and gristmill here in the mid-1800s. Swauger's gristmill ground wheat and buckwheat until 1859, and his sawmill remained active until 1890.

The park lies within the boundaries of the Savage River State Forest, Maryland's largest. Trees include red and white oak, wild cherry, sugar and red maple, birch, beech, basswood, white pine, hemlock, tulip, poplar, and hickory.

Fishing is a favorite in New Germany's small lake, which is stocked with trout, and swimmers enjoy the beach and bathhouse. Rental rowboats and paddleboats round out the lakefront amenities. New Germany's hiking trails double as cross-country ski trails during snow months.

New Germany State Park is five miles southeast of Grantsville, Maryland, on New Germany Road. Cabins available year-round. Rates: $32 to $63 per night, $137 to $367 per week. Cash and checks accepted. For summer rentals, a lottery-type drawing is held in mid-January at the Maryland Forest, Park, and Wildlife Service, Tawes

State Office Building, Annapolis, Maryland 21401. (301) 269-3771. Reservations for the rest of the year made through New Germany State Park. Cabins rented only for full weeks in summer; two-night minimum the rest of the year.

Massachusetts

~~~~

STATE PARK INFORMATION:
MASSACHUSETTS DEPARTMENT OF ENVIRONMENTAL
 MANAGEMENT
DIVISION OF FORESTS AND PARKS
100 CAMBRIDGE STREET
BOSTON, MA 02202
(617) 727-3180

TOURISM INFORMATION:
MASSACHUSETTS DEPARTMENT OF COMMERCE AND
 DEVELOPMENT
DIVISION OF TOURISM
100 CAMBRIDGE STREET
BOSTON, MA 02202
(617) 727-3201

STATE BIRD: *Chickadee*
STATE MAMMAL: *Right Whale*
STATE TREE: *American Elm*
STATE FLOWER: *Mayflower*
STATE FISH: *Cod*

MOHAWK TRAIL STATE FOREST
P.O. Box 7
CHARLEMONT, MA 01339
(413) 339-5504

More than six thousand acres of wooded mountain ridges, deep gorges, two excellent trout streams — Cold and Deerfield rivers — these are but some of the natural attractions at this northwestern Massachusetts state forest. A Mohawk warpath dating from the French and Indian Wars passes through the area; Mohawks used the trail to travel between what are now New York and Connecticut.

Mohawk Trail proudly displays one of the finest pine stands in the Northeast, with many trees soaring to heights of more than one hundred feet. Spruce, hemlock, gray birch, maple, oak, and beech fill out valleys and hillsides, and mountain laurel, wild rose, raspberry, and strawberry flourish. Miles of hiking trails rise through woodlands to magnificent overlooks on Todd Mountain and Hawks Mountain. Picnic areas line the banks of the Cold River, which is also the site of a swimming beach.

Mohawk's four fifty-year-old cabins occupy the south slope of Todd Mountain. Constructed by the Civilian Conservation Corps, two of these log cabins have a single room, and the others have three rooms. Each comes equipped with a fireplace or wood stove, an icebox, running water, electricity, and outdoor latrine, plus a picnic table and barbecue grill. In winter, a substantial hike may be necessary to reach these cabins.

Mohawk Trail State Forest is two miles west of Charlemont, Massachusetts, on Rte. 2. Cabins available year-round. Rates: $8 to $10 per night. Cash accepted. Reservations recommended six months in advance for fall. Cabins reserved only for full weeks in summer, two-night minimum the rest of the year.

MOUNT GREYLOCK STATE
  RESERVATION
P.O. Box 138
LANESBOROUGH, MA 01237
(413) 499-4262

BASCOM LODGE
P.O. Box 394
LANESBOROUGH, MA 01237
(413) 743-1591

Mount Greylock's summit reaches an elevation of 3491 feet, the highest spot in Massachusetts. Some believe the mountain takes its name from the gray, frosty aspect of its peak; it often receives the state's first snowfall. Others claim it bears the name of a legendary Chief Greylock, leader of the Woronoco Indians. In either case, Mount Greylock was definitely not the first name for this imposing edifice in western Massachusetts — before 1819 settlers called it Saddle Ball Mountain, a name inspired by its appearance from the south.

By the late 1800s, loggers had stripped timber from the mountain's entire east face, resulting in serious erosion and landslides. Fortunately, in 1885 the Greylock Park Association purchased four hundred acres around the summit, land that was later granted to the state with the stipulation that sufficient additional acreage be acquired to protect Greylock and its adjacent peaks forever. Today the park encompasses more than fifteen thousand acres.

Bascom Lodge, atop Mount Greylock, sleeps twenty-four people in six dormitory-style rooms, which share two community baths. Built by the Civilian Conservation Corps in the 1930s, this stone-and-log lodge features wide beams, enormous fireplaces, and a cheerful dining room.

A variety of birds nest on and around Mount Greylock, including thrushes, grouse, and owls. Hawks can be seen riding the air currents that swirl around the summit, while deer, bear, bobcat, raccoon, snowshoe hare, and woodchuck roam the forests. Northern hardwoods populate the mountain's lower reaches, including birch, beech, and ash. At the peak, weather has taken its toll on red spruce and balsam trees, which have been dwarfed and gnarled by the wind.

This park's thirty-five miles of hiking trails include a section of the famed Appalachian Trail and a path to a lovely waterfall, Money Brook Falls. The top of the War

Memorial Tower on Mount Greylock's summit presents an unrivaled vista of the surrounding mountain valleys and a view of five states.

Mount Greylock State Reservation is four miles north of Pittsfield, Massachusetts, on Rte. 7. Bascom Lodge open mid-May to mid-October. Rates: $8 per night per person. Cash and checks accepted. Reservations recommended two months in advance.

SAVOY MOUNTAIN STATE FOREST
RFD 2
NORTH ADAMS, MA 01247
(413) 663-8469

In the nineteenth century, a dam on Bulingame Brook furnished waterpower for a tannery and sawmill. Today, hiking, camping, fishing, and just appreciating nature constitute the business of this 10,500-acre state forest in northwest Massachusetts. Savoy Mountain consists of craggy peaks, rushing streams, and half a dozen lakes and ponds. Along the trails, the eighty-foot plunge of Tannery Falls impresses hikers, while Borden Mountain's fire tower offers a fine lookout on forests of fir, spruce, pine, beech, oak, and maple. An ice storm more than forty years ago created the stunted Crooked Forest, a unique natural phenomenon.

Trout, perch, and sunfish can be taken from Savoy's ponds and streams, which also hold stocked trout. Deer and beaver amble through the forest, beneath numerous species of game birds and songbirds. Smoke rises from the many sugarhouses once the first spring thaw starts the maple sap running.

Savoy Mountain State Forest has three one-room cabins, built by the Civilian Conservation Corps in the 1930s. Constructed of rough native logs, they sleep up to four people apiece on fold-up cots, and come equipped with picnic tables, iceboxes, drinking water, outdoor latrines, and either a wood stove or a fireplace. Visitors cook on outdoor grills and must supply their own firewood. These cabins can be reached only as weather permits, and winter hikes of half a mile are typical.

Savoy Mountain State Forest is half a mile east of

North Adams, Massachusetts, off Rte. 2. Cabins available year-round. Rates: $8 per night. Cash accepted. Reservations taken up to six months in advance, recommended six months in advance for fall. Cabins reserved only for full weeks in summer, two-night minimum for the rest of the year.

WILLARD BROOK STATE FOREST
P.O. BOX 111
WEST TOWNSEND, MA 01474
(617) 597-8802

The fall foliage is spectacular here! Willard Brook comprises gently rolling hills forested with hardwoods and hemlocks, trimmed with a dash of pine. Mountain laurel, azalea, dogwood, and scatterings of shadblow accent the woods. One of the best trout streams in eastern Massachusetts, Squannacook River, flows from west to east through this five-thousand-acre park near the New Hampshire border.

Civilian Conservation Corps workers erected Willard Brook's four cabins in the 1930s, using logs cut from the surrounding forest. Heated by wood stoves or fireplaces, they have one or three rooms, and all cooking takes place on outdoor barbecue grills. In winter, weather restricts road access, and visitors must hike in at least half a mile to reach the cabins.

Diverse wildlife inhabits this state forest, including cottontail rabbits, showshoe hares, gray squirrels, fox, raccoon, deer, ruffed grouse, and various waterfowl. Hikers and cross-country skiers take advantage of the many old roads that crisscross the tranquil terrain.

A favorite picnic spot is at picturesque Trap Falls, a fifteen-foot waterfall on Trap Falls Brook. Williard Brook, which spills into Damon Pond, teems with stocked trout and has a swimming beach and bathhouse. Each spring, canoeists take to the Squannacook River.

Willard Brook State Forest is on Rte. 119 near Ashby, Massachusetts. Cabins available year-round. Rates: $8 to $10 per night. Cash accepted. Reservations recommended two months in advance. Cabins reserved only for full weeks in summer, two-night minimum the rest of the year.

New Jersey

STATE PARK INFORMATION:
NEW JERSEY DEPARTMENT OF ENVIRONMENTAL
   PROTECTION
DIVISION OF PARKS AND FORESTRY
CN 404
TRENTON, NJ 08625
(609) 292-2797

TOURISM INFORMATION:
NEW JERSEY DIVISION OF TRAVEL AND TOURISM
CN 826
TRENTON, NJ 08625
(609) 292-2470

STATE BIRD: *Eastern Goldfinch*
STATE MAMMAL: *Horse*
STATE TREE: *Red Oak*
STATE FLOWER: *Purple Violet*

BASS RIVER STATE FOREST
BOX 118
NEW GRETNA, NJ 08224
(609) 296-1114

Bass River has the most varied overnight accommodations in the New Jersey park system, including cabins, shelters, and lean-tos. Set in a stand of oak and pine on the north shore of Lake Absegami, six half-century-old cabins display rough, wood-plank construction. Each has two bedrooms with double-deck bunk beds, a living room with stone fireplace, a full kitchen, and a bath with shower.

Also on the north shore stand six shelters, each containing two small bunk rooms and a living room heated by a Franklin stove. All cooking takes place on outdoor fireplaces, and the shelters do not have electricity. Six fully enclosed lean-tos line the lakefront, within walking distance of hot showers and a laundry room. The lean-tos come with picnic tables and fire rings.

This 18,208-acre state forest lies twenty-five miles north of the boardwalk at Atlantic City. Higher-level vegetation here consists of pitch pine, white oak, scarlet oak, sassafras, and holly. Common understory plants include mountain laurel, sheep laurel, highbush blackberry, bracken fern, huckleberry, and wintergreen.

A self-guided nature trail begins near the eastern arm of Lake Absegami, passing by a cross-section of typical pine and oak woods and a small white-cedar bog. While hiking the trail, you might encounter white-tailed deer, raccoons, or opossums. Overhead you may catch a glimpse of yellowthroats, pine warblers, robins, black-capped chickadees, and barn swallows.

Nearby attractions include the beaches and saltwater fishing at the New Jersey shore and crabbing at Tuckerton, New Jersey, some ten miles away. Riding stables in the area offer trail rides.

Bass River State Forest is twenty-five miles north of Atlantic City, New Jersey, off Rte. 9 and the Garden State Parkway. Cabins and camp shelters available April through October, lean-tos rented year-round. Rates: cabins, $30 per night; shelters, $15 per night; lean-tos, $10 per night. Cash and checks accepted. Reservations taken from in-

state residents starting in January, from nonresidents in March. Cabins and shelters rented only for full weeks in summer, two-night minimum the rest of the season.

Lean-to, Belleplain State Forest, New Jersey

BELLEPLAIN STATE FOREST
P.O. BOX 450
WOODBINE, NJ 08270
(609) 861-2404

Just thirty-five minutes north of the Victorian resort community of Cape May, New Jersey, and forty-five minutes southwest of the casinos and nightlife in Atlantic City, Belleplain State Forest comprises more than eleven thousand acres of young pine, oak, and southern white cedar in New Jersey's Pine Barrens. Beautiful native holly trees and masses of laurel, magnificent in bloom, line its roadsides and hiking trails.

This state forest centers on twenty-six-acre Lake Nummy, an abandoned cranberry bog. Civilian Conservation Corps workers toiled here during the Depression, dredging up by hand (and later by steam shovel) vegetation mired in the bog. Once large cedar logs were removed from the bog, the Corps milled them for lath, board, and shingles. They then dammed the stream feeding the lowlands, creating the splendid "cedar water" lake. Lake Nummy bears the name of the last Lenape Indian sachem (chief) to rule these forests; his remains are interred on Nummy Island.

Lake Nummy's north shore has a swimming beach, bathhouse, and playground equipment. Anglers fish Lake Nummy and the sixty-five-acre East Creek Lake for largemouth bass, pickerel, catfish, sunfish, perch, and (occasionally) smallmouth bass. Sailing is a favorite activity on East Creek Lake, and canoes can be rented at Lake Nummy. Belleplain is endowed with miles of trails and old sand roads suitable for hiking. Various oceanside beaches and fine restaurants are within a half hour's drive of this state forest.

Belleplain State Forest's lean-tos are wooden, one-room structures whose fronts are enclosed by insect screens in summer and clear acrylic "glass" in winter. Each features a picnic table and outdoor fireplace, plus an indoor wood heating stove for those cold winter nights.

On East Creek Lake's southern shore rests a former hunting lodge now available for groups of up to twenty-four visitors. This two-story, concrete-block structure has dormitory-style sleeping rooms, plus two small bedrooms, a large kitchen, a screened porch, and two bathrooms. A small beach and dock await at the lakefront.

Belleplain State Forest is two miles west of Woodbine, New Jersey, on Rte. 550. Lodge and lean-tos available year-round. Rates: lodge, $75 per night; lean-tos, $10 per night. Cash and checks accepted. Reservations taken starting in January for coming year. Lodge rented only for full weeks in summer, two-night minimum the rest of the year.

HIGH POINT STATE PARK
RR 4, Box 287
SUSSEX, NJ 07461
(201) 875-4800

In New Jersey's extreme northwest corner, along the crest of the Kittatinny Mountains and the Appalachian Trail, lies 14,056-acre High Point State Park. From the New York state line, High Point stretches southwesterly for eight miles, where it joins Stokes State Forest.

High Point Monument dominates the summit of Kittatinny Ridge, the highest elevation in New Jersey. This 220-foot monument, faced with New Hampshire granite, measures 34 feet square at its base and rests at 1803 feet above sea level. Westward across the Delaware River valley is an impressive view of Pennsylvania, with the Poconos looming in the distance. Sawmill Lake can be seen from atop the monument, while Lake Marcia's crystal-clear waters shimmer in the foreground.

High Point's two forty-year-old frame cabins occupy a thick woods at Lake Steenykill. Shaded by a mixture of hardwoods and hemlocks, highlighted with ferns and mountain laurel, these cabins sleep six people apiece in three bedrooms. Both have hot and cold running water, kitchen appliances, and fireplaces.

Cedar Swamp, practically an oasis of virgin woodland, supports large hemlocks, white pine, black spruce, and — surprisingly at this fifteen-hundred-foot elevation — a fine stand of mature white cedar. A sparkling beach on Lake Marcia invites bathers; this spring-fed, twenty-acre lake nearly sixteen hundred feet above sea level is cool and invigorating. Fishermen try their luck in all of High Point's lakes, and often bring home fine catches of sunfish, bass, and catfish. Sawmill Lake is stocked with trout each spring.

High Point State Park is seven miles north of Sussex, New Jersey, on Rte. 23. Cabins available mid-May to mid-October. Rates: $30 per night. Cash and checks accepted. In-state cabin reservations taken beginning in January, nonresident reservations starting in March. Cabins rented only for full weeks in summer, two-night minimum the rest of the season.

LEBANON STATE FOREST
NEW LISBON, NJ 08064
(609) 726-1191

In central New Jersey's historic Pine Barrens, Lebanon State Forest derives its name from the Lebanon Glass Works, established in 1862. Glassmaking was once a major industry here, thanks to readily available sand, wood for charcoal, and other raw materials. The fires eventually "burned out" when the supply of wood was exhausted, and operations were abandoned in 1867.

In the more than one hundred years since, forests have regenerated, and forestry practices have aided in preventing and controlling forest fires — the scourge of the Pine Barrens for centuries. Along Lebanon's streams there now lie acres of swampland covered with crowded stands of Atlantic white cedar, often as dense as four thousand trees per acre.

Three cabins in this park line a trail along the shores of Pakim Pond. This five-acre pond, developed from a former cranberry bog, takes its name from the Lenape Indian word for cranberry. Visitors loll, sun, and swim at Pakim Pond's popular beach.

Constructed of rough-hewn timber, Lebanon's forty-year-old cabins have kitchens with running water, electric appliances, and stone fireplaces. Each has a single living / sleeping room, with two double bunk beds. The cabins are equipped with half bathrooms; showers are available at a nearby bathhouse.

Miles of sand roads wander through the state forest, and canoes can be rented on streams throughout the area. Batona Hiking Trail, a well-marked footpath, starts in Lebanon State Forest and concludes at Evan's Bridge in Wharton State Forest, some forty miles away.

Lebanon State Forest is four miles south of New Lisbon, New Jersey, on Rte. 72. Cabins available April through October. Rates: $20 per night. Cash and checks accepted. Reservations from in-state residents taken starting in January, nonresident reservations beginning in March. Cabins rented only for full weeks in summer, two-night minimum the rest of the season.

Parvin State Park
RD 1, Box 374
Elmer, NJ 08318
(609) 692-7039

During World War II, while American servicemen and women relaxed at Atlantic City, Parvin State Park housed German prisoners of war some forty miles away. In 1952, Parvin once again assumed an unusual assignment, sheltering Kalmyck immigrants fleeing Soviet persecution in Siberia.

This 1125-acre park in southwestern New Jersey consists of upland woods and two man-made lakes, Parvin Lake and Thundergust Lake. A small stream, Muddy Run, feeds the larger Parvin Lake and eventually joins the Maurice River on its way to Delaware Bay. Early settlers dammed Muddy Run and Thundergust Brook to supply waterpower for gristmills and sawmills; one was owned by a family named Parvin.

Parvin State Park's Natural Area comprises dogwood, laurel, holly, magnolia, wild azalea, and numerous other flowering plants. Bird life abounds here, particularly during migrations. Several miles of foot trails meander through cedar swamps, holly groves, pine forests, and laurel thickets.

Visitors swim in both of this park's lakes, and rowboats and canoes can be rented from a livery on Parvin Lake's north shore. Fishermen are rewarded with stringers full of largemouth and calico bass, eastern chain pickerel, channel catfish, and carp. Golfers enjoy the nearby Centerton Golf Club.

Parvin's fifteen CCC-era cabins line the northwest shore of Thundergust Lake, under oaks, hickories, dogwoods, pines, cedars, and maples. These cabins share a private beach and accommodate up to four people apiece. Each has two bedrooms, kitchen appliances, hot and cold running water, and a bath with shower. All come with outdoor terraces; half have fireplaces, and the rest use wood stoves. Boat landings and outdoor barbecue grills also serve the cabins.

Parvin State Park is six miles west of Vineland, New Jersey, on Rte. 540. Cabins available April through

October. Rates: $20 per night. Cash and checks accepted. Reservations taken from in-state residents starting in January, from nonresidents beginning in March. Cabins rented only for full weeks in summer, two-night minimum the rest of the season.

STOKES STATE FOREST
RR 2, Box 260
BRANCHVILLE, NJ 07826
(201) 948-3820

This fifteen-thousand-acre forest in northwestern New Jersey straddles a transition zone, where a central forest of oak and hickory begins to give way to a northern forest of beech, birch, maple, and hemlock. Long ago, Indians often set fire to woodlands here to facilitate hunting and farming. At the dawn of the Industrial Revolution, the forest's exploitation continued with the conversion of wood into charcoal — the principal source of energy used to smelt iron ore in blast furnaces.

Today, Stokes's woods, streams, lakes, and ridges offer a variety of habitats for wildlife. Kittatinny Ridge, with its loose rocks, ledges, and bold outcrops, provides den sites for copperheads and eastern rattlesnakes. Located along the Atlantic flyway, this forest also serves as a resting area for thousands of migratory birds — predators and geese can be observed each fall from Sunrise Mountain, the forest's highest peak. In the valleys, shallow beaver ponds along Flatbrook and its tributaries offer a haven for flycatchers, herons, woodpeckers, and their prey.

Stocked annually by the state, Flatbrook presents some of New Jersey's finest trout fishing. Stony Lake's clear mountain waters attract swimmers to its beach, and small, nonmotorized boats can be launched at Lake Ocquittunk. Tillman Brook slides down long, well-worn channels and tumbles over huge boulders in delicate cascades.

Ten of Stokes's eleven wood cabins, built in the mid-1930s, sleep up to four people apiece; one accommodates up to eight. In the small cabins, one large room houses two single beds and a double-deck bunk bed, kitchen appliances, a sink with cold running water, and a fireplace.

A pit-type toilet with a separate outdoor entrance adjoins each cabin.

Stokes's largest cabin, accommodating up to twelve people, has two second-floor bunk rooms and a ground-floor living area, kitchen, and screened porch. The eleven single-story cabins line Lake Ocquittunk; the two-story cabin is a mile from the lakefront.

Stokes State Forest is five miles north of Branchville, New Jersey, on Rte. 206. Cabins available April to mid-December. Rates: $20 to $55 per night. Cash and checks accepted. Reservations taken from in-state residents starting in January, from nonresidents beginning in March. Cabins rented only for full weeks in summer, two-night minimum the rest of the season.

WHARTON STATE FOREST
RD 4, BATSTO
HAMMONTON, NJ 08037
(609) 561-0024

The Pine Barrens, a relatively level section of coastal plain in central New Jersey between the piedmont and the tidal strip, is so ecologically unique that it has been designated an International Biosphere Reserve. Indians apparently held in awe the strange, wild beauty of the region, yet there is evidence that they stayed away from here when possible. Even today, not unlike a desert, it both attracts and repels.

Flying over it or driving the long straight highways that transect it might give the impression of a vast wasteland. But once in the terrain — atop Apple Pie Hill fire tower, for example — the outlook to the four horizons reveals an unbroken carpet of forest, twinkling with the glimmer of small ponds. All seasons delight in the Pine Barrens: spring and summer with the beauty of countless bog flowers and the fragrance of sun-warmed pine and cedar, autumn with a colorful palette on a background of deep green, and winter with its snow-streaked, stark aspect.

Four rivers amble through this vast state forest: the Mullica, Batsto, Wading, and Oswego. Visitors swim at the beach on Atsion Lake, site of boat rentals and launching ramps (nonmotorized craft only).

A splendid pine forest engulfs Wharton's nine fifty-year-old cabins. Built of rough cedar logs, these simply furnished structures have bunk beds in two or three bedrooms, screened porches, electric kitchen appliances, and baths with showers. Plenty of firewood fuels their fireplaces.

Batsto Furnace, constructed in 1766, furnished munitions for both the Revolutionary War and the War of 1812. Ocean schooners once arrived here via the Mullica River to take on cargoes of water pipes for the new nation's cities. Today, tours of Batsto, located within Wharton State Forest, explore this community's many historic buildings, where local crafts-people demonstrate pioneer skills.

Wharton State Forest is eight miles east of Hammonton, New Jersey, on Rte. 542. Cabins available April through October. Rates: four-bunk cabins, $20 per night; eight-bunk cabins, $40 per night. Cash and checks accepted. Reservations taken from in-state residents starting in January, from nonresidents beginning in March. Cabins rented only for full weeks in summer, two-night minimum the rest of the season.

New York

~~~

STATE PARK INFORMATION:
NEW YORK STATE OFFICE OF PARKS, RECREATION
   AND HISTORIC PRESERVATION
EMPIRE STATE PLAZA
ALBANY, NY 12238
(518) 474-0456

TOURISM INFORMATION:
NEW YORK STATE DEPARTMENT OF COMMERCE
ONE COMMERCE PLAZA
ALBANY, NY 12245
(800) 225-5697 (calls from northeastern states)
(518) 474-4116 (all other calls)

STATE BIRD: *Bluebird*
STATE MAMMAL: *Beaver*
STATE TREE: *Sugar Maple*
STATE FLOWER: *Rose*
STATE FISH: *Brook Trout*

ALLEGANY STATE PARK
RD 1
SALAMANCA, NY 14779
(716) 354-2535 (park office)
(716) 354-2545 (cabins — Red House area)
(716) 354-2182 (cabins — Quaker area)

Southwestern New York's Allegany State Park encompasses sixty-five thousand acres of mountains and ridges within an oxbow of the Allegheny River. It is bordered on the east, north, and west by the Seneca Indians' Allegany Reservation, and on the south by Pennsylvania's Allegheny National Forest. Two types of timber predominate in this vast preserve. North- and west-facing slopes support northern hardwood forests of beech, sugar maple, red maple, and hemlock. Oaks, hickories, cucumber trees, and tulip trees overlie south- and east-facing slopes. Both types are interspersed with black cherry, white ash, yellow birch, black birch, and bigtooth aspen.

A favorite attraction here is a twenty-foot-high ledge called Bear Caves; the caves consist of cracks in huge blocks of conglomerate rock. Though bears do not inhabit the caves, black bears are conspicuous residents of the park.

Allegany features three man-made lakes: Science Lake, Red House Lake, and Quaker Lake. Anglers fish all three, plus numerous streams and beaver ponds, for bass, perch, sunfish, bullheads, and stocked trout. Red House and Quaker lakes have beaches open in summer, and nonmotorized boats ply their waters. Rowboats and bicycles can be rented at Red House. The state park also offers seventy-five miles of hiking trails, picnic areas, playing fields, and tennis courts. Hunting for deer, turkey, and small game is permitted during designated seasons.

Allegany State Park has 374 cabins for overnight guests — by far the most cabins in any New York state park. Standard equipment in these primitive cabins includes cots or bunks with mattresses for four to six people, and tables and chairs. Most are equipped with refrigerators, ranges, and gas or wood heaters. Many of these one- and two-room wood cabins are winterized, but none has indoor plumbing; pit toilets, community bathhouses, and water taps are nearby.

Allegany State Park is five miles west of Salamanca, New York, on Rte. 17. Cabins available year-round. Rates: $16 to $41 per night, $62 to $164 per week. Cash and checks accepted. Reservations taken starting in October for the coming year. Summer reservations recommended in January; determined by lotteries held mid-January to mid-March; taken on first-come, first-served basis after mid-March. Cabins rented only for full weeks in summer; two-night minimum the rest of the year.

Bear Mountain Inn, Bear Mountain State Park, New York

BEAR MOUNTAIN STATE PARK / HARRIMAN STATE PARK
BEAR MOUNTAIN, NY 10911
(914) 786-2701 *(regional office)*
(914) 786-2731 *(Bear Mountain Inn)*
(914) 351-2360 *(Harriman cabins)*

Just an hour's drive north of midtown New York City, these adjoining state parks are part of a chain of parks and historic sites on the west bank of the Hudson River, in both New York and New Jersey. With a combined area of more than fifty thousand acres, the two parks provide tranquil mountain retreats for those weary of the day-to-day grind of city life. The Palisades Interstate Parkway stretches invitingly from the George Washington

Bridge to Bear Mountain. During summer months, the excursion boat *Dayliner* steams daily from Manhattan up the Hudson to the parks.

Blessed with a score of lakes, these parks feature swimming beaches, boating, fishing, and just about every other form of water-oriented recreation. In winter, skiing, ice skating, and sledding are the preferred activities. Miles of trails wander the hilly woodlands, which turn brilliant with color in autumn.

Bear Mountain Inn, constructed of stone and timber in 1916, four stone lodges that date from the 1930s, and modern Overlook Lodge offer a total of sixty-one guest rooms at Bear Mountain State Park. Set on Hessian Lake, a deep, clear mountain lake popular for fishing and boating, the inn offers fine dining and a handsome lobby with hardwood floors, exposed wood ceiling and beams, and a massive stone fireplace.

Harriman State Park's forty-two cabins occupy ten acres of Lake Sebago's shoreline, which is heavily blanketed with oaks and maples. A beach serves the forty-five-year-old wood cabins, which contain cots with mattresses, two-burner gas stoves, and refrigerators. Each cabin has an outdoor fireplace and picnic table, but no running water. Bathhouses and pit toilets are nearby.

Points of interest in the area include the Franklin D. Roosevelt home at Hyde Park, Brotherhood Winery, and Washington Irving's home. The U.S. Military Academy at West Point is six miles north of Bear Mountain Inn. For a spectacular view of the Hudson highlands, take Perkins Memorial Drive to the top of Bear Mountain and climb Perkins Memorial Tower.

Bear Mountain State Park and Harriman State Park are off the Palisades Interstate Parkway, thirty-eight miles north of Manhattan. Cabins available mid-April to mid-October, lodges open year-round. Rates: cabins, $26 per night, $102 per week; lodge rooms, $50 per night for two people. Cash and checks accepted for cabins; cash, checks, Visa, and MasterCard for lodge rooms. Reservations for lodge rooms taken up to six months in advance. For cabins, summer reservations recommended in January; determined by lotteries held mid-January to mid-March;

taken on a first-come, first-served basis after mid-March. Cabins rented only for full weeks in summer; two-night minimum the rest of the season.

BUTTERMILK FALLS STATE PARK
RD 5
ITHACA, NY 14850
(607) 273-5761

Buttermilk Creek descends more than five hundred feet in a series of cascades and foaming rapids, while Pinnacle Rock, a spirelike stone formation, towers forty feet above the center of the stream. A natural pool at the base of Buttermilk Falls (one of ten major waterfalls in this park) provides swimmers with the feel of an old swimming hole. Upstream, a scenic trail circles Lake Treman.

Buttermilk's seven, fifty-year-old cabins are definitely rustic, with their wavy wooden exteriors and unfinished interiors. Oak, maple, beech, ironwood, hemlock, and white pine trees guard the cabins, which cuddle a hillside. Each of these one-room units has four beds with mattresses, a refrigerator, and a stove, plus an outdoor grill and picnic table. Running water and a bathhouse are nearby.

The earliest evidence of human habitation near Buttermilk Falls is the site of the Indian village of Coreorgonel — twenty-five log cabins once were surrounded by cultivated fields and plum and apple orchards. The Indians fled before the arrival of General John Sullivan's Continental Army, and the village was burned to the ground on September 4, 1779.

During the first part of the twentieth century, the area around Ithaca in western New York blossomed as a center of the movie industry. Its glacier-carved gorges and delightful glens served as backgrounds for many early films. The Dewitt Historical Society of Ithaca, housed in historic Clinton House, has exhibits that depict the intriguing history of this lush countryside.

Buttermilk Falls State Park is one mile south of Ithaca, New York, on Rte. 13. Cabins available mid-May to mid-October. Rates: $16 per night, $62 per week. Cash and *checks accepted. Summer reservations recommended in January; determined by lotteries held mid-January through mid-March; taken on a first-come, first-served basis after mid-March. Cabins rented only for full weeks in summer; two-night minimum the rest of the season.*

CANOE-PICNIC POINT STATE PARK
c/o CEDAR POINT STATE PARK
ROUTE 12
CLAYTON, NY 13624
(315) 654-2522

So you'd like to spend a couple of nights on a quiet island in the Saint Lawrence River? Then Canoe-Picnic Point State Park is just for you. Set on Grindstone Island in the Saint Lawrence, between New York and Canada, this park offers five thirty-year-old cabins built with rough-cut lumber and studding. Each accommodates up to four people and is equipped with a refrigerator and indoor plumbing. Outdoor fireplaces constitute the only cooking facilities. The cabins occupy a hillside on Canoe Point's northwest bank, are dwarfed by oak, walnut, and poplar trees, and have a view of the river.

Visitors travel to the island by boat, often departing from nearby Grass Point Marina or Wellesley Island. The park consists of rolling, stony terrain broken by cliffs, high slopes, and rock formations. Fishing is probably the most popular pastime here; anglers enjoy fine catches of pike, perch, and bass. Salmon wait to be reeled in several miles south of the park. Swimming is a favorite at nearby Grass Point Beach, and launching ramps are available throughout the area. Other activities include tours of Boldt Castle (on Heart Island), historic sites, and museums, tennis, excursion boat trips, and guided fishing expeditions.

Canoe-Picnic Point State Park is on Grindstone Island in the Saint Lawrence River, six miles northeast of Clayton, New York. Cabins available late May to mid-September. Rates: $16 per night, $62 per week. Cash and checks accepted. Summer reservations recommended in January; determined by lotteries held mid-January to mid-

March; taken on a first-come, first-served basis after mid-March. Cabins rented only for full weeks in summer; two-night minimum the rest of the season.

Cayuga Lake State Park
RD 3
Seneca Falls, NY 13148
(315) 568-5163

Fourteen cabins grouped on a plateau overlook the northern end of long, slender Cayuga Lake, in western New York's Finger Lakes region. These lakes lie in very deep basins, troughs gouged by glaciers. Since the ice retreated, forest has reclaimed the land, but there are fewer plant species than in englaciated areas to the south. Principal trees in this north-temperate forest include beech, maple, hemlock, birch, oak, hickory, and white pine.

Each of Cayuga Lake's cabins has kitchen appliances and an outdoor barbecue grill and picnic table. The thirteen smaller cabins sleep up to four people; the large one can accommodate up to six, and has the added ambience of a wood-burning fireplace. Constructed of wood, these fifty-year-old cabins have unfinished interiors, except for the large cabin, which has a partially finished interior. Hot showers, toilets, and running water await at the washhouse.

Tall oaks shade the sweeping lawns and beaches at Cayuga Lake, which is popular for swimming, fishing, and boating. The longest of the Finger Lakes, Cayuga Lake spans more than forty miles from north to south. Steam-powered paddleboats once brought vacationers from Ithaca and Aurora, New York, to a privately owned resort on this site, Wayne's Grove. During the late 1800s and early 1900s, crowds gathered at a three-story pavilion at Wayne's Grove for entertainment and socializing.

Several miles south of the park is the birthplace of the Iroquois chief Red Jacket; a granite monument honors this Indian orator and statesman. Also in the area is the Women's Rights National Historic Park, including the National Women's Hall of Fame and a museum. After touring the museum, you can stop by a local winery for a peek at wine-making and a sample of their product.

Cayuga Lake State Park is three miles east of Seneca Falls, New York, on Rte. 89. Cabins available mid-May to mid-October. Rates: $16 to $30 per night, $62 to $118 per week. Cash and checks accepted. Summer reservations recommended in January; determined by lotteries held mid-January to mid-March; taken on a first-come, first-served basis after mid-March. Cabins rented only for full weeks in summer; two-night minimum the rest of the season.

CHENANGO VALLEY STATE PARK
RD 2, Box 593
CHENANGO FORKS, NY 13746
(607) 648-5251

Chenango Valley State Park has two small lakes, and between the lakes, an esker — a narrow ridge of sand, gravel, and boulders deposited by a glacial stream. The lakes too have their origin in the glaciers that once covered this region with a thick layer of ice. As the climate warmed and glaciers melted, the meltwaters created depressions in the landscape called kettles. Both of Chenango Valley's lakes fill kettles.

Located in south-central New York, not far from the Pennsylvania border, Chenango Valley State Park has twenty-four two- and three-room cabins, each capable of sleeping up to four people. The cabins in this 1071-acre park have electricity, fireplaces or wood stoves, kitchen appliances, cold running water, and indoor toilets (hot showers available at a nearby bathhouse). For that summer cookout, take advantage of your private outdoor grill and picnic table.

The most popular spot on the shore of Chenango Lake is the swimming beach, where a snack bar and dining plaza overlook the water. Rowboats can be rented at this lake, which is stocked with rainbow, brown, and brook trout. Canoeing is a favorite on the Chenango River, which borders the park and offers miles of lush waterways. Other attractions include an eighteen-hole golf course and bicycling on the many paved roads.

A portion of the old Chenango Canal is still visible from several park locations. This canal, built in the 1830s, was a spur of the canal that connected Norwich and Binghamton. Fossil hunters search Page Brook for seashell fossils, which date from the era when shallow seas covered this terrain. Other points of interest in the area include the Baseball Hall of Fame at Cooperstown, New York, and the Corning Glass Center.

Chenango Valley State Park is twelve miles north of Binghamton, New York, on Rte. 369. Cabins available mid-April to late October. Rates: $29 per night, $116 per week. Cash and checks accepted. Summer reservations recommended in January; determined by lotteries held mid-January to mid-March; taken on a first-come, first-served basis after mid-March. Cabins rented only for full weeks in summer; two-night minimum the rest of the season.

DeWolf Point State Park
RD 1, Box 437
Alexandria Bay, NY 13607
(315) 482-2012

DeWolf Point State Park rests on Wellesley Island in the Saint Lawrence River, along an inland lake named the Lake of the Isle. This small (five-acre) park comprises impressive granite formations and modest hills. Five miles from Wellesley Island State Park, DeWolf is a satellite park that is managed and maintained by the former park's staff.

DeWolf Point's fourteen cabins line a rocky knoll overlooking Lake of the Isle. These frame, two-room cabins sleep up to four people apiece, and each has a refrigerator, table, bunk beds, and electricity, plus an outdoor fireplace and picnic table. Potable water is a short distance away, as is a community bathhouse.

Nearby attractions include Heart Island's magnificent Boldt Castle. George C. Boldt arrived in America from Prussia in the 1860s, the son of a poor family. He labored and prospered, and eventually owned the Waldorf-Astoria Hotel in New York and the Bellevue-Stratford in Philadelphia. Boldt put three hundred craftsmen to work building an opulent summer home for his beloved wife, Louise. But before the project was completed, Mrs. Boldt died, and a distraught George Boldt ordered work on the home stopped. The sculptures, tapestries, fine furniture, and Italian mantels were never put in place. Today visitors tour the empty rooms, spacious and ornate, imagining how this retreat would have looked had it been finished.

DeWolf Point State Park is thirty miles north of Watertown, New York, off I-81. Cabins available late May to early September. Rates: $16 per night, $62 per week. Cash and checks accepted. Summer reservations recommended in January; determined by lotteries held mid-January to mid-March; taken on a first-come, first-served basis after mid-March. Cabins rented only for full weeks in summer; two-night minimum the rest of the season.

FAIR HAVEN BEACH STATE PARK
FAIR HAVEN, NY 13064
(315) 947-5205

Fair Haven's beach, wooded hills, and bluffs line Lake Ontario. During the ice ages, great glaciers advanced southward from Canada, forming long, cigar-shaped hills called "drumlins" from compacted earth and boulders. Ever since, Lake Ontario's waves have pounded away at the base of the drumlins, eroding their sculpted cliffs. Material chipped away by waves has been redistributed to form the beaches that isolate Sterling Pond, Sterling Marsh, and other backwater areas near the lake. These areas provide habitats for rooted and floating plants, fish, amphibians, ducks, geese, muskrat, and beaver.

Cayuga and Seneca Indians lived here in the mid-1600s, and French traders subsequently came to barter with the Indians. By 1872, harbor development and the completion of the Southern Central Railroad had transformed Fair Haven into a shipping center, for unfinished wood products, stoves, apples, potatoes, coal, and milk. A large ice industry blossomed in response to the need to cool milk being shipped by rail. In 1944 and 1945, Fair Haven Beach State Park housed German prisoners of war.

Fair Haven's thirty wooden cabins line the shores of Sterling Pond and Sterling Marsh. These fifty-year-old structures sleep from four to six people in one to three rooms. Each has a refrigerator and an outdoor fireplace and picnic table; one has a stove. A bathhouse serves the cabins.

Water sports such as sailing, fishing, swimming, and boating prevail here, and rental boats and launching ramps are available. Park visitors also enjoy the hiking trails, picnic areas, playing fields, and playgrounds.

Fair Haven Beach State Park is one mile northeast of Fair Haven, New York, off Rte. 104A. Cabins available mid-May to mid-October. Rates: $16 to $30 per night, $62 to $118 per week. Cash and checks accepted. Summer reservations recommended in January; determined by lotteries held mid-January to mid-March; taken on a first-come, first-served basis after mid-March. Cabins rented only for full weeks in summer; two-night minimum the rest of the season.

FILLMORE GLEN STATE PARK
RD 4
MORAVIA, NY 13118
(315) 497-0130

During the ice ages, which ended about ten thousand years ago, great glaciers bulldozed out the deep valley of Owasco Lake and Owasco Inlet in western New York. Since the glaciers retreated, Dry Creek has poured down the steep valley and scraped out Fillmore Glen, forming five waterfalls and many unusual stone formations. Some stones have been eroded into rectangular chunks, and the remarkable Pinnacle is a section of cliff separated from the rest of a rock wall.

Fillmore Glen State Park offers an oasis of cool, dense woods within the long, narrow gorge. A gorge trail crosses a stream eight times via footbridges. New stonework here complements the renowned masonry of the Civilian Conservation Corps from the 1930s.

Visitors take a swim in the cool, stream-fed gorge pool, or hike through Fillmore's peaceful 908 acres. Fishing is popular in nearby Owasco Lake and Owasco Inlet.

Three frame cabins, dating from CCC days, each has a single room with four bunk beds and a refrigerator. Cooking takes place on an outdoor fireplace, near a picnic table, and a washhouse contains showers and toilets. The cabins line Dry Creek in the Owasco Valley, a few miles south of Owasco Lake.

Fillmore Glen bears the name of President Millard Fillmore, who was born about five miles from the park on January 7, 1800. A reconstructed cabin, similar to his birthplace, pays tribute to Fillmore, who is remembered for his opposition to slavery. Another intriguing attraction here is the "Cow Sheds" — a huge cliff recess next to Lower Falls where cattle rustlers reportedly hid their four-legged loot.

Fillmore Glen State Park is sixteen miles south of Auburn, New York, on Rte. 38. Cabins available mid-May to mid-October. Rates: $16 per night, $62 per week. Cash and checks accepted. Summer reservations recommended in January; determined by lotteries held mid-January to mid-March; taken on a first-come, first-served basis after mid-March. Cabins rented only for full weeks in summer; two-night minimum the rest of the season.

GILBERT LAKE STATE PARK
LAURENS, NY 13796
(607) 432-2114

Somewhat reminiscent of the Adirondacks, Gilbert Lake State Park incorporates 1569 wooded, hilly acres and reaches a peak elevation of 1800 feet. Its lowest elevation is 1510 feet at Gilbert Lake. Backwoods trails lead hikers to three smaller bodies of water: Lake of the Twin Fawns, Ice Pond, and Spring Pond. All four lakes teem with stocked brook and rainbow trout, and anglers also reel in catches of bullheads, pickerel, and bass. Swimming and rental rowboats round out the facilities at tranquil Gilbert Lake. Come winter, cross-country skiing, snowshoeing, ice skating, and snowmobiling draw many to this park; at least one cross-country ski race and clinic is conducted each season.

Gilbert Lake once stored water and furnished power for sawmills and cotton mills downstream, near the village of Laurens. At about 1900, extensive lumbering took place here, as narrow-gauge railroads hauled out timber.

A pleasing stream flows past thirty-three fifty-year-old

cabins, which sleep from four to six people. Each has cold running water, a gas cooking stove, a refrigerator, a bathroom, and a screened porch. Hot showers are available at a nearby camping area. Fireplaces take the nip out of a cool evening, and a picnic table and barbecue grill stand ready for those luncheon inspirations. Pines tower over the cabins, which are located at the northern end of Gilbert Lake.

Gilbert Lake State Park is twelve miles north of Oneonta, New York, off Rtes. 51 and 205. Cabins available mid-May to mid-October. Rates: $29 to $30 per night, $116 to $118 per week. Cash and checks accepted. Summer reservations recommended in January; determined by lotteries held mid-January to mid-March; taken on a first-come, first-served basis after mid-March. Cabins rented only for full weeks in summer; two-night minimum the rest of the season.

GREEN LAKES STATE PARK
FAYETTEVILLE, NY 13066
(315) 637-6111

Two glacial lakes at this western New York park, products of the last ice age, warrant special attention. Round Lake, designated a National Natural Landmark by the U.S. Department of the Interior, and Green Lake are two of the few meromictic lakes — lakes in which surface waters do not mix with bottom water — in the country. About ten thousand years ago, glacial ice began to recede to the north. Geologists have concluded that meltwater torrents from the great glacial waterfalls carved out the basins of these two lakes. Their unique greenish hue is due to their depth — 180 feet and 195 feet, respectively — and to their very clear water, which holds little suspended material.

Hiking around the lakes, visitors notice massive deposits of marl along the shorelines. A hilly watershed protects the lakes from wind activity that would mix their waters, as does a belt of white cedars fringing the shorelines. Surrounded by virgin timber, Round Lake was thought by Indians and early travelers to be bottomless.

Both lakes thrill fishermen with stocked trout. A beach

gives swimmers access to the cool waters of Green Lake, where rowboats can be rented. The park also offers an eighteen-hole golf course, complete with pro shop and rentals.

Green Lakes's seven cabins, which date from the Civilian Conservation Corps era, feature three rooms: a bedroom, a living room, and a kitchen. Wood-burning fireplaces provide the only heat in these cabins, which are equipped with cold running water, kitchen appliances, and screened porches. While they do have indoor toilets, the nearest hot showers are in a camping area. Resting on a secluded ridge above the lakes, the cabins also have outdoor grills and picnic tables.

Green Lakes State Park is seven miles east of Syracuse, New York, on Rte. 290. Cabins available Memorial Day to mid-October. Rates: $29 per night, $116 per week. Cash and checks accepted. Summer reservations recommended in January; determined by lotteries held mid-January to mid-March; taken on a first-come, first-served basis after mid-March. Cabins rented only for full weeks in summer; two-night minimum the rest of the season.

KRING POINT STATE PARK
ROUTE 1, BOX 42
REDWOOD, NY 13679
(315) 482-2444, 482-2593

Kring Point State Park comprises fifty-eight rocky acres wooded with ash, pine, and oak along the edge of the stately Saint Lawrence River, in northern New York. Two miles of shoreline, most of it pink crystalline rock, afford excellent views of the river, its islands, commerce, and recreation. At one end of the park is Goose Bay, a large, shallow inlet, rich in marsh and aquatic life.

Fishermen make excellent catches year-round in both the river and bay, and marinas with rental boats are available in the area. Kring Point's sand swimming beach attracts throngs on hot July days, and special programs, bands, and folk singers entertain throughout the summer season. Nearby attractions include Waterfun Village, an amusement park with a waterslide, and the charming community of Alexandria Bay, New York.

Eight cabins line the water's edge at Goose Bay, which is a major fish spawning area and waterfowl habitat. Each cabin sleeps up to eight people and has a refrigerator and an outdoor barbecue grill and picnic table. Two cabins also feature stoves, baths with showers, and hot and cold running water. These two "deluxe" cabins also have wood-burning fireplaces. All of Kring Point's thirty-five-year-old cabins are of wood construction.

Kring Point State Park is eight miles north of Alexandria Bay, New York, on Rte. 12. Cabins available May to mid-October. Rates: $16 to $34 per night, $62 to $134 per week. Cash and checks accepted. Summer reservations recommended in January; determined by lotteries held mid-January to mid-March; taken on a first-come, first-served basis after mid-March. Cabins rented only for full weeks in summer; two-night minimum the rest of the season.

LAKE ERIE STATE PARK
RD 1
BROCTON, NY 14716
(716) 792-9214

Three hundred and eighteen acres of parkland adjoin the lakeside cliffs of Lake Erie, in far western New York. Nearly three miles of park trails wander along the Lake Erie Escarpment, past a swimming beach, bicycle trails, and playgrounds. Boat-launching ramps edge into the water, and shore fishing is very popular.

Lake Erie's ten cabins consist of single rooms with kitchen alcoves and porches. Each has bunks for four people, electric heat, and cold running water. Built in 1951, these wood cabins feature paneled interiors and outdoor grills and picnic tables. Flush toilets and hot showers are available in a community bathhouse.

Attractions in the area include breathtaking Chautauqua Gorge, Chautauqua Lake — world-famous for its outstanding muskie fishing — and the Chautauqua Institute, which presents a full range of cultural activities such as dance, theater, and music. Nearby family-run wineries offer tours and wine tastings, and many museums and historic buildings dot the countryside. One of the most intriguing stops is at Sherman, New York, the site of a collection of structures that date from western New York's first settlement, including a 350-year-old log blockhouse that was erected by French explorers.

Lake Erie State Park is eight miles southwest of Dunkirk, New York, on Rte. 5. Cabins available mid-May to mid-October. Rates: $26 per night, $102 per week. Cash and checks accepted. Summer reservations recommended in January; determined by lotteries held mid-January to mid-March; taken on a first-come, first-served basis after mid-March. Cabins rented only for full weeks in summer; two-night minimum the rest of the season.

LAKE TAGHKANIC STATE PARK
RD
ANCRAM, NY 12502
(518) 851-3631

In the rolling hills of Columbia County in southeastern New York, about midway between the Hudson River and the Massachusetts state line, Lake Taghkanic State Park offers cool, blue water and lush greenery. Dr. McRa Livingston donated these 1570 acres to the state of New York in 1929, stipulating that both park and lake be named Lake Taghkanic. In 1933, a Civilian Conservation Corps camp constructed the lake's east beach, a bathhouse, camping and cabin areas, and a water tower.

Today, a second beach also delights the swimmers and sunbathers who flock here to savor the lake. Rowboats can be rented at the west beach, and are popular with anglers anxious to try their luck. Two hiking trails amble through thick forests.

Lake Taghkanic's thirty-three cabins and cottages date from CCC days, and vary in size from one to four bedrooms. White frame cottages line Lake Taghkanic's west shore; rough-wood cabins sprinkle the woods on the north side of the lake. Both cabins and cottages provide beds or bunks with mattresses, gas stoves, refrigerators, and running water. Some units feature wood-burning fireplaces.

Lake Taghkanic State Park is twelve miles east of Hudson, New York, off the Taconic State Parkway. Cabins and cottages available mid-May through October. Rates: $22 to $41 per night, $100 to $164 per week. Cash and checks accepted. Summer reservations recommended in January; determined by lotteries held mid-January to mid-March; taken on a first-come, first-served basis after mid-March. Cabins rented only for full weeks in summer; two-night minimum the rest of the season.

LETCHWORTH STATE PARK
CASTILE, NY 14427
(716) 493-2611 *(park office)*
(716) 493-2622 *(Glen Iris Inn)*

The precipitous walls of Genesee Gorge, the Genesee River rushing below, the plunge and spray of dramatic waterfalls contrasting with the silence of deep forests — all contribute to make Letchworth State Park one of the most striking examples of gorge and waterfall scenery in the eastern United States. Letchworth comprises more than fourteen thousand acres of land in a long, narrow strip following the Genesee River, about thirty-five miles southwest of Rochester, New York. Within the park, the Genesee roars over three major waterfalls, one of which is more than one hundred feet high. Each passing day, the river cuts deeper into the cliffs; some already approach heights of six hundred feet.

Letchworth's rock formations bear witness to millions of years of geological history. Layers of shale and sandstone were formed when this terrain lay under shallow seas. Later, tens of millions of years of erosion wore away the rock, gouging out river valleys. Genesee Gorge's seventeen miles of undulating canyons and valleys are the product of this great natural force.

Park visitors swim in several pools, and explore the spectacular landscape via hiking trails in the gorge and along cliffs and ridges. Anglers wet a line in the Genesee River.

Eighty-two cabins stand in five heavily forested cabin colonies, which are dispersed through the park. These wooden cabins range from one-room sleeping units with no running water or kitchen facilities to three-room structures with paneled interiors, kitchenettes, running water, electric heat, fireplaces, and screened porches.

Rocking chairs rest in the shade of the tall porch attached to the quaint, three-story Glen Iris Inn, built in 1859. Operated by the Pizzutelli family, the inn features twenty-one guest rooms, plus accommodations with kitchens at the Pinewood Lodge Motel. Glen Iris Inn also houses a popular restaurant that serves three meals daily in season.

Letchworth State Park is three miles south of Castile, New York, on Rte. 19A. Cabins available year-round, inn and motel open Easter through early November. Rates: cabins, $16 to $41 per night, $62 to $164 per week; inn and motel, $33 to $48 per night for two people. Cash and checks accepted. Summer cabin reservations recommended in January; determined by lotteries held mid-January to mid-March; taken on a first-come, first-served basis after mid-March. Cabins rented only for full weeks in summer; two-night minimum the rest of the year.

MILLS-NORRIE STATE PARK
STAATSBURG, NY 12580
(914) 889-4646

Mills Mansion, with its splendid grounds, architecture, and furnishings, is an elegant example of the great estates built by financial and industrial leaders of the early twentieth century. Inherited by Ruth Livingston Mills (the wife of Ogden Mills, a wealthy financier and philanthropist), the original home was remodeled and greatly enlarged in 1896 by the prestigious New York City architectural firm of McKim, Mead and White. Two large wings were added, and the exterior was embellished with balustrades, pilasters, and floral swags. The interior features marble fireplaces, oak paneling, and gilded ceilings and wall decorations. Elaborately carved furniture fills the mansion, as do Flemish tapestries and a collection of art objects from Europe, ancient Greece, and the Orient. Today, visitors tour this stunning Greek Revival residence on the east bank of the Hudson River, in southeastern New York.

Another distinctive attraction at Mills-Norrie State Park is the environmental center, which includes interpretive displays, live animals from the region, hands-on exhibits, and a weather station. The park's marina launches small boats and docks some of the largest and most beautiful pleasure craft cruising the Hudson. Two nine-hole golf courses and a friendly restaurant also serve park patrons; all feature commanding views of the Hudson valley.

Under a parasol of giant oaks are Mills-Norrie's ten two-bedroom cabins. These forty-five-year-old cabins sleep up to four people apiece on bunk beds, have stoves, refrigerators, and screened porches, and share a community bathhouse.

Mills-Norrie State Park is four miles north of Hyde Park, New York, on Rte. 9. Cabins available mid-May to late October. Rates: $29 per night, $116 per week. Cash and checks accepted. Summer reservations recommended in January; determined by lotteries held mid-January to mid-March; taken on a first-come, first-served basis after mid-March. Cabins rented only for full weeks in summer; two-night minimum the rest of the season.

NEWTOWN BATTLEFIELD RESERVATION
RD 2
ELMIRA, NY 14901
(607) 732-1096

This 321-acre park covers a large, wooded hill (elevation: 1507 feet) that overlooks the Chemung River Valley, in southwest New York. Many hiking trails diverge through Newtown's forest, passing abundant mountain laurel and the haunts of deer, wild turkey, grouse, hawks, and owls.

Not far from the park is the site of an important revolutionary war battle that helped open western New York to settlement. General John Sullivan's army defeated a band of Iroquois, British, and Loyalists there, and a monument at the summit of the park's hill memorializes the conflict.

Newtown's five cabins are grouped at the hilltop, engulfed by oaks, maples, beeches, and some conifers. These one-room cabins sleep up to four people apiece and are constructed of rough wood planking. They provide stoves and refrigerators, plus outdoor grills and fireplaces. Cabin guests use a centralized bathhouse.

Harris Hill Park, in nearby Big Flats, New York, is the home of the National Soaring Museum, which salutes a century of gliding and soaring. Sailplane rides are also available at several area locations. Other attractions include the wineries in Hammondsport, New York, and the Corning Glass Works in Corning, New York.

Newtown Battlefield Reservation is five miles south of Elmira, New York, on Rte. 17. Cabins available mid-May to mid-October. Rates: $16 per night, $62 per week. Cash and checks accepted. Summer reservations recommended in January; determined by lotteries held mid-January to mid-March; taken on a first-come, first-served basis after mid-March. Cabins rented only for full weeks in summer; two-night minimum the rest of the season.

ROBERT H. TREMAN STATE PARK
RD 10
ITHACA, NY 14850
(607) 273-3440

Treman State Park is an area of stunning beauty, with craggy gorges, deciduous and evergreen woodlands, and a dozen waterfalls. Lush forests reach from the flats up steep banks to gorge rims. Trails trace the winding gorge for nearly three miles, passing cascades that include 115-foot Lucifer Falls. This splendid, western New York scenery has served as the backdrop for several motion pictures.

Treman's fourteen cabins stand under the trees along Enfield Creek, just a short walk from a stream-fed pool beneath a waterfall that is a favorite with swimmers. The one- and three-room cabins, built in the 1930s, sleep four to six people. Each of these wood structures has a refrigerator and bunk beds inside, and a picnic table and fireplace outside. A bathhouse serves the cabins.

The Old Mill, a water-powered gristmill built in 1839, ground corn and wheat for area farmers until 1917. The mill serves today a museum of antique milling machinery. Each of its main floor beams, fourteen inches square and thirty-six feet long, was hewn from a single log.

Stop by nearby Watkins Glen State Park for an intriguing evening program called "Timespell." This sound-and-light spectacular, presented in Watkins Glen gorge, re-creates the history of the universe, using laser images, panoramic sound, and dazzling special effects.

Robert H. Treman State Park is three miles south of Ithaca, New York, on Rte. 327. Cabins available mid-May to mid-October. Rates: $16 to $30 per night, $62 to $118 per week. Cash and checks accepted. Summer reservations recommended in January; determined by lotteries held mid-January to mid-March; taken on a first-come, first-served basis after mid-March. Cabins rented only for full weeks in summer; two-night minimum the rest of the season.

ROBERT MOSES STATE PARK
P.O. Box 548
MASSENA, NY 13662
(315) 769-8663

Elms and marsh willows highlight the area at Moses State Park where fifteen two-bedroom cabins look out on Lake Saint Lawrence. Each has four single beds, a bath with shower, a stove, and a refrigerator. Built in the mid-1960s, these cabins are of frame-and-siding construction.

Robert Moses State Park comprises 2322 acres of land along the Saint Lawrence River, including Barnhart Island. Its rolling hills, river banks, wooded areas, and open fields are populated by deer, coyotes, an abundance of small game, songbirds, birds of prey, and waterfowl. Visitors marvel at the Eisenhower Lock and other components of the Saint Lawrence Seaway. Boating and fishing are popular on the river and on Lake Saint Lawrence; fine catches of northern pike, muskellunge, bass, and walleye are common. Swimmers test the waters from a lakefront beach, and boats can be rented at the marina.

Nearby points of interest include Upper Canada Village, a completely restored Canadian community circa 1800, just half an hour's drive from the park, and the Frederic Remington Museum in Ogdensburg, New York.

Robert Moses State Park is seven miles east of Massena, New York, on Rte. 131. Cabins available May through

September. Rates: $34 per night, $134 per week. Cash and checks accepted. Summer reservations recommended in January; determined by lotteries held mid-January to mid-March; taken on a first-come, first-served basis after mid-March. Cabins rented only for full weeks in summer; two-night minimum the rest of the season.

SELKIRK SHORES STATE PARK
PULASKI, NY 13142
(315) 298-5737

Bounded on the north by Big Salmon River and on the south by Grindstone Creek, Selkirk Shores State Park rests on 980 acres of level, wooded terrain on the shores of Lake Ontario. Nestled in a bend of the lake in central New York, due north of Syracuse, Selkirk Shores is renowned for its fishing. In spring, anglers come seeking rainbow and brown trout, steelheads, smelt, and bullheads. During summer, the preferred catches are bass, which can be pulled from the lake or either stream, and brook trout, which dart through the streams feeding Lake Ontario. Come fall, attention turns to coho and Chinook salmon; this region is known as the Salmon Capital of New York State.

Boat-launching ramps on the Big Salmon River and at nearby Mexico Point aid boaters heading for vast Lake Ontario, and rental boats can be secured in Port Ontario. Swimmers and sunbathers relax along a lakefront beach. Numerous trails explore Selkirk's forests of hard and soft woods, home of a substantial population of deer. Hikers take to the trails in warmer months, and cross-country skiers utilize the six miles of pathways in winter.

Three of Selkirk's twenty-eight wooden cabins offer lakefront or riverfront locations; the remainder occupy a peaceful forest. These fifty-year-old structures sleep from four to six people apiece and are equipped with gas stoves and electric refrigerators. After a day of fishing, hiking, or swimming, you can snuggle up in front of your cabin's fireplace or enjoy the night air out on the screened porch.

Selkirk Shores State Park is three miles west of Pulaski, New York, on Rte. 3. Cabins available late April to mid-October. Rates: $29 to $30 per night, $116 to $118 per *week. Cash and checks accepted. Summer reservations recommended in January; determined by lotteries held mid-January to mid-March; taken on a first-come, first-served basis after mid-March. Cabins rented only for full weeks in summer; two-night minimum the rest of the season.*

TACONIC STATE PARK
COPAKE FALLS, NY 12517
(518) 329-3997

Taconic State Park covers approximately five thousand acres in the foothills of eastern New York's Berkshire Mountains, right on the Massachusetts and Connecticut state lines. Oak, maple, birch, ash, and pine trees drape the rolling countryside, and Bash Bish Brook slides through the park. Taconic consists of two separate sections — the Copake Falls area and the Rudd Pond area — each of which has its own attractions.

Bash Bish Brook and Ore Pit Pond, at Copake Falls, rate highly with anglers seeking trout. The pond, once the site of iron-ore mining, has wading and swimming areas and a bathhouse. Copake Falls offers some thirty miles of hiking trails, including a popular path that extends one mile into Massachusetts to a most picturesque locale: Bash Bish Falls.

At Rudd Pond, water sports dominate, including swimming at a sandy beach, fishing, and rowboating (rentals available). In winter, activities such as ice-fishing, ice skating, snowmobiling, and cross-country skiing are favorites.

All twelve of Taconic State Park's cabins and cottages are found in the Copake Falls section of the park. The cabins line a bluff above Bash Bish Brook, while the cottages are surrounded by grassy lawns along the stream bank. The fifty-year-old wooden cabins have four rooms, including two bedrooms. Each sleeps up to four people and has kitchen appliances, cold running water, a flush toilet, and a screened porch. The seven cottages — which are more than 125 years old and once housed mill workers — sleep four to six people and are equipped with fireplaces, hot and cold running water, baths with showers, and kitchen appliances. Cabins and cottages alike have outdoor picnic tables and grills.

Taconic State Park is one-quarter mile east of Copake Falls, New York, on Rte. 344. Cabins and cottages available mid-May to late October. Rates: $29 to $41 per night, $116 to $144 per week. Cash and checks accepted. Summer reservations recommended in January; determined by lotteries held mid-January to mid-March; taken on a first-come, first-served basis after mid-March. Cabins rented only for full weeks in summer; two-night minimum the rest of the season.

TAUGHANNOCK FALLS STATE PARK
RD 3
TRUMANSBURG, NY 14886
(607) 387-6739

Taughannock Falls, for which this park is named, is one of the superior natural attractions in the Northeast. Exciting to behold in any season, the 215-foot waterfall dives through a rock amphitheater whose walls are 400 feet high. This state park borders the western shore of slender Cayuga Lake, one of the Finger Lakes of western New York.

Over the past million years, great continental glaciers advanced over Canada and the northern United States and retreated at least five times. The glaciers gouged deep troughs in existing river valleys, greatly steepening the slopes. The Finger Lakes formed in these troughs after the retreat of the last glacier, about ten thousand years ago. Streams that poured over the newly steepened slopes cut rapidly into the soft shale hillsides, thus creating today's scenic gorges.

A marina and launching ramps assist boaters and fishermen anxious to get out on forty-mile-long Cayuga Lake, which has depths of more than four hundred feet. Hiking trails lead park visitors to the falls and other scenic destinations.

Taughannock's sixteen cabins loll under mature oak and hemlock trees on a bluff overlooking the lake. The cabins have natural wood exteriors, rough interiors, stoves, and refrigerators. Each accommodates up to four people and has an outdoor picnic table and barbecue grill. They share a community bathhouse.

Taughannock Falls State Park is eight miles north of Ithaca, New York, on Rte. 89. Cabins available mid-May to mid-October. Rates: $16 per night, $62 per week. Cash and checks accepted. Summer reservations recommended in January; determined by lotteries held mid-January, to mid-March; taken on a first-come, first-served basis after mid-March. Cabins rented only for full weeks in summer; two-night minimum the rest of the season.

WELLESLEY ISLAND STATE PARK
RD 1, BOX 437
ALEXANDRIA BAY, NY 13607
(315) 482-2722

Wellesley Island State Park is a thirty-two-hundred-acre recreation facility in the middle of northern New York's Thousand Islands. Situated in the Saint Lawrence River, between New York and Canada, Wellesley Island is particularly rich in wildlife, hosting most all species common to a temperate deciduous forest. Its shorelines consist of either marsh or rock, with the exception of two areas that have been developed as beaches. Eel Bay, a large shallow inlet at the center of the park, essentially divides it into two separate land masses.

Wellesley's Minna Anthony Common Nature Center includes a museum, complete with collections of live fish, reptiles, and amphibians, an observation beehive, mounted waterfowl and birds of prey, decoys, geological specimens, and wild flowers. The nature center also incorporates six hundred acres of varied wildlife habitats bordered by the Saint Lawrence River, which range from wooded wetland and prairie to open granite knobs with pitch pine.

Ten cabins perch on a knoll with a view of the Canadian channel of the river. Each of these thirty-year-old frame cabins has a bedroom with two pairs of bunk beds and a large room for cooking and eating. They are equipped with refrigerators, wood-burning heating stoves, and electricity. An outdoor fireplace and picnic table adjoin each cabin, and hot showers and toilets are available at a central washhouse.

Wellesley Island features a large marina on the Saint Lawrence that has launching ramps, dock space, and rental boats. Anglers will be pleased by plentiful black bass, rock bass, northern pike, muskellunge, perch, and sunfish. Swimmers flock to the park's beaches, and two miles from the park is a state-owned, well-maintained nine-hole golf course. Countless restaurants and shops wait to be discovered in nearby Alexandria Bay, New York, along with charter boats and fishing guides.

Wellesley Island State Park is thirty miles north of Watertown, New York, off I-81. Cabins available year-round. Rates: $16 per night, $62 per week. Cash and checks accepted. Summer reservations recommended in January; determined by lotteries held mid-January to mid-March; taken on a first-come, first-served basis after mid-March. Cabins rented only for full weeks in summer; two-night minimum the rest of the year.

Pennsylvania

〜

STATE PARK INFORMATION:
PENNSYLVANIA DEPARTMENT OF ENVIRONMENTAL
  RESOURCES
BUREAU OF STATE PARKS
P.O. BOX 1467
HARRISBURG, PA 17120
(717) 787-6640

TOURISM INFORMATION:
BUREAU OF TRAVEL DEVELOPMENT
PENNSYLVANIA DEPARTMENT OF COMMERCE
416 FORUM BUILDING
HARRISBURG, PA 17120
(800) 847-4872
(717) 787-5453

STATE BIRD: *Ruffed Grouse*
STATE MAMMAL: *White-tailed Deer*
STATE TREE: *Eastern Hemlock*
STATE FLOWER: *Mountain Laurel*
STATE FISH: *Brook Trout*

Logging boomed here in central Pennsylvania in the mid-1800s; with ax and crosscut saw, loggers felled white-pine stands at a rapid clip. Draft animals, wagons, and primitive roads proved inadequate for removing the timber, so lumbermen turned to man's oldest highway, the river. To harness small headwater streams, loggers constructed a series of log-and-earth splash dams, each of which had a gate to release the amount of water required to "splash" logs into wider and deeper tributaries. By the 1880s, all of the white timber had been cut in what is today Moshannon State Forest.

Dague Nursery, established in 1911, championed reforestation of the area by providing pine seedlings. Peak production reached thirty-five million seedlings per year, and most of the pine plantations evident today in this 184,000-acre state forest are the result of this nursery and the Civilian Conservation Corps.

Black Moshannon State Park lies atop the Allegheny Front, within Moshannon State Forest. Hemmed in by mountains, this park's nucleus is 250-acre Black Moshannon Lake, one of the finest examples of a true bog in Pennsylvania.

Perch, bass, pike, muskie, and pickerel delight anglers at the lake, while trout fishermen enjoy their sport in Black Moshannon Creek. Ice-skating, ice fishing, snowmobiling, and cross-country skiing attract enthusiasts during colder months. A lodge, two Poma lifts, and beginner and intermediate slopes make Moshannon's downhill ski area a favorite.

Built in 1937 and 1938, thirteen cabins rest on a knoll overlooking the lake. These log cabins sleep from four to six people, in one or two rooms. Each has a stone fireplace and electric kitchen appliances, and the larger cabins feature wood stoves. A nearby bathhouse offers toilets and showers.

Black Moshannon State Park is seven miles east of Philipsburg, Pennsylvania, on Rte. 540. Cabins available *mid-April to late December. Rates: $41 to $59 per half week, $82 to $108 per week. Checks accepted. Lotteries three times a year determine cabin reservations; preference given to Pennsylvania residents. Cabins rented only for full weeks in summer.*

CLEAR CREEK STATE PARK
RD 1, Box 82
SIGEL, PA 15860
(814) 752-2368

A fresh mountain stream, Clear Creek, runs the entire length of this park and spills into the Clarion River. Anglers tangle with brook trout in the pristine creek, while the Clarion teems with northern pike, smallmouth bass, walleye, and a variety of others.

Snuggled between 10,000-acre Kittanning State Forest and 500,000-acre Allegheny National Forest, Clear Creek State Park occupies 1209 heavily wooded acres in northwest Pennsylvania. Mountain laurel and rhododendron thickets lie beneath white pines, hemlocks, oaks, and cherry trees.

Clear Creek has fifteen miles of well-maintained hiking trails, along which deer, turkey, and grouse can frequently be spotted. Swimmers utilize a four-hundred-foot beach at a one-acre, man-made lake. The Clarion River provides excellent canoeing, and numerous liveries service the area. One popular four-hour canoe trip proceeds from Clear Creek State Park to nearby Cook Forest State Park.

Constructed of log and chinking or lap siding, twenty-two cabins stand under red and white oaks, hemlocks, and white pines. The larger cabins front the Clarion River and have bunk beds, electric kitchen appliances, and fireplaces. Wood stoves heat the smaller cabins, which line Clear Creek. None comes equipped with running water.

Clear Creek State Park is four miles north of Sigel, Pennsylvania, on Rte. 949. Cabins available April to late December. Rates: $29 to $41 per half week, $58 to $82 per week. Checks accepted. Lotteries three times a year determine cabin reservations; preference given to Pennsylvania residents. Cabins rented only for full weeks in summer.

COOK FOREST STATE PARK
P.O. BOX 120
COOKSBURG, PA 16217
(814) 744-8407

Cook Forest State Park encompasses 6422 mountainous acres of sylvan beauty in western Pennsylvania, including a significant stand of virgin white pine and hemlock. Designated a National Natural Landmark, this virgin forest, which greeted European pioneers who arrived here three centuries ago, has survived forest fires and extensive logging in the area.

A small stream, Tom's Run, threads the park, emptying into the much larger Clarion River. Each year, the state stocks three miles of the stream with trout.

Longfellow Trail leads to Forest Cathedral, which holds majestic pines and hemlocks nearly two hundred feet tall. An overview of the entire region awaits at the top of a seventy-foot-high fire tower; for another breath-taking panorama, venture up to Seneca Rock's overlook on the Clarion River. Cook Forest's swimming pool is used heavily each summer, while canoeists slip down the peaceful Clarion. Hunters stalk deer, squirrels, and turkeys in the appropriate seasons.

Cook Forest offers two distinct types of cabins: Indian Cabins and River Cabins. The one-room Indian Cabins, set in a circle near the mouth of Tom's Run, are made of logs and have bunk beds, gas ranges, and electric refrigerators. Two contain wood-burning fireplaces; gas heaters warm the other nine. All share a modern bathhouse.

The River Cabins, also built of logs, cling to a thickly wooded hillside above the Clarion River. These thirteen Civilian Conservation Corps–era units have four rooms (including two bedrooms), fireplaces, kitchen appliances, and cold running water. One features an upstairs sleeping loft, all accommodate between six and eight people, and pit-type toilets are nearby.

Cook Forest State Park is on Rte. 36 in Cooksburg, Pennsylvania. Cabins available mid-April to late December. Rates: $33 to $60 per half week, $66 to $120 per week. Checks accepted. Lotteries three times a year determine *cabin reservations; preference given to Pennsylvania residents. Cabins rented only for full weeks in summer.*

COWANS GAP STATE PARK
HC 17266
FORT LOUDON, PA 17224
(717) 485-3948

Cowans Gap's ten cabins, constructed of timber and stone by the Civilian Conservation Corps in the 1930s, trace the south branch of Little Aughwick Creek. Mixed hardwoods populate the area, and fresh mountain breezes roam the valley. Each of these rough cabins has a fireplace and one-inch-thick wood paneling, creating a pioneer atmosphere. These two-bedroom units sleep up to four people on bunk beds, and each is equipped with an electric range and refrigerator. A central washhouse has hot showers and flush toilets.

Cowans Gap State Park, 1085 acres in south-central Pennsylvania's Tuscarora Mountains, adjoins Buchanan State Forest. In addition to splendid hiking, the park offers a forty-two-acre lake for swimming and sunbathing, and rowboats and paddleboats can be rented. The cool lake tantalizes anglers with its excellent trout supply, as well as plenty of bass, perch, and panfish.

Cowans Gap bears the name of Major Samuel Cowan, a British officer during the revolutionary war. After the conflict, he and his bride eloped and headed for Kentucky. Their wagon broke down en route, so they traded it to an Indian chief for the tract of land now known as Cowans Gap.

The park bustles with activity during cold weather: ice-skating and ice fishing on the frozen lake, and sledding and cross-country skiing. Sledding is particularly exhilarating on the three-quarter-mile run down Knobsville Road, which is closed to vehicular traffic in winter. Nearby is the birthplace of James Buchanan, fifteenth president of the United States and the only Pennsylvanian ever to occupy the White House.

Cowans Gap State Park is north of Fort Loudon, Pennsylvania, off Rte. 75. Cabins available mid-April through *late December. Rates: $49 per half week, $98 per week. Checks accepted. Lotteries three times a year determine cabin reservations; preference given to Pennsylvania residents. Cabins rented only for full weeks in summer.*

KOOSER STATE PARK
RD 4, Box 256
SOMERSET, PA 15501
(814) 445-8673

Kooser State Park's elevation ranges from twenty-three hundred to twenty-six hundred feet above sea level, providing summer temperatures six to eight degrees cooler than those in surrounding lowlands. The mountain climate also explains the winter snowfalls here, which typically reach 130 or 140 inches per season.

Because of the relatively cool climate, the primary tree species in Kooser State Park are northern hardwoods, such as eastern hemlock, American beech, yellow poplar, birch, and varieties of maple. Park underbrush consists mainly of rhododendrons and mountain laurel, along with ferns and mosses.

Located on the eastern slope of Laurel Mountain, in southwest Pennsylvania, the park derives its name from John Kooser, who settled at the far end of the park by a gushing spring in 1890. Earlier, a contingent of General Washington's army known as Coxes Army had crossed here during the Whiskey Rebellion.

Spring-fed Kooser Run, an excellent trout stream, courses through the park acreage. Kooser Lake, home of sizable populations of bass, perch, and bluegills, has a peaceful swimming beach. Hikers observe deer, turkeys, grouse, chipmunks, and occasionally a bear. Winter activities range from sledding and tobogganing on a steep slope to cross-country skiing and snowmobiling. Less than an hour's drive away churns the Youghiogheny River, a favorite with rafters and kayakers.

Within easy walking distance of the beach at Kooser Lake stand nine fifty-year-old cabins. Constructed of timber and stone, they have interior walls of log or thick wood paneling. Each cabin has kitchen appliances, bunk beds, and modest furnishings. Though the cabins are equipped with running water, the closest bathroom facilities are three comfort stations with pit toilets.

Kooser State Park is ten miles northwest of Somerset, Pennsylvania, on Rte. 31. Cabins available mid-April to late December. Rates: $38 to $49 per half week, $76 to $98 per week. Checks accepted. Lotteries three times a year determine cabin reservations; preference given to Pennsylvania residents. Cabins rented only for full weeks in summer.

LINN RUN STATE PARK
Box 527
LIGONIER, PA 15658
(412) 238-6623

When the state of Pennsylvania acquired this mountainous territory from Byers and Allen Lumber Company in 1909, it was the first major public purchase of denuded forest land in the Ohio River Basin. Today, confronted with its even-aged stand of red oak, tulip poplar, and maple, it is difficult to visualize this Laurel Mountain terrain as it must have appeared in 1909 — terrain that critics labeled a "waste land."

In an area that once had been clear-cut, slopes have been reforested and wildlife has been imported, including white-tailed deer from Michigan and New York. Varied topography and mixed hardwood and evergreen forests make Linn Run State Park a delight for hiking and picnicking.

Huge rock outcroppings along several trails afford splendid vistas, including views of adjoining Forbes State Forest. Linn Run, a small stream, spans the length of the park and is stocked annually with trout; May is a favorite fishing month.

Laurel Mountain Ski Area has earned a reputation as one of southwestern Pennsylvania's best facilities. Privately operated, the resort has twelve trails, a double chair lift, two Poma lifts, three rope lifts, and a lodge complete with ski school, rentals, and meals.

Linn Run meanders past ten cabins constructed by the Civilian Conservation Corps in the 1930s. These stone-

and-wood cabins have fireplaces (or a fireplace insert), bunk beds, and full kitchens. They sleep from two to six people, and are only a short walk away from running water and pit latrines.

Linn Run State Park is four miles south of Rector, Pennsylvania, on Linn Run Road. Cabins available mid-April to late December. Rates: $25 to $49 per half week, $50 to $98 per week. Checks accepted. Lotteries three times a year determine cabin reservations; preference given to Pennsylvania residents. Cabins rented only for full weeks in summer.

Cabin, Parker Dam State Park, Pennsylvania

PARKER DAM STATE PARK
RD 1, Box 165
PENFIELD, PA 15849
(814) 765-5082

Unbelievably dense pine and hemlock forests once attracted lumbermen to this region of western Pennsylvania. In 1875 John A. Otto, owner of a vast tract, hired William Parker to cut timber along Laurel Run, the primary stream in what is now Parker Dam State Park.

By the late 1800s, most of the white pine had been removed, so Otto sold this land to Thomas Proctor, owner of a tannery in nearby Penfield. Proctor used the bark of hemlock, chestnut, and chestnut oak trees to tan hides. In 1903 the Central Pennsylvania Lumber Company built a logging railroad up the Moose, Laurel, and Little Laurel runs, gaining access to stands previously out of reach. Many of the old railroad grades are still visible today; a logging exhibit and a life-size reproduction of a log slide inform visitors about this period in Pennsylvania's history.

One of three state parks in enormous Moshannon State Forest, Parker Dam's topography includes mixed hardwoods, second-growth timber, and swamp meadows. White-tailed deer, black bear, wild turkey, ruffed grouse, fox, and beaver abound here; they can be viewed by alert hikers on more than two hundred miles of dirt roads and ninety miles of trails.

Sixteen cabins, each of which sleeps from four to eight people, are clustered along Mud Run, a tributary of Parker Dam Lake. Some of these CCC-era accommodations are log cabins built of heavy chestnut timbers; others were constructed with craggy fieldstones. Each has an electric range and refrigerator, a fireplace, and bunk-style beds. Wood-burning stoves heat the cabins, and running water and restrooms are nearby.

Parker Dam Lake, twenty acres in area, is the focal point of summer activities that include swimming, boating, and fishing. Nonmotorized and electric-powered craft slip silently across the surface, and rowboats can be rented. Stocked with brook and rainbow trout, Parker Dam Lake also rewards fishermen with stringers of bluegill, crappie, and catfish. Each fall, the northern portion of the park hosts archery hunting for deer; winter brings ice fishing, ice-skating, sledding, tobogganing, and snowmobiling.

Parker Dam State Park is two miles south of Penfield, Pennsylvania, off Rte. 153. Cabins available mid-April through late December. Rates: $46 to $65 per half week, $92 to $130 per week. Checks accepted. Lotteries three times a year determine cabin reservations; preference given to Pennsylvania residents. Cabins rented only for full weeks in summer.

PROMISED LAND STATE PARK
RD 1, Box 96
GREENTOWN, PA 18426
(717) 676-3428

When a group of early Shakers decided to settle here in northeast Pennsylvania, they did so because of the promise of the land, its agricultural patential. Once settled, they quickly discovered that the rocky soil was incapable of supporting gardening, much less farming. The members of this religious group soon continued westward, but not before, tongue in cheek, they had christened the area "the promised land."

Only one hundred miles from Philadelphia and New York City, this 2971-acre state park is encircled by 8000 acres of state forest. The landscape's mixed hardwoods consist of beech, birch, and maple, along with some hemlock and white pine. Streams and rock outcroppings highlight the topography here, and several rapids and waterfalls occur along Wallenpaupack Creek.

Promised Land's two man-made lakes have swimming beaches with lifeguards, and rental rowboats and canoes and boat-launching ramps are available. Anglers discover bass, pickerel, walleye, muskellunge, perch, and catfish in good quantities.

Hikers travel twenty-three miles of trails, including a path to Bruce Lake, which was created ten thousand years ago, when one of the last glaciers in the area dammed a valley with till.

Promised Land's twelve cabins, built by Civilian Conservation Corps workers, line a south-facing ridge near a stream flowing from Promised Land Lake. Fabricated either of wood beams or of log and stone, the cabins sleep from two to four people on bunk beds. All have fireplaces, and most have wood stoves. Each is equipped with kitchen appliances, a porch with a picnic table, and a stone fire ring. A shared modern bathhouse provides restrooms and showers.

Promised Land State Park is ten miles north of Canadensis, Pennsylvania, on Rte. 390. Cabins available mid-April to late December. Rates: $38 to $49 per half *week, $76 to $98 per week. Checks accepted. Lotteries three times a year determine cabin reservations; preference given to Pennsylvania residents. Cabins rented only for full weeks in summer.*

RALPH STOVER STATE PARK
RR 1, BOX 209L
PIPERSVILLE, PA 18947
(215) 297-5090

Ralph Stover State Park, located in Bucks County in eastern Pennsylvania, marks the site of a water-powered gristmill of the late 1700s. Named for the man who owned and operated the mill, this park preserves remnants of the old structure, including the mill race that diverted water from Tohickon Creek to turn the grinding stones.

Since the gift of this property to the state by Stover heirs in 1931, other territory, known as High Rocks, has been added through the generosity of author James Michener. High Rocks features two-hundred-foot sheer cliffs overlooking a creek and tranquil valley, and attracts climbing and rappelling enthusiasts.

Tohickon Creek, usually a shallow, undulating stream, holds smallmouth bass, sunfish, carp, and eels, plus stocked trout. When high-water conditions exist due to heavy rainfall or water released from Lake Nockamixon, this placid stream is transformed into a white-water adventure, challenging rafters, canoeists, and kayakers.

Ralph Stover's six frame and stone cabins dominate a hillside a few hundred feet from Tohickon Creek. Shaded by hemlock, oak, walnut, and ash, these fifty-year-old, one-room cabins sleep four people apiece on double bunks. Each cabin features a full kitchen and a fireplace, and on the patio are a picnic table and a stone barbecue grill. Showers and restrooms are a short distance away.

Visitors to Ralph Stover enjoy its proximity to many fine restaurants and shops. Also nearby is Roosevelt State Park, which contains a stretch of the sixty-mile Delaware Canal. This remnant of the great towpath-canal era of the nineteenth century appears today almost as it did during its hundred years of commercial operation.

Ralph Stover State Park is two miles north of Point Pleasant, Pennsylvania, off Rte. 32. Cabins available mid-April to late December. Rates: $25 per half week, $50 per week. Checks accepted. Lotteries three times a year determine cabin reservations; preference given to Pennsylvania residents. Cabins rented only for full weeks in summer.

S. B. ELLIOTT STATE PARK
c/o PARKER DAM STATE PARK
RD 1, Box 165
PENFIELD, PA 15849
(814) 765-7271 *(park office)*
(814) 765-5082 *(cabin reservations)*

Gently rolling hills at S. B. Elliott State Park harbor mixed oak trees with an understory of red maple and mountain laurel. The park rests atop the Allegheny Plateau in western Pennsylvania, at about 2150 feet elevation. No streams or lakes occur in the park, although its spring and swamps do feed several nearby creeks.

Simon B. Elliott, an early conservationist and Pennsylvania legislator, promoted the idea of planting trees here, to replenish lands devastated by logging. In 1933, the Civilian Conservation Corps set up camp along the edge of the forest nursery. Their labor resulted in Elliott's cabins, pavilions, roads, and trails.

Today, hikers scour the hilltop, while backpackers follow the Quehanna Trail system for up to seventy-five miles of exploration. Fishing for stocked and native trout in area streams satisfies anglers. During winter months, snowmobilers power along specified routes.

S. B. Elliott's six cabins, built in 1935, shelter overnight guests on the park's southern edge. Stepping out of these chestnut or stone structures, you face dense woodlands, lush and green. Each cabin includes kitchen appliances, a fireplace, a wood-burning stove, and an outdoor porch with picnic table. Sleeping four to eight people apiece, these cabins have individual pit privies, and a centralized water tap is nearby.

S. B. Elliott State Park is nine miles north of Clearfield, Pennsylvania, off Rte. 153. Cabins available mid-April to late December. Rates: $28 to $47 per half week, $56 to $94 per week. Checks accepted. Lotteries three times a year determine cabin reservations; preference given to Pennsylvania residents. Cabins rented only for full weeks in summer.

WORLDS END STATE PARK
P.O. Box 62
FORKSVILLE, PA 18616
(717) 924-3287

The journey up a steep slope on the first road here prompted early travelers to muse that they were surely at the "end of the world." From that, the mountains of north-central Pennsylvania came to be known as the Endless Mountains.

A sharp-walled, snaking canyon has been cut into the rugged Appalachian Plateau by glacial action and Loyalsock Creek. Dogwood and mountain laurel enhance Worlds End's sturdy forests of cherry, beech, maple, and birch. The state stocks the creek with trout, and wildlife here typifies that of mountain regions: deer, rabbit, turkey, grouse, fox, wildcat, and bear.

Kayakers revel in the rapids and fast action of the creek, which is too rough for open canoes. A small dam on Loyalsock Creek backs up a swimming area, where lifeguards watch over park guests in summer.

Backpackers often use Worlds End as a base while exploring rocky Loyalsock Trail, a fifty-seven-mile route stretching from Loyalsockville to Laporte, Pennsylvania. For spectacular scenery, you can also follow mountain roads to Canyon Vista or nearby High Knob Overlook; in June the mountain laurel bloom, and autumn colors are splendid.

Gathered at the bottom of Loyalsock Gorge along the creekbed, Worlds End's nineteen cabins come in three different designs: log, frame with rough hemlock lapboard siding, and stone and frame with hemlock siding. These fifty-year-old cabins sleep from two to six people and are equipped with kitchens and bunk beds. Each cabin has a wood-burning fireplace, most have wood stoves, and five of the larger structures come with a second fireplace, on the porch. Water is hand-pumped from wells, and pit toilets serve the cabin area.

Worlds End State Park is two miles east of Forksville, Pennsylvania, on Rte. 154. Cabins available mid-April to late December. Rates: $25 to $46 per half week, $50 to $92 per week. Checks accepted. Lotteries three times a year determine cabin reservations; preference given to Pennsylvania residents. Cabins rented only for full weeks in summer.

The
SOUTHEAST

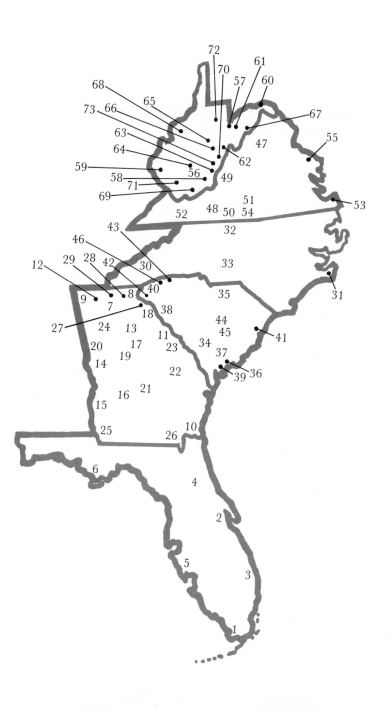

Florida

STATE PARK INFORMATION:
FLORIDA DEPARTMENT OF NATURAL RESOURCES
EDUCATION AND INFORMATION
3900 COMMONWEALTH BOULEVARD
TALLAHASSEE, FL 32303
(904) 488-7326

TOURISM INFORMATION:
FLORIDA DEPARTMENT OF COMMERCE
OFFICE OF VISITOR INQUIRY
126 VAN BUREN STREET
TALLAHASSEE, FL 32301
(904) 487-1462

STATE BIRD: *Mockingbird*
STATE MAMMALS: *Porpoise and Manatee*
STATE TREE: *Sabal Palm*
STATE FLOWER: *Orange Blossom*
STATE FISH: *Largemouth Bass*

EVERGLADES NATIONAL PARK
P.O. Box 279
HOMESTEAD, FL 33030
(305) 247-6211

FLAMINGO INN
EVERGLADES PARK CATERING
FLAMINGO, FL 33030
(813) 695-3101
(305) 253-2241

A freshwater river six inches deep and fifty miles wide creeps seaward through the Everglades on a riverbed that slopes ever so gradually. During the wet season the water may seem to be still, but it is flowing, dropping one foot per mile and finally emptying into Florida Bay at Florida's extreme southern tip.

The importance and uniqueness of the Everglades ecosystem have been recognized through its designation as an International Biosphere Reserve and a World Heritage Site. Nearly constant warm, sunny weather makes this park a year-round attraction, but there are two distinct seasons. Summer is wet; winter, dry. Heavy rains fall in intense storms from late May through October. The warm, humid conditions bring numerous insects, including mosquitoes, and precipitation can exceed fifty inches per year.

Exploring by hiking trail or boat, visitors to this tropical wonderland are rewarded with abundant and intriguing wild creatures. The Everglades may be best known for its variety of bird life. You can observe roseate spoonbills, large pink birds that often are mistaken for flamingos. Reddish egrets and rare great white herons live and breed in Florida Bay; about fifty pairs of southern bald eagles nest along the coast. Other rare and endangered species found in the park include Florida panther, manatee, brown pelican, green sea turtle, short-tailed hawk, and crocodile.

Gumbo Limbo Trail twists through a hardwood hammock, a junglelike grove of tropical trees and smaller plants. Statuesque royal palms, gumbo limbo trees, wild coffee, and lush aerial gardens of ferns and orchids grow in this dense, moist forest. Pa-hay-okee Overlook Trail leads to an observation tower offering a view of the vast "river of grass" — the glades that gave this park its name. Muhly grass, Everglades beard grass, arrowhead, and many others grow here. Patient observers may see red-shouldered hawks, red-winged blackbirds, common yellowthroats, vultures, and an occasional alligator.

Flamingo Inn graces the southern edge of the Everglades, along the shore of Florida Bay, where the shoreline is dotted with gracefully arched palm trees. Accommodations here include sixteen one-bedroom frame cabins and a modern resort inn that holds sixty-eight standard rooms, thirty-four first-class quarters, and two deluxe suites. Flamingo's cabins are fully furnished and have practical kitchenettes, heating, air conditioning, and large picture windows.

At the inn, constructed of concrete block a quarter of a century ago, Flamingo's dining room rises through three levels; all tables overlook the bay. Tropical and subtropical plants and flowers set the mood in this fine restaurant, open November through May.

Other facilities at this resort include a large, fully screened swimming pool and a screened lounge. At the marina, rental boats, ocean bay fishing, dockage, and launching ramps are available. Visitors can also hop on a tram tour or boat tour of this impressive parkland.

Everglades National Park is twelve miles southwest of Homestead, Florida, on Rte. 27. Cabins and inn open year-round. Rates: cabins, $41 to $55 per night; inn, $33 to $95 per night for two people. Cash, Visa, MasterCard, and American Express accepted. Cabin reservations recommended six to eight months in advance, inn reservations recommended one month in advance for winter.

BLUE SPRING STATE PARK
HONTOON ISLAND CABINS
ROUTE 3
ORANGE CITY, FL 32763
(904) 775-3663 *(park office)*
(904) 734-7158 *(cabin reservations — allow phone to ring repeatedly)*

Timucuan Indians first inhabited 1650-acre Hontoon Island, which is bordered by the Saint Johns River on the north and east, Snake Creek on the south, and Hontoon Dead River on the west. From the Saint Johns they gathered snails — a staple of their diet — and the discarded shells form two large mounds still visible at this northeast Florida park.

After the Civil War, large numbers of northerners arrived at Jacksonville, the mouth of the Saint Johns River. From there, a great wave of settlers and tourists advanced upriver aboard steamers. At Blue Spring, they discovered one of the first steamboat landings in the region and orange groves, all owned by Louis Thursby, who anticipated a boom here in the 1870s and 1880s.

The oranges displayed at Thursby's landing lured newcomers, and promoters claimed that one acre of oranges in Florida was worth fifty acres of wheat in Iowa. The steamboat era on the Saint Johns came to an abrupt end in 1886, however, with the arrival of the much faster railroad. Thursby's two-story frame house is today a museum, restored to its appearance during the steamboat heyday of the 1870s and 1880s.

Other activities at Blue Spring include swimming in Blue Spring Run, canoeing on the Saint Johns and its tributaries (rentals available), hiking through pine flatwoods, cypress swamps, and palm and oak hammocks, and fishing for largemouth bass, bluegill, speckled perch, and channel catfish. Be sure to watch for one of Florida's most remarkable mammals in the seventy-two-degree water of Blue Spring Run — the gentle manatee, which grows to fifteen feet in length and almost two thousand pounds in weight. These endangered vegetarians escape the chilled waters of the Saint Johns River each year from November through April.

To reach Hontoon Island's six cabins, visitors travel by car, in their own boats, or on a passenger ferry. Under shady, tropical vegetation, these one-room cabins sleep up to six people apiece and have screened porches and electricity. Right outside are picnic tables, cold running water, and barbecue grills, which are the only cooking facilities here.

Hontoon Island is six miles southwest of DeLand, Florida, on River Ridge Road. Cabins available year-round.

Rates: $8 to $10 per night. Cash and checks accepted. Reservations taken up to sixty days in advance, recommended thirty to sixty days in advance for summer and holidays.

JONATHAN DICKINSON STATE PARK
14800 S.E. FEDERAL HIGHWAY
HOBE SOUND, FL 33455
(305) 546-2771 *(park office)*
(305) 746-5804 *(cabin reservations)*

Throughout the year, rangers guide visitors of this southeast Florida park to the Trapper Nelson Interpretive Site on the Loxahatchee River. The site, which can only be reached by canoe or tour boat, is named for one of the region's most colorful residents. Harsh New Jersey winters drove Nelson to Florida as a young man, and he settled in the wilderness on the river's northwest fork. He established a private zoo, and excursion boats soon were traveling upriver from Palm Beach so that visitors could see the powerful man who wrestled alligators and devoured raw possum.

Jonathan Dickinson State Park consists of 10,284 acres of woodlands and wetlands, including freshwater creeks and a massive river swamp. Not far from the Atlantic coast, this park hosts such endangered animals as bald eagles, scrub jays, manatees, and Florida sandhill cranes. Dickinson's slash-pine flatwoods comprise a canopy of slash pines and an understory of oaks and palmettos. In the days before this area became parkland, settlers sought out the hard, termite-resistant pines for home-building. For a splendid view of these Florida flatlands, you can climb the observation tower to an elevation of 111 feet above sea level.

Constructed in the 1970s, Dickinson's seven wood cabins have single bedrooms, baths with showers, and kitchen/living areas. They sleep up to six people apiece, and have heating and air conditioning. Set just up from the river, surrounded by slash pine, saw palmetto, and cabbage palm, these cabins feature outdoor picnic tables and barbecue grills.

Named for a Quaker who was shipwrecked five miles from here in 1696, Jonathan Dickinson State Park has a roped-off sandy beach on the Loxahatchee River. Anglers pursue sheephead, bass, catfish, snook, bream, tarpon, and mangrove snapper.

Jonathan Dickinson State Park is one mile south of Hobe Sound, Florida, on Rte. 1. Cabins available year-round. Rates: $35 per night, $200 per week for two people. Checks accepted. Reservations taken up to three months in advance.

Mike Roess Gold Head Branch State Park
Route 1, Box 545
Keystone Heights, FL 32656
(904) 473-4701

Fourteen cabins perch on a hilltop, looking down on picturesque Lake Johnson. Live oaks and longleaf pines ring the cabins, which include wooden CCC-era structures and modern concrete-block units. Each of the nine cabins built by the Civilian Conservation Corps in the 1930s has a kitchen, a bath, and a sleeping / living area, plus a fireplace. The block cabins feature separate bedrooms; both kinds are equipped with electric heat, screened porches, grills, and picnic tables.

Set in the northeastern part of the state, between Jacksonville and Gainesville, this 1561-acre park lies on high, dry hills in Florida's Center Ridge. Springs issue from a deep ravine to form a stream — Gold Head Branch — which flows into Lake Johnson. Within the ravine, diverse hardwoods create a shady hammock that is carpeted with ferns. The turpentine industry once operated here, as evidenced by the "catfaces" (scars) still present on many pine trees.

Lake Johnson, the largest of five lakes in this park, has a swimming beach and a boat-launching ramp. Fishermen delight in this park's productive waters, which are loaded with bass, bream, and perch. Quiet hikers are apt to spot deer, fox, wading birds, and an occasional black bear.

Mike Roess Gold Head Branch State Park is six miles east of Keystone Heights, Florida, on Rte. 21. Cabins available year-round. Rates: $30 per night. Cash and checks accepted. Reservations taken up to four months in advance, recommended that early for summer and holidays.

MYAKKA RIVER STATE PARK
ROUTE 1, BOX 72
SARASOTA, FL 33583
(813) 924-1027

Florida's "coastal lowlands" extend from the Gulf of Mexico shoreline to an elevation of one hundred feet above sea level, which can be as far as sixty miles inland. This flat terrain consists of thin sandy soil over a base of limestone. The Myakka River originates in and meanders through this level territory in southwest Florida until it spills into the gulf. The river's waters come entirely from rainfall, which occurs primarily in summer. Within this state park, the river fills two lakes and several broad marshes.

Myakka River State Park, seventeen miles from the gulf, has a reputation as one of the finest wading-bird sanctuaries in the United States, and wintering birds visit in huge numbers. Bald eagles and ospreys rate among the more spectacular sights, along with wood storks, white pelicans, and roseate spoonbills. Alligators and otters also call this park home.

Myakka's ecosystem has been threatened by the introduction of exotic plants and animals, particularly feral pigs. Although visitors sometimes refer to these animals as "wild boars," they are in fact domestic pigs that have gone wild. They multiply rapidly and feed on acorns, thereby depriving deer and turkey of one of their primary foods.

Constructed by Civilian Conservation Corps workers in the mid-1930s, Myakka's five cabins are built of sabal-palm logs. Each cabin accommodates up to six people, on two double beds and a "sleeper sofa," and has kitchen appliances, a bath with shower, and a fireplace. The cabins are equipped with heating and air conditioning, and on each cabin's back porch is a picnic table.

Canoes and bicycles can be rented at Myakka River State Park, and the many trails challenge hikers. A seventy-five-hundred-acre wilderness preserve has been established in the park; a limited number of visitors enter the preserve each day on foot or in nonmotorized boats.

Myakka River State Park is seventeen miles east of Sarasota, Florida, on Rte. 72. Cabins available year-round. Rates: $30 per night. Cash and checks accepted. Reservations taken up to four months in advance, recommended that early for winter.

T. H. Stone Memorial–Saint Joseph Peninsula State Park
P.O. Box 909
Port Saint Joe, FL 32456
(904) 227-1327

A thin earthen strand that stretches out into the Gulf of Mexico in northwest Florida, this pristine, 2516-acre park is almost entirely surrounded by water. Bordered by the gulf and Saint Joseph Bay, the park comprises miles of white sand beaches, striking dune formations, and a heavily forested interior.

Indians once inhabited this land of small freshwater and saltwater marshes, reaping the bounty of abundant shell-fish from the shallow bay waters. Octopi, bay scallops, hermit crabs, fiddler crabs, and horseshoe crabs teem in the bay, while vast numbers of sea trout lurk in the grass flats. Across the narrow peninsula, on the gulf side, surf anglers pull in cobia, bluefish, redfish, whiting, speckled trout, and flounder.

Swimmers frolic along the beaches, near the tallest dunes on the Florida coast. A marina and boat-launching ramp provide access to the bay, as do rental catamaran sailboats. Hikers wander the beach and bay shore or the 1650-acre wilderness preserve in the center of this peninsula, which is populated with sand pine, slash pine, live oak, sabal palm, and red cedar. More than two hundred different species of birds have been spotted here, and shore and wading birds are particularly numerous. In fall, this park is one of the best locations in the eastern United States to observe monarch butterflies and migrating hawks.

Eight modern wooden cabins rest on the bay side of the peninsula, not far from the wilderness preserve. Each of the cabins accommodates up to seven people. They feature kitchens, baths, and dining areas. Set just back from the water's edge, the cabins have both heating and air conditioning.

T. H. Stone Memorial–Saint Joseph Peninsula State Park is south of Port Saint Joe, Florida, on Rte. 30. Cabins available year-round. Rates: $50 per night. Cash and checks accepted. Reservations taken up to four months in advance, recommended that early for March through October.

Georgia

~~~~

STATE PARK INFORMATION:
GEORGIA STATE PARKS AND HISTORIC SITES
270 WASHINGTON STREET, SW, ROOM 817
ATLANTA, GA 30334
(404) 656-3530

TOURISM INFORMATION:
TOURISM DIVISION
GEORGIA DEPARTMENT OF INDUSTRY AND TRADE
P.O. BOX 1776
ATLANTA, GA 30301
(404) 656-3590

STATE BIRD: *Brown Thrasher*
STATE TREE: *Live Oak*
STATE FLOWER: *Cherokee Rose*
STATE FISH: *Largemouth Bass*

AMICALOLA FALLS STATE PARK
STAR ROUTE
DAWSONVILLE, GA 30534
(404) 265-2885

Amicalola Falls, at the southern end of the Appalachian Mountains in northern Georgia, is the state's highest waterfall. Formed by a clear stream that dives 729 feet in a series of thunderous cascades, the falls can be viewed at a breathtaking angle from an observation platform. A boardwalk places you on the verge of the falls, where its beauty and power produce a transcendent pleasure. To the Cherokees, *Amicalola* meant "tumbling waters."

The Appalachian Trail stretches 2052 miles from Mount Katahdin, Maine, to Springer Mountain, Georgia, which is eight miles from this park via an approach trail. Amicalola's hiking trails range from steep to extremely steep, thanks to the mountainous terrain. The slopes support pine, hemlock, and dogwoods, along with rhododendron, mountain laurel, and flame azaleas. Scattered throughout the hills are the remains of old moonshine stills.

Amicalola's fifteen cabins have from one to three bedrooms and sleep up to ten people. Ten cabins that overlook Little Amicalola Creek offer scenic mountain vistas, while five at a lower level give the best views of the falls. All feature gas heat, electric stoves and refrigerators, and outdoor picnic tables and grills. Ten have fireplaces, some have rear patios, and five come with porch swings.

The nearby Etowah, Chestatee, and Amicalola rivers all provide splendid rafting, tubing, and canoeing, and liveries and guided river-running trips are available. Trout fishing is another favorite in this park, which is bordered by the Chattahoochee National Forest. Dahlonega Gold Museum, just a few minutes' drive from Amicalola Falls State Park, preserves the history and lore of our nation's first major gold rush: thousands flocked to northeast Georgia in 1828–1829 to seek their fortune.

Amicalola Falls State Park is eighteen miles north of Dawsonville, Georgia, on Rte. 52. Cabins available year-round. Rates: $30 to $48 per night. Cash, checks, Visa, and

MasterCard accepted. Reservations taken up to 11 months in advance, recommended that early for October. Cabins reserved only for full weeks in summer; two-night minimum the rest of the year.

BLACK ROCK MOUNTAIN STATE PARK
MOUNTAIN CITY, GA 30562
(404) 746-2141

A sheer cliff of black granite, Black Rock Mountain has long lured hikers and climbers to northeastern Georgia. At an elevation of thirty-six hundred feet above sea level, this is the highest state park in Georgia; it presents the flora, fauna, and scenic beauty of the southernmost portion of the Appalachians, North America's oldest mountain chain. Each year, countless visitors return to Black Rock just to gaze from a magnificent overlook, where at night you can see the lights of thirteen cities twinkling in the distance.

Five Black Rock cabins line the edge of the mountain, five more look out on the community of Mountain City, and five others nestle in a wooded setting. These two- and three-bedroom cabins show off high ceilings, modern baths and kitchens, ceiling fans, and electric heat. Five include fireplaces, another five contain wood stoves, and all have outdoor grills and picnic tables. Black Rock's cabins accommodate up to ten people apiece and feature spacious back porches.

Spring brings blooms of rhododendrons, lady's slippers, mountain laurel, flame azalea, and other treats to the park. Red foxes, bears, and owls inhabit this rugged, mountainous terrain, along with rabbits and raccoons. Black Rock's three hiking trails range in length from fifteen hundred feet to six miles, and one leads to a tranquil waterfall. A seventeen-acre lake hosts trout, bass, and bream, and there are eleven other lakes in the area. Other attractions near the park include golf, tennis, horseback riding, rafting, swimming, hang gliding, and snow-skiing in winter.

Black Rock Mountain State Park is three miles north of Clayton, Georgia, off Rte. 441. Cabins available year-round. Rates: $38 to $48 per night. Cash, checks, Visa, *and MasterCard accepted. Reservations taken up to eleven months in advance, recommended that early for fall and holidays. Cabins reserved only for full weeks in summer; two-night minimum the rest of the year.*

CLOUDLAND CANYON STATE PARK
ROUTE 2
RISING FAWN, GA 30738
(404) 657-4050

Step out of your two- or three-bedroom cabin at Cloudland, and you're within yards of a spectacular canyon on the western edge of historic Lookout Mountain. Oak, hickory, and pine trees shade the five board-and-batten and eleven log cabins here, each of which is equipped with a kitchenette and one and a half or two full bathrooms. You can take the chill out of an autumn evening with a blazing fire in the fireplace, or unwind in a peaceful rocking chair. All Cloudland cabins are heated, and the newer, log units feature air conditioning and screened porches.

Loblolly pine, red oak, maple, hemlock, and cedar populate this mountainous countryside in northwestern Georgia, where waterfalls tumble seven hundred to eight hundred feet to the canyon floor below. An occasional fox, bobcat, deer, or wild boar is spotted here, and rabbits and squirrels abound.

Cloudland's network of trails consists of seven miles of footpaths, most of which descend into the canyons. In fall, changing colors create eye-catching panoramas on the rugged hillsides.

Three miles from here is one of the South's most popular hang-gliding launching points, the site of the 1981 National Hang Gliding Cup competition. Also in the area are Point Park, which is part of the Chickamauga Battlefield, and Ruby Falls, a cavern eighty feet underground.

Cloudland Canyon State Park is twenty miles northwest of LaFayette, Georgia, off Rte. 136. Cabins available year-round. Rates: $38 to $48 per night. Cash, checks, Visa, and MasterCard accepted. Reservations taken up to eleven months in advance, recommended six months in advance for June through November.

Georgia / 85

CROOKED RIVER STATE PARK
3092 Spur 40
Saint Marys, GA 31558
(912) 882-5256

Eleven gray frame cabins overlook the Crooked River and a saltwater marsh, which provide excellent crabbing, shrimping, and fishing. These two- and three-bedroom cabins sleep from eight to twelve people apiece. Each has a fireplace, a complete kitchen, a bath, an outdoor picnic table and grill, and a screened porch. Five of the cabins stand in a meadow, the remainder under a thick cover of trees.

Not far from the Atlantic Ocean, Crooked River State Park occupies level southeastern Georgia terrain that is wooded with slash and longleaf pine, dogwood, holly, cedar, and oak. Situated near a migratory flyway, the park boasts of fine birding. Armadillos, marsh rabbits, raccoons, and gopher tortoises are also prevalent, and an occasional deer is spotted. Mushrooms of unusual color and size sprinkle the landscape, along with abundant palmetto.

A boat ramp slides into the Crooked River, providing access to this fast-moving tidal stream and the Intracoastal Waterway. A swimming pool and a miniature golf course round out Crooked River's recreational offerings.

Three miles from this park stand the ruins of the McIntosh Sugar Works. Other attractions nearby include Kings Bay Submarine Base and Cumberland Island National Seashore; the latter is accessible by excursion boat.

Crooked River State Park is ten miles east of Kingsland, Georgia, off I-95. Cabins available year-round. Rates: $38 to $48 per night. Cash, checks, Visa, and MasterCard accepted. Reservations taken up to eleven months in advance, recommended three to six months in advance for summer and holidays. Cabins reserved only for full weeks in summer; two-night minimum the rest of the year.

ELIJAH CLARK STATE PARK
ROUTE 4, BOX 293
LINCOLNTON, GA 30817
(404) 359-3458

This state park bears the name of General Elijah Clark, a legendary frontiersman who led an up-country militia during the revolutionary war. A log-cabin replica of Clark's home re-creates the pioneer days here in northeastern Georgia.

Clinging to the western shore of Clark Hill Lake, this 447-acre preserve blends history with recreation in serene surroundings. Clark Hill Lake, one of the ten most popular Army Corps of Engineer lakes in the nation, attracts six million visitors annually. Healthy populations of black, white, and striped bass, along with crappie, bluegill, and sauger, are responsible for the interest in this lake, as are its pleasurable boating and swimming. The park has four launching ramps and a supervised beach. Its hills, wooded with oak, hickory, sweet gum, dogwood, and pine, and inhabited by deer, turkey, fox, raccoon, and squirrel, hem in the seventy-thousand-acre reservoir.

Clark's twenty contemporary, wooden cabins rest within seventy-five yards of the lake, and feature fireplaces, heating, and air conditioning. Each sleeps up to eight people in two bedrooms. Stocked with up-to-date kitchens and baths, these cabins also have outdoor picnic tables and barbecue grills. Half have screened porches; the others, open sun decks.

Elijah Clark State Park is seven miles east of Lincolnton, Georgia, off Rte. 378. Cabins available year-round. Rates: $38 to $42 per night. Cash, checks, Visa, and MasterCard accepted. Reservations taken up to eleven months in advance, recommended that early for April through September. Cabins reserved only for full weeks in summer; two-night minimum the rest of the year.

FORT MOUNTAIN STATE PARK
ROUTE 7, BOX 1-K
CHATSWORTH, GA 30705
(404) 695-2621

Fort Mountain State Park's fifteen cabins are surrounded by a mixture of deciduous trees and some evergreens. These one- and two-bedroom cabins feature stained wood siding and brick or rock fireplaces. Five have air conditioning, all are heated, and each has its own outdoor barbecue grill and picnic table.

From your cabin's deck or screened porch, you can enjoy the splendid scenery near the summit of Fort Mountain, the most prominent peak of the Cohutta range at the terminus of the Blue Ridge Mountains in north-central Georgia. Small spring-fed streams and challenging hiking trails thread the rugged terrain. At an elevation of 2854 feet, this 2526-acre park serves as a habitat for deer, foxes, black bears, groundhogs, rabbits, and raccoons. Birding enthusiasts discover hawks, owls, crows, indigo buntings, evening grosbeaks, American goldfinches, and robins, among others.

Fort Mountain displays spectacular foliage in mid-to-late October, in woods thick with poplar, oak, birch, and honey locust. The springtime landscape explodes with dogwood, violets, wild iris, wild azalea, mountain laurel, and trilliums; summer continues the pageantry with the bloom of rhododendrons, daisies, and black-eyed Susans.

This park's sixteen-acre, man-made lake is a pleasant site for bank fishing, swimming, paddleboat rentals, and sunbathing. Nearby recreational opportunities include canoeing, rafting, and horseback riding. Several attractions in the vicinity merit notice: the Chief Vann House, the restored nineteenth-century home of a wealthy Cherokee Indian whose family intermarried with Scottish immigrants (thirteen miles from the park); New Echota, the capital of the Cherokee Nation for half a century (eighteen miles from the park); and the Cohutta Wilderness Area, known for its fine backpacking trails and trout fishing (fourteen miles from the park). Also of interest is the 855-foot-long, man-made rock wall on the peak of Fort Mountain. Averaging two to three feet in height and twelve feet in width, it zigzags across the mountain crest, bounded on both sides by sheer cliffs. Its origin and purpose are unknown.

Fort Mountain State Park is seven miles east of Chatsworth, Georgia, on Route 52. Cabins available year-round. Rates: $38 to $48 per night. Cash, checks, Visa, and MasterCard accepted. Reservations taken up to eleven months in advance, recommended that early for fall foliage season and holidays. Cabins reserved only for full weeks in summer; two-night minimum the rest of the year.

FORT YARGO STATE PARK
Box 764
WINDER, GA 30680
(404) 867-3489 *(park office)*
(404) 867-5313 *(Will-A-Way Recreation Area)*

The old log fort for which this park is named was built in 1792. It was one of four blockhouses erected by the Humphries brothers on the northeast Georgia frontier, to protect early settlers from the Creeks and Cherokees. Still standing, its hand-hewn logs of virgin pine are now as hard as concrete, and numerous bullet holes from heavy-caliber guns appear in the timber. About one hundred feet from the fort flows a fine spring.

Recreation here centers around Fort Yargo's lake, which was completed in 1967 as part of the Marbury Creek Watershed Project. Swimming, boating (maximum ten horsepower), and fishing for bass, bream, catfish, and crappie are all popular pastimes. Anglers occasionally reel in bass as large as fifteen pounds, and boat-launching ramps are provided. Other Fort Yargo activities include tennis (on three courts), miniature golf, and hiking the nineteen hundred acres of pines and hardwoods.

A unique feature here is Will-A-Way Recreation Area, a three-hundred-acre complex on the lake's north shore that is devoted solely to the needs of the handicapped. Steep slopes, uneven walks, steps, and narrow doorways have been eliminated, allowing handicapped individuals full access to the facilities. Boating on pontoon craft equipped with electric motors, swimming, and fishing are typical lakefront activities at Will-A-Way, while others enjoy shuffleboard, horseshoes, miniature golf, and a half-mile nature trail.

Will-A-Way's three cabins, completely accessible, sleep up to six people apiece. Each has five rooms, including two bedrooms and a modern kitchen, heating, air conditioning, and a fireplace. Engulfed by tall trees, the cabins stand a short distance from the lakeshore.

Fort Yargo State Park is one mile south of Winder, Georgia, on Rte. 81. Cabins available year-round. Rates: handicapped, $26 per night; nonhandicapped, $38 to $42 per night. Cash, checks, Visa, and MasterCard accepted. Reservations taken up to eleven months in advance, recommended two to four months in advance for May through October. Cabins reserved only for full weeks in summer; two-night minimum the rest of the year.

FRANKLIN D. ROOSEVELT STATE PARK
P.O. BOX 749
PINE MOUNTAIN, GA 31822
(404) 663-4858

Poised atop one of the most picturesque mountains in the Southeast, this park is named after President Roosevelt, who visited here often while staying at the Little White House in nearby Warm Springs. He enjoyed picnics at Dowdell's Knob, a spur off the mountain, and the cooking grill he had constructed there still serves park guests. Roosevelt died at the Little White House in 1945, twelve miles from this west-central Georgia park.

Roosevelt State Park comprises ten thousand acres on Pine Mountain, where Virginia white-tailed deer, quail, and turkey abound. Each fall, wild ducks migrate to Roosevelt's lakes, after the plentiful largemouth bass, bream, and catfish have been left in peace by fishermen. (Anglers may also be drawn to the outstanding bass and crappie fishing at West Point Lake, eighteen miles from Roosevelt.) Swimming enthusiasts take advantage of a unique pool, built of native fieldstone in the shape of the Liberty Bell. Golf, tennis, and year-round nature programs are available at the adjoining Calloway Gardens resort.

Roosevelt's four rustic rock cabins line the edge of the

mountain, overlooking the valley below. Near the park's lakes, sixteen log and five newer board-and-batten units nestle under oaks and pines; some are along the water's edge. The rock and log cabins have heating, and a few come with screened porches, while the modern cabins offer both heating and air conditioning. All the cabins feature cozy fireplaces, kitchens, and baths; they sleep from two to eight people apiece.

This mountaintop terrain was a portion of the territory ceded to the Creek Indians by treaties in 1825 and 1826. Kings Gap, almost precisely at Roosevelt's geographic center, was a pass on the famed Indian Trail, later to be used by stagecoaches.

Franklin D. Roosevelt State Park is three miles south of Pine Mountain, Georgia, on Rte. 190. Cabins available year-round. Rates: $30 to $42 per night. Cash, checks, Visa, and MasterCard accepted. Reservations taken up to eleven months in advance, recommended three to four months in advance for holiday weekends and summer. Cabins reserved only for full weeks in summer; two-night minimum the rest of the year.

GEORGE T. BAGBY STATE PARK
ROUTE 2, BOX 116
GEORGETOWN, GA 31754
(912) 768-2660

The fish that reside in Lake Walter F. George have a widespread reputation for being quick, clever, and tasty. Each year, anglers come to Bagby State Park to try their luck at this southwestern Georgia reservoir. Set on Pataula Creek in the lake's backwaters, the park offers teeming crappie, black bass, white bass, hybrid bass, catfish, bream, and carp. Waterskiers share the narrow, slender reservoir and its boat ramps with fishermen.

Pines and hardwoods blanket the level terrain here, which is home to deer, bobcats, raccoons, and squirrels. Migratory birds alight at the nearby Eufaula National Wildlife Refuge.

Bagby State Park's five wood-sided cabins rest on a slight incline about 150 feet from the water's edge, shaded by tall trees. These two-bedroom cabins accommodate up to eight people apiece and include central heating and air conditioning. Each has a complete kitchen, a fireplace, and an outdoor barbecue grill and picnic table.

A marina one-and-a-half miles from Bagby State Park rents boats and motors and sells marine supplies. Other area attractions include the quaint southern communities of Eufaula and Cuthbert, Georgia, the sites of many historic homes and buildings.

George T. Bagby State Park is fifteen miles north of Fort Gaines, Georgia, on Rte. 39. Cabins available year-round. Rates: $38 to $42 per night. Cash, checks, Visa, and MasterCard accepted. Reservations taken up to eleven months in advance, recommended three to five months in advance for March through July. Cabins reserved only for full weeks in summer; two-night minimum the rest of the year.

GEORGIA VETERANS MEMORIAL STATE PARK
ROUTE 3
CORDELE, GA 31015
(912) 273-2190

The centerpieces at Georgia Veterans Memorial are indoor and outdoor military displays that honor the men and women who served the United States in conflicts as far back as the French and Indian Wars. After touring the museum, you can head outside for a close-up look at tanks, artillery pieces, and aircraft, including an impressive B-29 bomber.

Georgia Veterans Memorial State Park fills a peninsula on Lake Blackshear, which is the site of fishing, swimming, and boating. Three public launching ramps aid boaters; in addition to a lakefront beach, the park also has a large swimming pool. A thirteen-thousand-acre impoundment of the Flint River, the lake boasts some of the best fishing in Georgia: largemouth, smallmouth, hybrid, striped, and white bass, bream, catfish, white perch, crappie, carp, and gar all await skillful anglers.

Ten two-bedroom cabins trace the lakeshore and are surrounded by large oaks and pines. Half of these wood cabins have screened porches; the others, sun decks. All are heated and air-conditioned. Each cabin sleeps up to eight people, and features a complete kitchen, a fireplace and a bath with shower.

Hiking this park, you might encounter deer, quail, doves, ducks, and geese, and maybe an alligator or bald eagle. Plains, Georgia, the home of former president Jimmy Carter, is thirty miles from Georgia Veterans, and historic Andersonville lies at about the same distance. Andersonville held the largest Confederate military prison during the Civil War; during its fourteen-month existence, more than forty-five thousand Union soldiers were confined there. Of these, twelve thousand died from disease, malnutrition, overcrowding, and exposure. A museum depicts the events that took place at Andersonville more than a century ago.

Georgia Veterans Memorial State Park is nine miles west of Cordele, Georgia, on Rte. 280. Cabins available year-round. Rates: $38 to $42 per night. Cash, checks, Visa, and MasterCard accepted. Reservations taken up to eleven months in advance, recommended four months in advance for April through October. Cabins reserved only for full weeks in summer; two-night minimum the rest of the year.

HARD LABOR CREEK STATE PARK
P.O. BOX 247
RUTLEDGE, GA 30663
(404) 557-2863 *(park office)*
(404) 557-2143 *(golf manager)*

Prestigious *Golf* magazine rates the eighteen-hole course at Hard Labor Creek as one of the most beautiful and challenging public courses in the country. The facility features an attractive clubhouse, where carts and clubs can be rented.

Anglers, meanwhile, will want to wet a line in 275-acre Lake Rutledge, for bass, bream, crappie, and catfish. Rental boats and a swimming beach are also available. Hikers on Hard Labor Creek State Park's trail discover huge granite outcrops and natural rock gardens that are smothered in gray lichens and green mosses. Rocky Creek and Still Branch course through thick stands of sweet gum, oak, poplar, beech, locust, hickory, persimmon, and walnut. In spring, the mountain laurel, dogwood, and redbud come alive with red, white, and pink blooms.

Hard Labor Creek's twenty cabins line both sides of a road that leads from a hilltop to a second lake, Lake Brantley. These wood-sided, two-bedroom cabins sleep up to eight people. Each has a kitchen, a bath, a fireplace, heating, and air conditioning, and most offer screened porches.

This north-central Georgia park receives its name from a bold stream that cuts an easterly course through the heavily forested countryside and joins the Apalachee River about twenty-five miles from here. The origin of Hard Labor Creek's name, though, is in dispute. Some claim it referred to slaves who tilled the bottomland fields in intense summer heat. Others are convinced that the name derived from Indians who found the stream difficult to ford at high water.

Nearby Madison — described by many as the "prettiest town in Georgia" — contains a wealth of antebellum houses. Spared during Union general William T. Sherman's famous march to the sea, Madison now features the Madison-Morgan Cultural Center, which houses a beautifully restored auditorium, art galleries, a historical museum, and a schoolroom museum — all in a fine old Romanesque Revival building that dates from 1895.

Hard Labor Creek State Park is two miles north of Rutledge, Georgia, off Rte. 278. Cabins available year-round. Rates: $38 to $42 per night. Cash, checks, Visa, and MasterCard accepted. Reservations taken up to eleven months in advance, recomendmed six to eleven months in advance for April through October. Cabins reserved only for full weeks in summer; two-night minimum the rest of the year.

Hart State Park
1515 Hart Park Road
Hartwell, GA 30643
(404) 376-8756

Colorful spinnakers billow as sleek sailboat hulls slice through Lake Hartwell, counterpointed by the sound of ski boats. Large and lovely, Lake Hartwell greets visitors at the northeast corner of Georgia's piedmont region. Largemouth bass, black crappie, bluegill, bream, and walleyed pike lurk in the sparkling waters of this fifty-six-thousand-acre reservoir, which has a thousand miles of shoreline and many quiet coves. Launching ramps and a beach with diving dock are available here; boats and barges can be rented nearby. Ten minutes away, at the stocked waters behind the dam on the Savannah River, abundant trout await anglers.

Hart State Park's five mobile homes line a small cove on Lake Hartwell's southern shore. Oaks, sweet gums, black gums, cedars, pines, and willows create a backdrop for these accommodations, which sleep up to six people. Each two-bedroom mobile home contains kitchen appliances, central heating and air conditioning, and a modern bathroom. Not far from the lapping lake waters, these units have individual barbecue grills and picnic tables.

Nearby attractions include the Elberton Granite Museum and Exhibit in Elberton, Georgia — "Granite Capital of the World" — and train rides on the Red Carpet Line. Visitors relive the 1920s and 1930s for a few hours when they hop aboard an old-fashioned train pulled by a 1925 steam locomotive. The Red Carpet Line huffs and puffs through twenty rolling and picturesque miles of Georgia countryside.

Hart State Park is two miles east of Hartwell, Georgia, off Rte. 29. Mobile homes available year-round. Rates: $26 to $30 per night. Cash, checks, Visa, and MasterCard accepted. Reservations taken up to eleven months in advance, recommended two to four months in advance for summer. Mobile homes reserved only for full weeks in summer; two-night minimum the rest of the year.

INDIAN SPRINGS STATE PARK
INDIAN SPRINGS, GA 30231
(404) 775-7241

Centuries ago, Creek Indians used the sulphur springs here in central Georgia to heal their sick and ward off evil spirits. White settlers discovered the springs in 1792; later, two historic treaties between the Indians and the state of

Georgia were signed here. After signing the treaties, Indian Chief General William McIntosh was slain by enraged Creeks, who felt he had betrayed them. In the late 1800s, several large hotels constructed at the springs attracted thousands of well-to-do northerners each summer.

A 105-acre lake lures swimmers to its sandy beach, and fishermen to its supply of largemouth bass, crappie, perch, and catfish. Rowboats and paddleboats can be rented at the lakefront. Other amenities at Indian Springs State Park include an Indian museum, miniature golf, picnic areas, and playgrounds.

Bordered on the north by Aboothlacoosta Creek and on the south by Hoethleyoholo Creek, this park has 510 acres of woodland — some level, some hilly — and a vast array of wild flowers. A modest waterfall tumbles over the lake's spillway.

Indian Springs State Park's ten cabins — five rustic, five modern — feature fireplaces and central heating and air conditioning. Each cabin has two bedrooms, a living / dining / kitchen combination, and a bath. Half of these cabins line the lakefront, while the remainder stand in a quiet forest; each accommodates up to eight people.

Indian Springs State Park is four miles south of Jackson, Georgia, on Rte. 42. Cabins available year-round. Rates: $38 to $42 per night. Cash, checks, Visa, and MasterCard accepted. Reservations taken up to eleven months in advance, recommended that early for summer. Cabins reserved only for full weeks in summer; two-night minimum the rest of the year.

JOHN TANNER STATE PARK
354 TANNERS BEACH ROAD
CARROLLTON, GA 30117
(404) 832-7545

In the gentle hills of northwestern Georgia, John Tanner State Park encompasses both a twelve-acre fishing lake and a twenty-four-acre recreation lake that is blessed with the largest sand beach in the Georgia state-park system. Once a private resort, John Tanner also features rental canoes and paddleboats, miniature golf, rental bicycles, and a one-mile bike trail. Private fishing boats glide across the smaller lake (electric motors only) and tie up at its dock.

Six motel-type accommodations face the larger lake; they are fifty feet from the water, under towering trees. Each one-bedroom unit sleeps up to six people on two double beds and a fold-out sofa. Heated and air-conditioned, these units also have baths with showers, living rooms, dining areas, and kitchenettes.

John Tanner State Park is six miles west of Carrollton, Georgia, on Rte. 16. Motel units available year-round. Rates: $26 to $30 per night. Cash, checks, Visa, and MasterCard accepted. Reservations taken up to eleven months in advance, recommended four to six weeks in advance for summer. Motel units reserved only for full weeks in summer; two-night minimum the rest of the year.

LITTLE OCMULGEE STATE PARK
P.O. Box 97
McRAE, GA 31055
(912) 868-2832

Little Ocmulgee State Park rises from high sandhills in south-central Georgia, the habitat of the gopher turtle and the endangered indigo snake. This beautiful parkland owes its existence to local folks who, during the Depression, began donating land bordering the Little Ocmulgee River for a recreational facility that would ease the bleak times. A dam created a 265-acre lake that is hemmed in by the park. Civilian Conservation Corps workers constructed many of the buildings here, including the hand-hewn timber visitor center. Long before this was a park, Creek Indians inhabited the area, and called the river "Au che ha chee."

Hiking Ocmulgee's trails, you wander through pines, dogwoods, magnolias, and oaks, many draped with Spanish moss. Fox, deer, or rabbit may scurry by, while vultures, red-tailed hawks, and pileated woodpeckers fly overhead. In these pastoral surroundings, the eighteen-hole Wallace Adams Golf Course offers challenging fairways and manicured greens.

Fishing enthusiasts will be down at the lake, wetting a

line for bass, crappie, shellcrackers, perch, bream, and catfish. A swimming pool, tennis courts, picnic shelters, and an airstrip complete the facilities at Little Ocmulgee State Park.

Visitors choose between modern and rustic cabins here. Five cabins that date from the 1940s feature cathedral ceilings with exposed beams, and pine paneling. Each of these one-bedroom cabins has heating, air conditioning, a stove, and a refrigerator, plus a delightful lake view through a wall of glass. Furnished with oak and pine, five newer cabins offer two bedrooms, full kitchens, and a setting among tall shade trees.

Little Ocmulgee State Park is three miles north of McRae, Georgia, on Rte. 441. Cabins available year-round. Rates: $30 to $42 per night. Cash, checks, Visa, and MasterCard accepted. Reservations taken up to eleven months in advance, recommended eight months in advance for May through November. Cabins reserved only for full weeks in summer; two-night minimum the rest of the year.

MAGNOLIA SPRINGS STATE PARK
ROUTE 5, Box 488
MILLEN, GA 30442
(912) 982-1660

During the Civil War, Magnolia Springs was the site of Camp Lawton, a Confederate POW camp built to absorb the overflow from Andersonville Prison. In the 113 days between August 5 and November 25, 1864, a forty-three-acre stockade was planned, constructed, armed, used, and abandoned. The prison, under the command of Captain D. W. Vowles, received 10,229 prisoners. The victorious Union general William T. Sherman, heading southeastward from Atlanta, forced the camp's abandonment.

Remnants of Camp Lawton can still be found, here in eastern Georgia. Two huge timbers recovered from a stream were once part of the stockade walls at the compound General John H. Winder called "the largest prison in the world." On a hill that afforded a clear field of fire over the entire facility stands an impressive earthwork.

Magnolia Springs State Park has long been famous for its spring, which gushes nine million gallons of crystal-clear water daily. Flowing in a waterway twelve to fifteen feet deep, the water is almost as cold as ice; it forms a beautiful pool lined with unusual aquatic plants.

Five frame cabins border a forest of oaks and pines in a secluded section of this park, not far from the twenty-eight-acre Upper Lake. These two- and three-bedroom cabins sleep from eight to twelve people, and are heated and air-conditioned. Each has a modern bath, a kitchen, a screened porch, and a fireplace, plus an outdoor picnic table and grill.

Bass, catfish, bream, and perch reward anglers at both of Magnolia Springs's lakes, and waterskiing is popular on Upper Lake. Swimmers enjoy a large pool, and bicycles and boats can be rented. The park, home of eight species of woodpeckers, offers fine birding and wildlife observation.

Magnolia Springs State Park is five miles north of Millen, Georgia, on Rte. 25. Cabins available year-round. Rates: $38 to $48 per night. Cash, checks, Visa, and MasterCard accepted. Reservations taken up to eleven months in advance. Cabins reserved only for full weeks in summer; two-night minimum the rest of the year.

MISTLETOE STATE PARK
ROUTE 1, BOX 117F
APPLING, GA 30802
(404) 541-0321

Once the home of the Savannah Indians and later of the Euchees, this northeast Georgia territory subsequently served as cropland for fine southern plantations. However, poor farming techniques reduced its agricultural potential and created erosion ditches, such as the one called Miscalculation Canyon. Mistletoe State Park does offer, as you might expect, abundant quantities of affection-inspiring mistletoe.

Loblolly pine today covers much of Mistletoe's 1924 acres; it is mixed with hardwood stands that are highlighted by dogwood and wax myrtle. Following the coves of Clark

Hill Lake's southern shore, Mistletoe State Park features a white-sand swimming beach, boating, and excellent fishing for crappie, white and black bass, bream, and catfish. Landlubbers enjoy a hike through the level, wooded terrain or a spin on a rental bicycle. Hikers will definitely want to admire scenic Cliatt Creek close-up.

Mistletoe's ten-year-old cabins line the banks of the gurgling creek. These two-bedroom cabins accommodate up to eight people and have electric heating and air conditioning. Each includes two bathrooms, a kitchen, a dining area, a living room with fireplace, and two screened porches with comfortable rocking chairs. A boat ramp is provided for cabin guests.

Mistletoe State Park is fifteen miles north of Thomson, Georgia, on Rte. 150. Cabins available year-round. Rates: $38 to $42 per night. Cash, checks, Visa, and MasterCard accepted. Reservations taken up to eleven months in advance, recommended six months in advance for April through Labor Day. Cabins reserved only for full weeks in summer; two-night minimum the rest of the year.

RED TOP MOUNTAIN STATE PARK
ROUTE 2
CARTERSVILLE, GA 30120
(404) 974-5184

Visitors to Red Top Mountain State Park find the region rich in Cherokee Indian lore and Civil War history. Situated on a 1950-acre peninsula along Lake Allatoona, Red Top provides tranquility and recreation in the red-clay hills forty miles northwest of Atlanta.

This splendid acreage was developed in the 1950s, and has since become one of the most popular state parks in Georgia. Guarded by gentle hills, the lake is an ideal spot for swimming, fishing, boating, and skiing in deep blue water. In addition to launching ramps, Red Top Mountain State Park boasts a 360-foot beach along the 11,860-acre lake. From the water, boating enthusiasts can explore 270 miles of shoreline. Three hiking trails traverse the peaceful terrain here.

All of Red Top's eighteen frame cabins are within

walking distance of the water's edge. Each of these two-bedroom structures has heating, air conditioning, and a fireplace. They provide electric stoves and refrigerators, and outdoors there are barbecue grills and picnic tables. Some feature sun decks; others, covered porches, and each sleeps up to eight people.

Nearby attractions include the nightlife, culture, sports, and restaurants in Atlanta. Six miles away is the William Weinman Mineral Center and Museum. Designed as Georgia's showplace of geologic history, Weinmans displays a collection of 600 cut and polished stones and 325 minerals from around the world.

Red Top Mountain State Park is six miles south of Cartersville, Georgia, off I-75. Cabins available year-round. Rates: $38 to $42 per night. Cash, checks, Visa, and MasterCard accepted. Reservations taken up to eleven months in advance, recommended three months in advance for summer. Cabins reserved only for full weeks in summer; two-night minimum the rest of the year.

SEMINOLE STATE PARK
ROUTE 2
DONALSONVILLE, GA 31745
(912) 861-3137

Seminole State Park, located in the extreme southwestern corner of Georgia, bears the name of Indians who lived here prior to the advent of white settlers. A Spanish mission, Santa Cruz de Sabacola el Menor, was established near the confluence of the Chattahoochee and Flint rivers in 1675. The site of Sabacola, now under the waters of Lake Seminole, was abandoned in 1724 after an Indian raid.

Lake Seminole backs up behind Jim Woodruff Lock and Dam, which provides navigable waters in a channel nine feet deep and one hundred feet wide. Averaging fifteen feet or less in depth, the lake is shallow in comparison with Georgia's other big lakes, but the natural lime sink ponds it has flooded hold a greater number of fish species than any other lake in the state. Fishermen launch their boats at Kelly's Marina, a mile from the park, in pursuit of crappie, catfish, bream, and shellcracker. A beach attracts swimmers, and rental fishing boats and pontoon boats are available at the marina.

Seminole's ten cabins line the lakefront, and are sprinkled amid pine trees. These wood-sided cabins sleep up to six people apiece, and feature heating and air conditioning. Each has two bedrooms, two baths, kitchen appliances, and dishes. You can toss steaks or burgers on the outdoor barbecue grill, or enjoy a rocking chair on the screened porch.

Pine, oak, dogwood, sycamore, persimmon, and huckleberry trees populate Seminole's level landscape, where raccoon, fox, deer, and alligators can be observed. Hunting for quail, dove, duck, rabbit, and squirrel takes place just outside the park.

Seminole State Park is sixteen miles south of Donalsonville, Georgia, on Rte. 39. Cabins available year-round. Rates: $38 to $42 per night. Cash, checks, Visa, and MasterCard accepted. Reservations taken up to eleven months in advance, recommended nine months in advance for spring. Cabins reserved only for full weeks in summer; two-night minimum the rest of the year.

STEPHEN C. FOSTER STATE PARK
ROUTE 1
FARGO, GA 31631
(912) 637-5274

Stephen C. Foster State Park occupies Jones Island within the Okefenokee National Wildlife Refuge, in southeastern Georgia. It is one of three primary entrances into the deep, dark, mysterious Okefenokee Swamp.

Pine, cypress, bay, sweet gum, magnolia, live oak, and black gum trees blanket the island, which is home to deer, raccoons, and alligators. Foster State Park serves as an access point for more than twenty-five miles of lakes and waterways throughout the swamp. Along those waterways, you might spot egrets, herons, wood ducks, and pileated woodpeckers. Visitors also tour a museum, walk along an elevated boardwalk, and travel by boat to nearby Billy's Island.

The swamp's lush vegetation and black waters are the habitat for more than 225 species of birds, 41 species of mammals, 54 different reptiles, and more than 60 species of fish and amphibians. Among those fish, Okefenokee offers sizable catches of bass, pickerel, bream, and perch. Rental boats and canoes are available, as is a launching ramp, here in one of the most primitive wilderness areas in the United States.

On a wooded section in the center of the island, Foster's nine wood-sided cabins feature two bedrooms and sleep up to eight people apiece. Each is equipped with kitchen appliances, central heat and air conditioning, and a screened porch. You can barbecue the day's catch on an outdoor grill and dine at a shaded picnic table.

Stephen C. Foster State Park is seventeen miles north of Fargo, Georgia, on Rte. 177. Cabins available year-round. Rates: $38 to $42 per night. Cash, checks, Visa, and MasterCard accepted. Reservations taken up to eleven months in advance, recommended that early for spring. Cabins reserved only for full weeks in summer; two-night minimum the rest of the year.

TUGALOO STATE PARK
ROUTE 1, BOX 300
LAVONIA, GA 30553
(404) 356-4362

"Tugaloo" comes from an Indian name for a river that once flowed freely near this land, prior to the construction of Hartwell Dam. Tugaloo State Park is one of several state parks along the Hartwell Reservoir, in northeastern Georgia. It rests on a rolling peninsula that dips and rises, giving sparkling views of the water in every direction. Founded in 1965 on the lake's western edge, Tugaloo was the first state park to be developed along the reservoir's 962-mile shoreline.

Tugaloo's twenty contemporary cabins, built of wood, hug the waterfront and share the boat docks that are interspersed among them. Oak, hickory, and pine tower above the cabin area, as they do the rest of this 393-acre park. Each of these two-bedroom cabins accommodates up to eight people and has an outdoor picnic table and grill. Meals can also be prepared in the modern kitchens. Most of Tugaloo's cabins have a single bath, though some are equipped with a bath and a half. Sixteen feature fireplaces; four have Franklin stoves. Those with screened porches and high-backed rockers provide the perfect place to enjoy the scenery.

Fishing, swimming, and boating are the recreational mainstays here, along with hiking on two nature trails. Fishermen appreciate the fine year-round catches of large-mouth bass and other species. Visitors often gather at the group shelter for bluegrass music or clogging.

Tugaloo State Park is seven miles northeast of Lavonia, Georgia, off Rte. 328. Cabins available year-round. Rates: $38 to $42 per night. Cash, checks, Visa, and MasterCard accepted. Reservations taken up to eleven months in advance, recommended nine to eleven months in advance for October weekends, summer, and holidays. Cabins reserved only for full weeks in summer; two-night minimum the rest of the year.

UNICOI STATE PARK
P.O. Box 256
HELEN, GA 30545
(404) 878-2201 *(park office)*
(404) 878-2824 *(cabin and lodge reservations)*

A forty-seven-acre meadow traversed by a trout stream is within one thousand feet of Unicoi's lodge. Modern in design and incorporating a stained-cedar exterior, this handsome structure holds one hundred guest rooms. Exposed ceilings accent the spacious lobby, and the lodge restaurant looks out on vistas of northeast Georgia's mountain forest.

Twenty of Unicoi's cabins cling to the slopes above Unicoi Lake, while five unusual barrel-shaped cabins populate a hillside covered with oak, poplar, maple, and pine. These "barrel" cabins feature weathered wood exteriors. All Unicoi cabins include fully equipped kitchens and bathrooms, plus outdoor barbecue grills. They range from one to three bedrooms, and most have fireplaces.

Unicoi State Park's 1081 acres contain many hiking

trails, which wind through rhododendron and mountain laurel and past numerous waterfalls. Anna Ruby Falls, in the adjacent Chattahoochee National Forest, can be admired from its base, where water cascades down from two hundred feet above. Two beaches edge the park's cool, fifty-three-acre mountain lake; canoes and other non-motorized boats are available for rent. Unicoi's craft shop offers one of the largest quilt displays in the region.

Once inhabited by Cherokee Indians, the parkland was later the site of early gold-mining operations. Nearby attractions include the alpine village of Helen, Georgia, site of festivals, hot-air balloon races, shops, and restaurants. Brasstown Bald, Georgia's highest peak, is twenty miles away, and Tallulah Gorge, a thousand-foot-deep geological marvel, is only thirty miles from Unicoi.

Unicoi State Park is two miles north of Helen, Georgia, on Rte. 356. Cabins and lodge open year-round. Rates: cabins, $30 to $48 per night; lodge, $34 to $37 per night for two people. Cash, checks, Visa, and MasterCard accepted. Reservations taken up to eleven months in advance, recommended six to eleven months in advance for fall weekends and summer. Cabins reserved only for full weeks in summer; two-night minimum the rest of the year.

VOGEL STATE PARK
ROUTE 1, BOX 97
BLAIRSVILLE, GA 30512
(404) 745-2628

The Blue Ridge Mountains envelop Vogel State Park, in northern Georgia. Within a few hours' drive are numerous mountains, lakes, waterfalls, white-water rivers, ski resorts, and enchanting communities. Vogel lies near the heart of the Chattahoochee National Forest, and Brasstown Bald — the highest summit in the state — is thirteen miles away. DeSoto Falls, Cooper Creek, Anna Ruby Falls, Dukes Creek Falls, and Raven Cliffs all attract nature lovers to this region. Richard Russell Scenic Highway begins a few miles north of the park and climbs a crest of the Blue Ridge at Hog Pen Gap, providing frequent overlooks along the way. This twenty-mile highway con-nects Vogel with Unicoi State Park and Helen, Georgia, a community known for its alpine architecture, atmosphere, and cuisine.

Vogel State Park's thirty-six cabins fall into three groups: fifty-year-old log structures built by the Civilian Conservation Corps, twenty-year-old cabins slightly smaller than the CCC-era units, and modern two- and three-bedroom cabins. The log cabins line Lake Trahlyta's western shore; the smaller cabins are located south of the lake, some along Wolf Creek; and the newer cabins gather on the lower slopes of a ridge that forms the park's eastern boundary. Because of the ridge's steep angle, the back porches of these latter cabins stand about ten feet off the ground, giving splendid views of the hillside. All Vogel cabins include fireplaces, heating, kitchens, and baths, and they sleep up to ten people.

A dam across Wolf Creek created the twenty-two-acre Lake Trahlyta, named for a Cherokee princess. Stocked rainbow trout, bass, bream, and catfish satisfy fishermen, while swimming and rental paddleboats please other guests. Vogel's hiking trails lead to waterfalls, scenic overlooks, and the neighboring peaks of Blood Mountain and Slaughter Mountain. The park's flora are typical of the southern Appalachians: forests of hickory, pine, red oak, poplar, and maple. In spring and summer, such mountain wild flowers as Solomon's seal, jack-in-the-pulpit, Indian pink, trillium, and lily highlight the landscape.

Vogel State Park is eleven miles south of Blairsville, Georgia, on Rtes. 19 and 129. Cabins available year-round. Rates: $30 to $48 per night. Cash, checks, Visa, and MasterCard accepted. Reservations taken up to eleven months in advance, recommended that early for summer, October, and all weekends. Cabins reserved only for full weeks in summer; two-night minimum the rest of the year.

North Carolina

STATE PARK INFORMATION:
NORTH CAROLINA DIVISION OF PARKS AND
    RECREATION
P.O. BOX 27687
RALEIGH, NC 27611
(919) 733-4181

TOURISM INFORMATION:
NORTH CAROLINA TRAVEL AND TOURISM DIVISION
430 NORTH SALISBURY STREET
RALEIGH, NC 27611
(919) 733-4171

STATE BIRD: *Cardinal*
STATE MAMMAL: *Gray Squirrel*
STATE TREE: *Longleaf Pine*
STATE FLOWER: *Dogwood*
STATE FISH: *Channel Bass*

Rocky Knob Cabin, Blue Ridge Parkway, North Carolina

BLUE RIDGE PARKWAY
700 NORTHWESTERN BANK
BUILDING
ASHEVILLE, NC 28801
(704) 258-2850

PEAKS OF OTTER LODGE
VIRGINIA PEAKS OF OTTER
COMPANY
P.O. BOX 489
BEDFORD, VA 24523
(703) 586-1081

ROCKY KNOB CABINS
NATIONAL PARK
CONCESSIONS, INC.
MILE POST 174
MEADOWS OF DAN, VA 24120
(703) 593-3503
(919) 982-2988 (winter)

BLUFFS LODGE
NATIONAL PARK
CONCESSIONS, INC.
MILE POST 241
LAUREL SPRINGS, NC 28644
(919) 372-4499
(919) 982-2988 (winter)

PISGAH INN
PARKWAY INN, INC.
P.O. DRAWER 749
WAYNESVILLE, NC 28786
(704) 235-8228

Not a park in the traditional sense, the Blue Ridge Parkway extends 469 miles through the southern Appalachians, past vistas of quiet natural beauty and lush rural landscapes. Designed by the National Park Service especially for motor recreation, the parkway leisurely links a series of mountain crests from Shenandoah National Park in northern Virginia to Great Smoky Mountains National Park on the North Carolina–Tennessee border.

The Southern Highlands are a land of forested mountains, exquisite during flowering spring, cool in green summer, resplendent in red fall. Cruising at the maximum speed of forty-five miles per hour, your views are enlivened by highland farms, whose split-rail fences, weathered cabins, and gray barns evoke the "hill culture" along these three-thousand-foot crests. Rhododendron, azalea, white pine, and other native plants border the roadsides, creating pastoral settings.

Hiking trails branch off from scenic overlooks, allowing close-up exploration of forests, meadows, and trout-rich streams. In southern Virginia, rustic Mabry Mill is powered by springwater rushing down a white-oak flume, turning a massive waterwheel that drives the grinding stones. Grain and corn are reduced to flour and meal, both of which are available for purchase. Along with the mill, a blacksmith shop, sawmill, sorghum vats, and apple-butter kettles make up this slice of mountain history.

Overnight accommodations can be found at four locations along Blue Ridge Parkway, as well as in neighboring towns. Peaks of Otter Lodge, at mile post 86 near Bedford, Virginia, holds fifty-eight rooms and three suites in a rough-cut pine structure. Each guest room features a splendid view of lake and mountains, and second-floor accommodations have cathedral ceilings with exposed beams. Snug between Sharp Top and Flat Top mountains, the main lodge has a sun porch with fireplace, an English-style pub, and a dining room renowned for prime rib, trout, and blackberry cobbler. *Rates: $50 per night for two people. Cash, checks, Visa, and MasterCard accepted. Reservations taken starting in October for the coming year; recommended that early for the next foliage season.*

Near Meadows of Dan, Virginia, at mile post 174, Rocky Knob's seven cabins line the edge of a thick woods, cooled by pleasant breezes. Just two miles from Mabry Mill, these frame cabins sleep up to four people apiece on two double beds. Each is equipped with kitchen appliances and running water, and they share a central bathouse. Built in the 1930s, these cabins are available Memorial Day to Labor Day. *Rates: $24 per night for two people, two-night minimum stay. Cash, checks, Visa, and Master-*

Card accepted. Reservations taken up to a year in advance, recommended one to two months in advance.

At mile post 241, near Laurel Springs, North Carolina, is the twenty-four-room Bluffs Lodge, set on a hillside at 3750 feet above sea level with a fine view of meadows and mountains. A massive outdoor fireplace on the breeze-way patio takes the chill out of an autumn evening. This timber lodge, open May through October, sleeps two people in each of its guest rooms, which have tile baths and showers. Regional dishes please the palate at nearby Bluffs Coffee Shop. *Rates: $42 per night for two people. Cash, checks, Visa, and MasterCard accepted. Reservations taken up to one year in advance, recommended one to two months in advance.*

At mile post 408.6, near Waynesville, North Carolina, Pisgah Inn offers fifty-one guest rooms and dining on the likes of fresh trout, country ham, chicken cordon bleu, and prime rib. The inn is open May through October, and the latter month is particularly popular because of magnificent foliage displays. *Rates: $45 per night for two people. Cash, Visa, and MasterCard accepted. Reservations taken up to one year in advance, recommended four to six months in advance.*

CAPE LOOKOUT NATIONAL
   SEASHORE
P.O. BOX 690
BEAUFORT, NC 28516
(919) 728-2121, 728-4121

MORRIS MARINA, FERRY,
   AND KABIN KAMPS
STAR ROUTE BOX 76J
ATLANTIC, NC 28511
(919) 225-4261

Cape Lookout consists of a narrow ribbon of sand that stretches from Ocracoke Inlet southwest to Beaufort Inlet. These barrier islands, fifty-five miles long in all, separate the Atlantic Ocean from the North Carolina coastline with wide beaches and dunes covered only by scattered grasses, and long expanses of salt marsh.

Wind, waves, and currents continually struggle to re-shape these low-lying islands; each strong storm makes extensive renovations. Only the most tenacious plants survive this constant battle; grasses such as sea oats use their deep roots to anchor in the sand.

Human beings have found this environment difficult yet bountiful. A map dating from 1590 refers to Cape Lookout as *promontorium tremendum* — "horrible headland" — in recognition of its treacherous shoals. Nonetheless, fishing and whaling have been important industries for centuries on the Outer Banks, a tradition that continues with modern commercial fishing.

But it's sport fishing in the Atlantic surf that attracts visitors here, as catches of flounder, trout, puppy drum, large drum, pompano, and whiting are common. Swimming, surfing, shelling, sunbathing, and hiking are other Cape Lookout attractions, and dune buggies and three-wheelers roam the low dunes.

Captain Don Morris operates a ferry between his marina at Core Sound (on the mainland) and his seventeen cabins on the island (round-trip rates: $50 per automobile plus $10 per person). These rough wood cabins range in age from twenty to forty years. All are equipped with bunk beds, gas stoves, and baths, several with hot water and showers. Sleeping from four to twelve people apiece, the cabins have one, two, or three rooms.

Other points of interest include historic Portsmouth Village at the northern tip of this windswept barrier island. Here, heavily laden ships coming in from the Atlantic once met shallow-draft vessels capable of transporting cargo through the waters of Ocracoke Inlet. From its founding in 1753 until its demise during the Civil War, Portsmouth grew rapidly as a transshipment point for goods destined for New Bern, Bath, and other North Carolina ports.

Cape Lookout National Seashore is east of Beaufort, North Carolina, off Rte. 70. Cabins available March through November. Rates: $24 to $90 per night. Cash and checks accepted. Reservations taken up to one year in advance, recommended three to six months in advance for spring and fall.

HANGING ROCK STATE PARK
P.O. Box 186
DANBURY, NC 27016
(919) 593-8480

Hanging Rock State Park takes its name from its most prominent topographical feature, an enormous quartzite boulder that juts two hundred feet out of a hillside. Clear, sparkling mountain streams, breathtaking cascades, and peaceful waterfalls highlight this north-central North Carolina park's many hiking trails. The trail leading to Hanging Rock rises steeply to a vista across the Dan River valley to the Blue Ridge Mountains. Upper Cascades Trail drops through sand ridges and pines to a moist stream bank overhung with giant hemlocks. Here, edged by mountain galax and beds of rhododendron, a stream plunges one hundred feet in a series of short falls.

Hanging Rock's twelve-acre lake is popular with swimmers, anglers, and boaters, and rental rowboats are available. Amateur climbers flock to Moore's Knob, while others head for Balanced Rock, which appears to be precariously perched on a ridgetop.

Six frame cabins stand in this park's forest, away from noise and distractions. Each has two bedrooms, a bathroom, kitchen appliances, and a living room. Window screens let cool mountain air drift through the cabins, which sleep up to six people apiece.

Hanging Rock State Park is one of the few places where Canadian and Carolina hemlock grow side by side; the unusual table mountain pine, noted for its long, prickly scales, can also be found here. Hummingbirds often nest over the waterfalls, and the calls of screech owls and whippoorwills fill the evening air.

Hanging Rock State Park is five miles west of Danbury, North Carolina, off Rte. 1101. Cabins available April through October. Rates: $25 per night, $150 per week. Checks accepted. Reservations taken starting in January. Cabins rented only for full weeks in summer.

MORROW MOUNTAIN STATE PARK
ROUTE 5, BOX 430
ALBEMARLE, NC 28001
(704) 982-4402

More than 400 million years ago, volcanic islands emerged from the shallow seas that had covered the Carolina Slate Belt. The hard rocks produced by lava flows, basalt and rhyolite, resisted erosion by the Pee Dee River more effectively than did the softer volcanic slate that underlies much of the region. This difference in erosion rates created the rugged Uwharrie Mountains.

Excavated villages indicate that Indians settled along the riverbanks here ten thousand years ago, remaining in the area until the early 1700s. They fished, farmed the rich lowlands, and quarried rhyolite (volcanic flint) from nearby hilltops — especially Morrow Mountain — for tool-making and trading with other tribes.

Today, half a dozen trails climb this mountain acreage. Three Rivers Trail winds past swampy woodlands to a riverbank, skirts an open marsh, and tops a small hill overlooking the confluence of the Yadkin, Pee Dee, and Uwharrie rivers. Along Fall Mountain Trail, you have an excellent chance of spotting kingfisher, great blue heron, osprey, wood duck, or pileated woodpeckers. Boat-launching ramps enter the Pee Dee River just around a bend from Lake Tillery. Swimmers in this park frolic in a modern pool.

Morrow Mountain's six rough wood cabins, built in the late 1950s, accommodate up to six people in two bedrooms and a sofa bed. Shaded by oaks, beeches, and tulip poplars, the cabins feature electric kitchens, hot and cold water, fireplaces, and pleasant screened porches.

Morrow Mountain State Park is seven miles east of Albemarle, North Carolina, on Rte. 1719. Cabins available April through October. Rates: $25 per night, $150 per week. Checks accepted. Reservations taken starting in January. Cabins rented only for full weeks in summer.

South Carolina

~~~

STATE PARK INFORMATION:
SOUTH CAROLINA DIVISION OF STATE PARKS
1205 PENDLETON STREET
COLUMBIA, SC 29201
(803) 758-3622

TOURISM INFORMATION:
SOUTH CAROLINA DIVISION OF TOURISM
P.O. BOX 71
COLUMBIA, SC 29202
(803) 758-8735

STATE BIRD: *Carolina Wren*
STATE MAMMAL: *White-tailed Deer*
STATE TREE: *Palmetto*
STATE FLOWER: *Yellow Jessamine*
STATE FISH: *Striped Bass*

BARNWELL STATE PARK
ROUTE 2, BOX 147
BLACKVILLE, SC 29817
(803) 284-2212

Settled by transplanted Virginians and known as Red Hill during the American Revolution, the town of Barnwell is the county seat in a southwest South Carolina area of swamps, rivers, and pine forests. Race horses graze in pastures and train for spring races and (with luck) national glory later in the season. In Barnwell's courthouse square stands an unusual vertical sundial, believed to be the only one of its kind in the country. Just out of town is Healing Springs, whose waters are reputed to have medicinal properties.

Five miles south of the springs, Barnwell State Park comprises 307 acres of level terrain and upland forests of pines and hardwoods. A small swamp fed by Toby Creek holds several species native to the Sandhills, such as scrub oak. The park incorporates two small, tranquil lakes, the larger of which has a swimming beach, bathhouse, and rental boats, and a two-mile nature trail.

The park's five two-bedroom cabins have unusual, octagonal shapes and natural wood siding. Each sleeps up to six people, and has heating, air conditioning, and electric appliances. An outdoor picnic table and barbecue grill set the scene for a family cookout. Encircled by trees, the cabins are within easy walking distance of the lakes and beach.

Barnwell State Park is three miles south of Blackville, South Carolina, on Rte. 3. Cabins available year-round. Rates: $25 per night, $150 per week. Cash and checks accepted. Reservations taken starting in November for the following year. Weekend reservations must be for three nights; cabins rented on daily basis if not reserved.

CHERAW STATE PARK
P.O. Box 888
CHERAW, SC 29520
(803) 537-2215

South Carolina's first and largest state park, Cheraw embraces approximately seven thousand acres in the state's Sandhills region. The Sandhills consist of ancient dunes formed when the Atlantic coastline was far inland from its present location. Over a period of millions of years, the ocean receded to the east and then returned to the Sandhills at least four times. Later, pines and scrub oak sprouted in the dunes. Remains of these dunes can still be seen along a line reaching from Cheraw (in northeast South Carolina) to North Augusta (on the southwestern edge of the state).

Civilian Conservation Corps workers labored at Cheraw in the 1930s. Soon after, the National Park Service acquired 6657 acres adjoining the park and established Cheraw National Fish Hatchery, which raises bass, redear sunfish, channel and albino catfish, longnose gar, and Israeli carp. Visitors tour this intriguing facility.

Picturesque Lake Juniper, a three-hundred-acre, three-mile-long expanse of clear water at the center of this park, offers a swimming beach, fishing, and rental boats. Cheraw's natural landmarks include cedar bogs, trees containing the nests of red-cockaded woodpeckers, beaver colonies, and the only Hudsonia shrubs south of Pennsylvania. A sizable flock of Canada geese winters at Lake Juniper. Four miles away, the town of Cheraw, known as one of the prettiest communities in Dixie, has many historic homes and buildings.

Eight wood-sided cabins, constructed during CCC days, loll under tall pines on a gentle slope. These three-room cabins accommodate up to six people on double beds and fold-out couches. Heated and air-conditioned, each contains a fully equipped kitchen and an outdoor barbecue grill and picnic table, and most have screened porches.

Cheraw State Park is four miles southwest of Cheraw, South Carolina, on Rte. 1. Cabins available year-round. Rates: $15 per night, $90 per week. Cash and checks ac-

cepted. Reservations taken starting in November for the following year. Weekend reservations must be for three nights; cabins rented on a daily basis if not reserved.

EDISTO BEACH STATE PARK
ROUTE 1, Box 84
EDISTO ISLAND, SC 29438
(803) 869-2156

Beachcombers delight in the large number of shells discovered on Edisto Island, including occasionally the petrified remains of strange creatures that roamed this land long before man. Fossilized bone fragments from bison, mastadons, giant armadillos, three-toed horses, and other exotic species have all been collected along this shore, located toward the southern end of South Carolina's Atlantic coast.

Edisto Beach State Park's 1225 acres include a sandy strip of beach on the Atlantic, deep green woods, and an expanse of open salt marsh. This island park also boasts some of South Carolina's tallest palmetto trees, which rise above semitropical undergrowth.

The park and island take their name from the Edisto Indians, a peaceful agrarian tribe who lived here as long ago as four thousand years and left mounds of shells. No one knows if these shell mounds were burial grounds, ceremonial sites, or even refuse heaps, and it's possible that different mounds served each of these functions. During Prohibition, ships from the Caribbean slipped into quiet inlets here and unloaded their illegal cargoes under cover of darkness.

Perhaps Edisto Beach's most remarkable ecosystem, the salt marsh hosts diverse life forms. Some, such as shrimp, live and spawn in the sea, but come to the shallow, productive waters of the tidelands to mature. Others, such as fiddler crabs, spawn in the marshes, mature at sea, and later return to the marsh, taking up residence in small holes in the mud.

Constructed of wood, Edisto Beach's five cabins have four rooms, including two bedrooms. They sleep six people and are both heated and air-conditioned. These forty-five-year-old cabins line the shore of a bay; they are equipped with kitchen appliances, hot and cold running water, and screened porches.

As you would expect, this oceanfront park offers swimming and fishing, and fine seafood restaurants and deep-sea fishing charters are nearby. Historic Charleston is forty-five miles away.

Edisto Beach State Park is forty-five miles southwest of Charleston, South Carolina, on Rte. 174. Cabins available year-round. Rates: $25 to $28 per night, $150 to $168 per week. Cash and checks accepted. Reservations taken starting in November for the following year. Weekend reservations must be for three nights; cabins rented on a daily basis if not reserved. Cabins rented only for full weeks in summer.

GIVHANS FERRY STATE PARK
ROUTE 3, BOX 49
RIDGEVILLE, SC 29472
(803) 873-0692

Givhans Ferry State Park, 1235 acres of coastal plain in southeast South Carolina, overlooks the Edisto River. A diverse mix of vegetation exists here, pines and hardwoods standing not far from cypress, tupelo, and rare spruce pine. Anglers and hikers enjoy the river, where fish await bait and hook, and trails trace the banks.

The riverbank is also the location of four forty-five-year-old cabins, grouped together in the shade of tall trees. Each of these four-room cabins sleeps up to six people, in two bedrooms and on a fold-out couch. Furnished with full kitchens, heating, air conditioning, and fireplaces, the cabins also offer outdoor picnic tables and barbecue grills.

In addition to enjoying the beauty of Givhans Ferry State Park, visitors can also travel forty miles east to Charleston, South Carolina, a beautiful colonial port city where doll-like pastel houses peek at you from behind lacy iron grates. Seventy-three Charleston buildings predate the revolutionary war, 136 were constructed before 1800, and 600 others existed by the 1840s. As you stroll the quiet side streets and alleyways, cross spacious piazzas, visit antique shops and boutiques, and sample fine cuisine in many outstanding restaurants, it's difficult not to be charmed by Charleston.

Givhans Ferry State Park is sixteen miles west of Summerville, South Carolina, on Rte. 61. Cabins available year-round. Rates: $20 per night, $120 per week. Cash and checks accepted. Reservations taken starting in November for the following year. Weekend reservations must be for three nights; cabins rented on a daily basis if not reserved.

HICKORY KNOB STATE RESORT PARK
ROUTE 1, BOX 199-B
MCCORMICK, SC 29835
(803) 443-2151

Hickory Knob State Resort Park, overlooking Clarks Hill Lake, adjoins the seemingly endless, seventy-five-thousand-acre Sumter National Forest in western South Carolina. Anglers find the lake's seventy thousand acres loaded with hybrid, white, and largemouth bass, as well as crappie and other panfish. Rental fishing boats are also available.

In the spring of 1982, Hickory Knob unveiled its 6560-yard, eighteen-hole golf course. This glorious tree-lined course challenges experts and duffers alike, along lush stands of pine, oak, and hickory and clear streams. A pro shop with rental carts and equipment rounds out this fine facility. Other Hickory Knob attractions includes hiking, bicycle riding (rentals available), swimming, tennis on two lighted courts, and archery, trap, and skeet ranges.

Hickory Knob's eleven hundred acres include accommodations in sixty lodge rooms and nine duplex cabins, all of which have color TVs. Each cabin has one bedroom with two double beds, plus a sofa bed in the living room. Half of the cabins feature fireplaces, and all are equipped with kitchenettes. Constructed of vertical wood planking, Hickory Knob's cabins line a bluff overlooking the lake, under tall pines. Twenty lodge rooms also face the lake-front, while the rest afford views of wooded hills.

Hickory Knob State Resort Park is eight miles southwest of McCormick, South Carolina, off Rte. 378. Cabins and *lodge open year-round. Rates: cabins, $45 per night, $270 per week; lodge, $30 to $34 per night for two people. Cash, checks, and Visa accepted. Cabins rented only for full weeks in summer.*

HUNTING ISLAND STATE PARK
ROUTE 1, Box 668
FROGMORE, SC 29920
(803) 838-2011

As early as 1859, a brick lighthouse on Hunting Island guided vessels along the Atlantic coast. By the late 1860s, beach erosion had destroyed that first beacon. Concerned about the erosion, the U.S. Coast Guard built a replacement lighthouse one-quarter mile from the shoreline. This new structure, erected of cast-iron plate, featured a design that would allow it to be moved, if necessary. By 1889, the sea had cut away the northern end of the island, forcing relocation of the lighthouse to its present site. Located midway between Charleston, South Carolina, and Savannah, Georgia, Hunting Island State Park contains this hundred-year-old lighthouse.

Hunting Island, one of South Carolina's most popular parks, attracts more than one million visitors annually. Approximately three miles long and one mile wide, the park encompasses some five thousand acres of beach, forest, and marsh. The island earned its name because it once was the site of hunting for deer, raccoon, and waterfowl.

With more than three miles of beach on the Atlantic Ocean, well-developed dune vegetation, maritime forests, and extensive salt marshes, the island has diverse natural appeal. Park visitors frequently encounter white-tailed deer and raccoon, and more than 125 species of birds have been sighted here, including significant numbers of herons, gulls, terns, and egrets.

Some sections of the smooth, sandy beach serve swimmers and surfers; others are set aside for surf-fishing. During summer and fall, fine catches of whiting, spot, trout, bass, and drum exhilarate anglers.

Hunting Island's fourteen cabins, most of which were

built in the late 1950s, have heating, air conditioning, full kitchens, and hot and cold running water. Five feature fireplaces, some have screened porches, and nine front the beach under scattered palmettos and pines.

Nearby attractions include the many historic sites in Beaufort, South Carolina, some twenty minutes away. These include the Beaufort Arsenal Museum, built in 1795, and Parris Island Museum.

Hunting Island State Park is sixteen miles east of Beaufort, South Carolina, on Rte. 21. Cabins available year-round. Rates: $33 to $50 per night, $198 to $300 per week. Cash and checks accepted. Reservations taken starting in November for the following year. Cabins rented only for full weeks in summer; weekend reservations must be for three nights. Cabins rented on a daily basis if not reserved.

KEOWEE-TOXAWAY STATE PARK
SUNSET, SC 29685
(803) 868-2605

Once the center of the Lower Cherokee Indian civilization, the Keowee-Toxaway area is still rich in Indian heritage. Extensive archaeological work prior to the flooding of Lake Keowee yielded countless artifacts, many of which are displayed in the park's interpretive center and in four outdoor kiosks along a quarter-mile nature trail.

Set in the northwest corner of the state amid sparkling lakes and the foothills of the Appalachian highlands, South Carolina's Keowee-Toxaway State Park is bisected by the Cherokee Foothills Scenic Highway (Route 11). Extending from near the North Carolina border in a 130-mile crescent to the Georgia line, this highway threads mountain forests. Historical and recreational attractions along the way include Cowpens National Battlefield, where, in 1781, Americans handed the British their most devastating defeat of the Southern campaign; Poinsett Bridge, a massive stone bridge with a pointed arch of wedge-shaped rock; and Sumter National Forest.

Keowee-Toxaway's single cabin, a three-bedroom, wood-sided structure enveloped by tall pines and hardwoods near Lake Keowee, sleeps up to ten people. This deluxe cabin features two fireplaces, heating, air conditioning, a full kitchen, and an outdoor picnic table and barbecue grill.

Fishermen will want to try their luck in Lake Keowee, while others might prefer the adventure of Raven Rock Hiking Trail. This four-mile trail emerges from thick woodlands at a point looking down more than three hundred feet onto the lake. Not far from the park thunders Whitewater Falls, one of the highest waterfalls in the Southeast.

Keowee-Toxaway State Park is twenty miles northeast of Walhalla, South Carolina, on Rte. 11. Cabin available year-round. Rates: $50 per night, $300 per week. Cash and checks accepted. Reservations taken starting in November for the following year. Weekend reservations must be for three nights; cabin rented on a daily basis if not reserved.

MYRTLE BEACH STATE PARK
U.S. 17-S
MYRTLE BEACH, SC 29577
(803) 238-5325

This 312-acre oceanfront state park lies in the heart of South Carolina's Grand Strand — fifty-five miles of deep blue waters and white-sand beaches toward the northern end of the state's Atlantic coast. Cherry Grove, Ocean Drive, Crescent, Windy Hill, Atlantic, Myrtle Beach — these are some of the most popular resorts along the East Coast, captivating countless thousands of visitors annually.

At the center of all of this, Myrtle Beach State Park offers five frame cabins, painted white, facing the surf. Pines form the backdrop for these forty-five-year-old structures, and sand dunes and sea oats edge the beach. Each cabin has a large screened porch, for admiring the ocean, and outdoor picnic tables and barbecue grills. These two-bedroom units accommodate up to six people and have full kitchens, heating, and air conditioning. A former park store, near the park's camping area, has been converted into two apartments, which are also available for overnight guests.

The Atlantic naturally dominates park activities; sunbathing, swimming, and fishing are all favorites. For those who prefer, Myrtle Beach State Park also has a swimming pool, and anglers can choose between a fishing pier and surf-fishing in their pursuit of channel bass, flounder, spots, and whiting. Bait, tackle, and rental rods are available at the snack bar. Sport charter boats for bill-fishing and bottom fishing depart daily from the surrounding coastal villages, and crabbing is yet another popular pastime. As you would expect of a resort as renowned as Myrtle Beach, the area hosts a nearly unlimited number of fine restaurants serving everything from fresh seafood to southern specialties.

Myrtle Beach State Park is three miles south of Myrtle Beach, South Carolina, on Rte. 17. Cabins and apartments available year-round. Rates: $25 to $40 per night, $120 to $240 per week. Cash and checks accepted. Reservations taken starting in November for the following year. Weekend reservations must be for three nights; cabins and apartments rented only for full weeks in summer. Lodging rented on a daily basis if not reserved.

OCONEE STATE PARK
STAR ROUTE
WALHALLA, SC 29691
(803) 638-5353

Populated by tall trees on a high plateau between Stump House Mountain and Station Mountain in northwest South Carolina, Oconee State Park presents a restful retreat. From vantage points here in the heart of mountain country, you can look out over South Carolina's Choe Valley, Rabun Bald in Georgia, and Satoola and Whiteside mountains in North Carolina.

Park visitors congregate at a crystal-clear, twenty-acre lake fed by two mountain streams. Well-stocked with bass and bream for fishing, the lake has a sandy bottom and grassy beach ideal for swimming, while paddleboats splash by.

Constructed in the late 1930s, Oconee's nineteen wooden cabins have two bedrooms, and a few have sleeping lofts. Some feature log construction, others have lakefront views, but all offer the tranquility of a wood-burning fireplace. These cabins accommodate from four to eight people in one or two bedrooms, and are heated and air-conditioned.

Oconee's 1165 acres exude the sights and sounds of a forest in the Blue Ridge Mountains. Rhododendron, mountain laurel, and dogwood bloom in spring and early summer, filling the woods with magnificent pink and white blossoms. In fall, rolling hills explode with bursts of color — red, orange, gold, and yellow.

Many day trips can be made from Oconee: to excellent nearby trout streams, for example, or to the U.S. Fish and Wildlife Service's fish hatchery, one of the world's largest. To the south, look for Stump House Mountain Tunnel and Issaqueena Falls; to the north, there's Whitewater Falls, one of the highest waterfalls in the eastern United States. To the east stands Oconee Station, the oldest building in Oconee County, while to the west lies the Chattooga River, a National Wild and Scenic River.

Oconee State Park is twelve miles northwest of Walhalla, South Carolina, on Rte. 107. Cabins available year-round. Rates: $28 to $38 per night, $168 to $228 per week. Cash and checks accepted. Reservations taken starting in November for the following year. Weekend reservations must be for three nights; cabins rented only for full weeks in summer. Cabins rented on a daily basis if not reserved.

PLEASANT RIDGE STATE PARK
P.O. BOX 2
CLEVELAND, SC 29635
(803) 836-6589

An unspoiled wilderness awaits in South Carolina's piedmont, home of wild rivers, dense forests, and picturesque waterfalls. One of a number of northwest South Carolina parks along the Cherokee Foothills Scenic Highway, Pleasant Ridge State Park consists of three hundred acres of steep terrain that is thickly wooded and profusely covered with shrubs and wild flowers. At the end of the park road, tucked away among poplar, sweet gum, maple, pine, and sycamore trees lies a three-acre lake perfect for swimming and fishing. Paddleboats can also be rented at this quiet lake, and Pleasant Ridge's two cabins enjoy lakefront locations.

These ten-year-old, wood-sided cabins have four rooms, including two bedrooms, and will sleep up to six people apiece. Each has a fireplace, a full kitchen, electric heat, air conditioning, and an outdoor barbecue grill and picnic table.

In spring and summer at Pleasant Ridge, the woods come alive with dogwood, rhododendron, mountain laurel, wild azalea, and honeysuckle. Come autumn, an entirely different spectrum of colors overpowers the landscape. Hiking trails here climb hills and ridges and wander through ravines thick with vegetation.

Pleasant Ridge State Park is twenty-two miles northwest of Greenville, South Carolina, on Rte. 11. Cabins available year-round. Rates: $25 per night, $150 per week. Cash and checks accepted. Reservations taken starting in November for the following year. Weekend reservations must be for three nights; cabins rented on a daily basis if not reserved.

POINSETT STATE PARK
WEDGEFIELD, SC 29168
(803) 775-1231

Poinsett State Park bears the name of the famed South Carolina naturalist, statesman, and educator Joel Robert Poinsett. He's probably best remembered as the man who brought the Christmas flower home from the wilds of Mexico — a flower fellow scientists called poinsettia.

The road to Poinsett crests hills covered with giant hardwoods, pines, and Spanish moss. Lying in the center of the state, between the Sandhills and coastal plain, the rolling terrain of the park stands in contrast to the flat surrounding countryside. Ancient marine deposits of fuller's earth and coquina are other intriguing features here.

Fuller's earth, a sedimentary formation high in silica, derives its name from its first use by "fullers," who processed cloth. This substance absorbed the "yolk" or natural oils and greases from wool. Modern uses of fuller's earth include as a body for lubricants and as a base for cosmetics.

The rock used to construct the bathhouse and other structures at Poinsett, coquina, had its origin thousands of years ago when seas covered the coastal plain. The skeletal remains of marine animals such as oysters and corals accumulated on beaches and in shallow waters, and were broken into fragments by wave action. Coquina is rock composed of such shell fragments; the name derives from the Spanish word for "shell."

Two creeks ripple through Poinsett State Park: Campbell's Creek and Shank's Creek. Man-made Christmas Mill Lake has pleased swimmers and anglers since before the American Revolution. Fishermen try their luck for largemouth bass, and paddleboats and canoes can be rented, but no private boats are permitted.

Poinsett's four cabins inhabit a stand of trees not far from Shank's Creek. Next to each of these CCC-era wooden units is a picnic table and grill. Inside you'll find one or two bedrooms, simple furnishings, electric kitchens, and hot and cold running water. Heating and air conditioning provide comfort for all seasons, and a fireplace gives a homey ambience.

Poinsett State Park is eighteen miles southwest of Sumter, South Carolina, off Rte. 261. Cabins available year-round. Rates: $15 to $20 per night, $90 to $120 per week. Cash and checks accepted. Reservations taken starting in November for the following year. Weekend reservations must be for three nights; cabins rented on a daily basis if not reserved.

SANTEE STATE RESORT PARK
ROUTE 1, BOX 255-A
SANTEE, SC 29142
(803) 854-2408

More than 171,000 acres of water in Lake Marion and Lake Moultrie (the Santee-Cooper Lakes) challenge fishermen to break one of two world- and eight state-record catches established here. These lakes, famous as the home of landlocked striped bass weighing more than fifty pounds — the king of freshwater fighting fish — also

Cabins, Santee State Resort Park, South Carolina

have produced world-record black crappie and channel catfish. Other species abundant in the lakes include large-mouth bass, white bass, black bass, and bream. But fishing is far from the only activity here; nonanglers come for swimming, sailing, and waterskiing.

Santee State Resort Park hugs the banks of Lake Marion, in eastern South Carolina. Its thirty unique "rondette" (octagonal-shaped) redwood cabins sleep six people apiece. Ten of these cabins rest on a pier over the lake, and each of these ten has a private boat dock. The other twenty line a dense, moss-draped, wooded chunk of lakeshore, and they too feature docking facilities. All cabins are completely furnished, heated, and air-conditioned, and each has a kitchen and hot and cold running water. Those on shore also have redwood decks with outdoor tables and grills.

Thousands of acres of timberland in Santee-Cooper Country, as the area is called, nurture deer, turkey, dove, pheasant, goose, duck, and rabbit. Several nearby golf courses delight enthusiasts, and boats and bicycles can both be rented inside the park. Revolutionary war battle sites and pre-Civil War homes and churches give a flavor of the area's rich history.

Santee State Resort Park is three miles northwest of Santee, South Carolina, off Rte. 301. Cabins available year-round. Rates: $36 to $39 per night, $216 to $234 per week. Cash, checks, Visa, and MasterCard accepted.

Reservations taken starting in November for the follow-ing year. Cabins rented only for full weeks in summer; weekend reservations must be for three nights. Cabins rented on a daily basis if not reserved.

TABLE ROCK STATE PARK
ROUTE 3
PICKENS, SC 29671
(803) 878-9813

Long before the coming of white settlers, Indians chris-tened the area around Table Rock State Park "Sah-ka-na-ga," the Great Blue Hills of God. They believed that a gigantic chieftain sat upon a nearby rise called the "stool" and dined from a "table" nearly thirty-two hundred feet high — hence the name for this flat-topped mountain, Table Rock.

Against the backdrop of northwest South Carolina's natural beauty, Table Rock's 3069 acres extend over green mountains into dark valleys, shadowed by neighboring peaks. Rhododendron, mountain laurel, dogwood, and hundreds of other species add their brilliance to cool forests of pines and mixed hardwoods.

Activity focuses on Pinnacle Lake, a shimmering, thirty-six-acre body of water with a swimming beach, bathhouse, and rental boats. Table Rock's trail system, designated a National Recreational Trail, commences at the nature center. One path climbs to the summit of Table Rock Mountain, while another twists its way to the even taller Pinnacle Mountain. A three-mile trail con-nects the two peaks, completing a ten-mile hiking tour that passes blue granite boulders, sheer thousand-foot cliffs, a mountain stream and its spectacular waterfall, and several smaller cascades.

Most of this park's fifteen cabins inhabit a hillside a short distance from Pinnacle Lake. Made either of logs or of rough wood planking, the cabins have from one to three bedrooms and sleep from four to twelve people. All are equipped with refrigerators, ranges, hot and cold running water, fireplaces, and outdoor barbecue grills and picnic tables. Some include screened porches.

Table Rock State Park is sixteen miles north of Pickens, South Carolina, on Rte. 11. Cabins available year-round. Rates: $28 to $39 per night, $168 to $234 per week. Cash and checks accepted. Reservations taken starting in November for the following year. Cabins rented only for full weeks in summer; weekend reservations must be for three nights. Cabins rented on a daily basis if not reserved.

Virginia

STATE PARK INFORMATION:
VIRGINIA DIVISION OF PARKS AND RECREATION
1201 WASHINGTON BUILDING
CAPITOL SQUARE
RICHMOND, VA 23219
(804) 786-2132

TOURISM INFORMATION:
VIRGINIA DIVISION OF TOURISM
202 NORTH NINTH STREET, SUITE 500
RICHMOND, VA 23219
(804) 786-4484

STATE BIRD: *Cardinal*
STATE TREE: *Flowering Dogwood*
STATE FLOWER: *Flowering Dogwood*

Cabin, Shenandoah National Park, Virginia

SHENANDOAH NATIONAL PARK
LURAY, VA 22835
(703) 999-2266

ARA VIRGINIA SKY-LINE COMPANY, INC. (CABINS AND LODGES)
P.O. BOX 727
LURAY, VA 22835
(703) 999-2211, 999-2221 *(current-year reservations)*
(703) 743-5108 *(following-year reservations)*

POTOMAC APPALACHIAN TRAIL CLUB (CABINS)
1718 N STREET, NW
WASHINGTON, D.C. 20036
(202) 638-5306 *(weeknights, 7:00 to 10:00 P.M. only)*

Shenandoah National Park lies astride a stunning section of the Blue Ridge, the eastern rampart of the Appalachian Mountains. In a valley to the west flows the Shenandoah River, while to the east can be seen the pastoral, rolling Piedmont country. Offering spectacular vistas of this terrain and its neighboring valleys is Skyline Drive, which runs along the Blue Ridge the length of the park.

Over the course of centuries of residence by mountain

farmers who cleared land, hunted wildlife, and grazed sheep and cattle, the ridge suffered as its forests shrank, game animals disappeared, and soil wore out. Once this 195,000-acre national park was established in the 1930s, the cropland soon became overgrown with shrubs, locusts, and pines; these were eventually replaced by oak, hickory, and other trees that constitute a mature deciduous forest. Today, more than 95 percent of the park is woodland, with a hundred species of trees present. At Big Meadows, which is maintained as open land through managed fires, an abundance of wild flowers, strawberries, and blueberries lures both humans and wildlife.

Deer, bear, bobcat, turkey, and other animals that were rare or absent have now returned. Approximately two hundred types of birds have been spotted in the park, including such permanent residents as the ruffed grouse, barred owl, raven, woodpecker, and junco.

Shenandoah's spring begins in March with blooming red maple, serviceberry, and hepatica, and the appearance of chipmunks and groundhogs. The leafing of trees with green moves up the ridges at a rate of one hundred feet per day, until it reaches the peaks in late May.

Summer brings a mantle of deep green to hilltops and hollows, where catbirds, chestnut-sided warblers, indigo buntings, and towhees abound. Brilliant colors and clear, crisp days announce the arrival of fall, as does the southward migration of birds, particularly the large numbers of hawks that move along the ridge. Come winter, leafless trees provide unobstructed views of distant valleys, enhanced by frequent blankets of snow.

In addition to touring Skyline Drive, visitors can discover this park via more than five hundred miles of hiking trails, which vary from short leg-stretchers to a ninety-five-mile segment of the Appalachian Trail. Fishing the rushing creeks and streams for native brook trout rewards those willing to hike to Shenandoah's tree-lined waterways.

ARA Virginia Sky-Line Company offers cabins and lodge accommodations at three sites along Skyline Drive. At the drive's highest elevation, Skyland Lodge has 150 motel-type rooms and eight sleeping cabins (no kitchens). Built in the early 1950s, the lodge complex includes a glass-walled dining room with a view of the valley and a lounge that hosts live entertainment.

Big Meadows Lodge, set on a high plateau overlooking the Shenandoah Valley, has a total of ninety-three rooms in its main lodge building, motels, and cabins. Constructed in 1939 of stone and native chestnut, the lodge features a fine restaurant, a lounge with a rock fireplace, and striking floors of flagstone and random-width oak. On a clear day, dining-room guests take in a forty-mile, panoramic view across the entire Appalachian Range into West Virginia. Each motel room at Big Meadows contains two double beds and a private bath, and some offer scenic views.

Big Meadows's five cabins have wood-burning fireplaces but no cooking facilities. Additional cabins are available at Lewis Mountain; they are equipped with indoor baths and electric heat.

Shenandoah National Park is nine miles east of Luray, Virginia, on Rte. 211. Lodging available at Skyland Lodge early April through October; Lewis Mountain, late April through October; Big Meadows, mid-May through October. Rates: $25 to $48 per night for two people. Cash, checks, Visa, MasterCard, and American Express accepted. Reservations taken starting in early May for the following year, recommended at least three months in advance.

Potomac Appalachian Trail Club maintains six cabins in Shenandoah National Park for use both by club members and the general public. Some of these cabins were built by club members, some by rangers or the Civilian Conservation Corps, and still others served as homes for early settlers. All are rustic, having bunks and mattresses, tables, chairs, and cooking utensils, but no running water or electricity.

A substantial hike is usually required to reach a PATC cabin, with distances of one to four miles common. Although most weekend reservations go to club members, nonmembers can often secure weekday reservations throughout the year.

Potomac Appalachian Trail Club cabins available year-round. Rates: $6 to $12 per night for two people. Cash and checks accepted. Reservations taken up to three weeks in advance; phone reservations recommended.

CLAYTOR LAKE STATE PARK
ROUTE 1, BOX 267
DUBLIN, VA 24084
(703) 674-5492 (park office)
(804) 490-3939 (cabin reservations)

Western Virginia's twenty-one-mile-long Claytor Lake backs up behind a dam on the New River, which is ironically the oldest river in the Western Hemisphere. Built in 1939 by the Appalachian Power Company for hydroelectric power, the lake now has a sandy swimming beach and a marina that rents boats. It is popular for swimming, waterskiing, and fishing for catfish, perch, crappie, walleye, and bass. Claytor Lake State Park juts out into the lake on a wooded peninsula. The park's riding stable has saddle horses ready to hit the trails, including one trail that tops a limestone cliff above the lake.

Claytor Lake's administrative office occupies a historic structure built by Haven B. Howe in the late 1870s. The Howe House, constructed of handsome brick that was kiln-dried on the premises, features interior woodwork of walnut, maple, birch, and pine. Visitors tour this magnificent former residence to admire the outstanding craftsmanship employed in its construction.

Engulfed by an eastern deciduous forest, a dozen concrete-block cabins follow the lakeshore along this park's southern boundary. These two-bedroom cabins sleep up to six people apiece and have kitchens, baths, screened porches, and fireplaces.

Claytor Lake State Park is on Rte. 660 between Radford and Dublin, Virginia. Cabins available early May to early October. Rates: $25 per night, $150 per week. Cash and in-state checks accepted. Reservations taken up to fifty-one weeks in advance, recommended that early for summer. Cabins reserved only for full weeks; rented for less than a week if not reserved.

DOUTHAT STATE PARK
ROUTE 1, BOX 212
MILLBORO, VA 24460
(703) 862-7200 (park office)
(804) 490-3939 (cabin reservations)

Trout fishermen flock to Douthat State Park in the Allegheny Mountains to sample Wilson Creek's and Douthat Lake's stocked waters. Bass, chain pickerel, and sunfish also inhabit the lake and mountain streams in this state park, which is spread over 4493 acres of craggy ridges in central Virginia. Oak, hickory, and white-pine forests dominate the landscape, although birch, hemlock, beech, poplar, and maple trees thrive in deep hollows. Douthat's major understory plant is witch hazel, along with mountain laurel, rhododendron, and fetterbush. Blueberry, huckleberry, blackberry, and even an occasional wineberry highlight this parkland.

Douthat's three streams and fifty-acre lake form the headwaters of the Wilson Creek watershed, in this secluded valley between Beards Gap Mountain and Middle Mountain. Challenging hiking trails crisscross the park and the adjacent George Washington National Forest, guiding hikers to many scenic overlooks.

In addition to fishing, Douthat Lake hosts swimming and boating, and rental boats are available. The lakefront also offers launching ramps, but no gas-powered motors are permitted.

Douthat's visitor center, open in summer, displays rocks, plants, and wildlife indigenous to a mountain environment; nearby, blacksmithing demonstrations take place at the smithy's shop. If you've worked up an appetite, stop by the park restaurant for good food and a fine view of the lake.

Shaded by tall trees, some of Douthat's cabins line Wilson Creek, while others follow the lakeshore. Civilian Conservation Corps workers built the log cabins in the 1930s, and the concrete-block units were added in the 1940s and 1950s. The cabins range in size from one-room to two-bedrooms units, and sleep from two to six people. All have kitchens and fireplaces, and the concrete-block cabins include screened porches. Douthat also rents a six-bedroom, log lodge that can accommodate twelve people. It features two bathrooms, a fireplace, and a patio with a lake view.

Douthat State Park is six miles north of Clifton Forge, Virginia, on Rte. 629. Cabins and lodge available early May to early October. Rates: cabins, $20 to $30 per night, $95 to $180 per week; lodge, $85 per night, $375 per week. Cash and in-state checks accepted. Reservations taken up to fifty-one weeks in advance, recommended that early for summer. Cabins reserved only for full weeks; rented for less than a week if not reserved.

FAIRY STONE STATE PARK
ROUTE 2, BOX 134
STUART, VA 24171
(703) 930-2424 *(park office)*
(804) 490-3939 *(cabin reservations)*

Lodged in the foothills of the Blue Ridge Mountains in southern Virginia, this 4570-acre park derives its name from unique iron-aluminum-silicate crystals found in the ground near its southern tip. These "fairy stone" crystals, produced by a precise combination of heat and pressure during the creation of a mountain, commonly occur in pairs. When they intersect at right angles, they create a Latin or Maltese cross; at other angles, a Saint Andrew's cross. Legend has it that these stone crosses formed from the tears of elfin fairies who wept at the news of Christ's death. For many years, people held the little crosses in superstitious awe, firm in the belief that they protected the wearer against witchcraft, sickness, and accidents.

In addition to prospecting for fairy stones, visitors here can swim in a man-made lake and rent paddleboats and rowboats at the boat dock. Private boats can be launched at the park's ramps, but no motorized craft are permitted. Saddling up at the stables, you can ride through more than twenty miles of bridle and hiking paths — good places to observe deer, raccoons, and turkeys.

Fairy Stone's twenty-five cabins populate two peninsulas on the lake's south shore; some are right at the water's edge. The log cabins date from the 1930s, and the cinder-block units were constructed twenty years later. Cabin floor plans include one-room, one-bedroom, and two-bedroom models, sleeping from two to six people. All have full kitchens and fireplaces.

Fairy Stone State Park is ten miles west of Bassett, Virginia, on Rte. 346. Cabins available early May to early October. Rates: $16 to $25 per night, $80 to $150 per week. Cash and in-state checks accepted. Reservations taken up to fifty-one weeks in advance, recommended that early for summer. Cabins reserved only for full weeks; rented for less than a week if not reserved.

GOODWIN LAKE–PRINCE EDWARD STATE PARK
ROUTE 2, BOX 70
GREEN BAY, VA 23942
(804) 392-3435 *(park office)*
(804) 490-3939 *(cabin reservations)*

Blessed with two freshwater lakes — Goodwin Lake and Prince Edward Lake — this park specializes in water activities, such as swimming, boating, and fishing. Lifeguards oversee beaches on both lakes, and visitors can rent paddleboats and rowboats. A boat-launching ramp serves Prince Edward Lake, but no gas-powered vessels are permitted.

This southern Virginia park's six concrete-block cabins, built approximately thirty-five years ago, have two bedrooms, living rooms, baths with showers, and kitchens with electric appliances. The cabins accommodate up to six people apiece, and each has a wood-burning fireplace. From screened porches on three of these cabins, you can savor a view of Prince Edward Lake; the other three porches frame a glimpse of pine forest and abundant dogwood.

Hiking trails circle and connect the two lakes, and a bicycle trail meanders through hills covered by pines and hardwoods. Twin Beech Interpretive Trail identifies numerous plant species found here, including oak, hickory, dogwood, beech, and tulip poplar trees.

Goodwin Lake-Prince Edward State Park is three miles west of Burkeville, Virginia, on Rte. 360. Cabins available *early May to early October. Rates: $25 per night, $150 per week. Cash and checks accepted. Reservations taken up to fifty-one weeks in advance, recommended that early for summer. Cabins reserved only for full weeks; rented for less than a week if not reserved.*

HUNGRY MOTHER STATE PARK
ROUTE 5, BOX 109
MARION, VA 24354
(703) 783-3422 *(park office)*
(804) 490-3939 *(cabin reservations)*

The legend of Hungry Mother says that an Indian raiding party once attacked a settlement here, kidnapping women and children, including Molly Marley and her boy. The two eventually escaped from the Indians, but, after eating only berries for days, Molly collapsed at the foot of a mountain (now known as Molly's Knob). Her worried child wandered down a creek until he found a group of houses, and croaked to the occupants the words "Hungry — Mother!" A search party was formed, but by the time they found Molly, it was too late.

Adjacent to Jefferson National Forest in the Allegheny Mountains, Hungry Mother State Park comprises 2180 wooded acres in southwest Virginia. Hikers negotiate Molly's Knob Trail into the mountain highlands, discovering panoramic views of the parkland below and nearby Big Walker Mountain. Hungry Mother's placid, 108-acre lake describes six miles of shoreline, where fishermen wet a line for bass, crappie, bluegill, perch, catfish, and carp. A sand beach, bathhouse, and rental paddleboats and rowboats round out the lakefront facilities. Horseback riders enjoy leisurely journeys through this park's stands of oak, hickory, maple, locust, and pine.

Hungry Mother's twenty-five cabins, most of them two-bedroom units, rest on both sides of the lake. The log cabins here were built in the 1930s, the frame cabins were added in the 1940s, and the concrete-block units date from the 1950s. All feature fireplaces, kitchens, and baths with showers.

Nearby attractions include the world-renowned Barter Theatre in Abingdon and the quaint mountain town of

Marion. A yellow stripe down the middle of State Street separates the twin cities of Bristol, Virginia, and Bristol, Tennessee.

Hungry Mother State Park is three miles north of Marion, Virginia, on Rte. 16. Cabins available early May to early October. Rates: $16 to $25 per night, $80 to $150 per week. Cash and in-state checks accepted. Reservations taken up to fifty-one weeks in advance, recommended that early for summer. Cabins only reserved for full weeks; rented for less than a week if not reserved.

SEASHORE STATE PARK
2500 SHORE DRIVE
VIRGINIA BEACH, VA 23451
(804) 481-2131 (park office)
(804) 490-3939 (cabin reservations)

Within a matter of minutes, you can travel from exotic lagoons, graced with bald cypress trees that are draped with Spanish moss, to giant sand dunes whipped by the winds and pounding surf of the Atlantic Ocean. Seashore State Park's 2770 acres fill a peninsula in southeast Virginia that is bordered by Chesapeake Bay, Broad Bay, and the Atlantic.

Seashore's visitor center contains varied wildlife and plant exhibits, featuring species indigenous to this semi-tropical environment. It also serves as the starting point for a system of footpaths and bicycle trails. Crabbing, fishing, and boating center on the Narrows, off the channel between Broad Bay and Linkhorn Bay, while swimming enthusiasts take advantage of a beach on Chesapeake Bay.

Six cabins here are of frame construction; the other fourteen were built of concrete block. These two-bedroom cabins accommodate up to six people apiece and are equipped with kitchens, baths with showers, screened porches, and fireplaces.

The parkland as it appears today has taken shape fairly recently — probably during the last twenty-five thousand years. Shifting ocean currents have steadily deposited sand along the Cape Henry shoreline, extending the cape farther out into Chesapeake Bay. What once were beach dunes have been transformed into grasslands, then into dune scrub areas, and eventually into the beginnings of complex forests. The lowlands left behind by the advancing beach become pools, swamps, or marshes.

Nearby attractions include the resort of Virginia Beach and the international shipyards at Norfolk. Saltwater fishing expeditions depart from the area, or you might prefer a tour of colonial Williamsburg.

Seashore State Park is on Rte. 60 at Cape Henry in the city of Virginia Beach, Virginia. Cabins available early May to late September. Rates: $30 per night, $180 per week. Cash and in-state checks accepted. Reservations taken up to fifty-one weeks in advance, recommended that early for summer. Cabins reserved only for full weeks; rented for less than a week if not reserved.

STAUNTON RIVER STATE PARK
ROUTE 2, BOX 295
SCOTTSBURG, VA 24589
(804) 572-4623 *(park office)*
(804) 490-3939 *(cabin reservations)*

The Occoneechee Indians once inhabited this 1287-acre peninsula at the confluence of the Roanoke (also known as the Staunton) and Dan rivers, in south-central Virginia. But the mighty warriors of the Occoneechee tribe were virtually annihilated in 1676, when Nathaniel Bacon sought vengeance for the massacre at Jamestown. Bacon's band wiped out most of the Indians; only a handful escaped to what is now North Carolina.

About ten miles north of here, at Staunton River Railroad Bridge, seven hundred Confederate soldiers defeated a Union force of some two thousand men on June 25, 1864, protecting the vital Richmond-Danville railroad line. Later in the 1800s, a religious sect known as the Christian Social Colony established a communal settlement at the fork of the two rivers, but disbanded during the first winter because of inadequate food supplies.

Today, the forty-eight-thousand-acre John H. Kerr Reservoir, also called Buggs Island Lake, extends thirty-nine miles up the Roanoke along eight hundred miles of wooded, cove-studded shoreline. Visitors at Staunton River explore River Bank Trail and other paths, swim in a modern pool, play tennis, and enjoy fishing and boating on the lake and rivers.

Staunton's seven cabins rest beneath trees on a high bluff above the river, near the tip of the peninsula. Built in the 1930s by the Civilian Conservation Corps, these rough-wood cabins sleep up to six people, in one- and two-bedroom designs. All come with fireplaces, baths with showers, and fully equipped kitchens.

Staunton River State Park is ten miles southeast of Scottsburg, Virginia, on Rte. 344. Cabins available May through September. Rates: $17 to $25 per night, $85 to $150 per week. Cash and in-state checks accepted. Reservations taken up to fifty-one weeks in advance, recommended that early for summer. Cabins reserved only for full weeks; rented for less than a week if not reserved.

WESTMORELAND STATE PARK
ROUTE 1, BOX 53-H
MONTROSS, VA 22520
(804) 493-8821 *(park office)*
(804) 490-3939 *(cabin reservations)*

Set in the eastern Virginia countryside, Westmoreland State Park adjoins Stratford, the birthplace of General Robert E. Lee, and is only eight miles from Wakefield, site of George Washington's birth. Washington came into the world at his father's tobacco farm on February 22, 1732, and lived there until age three and again during his teens. Today, the National Park Service operates a colonial farm at Wakefield, where eighteenth-century plantation life is re-created.

Nearby Stratford Hall was built in the 1720s by Thomas Lee, a planter, burgess, and acting governor of Virginia. Two of Lee's sons signed the Declaration of Independence, and a third introduced the motion for independence in the Continental Congress.

Westmoreland State Park follows the Northern Neck, a peninsula that divides the Potomac and Rappahannock rivers. Its Beach Trail traces the Potomac along Horsehead Cliffs, and then turns inland through forests regenerated after decades of plantation farming. Numerous other trails cover the landscape here, taking hikers past Yellow Swamp and Rocky Pond and to an observation tower. Westmoreland's Olympic-size pool fronts the Potomac, and fishermen and boaters take advantage of launching ramps and rental boats.

Cabins at this park range from one-room overnight cabins with no cooking facilities or bathrooms (bathhouse nearby) to two-bedroom units that have fireplaces, kitchens, and baths with showers. Constructed of logs, concrete blocks, or wood frame, Westmoreland's thirty cabins dot the landscape, some along the Potomac. A twelve-person group lodge can also be rented.

Westmoreland State Park is six miles west of Montross, Virginia, on Rte. 3. Cabins available early May to early October. Rates: $6 to $15 per night, $42 to $108 per week. Cash and in-state checks accepted. Reservations taken up to fifty-one weeks in advance, recommended that early for summer. Cabins reserved only for full weeks in summer; rented for less than a week if not reserved.

West Virginia

STATE PARK INFORMATION:
WEST VIRGINIA DEPARTMENT OF NATURAL
   RESOURCES
DIVISION OF PARKS AND RECREATION
STATE CAPITOL-SP
CHARLESTON, WV 25305
(800) 642-9058 (in-state calls)
(800) 624-8632 (calls from neighboring states)
(304) 348-2764, 348-2766 (all other calls)

TOURISM INFORMATION:
WEST VIRGINIA OFFICE OF ECONOMIC AND
   COMMUNITY DEVELOPMENT
TRAVEL DEVELOPMENT DIVISION
STATE CAPITOL-SP
CHARLESTON, WV 25305
(800) 624-9110 (calls from eastern states)
(304) 348-2286 (all other calls)

STATE BIRD: *Cardinal*
STATE MAMMAL: *Black Bear*
STATE TREE: *Sugar Maple*
STATE FLOWER: *Rhododendron*
STATE FISH: *Brook Trout*

BABCOCK STATE PARK
ROUTE 1, BOX 150
CLIFFTOP, WV 25822
(800) 642-9058 (in-state calls)
(800) 624-8632 (calls from neighboring states)
(304) 438-6205 (all other calls)

A fast-flowing mountain trout stream, replete with waterfalls in a canyon strewn with massive boulders, typifies the serene yet rugged beauty of Babcock State Park. Along those churning waters stands Glade Creek Gristmill, a recently constructed "old" mill that was created by combining parts and pieces of several ailing mills. Its basic structure came from Stoney Creek Gristmill, which dates from 1890, and was moved piece by piece to Babcock from Campbelltown, West Virginia. The overshot waterwheel was salvaged from Spring Run Mill, while other parts are courtesy of Roaring Creek Mill. A working monument to more than five hundred mills that prospered in West Virginia at the turn of the century, Glade Creek sells freshly ground cornmeal and buckwheat flour.

In addition to trout fishing and the historic mill, this four-thousand-acre park in southern West Virginia offers more than twenty miles of hiking trails, including the popular Island in the Sky Trail, which rises to a vista over Glade Creek. In late spring and early summer, visitors delight at a colorful montage of wild flowers, especially purple and pink varieties of rhododendron. Paddleboats, rowboats, and sailboats can be rented at Babcock's nineteen-acre Boley Lake — also a favorite with fishermen — while swimmers enjoy a large pool. Volleyball, tennis, archery, shuffleboard, and horseshoes are other pursuits in the park.

Accommodations here include thirteen log cabins, five frame cabins, and eight economy cabins. The economy cabins, which sleep up to four people apiece, have living / dining / bedrooms with built-in double bunks, and small baths with showers. The larger log and frame cabins each sleep up to six people and have fully equipped kitchens, baths with ceramic-tile showers, and fireplaces.

Babcock State Park is south of Clifftop, West Virginia, on Rte. 41. Cabins available late April to late October.

Rates: range from $42 to $69 for the first night, to $162 to $284 per week. Cash, checks, Visa, and MasterCard accepted. Reservations taken up to one year in advance from West Virginia residents, ten months in advance from nonresidents. Cabins rented only for full weeks in summer.

BLACKWATER FALLS STATE PARK
DRAWER 490
DAVIS, WV 26260
(800) 642-9058 (in-state calls)
(800) 624-8632 (calls from neighboring states)
(304) 259-5216 (all other calls)

Plunging from a height equivalent to five stories, the famous falls on the Blackwater River are a spectacular sight. Below, the river careens through Blackwater Canyon, a deep gorge filled with an almost impassable jumble of monstrous boulders. Observation points afford panoramic views of this steep, half-mile-wide canyon, and stairways and boardwalks lead to the base of the falls for an awe-inspiring, close-up look.

Blackwater Lodge, built of rustic stone and wood, commands a sweeping view from its perch on the canyon's forested south rim. The lodge offers fifty-five air-conditioned guest rooms — each of which has a private bath, telephone, and color television — as well as a restaurant, a lounge, and a recreation room. Also on the south rim under tall trees are twenty-five deluxe wood cabins, with handsome paneled walls, stone fireplaces, and forced-air heating. These cabins accommodate up to eight people apiece and feature modern kitchens.

Spring wild flowers, autumn colors, and deep winter snows lure hikers, artists, photographers, and skiers to Blackwater country. One of the trails here, only a hundred yards from the lodge, crosses a footbridge over the stunning Falls of Elakala. Others make for excellent day hikes, and the surrounding Monogahela National Forest has many trails suitable for backpacking. A sandy beach at fourteen-acre Lake Pendleton delights swimmers and sunbathers during hot weather.

Blackwater Falls State Park is just east of Davis, West

Virginia, on Rte. 93. Cabins and lodge open year-round.
Rates: cabins, range from $58 to $91 for the first night, to
$233 to $411 per week. Lodge, $37 per night for two
people. Cash, checks, Visa, and MasterCard accepted.
Reservations taken up to a year in advance from West
Virginia residents, ten months in advance from non-
residents. Cabins rented only for full weeks in summer.

BLUESTONE STATE PARK
BOX 3, ATHENS STAR ROUTE
HINTON, WV 25951
(800) 642-9058 (in-state calls)
(800) 624-8632 (calls from neighboring states)
(304) 466-1922 (all other calls)

Some of the best white-water canoeing and rafting in all
of West Virginia takes place on the New River, not far
from Bluestone State Park's forested, mountainous terrain. Grandview State Park, also nearby, hosts annual
outdoor performances of two popular musical dramas:
The Hatfields and McCoys and *Honey in the Rock.*

Splendid peaks encircle southern West Virginia's two-
thousand-acre Bluestone Lake, the state's second-largest
lake. It satisfies anglers with stringers of bluegill, largemouth and smallmouth bass, crappie, and catfish, and
water-skiers and pleasure boaters with its clear waters. Bluestone's marina rents canoes and motorboats, and on hot
summer days, visitors can cool off in the park's pool. For
the hunting enthusiast, an adjacent twenty-thousand-acre
public hunting area offers varied game seasons throughout
the year.

Overnight guests at Bluestone retire in style in twenty-
five deluxe, dark-stained wood cabins, each of which has
distinctive interior decor, hardwood floors, and a stone
fireplace. The cabins, which sleep up to six people apiece,
feature kitchens with modern appliances and cabinets
crafted from native woods. Many offer shaded decks.

Bluestone State Park is five miles south of Hinton,
West Virginia, on Rte. 20. Cabins available late March
to mid-December. Rates: range from $47 to $69 for the
first night, to $222 to $349 per week. Cash, checks, Visa,

and MasterCard accepted. Reservations taken up to one year in advance from West Virginia residents, ten months in advance from nonresidents. Cabins rented only for full weeks in summer.

CABWAYLINGO STATE FOREST
ROUTE 1
DUNLOW, WV 25511
(800) 642-9058 (in-state calls)
(800) 624-8632 (calls from neighboring states)
(304) 385-4255 (all other calls)

This 8123-acre state forest at the western end of West Virginia bears parts of the names of the four counties it primarily serves: Cabell, Wayne, Lincoln, and Mingo. Its thirteen cabins feature old-fashioned log construction, charming fireplaces, complete kitchens, and baths with tile showers.

Cabwaylingo entertains visitors in a crystal-clear concrete swimming pool and a children's wading pool, both of which are near a bathhouse. Hunting and fishing are favorite activities here, and miles of trails lead hikers through heavily wooded terrain, past picturesque creeks and streams.

Cabwaylingo State Forest is six miles south of Dunlow, West Virginia, off Rte. 152. Cabins available late May to late October. Rates: range from $35 to $55 for the first night, to $135 to $220 per week. Cash, checks, Visa, and MasterCard accepted. Reservations taken up to one year in advance from West Virginia residents, ten months in advance from nonresidents. Cabins rented only for full weeks in summer.

CACAPON STATE PARK
BERKELEY SPRINGS, WV 25411
(800) 642-9058 (in-state calls)
(800) 624-8632 (calls from neighboring states)
(304) 258-1022 (all other calls)

Cacapon State Park is a long, narrow, 6115-acre preserve extending from the Virginia state line across West Virginia's eastern panhandle almost to the Maryland border.

It centers around Cacapon Mountain, whose formidable bulk dominates the view from anywhere in the broad plain beneath it. Hiking and bridle trails climb to this green mountain's summit.

The park's menu of summer activities includes swimming, boating, fishing, tennis, and nature programs presented by staff naturalists. Paddleboats and rowboats can be rented, and saddle horses are available.

Situated in rolling foothills, Cacapon Lodge overlooks an eighteen-hole golf course designed by Robert Trent Jones. This air-conditioned lodge has fifty guest rooms, each of which has fine paneling, a television, a telephone, and a private bath. In the black-walnut–paneled lounge, a wood-burning fireplace lends a cheerful ambience.

Another eleven rooms await in a truly rustic setting, the Old Inn. Built of rough-hewn logs, this unique structure recaptures the pioneer atmosphere, with its wrought-iron hardware, stone chimneys, and classic veranda. Chestnut and knotty pine cover the walls of the guest rooms, which are small and low-ceilinged in the Colonial style; some share connecting baths.

Cacapon also offers cabins that range from economy to deluxe units. The deluxe cabins feature native-wood paneling, fireplaces, and complete kitchens. Standard cabins typically have log construction, fireplaces, baths with showers, and kitchens with modern appliances. In the six economy cabins, living area, dining area, and kitchen are combined in one room; there is also a small bath with shower.

Cacapon State Park is six miles south of Berkeley Springs, West Virginia, on Rte. 522. Lodge and deluxe cabins available year-round, standard cabins available late April to late October, Old Inn and economy cabins open only in summer. Rates: lodge, $28 to $37 per night for two people; Old Inn, $23 to $27 per night for two people; cabins, range from $42 to $91 for the first night, to $162 to $411 per week. Cash, checks, Visa, and MasterCard accepted. Reservations taken up to one year in advance from West Virginia residents, ten months in advance from nonresidents. Cabins rented only for full weeks in summer.

CANAAN VALLEY STATE PARK
ROUTE 1, BOX 39
DAVIS, WV 26260
(800) 642-9058 *(in-state calls)*
(800) 624-8632 *(calls from neighboring states)*
(304) 866-4121 *(all other calls)*

With a climate more like Canada's than like what one expects of the mid-Appalachian highlands, it's not surprising that winter sports dominate the activity at Canaan Valley State Park. Alpine skiers thrive in the cold temperatures and abundant snowfall at Canaan, which features an 850-foot vertical drop in its landscape, chair lifts, and modern snowmaking equipment. Cross-country skiers discover more than twenty miles of winter trails, while ice skaters glide across a lighted outdoor rink. This eastern West Virginia park, some thirty-two hundred feet above sea level, is circled by forty-two-hundred-foot peaks.

During warmer months, golfers playing the acclaimed eighteen-hole course (with the majestic Alleghenies as a backdrop) often catch a glimpse of Canada geese and white-tailed deer. You can swim or sunbathe at a heated outdoor pool, play tennis on one of six lighted courts, or roller-skate under the lights.

Canaan's guest accommodations include 250 rooms within the lodge complex and fifteen deluxe cabins set in a secluded forest. These wood-sided cabins have two, three, or four bedrooms, fireplaces, and completely equipped kitchens. The main lodge features a spacious dining room, a coffee shop, and a lounge.

Canaan Valley State Park is eleven miles south of Davis, West Virginia, on Rte. 32. Cabins and lodge open year-round. Rates: cabins, range from $77 to $97 for the first night, to $342 to $467 per week; lodge, $39 to $48 per night for two people. Cash, checks, Visa, and Master-Card accepted. Reservations taken up to one year in advance from West Virginia residents, ten months in advance from nonresidents. Cabins rented only for full weeks in summer.

CASS SCENIC RAILROAD
P.O. Box 75
CASS, WV 24927
(800) 642-9058 (in-state calls)
(800) 624-8632 (calls from neighboring states)
(304) 456-4300 (park office)

A specially designed steam locomotive that once hauled logging trains now climbs from the old lumber town of Cass, West Virginia, to the summit of Bald Knob, the second highest mountain in the state. Here you can find spruce trees in abundance, the snowshoe hare, moss and lichen, and other flora and fauna typical of locales eight hundred miles to the north. For this reason, Bald Knob has been called "a bit of Canada gone astray."

The railroad's open passenger coaches are old logging flatcars, converted for their present use. The railroad itself was built in 1902 to reap the harvest of the forested mountains; by the time logging was discontinued here in 1960, it had removed two billion board feet of timber from the cloud-covered ridges. Today the railroad provides breathtaking mountain scenery for passengers on its Tuesday-through-Sunday summer runs and fall weekend excursions.

Originally built as lodging for the turn-of-the-century logging camp at Cass, the park's five cabins have been completely refurbished. These rustic cabins accommodate up to six people apiece and feature modern bathrooms and fully equipped kitchens. Energy-efficient woodstoves and electric heaters warm these intriguing structures.

Nearby attractions in "Cass Country" include the National Radio Astronomy Observatory, where massive radio telescopes search the heavens, and the Cass Country Store, formerly the world's largest company store. The park contains a wildlife museum that displays mounted animals native to the area, and a history museum dedicated to the region's logging and railroad past.

Cass Scenic Railroad is twenty-seven miles north of Marlinton, West Virginia, off Rte. 28. Cabins available year-round. Rates: range from $69 for the first night to $284 per week. Cash, checks, Visa, and MasterCard accepted. Reservations taken up to one year in advance

*from West Virginia residents, ten months in advance
from nonresidents. Cabins rented only for full weeks in
summer.*

GREENBRIER STATE FOREST
STAR ROUTE, BOX 125
CALDWELL, WV 24925
(800) 642-9058 (in-state calls)
(800) 624-8632 (calls from neighboring states)
(304) 536-1944 (all other calls)

Near the acclaimed resort town of White Sulphur Springs
and the world-famous Greenbrier Hotel, this state forest
encompasses 5130 acres in southern West Virginia, including Kates Mountain. Myriad hiking trails climb the
mountain's ridges to breathtaking scenic overlooks.

Greenbrier State Forest's twelve log cabins rate as
some of the most comfortable and popular in West Virginia. Each features a stone fireplace, a stove, a refrigerator, a bath with shower, and all linens and blankets.

Visitors to the state forest take advantage of a spacious
swimming pool, and children burn up energy on extensive
playground equipment. Hunting is permitted in the forest
during specified seasons, and fishermen try their luck in
nearby Greenbrier River.

*Greenbrier State Forest is two miles west of White
Sulphur Springs, West Virginia, off Rte. 60. Cabins available late April to late October. Rates: range from $42 to
$69 for the first night, to $162 to $284 per week. Cash,
checks, Visa, and MasterCard accepted. Reservations
taken up to one year in advance from West Virginia
residents, ten months in advance from nonresidents.
Cabins rented only for full weeks in summer.*

HAWKS NEST STATE PARK
P.O. Box 857
ANSTED, WV 25812
(800) 642-9058 (in-state calls)
(800) 624-8632 (calls from neighboring states)
(304) 658-5212 (all other calls)

Spectacular views of the New River Gorge bless Hawks
Nest State Park, located in an area of southern West
Virginia that many refer to as the "Grand Canyon of the

East." Hawks Nest's thirty-one room lodge affords a splendid view of the gorge, which is sixty miles long and more than one thousand feet deep in places. Below the lodge, the river widens into peaceful Hawks Nest Lake. Beyond the lake, a narrow canyon accelerates the flow of water, creating one of the most challenging wild-water stretches in the country.

Hawks Nest's dining room has a view of the marina and lake below; an intriguing aerial tramway links the lodge with the docks and marina, where rowboats and paddleboats are rented. Some of the lodge's guest-room balconies face the gorge and lake, while others overlook a swimming pool. Tennis courts complement the lodge complex. Indian and pioneer artifacts collected in this region are displayed in the park's museum.

Hawks Nest State Park is just west of Ansted, West Virginia, on Rte. 60. Lodge open year-round. Rates: $28 to $37 per night for two people. Cash, checks, Visa, and MasterCard accepted. Reservations taken up to one year in advance from West Virginia residents, ten months in advance from nonresidents.

HOLLY RIVER STATE PARK
P.O. BOX 8
HACKER VALLEY, WV 26222
(800) 642-9058 (in-state calls)
(800) 624-8632 (calls from neighboring states)
(304) 493-6353 (all other calls)

Constructed either of natural stone or of logs, Holly River's nine cabins sit peacefully among thickets of rhododendron and sturdy hemlocks, while small streams gurgle by. Each cabin sleeps up to four people and features a stone fireplace, a bath with shower, and a fully equipped kitchen.

Should you tire of preparing your own meals, drop in at the wood-paneled restaurant and have dinner next to a blazing fire. Or, take a short trip to Helvetia, West Virginia, a quaint community settled by Swiss immigrants that incorporates a restaurant, gift shop, and a cheese house.

Squeezed in a narrow valley in central West Virginia, this 8101-acre park includes heavily forested peaks, some of which reach almost three thousand feet. Known for its heavy annual rainfall, Holly River harbors such varied wild flowers as flame azalea, pink lady's slipper, Indian paintbrush, wild geranium, Dutchman's breeches, and Solomon's seal. Abundant rainfall also accounts for the mountain streams that course through the boulder-strewn beds of Buck Run and Laurel Fork; the latter is a tributary of Holly River and a fine trout stream.

Trails lead to two roaring waterfalls, Tecumseh and Tenskwatawa, that were named for famous Indian chiefs. You might prefer the brisk climb to Potato Knob, which is acclaimed for its panoramic view. After your hike, you can cool off in Holly River's pool. Adjacent to the swimming pool are basketball courts, an archery range, and excellent shuffleboard, croquet, and tennis facilities.

Holly River State Park is twenty miles north of Webster Springs, West Virginia, on Rte. 20. Cabins available late April to late October. Rates: range from $42 to $58 for the first night, to $162 to $238 per week. Cash, checks, Visa, and MasterCard accepted. Reservations taken up to one year in advance from West Virginia residents, ten months in advance from nonresidents. Cabins rented only for full weeks in summer.

KUMBRABOW STATE FOREST
P.O. Box 65
HUTTONSVILLE, WV 26273
(800) 642-9058 *(in-state calls)*
(800) 624-8632 *(calls from neighboring states)*
(304) 335-2219 *(all other calls)*

Kumbrabow takes its name from three prominent families — Kump, Brady, and Bowers — that were instrumental in the early development of this central West Virginia state forest. The 9431-acre tract has the highest elevation of any state forest in West Virginia, reaching almost four thousand feet above sea level.

Long before the state acquired it, the forest contained exquisite stands of virgin spruce and hemlock. Then, during the lumbering years, a standard-gauge logging train hauled timber from the head of the back fork of Elk River to the town of Mill Creek. Since then, the state has steadily replenished the forest.

Numerous hiking trails drift through thick second growth, where hunters stalk deer, bear, turkey, and ruffed grouse. Fishermen flock to Mill Creek, a natural trout stream that is also stocked each spring, thereby enhancing the catches in its swift, cold waters.

Kumbrabow's five cabins are rustic, with gas lamps, wood-burning cooking stoves and fireplaces, and gas refrigerators. Water comes from a nearby well, and restroom facilities are outside. These log cabins re-create the texture of pioneer life in this cool forest.

Kumbrabow State Forest is seven miles south of Huttonsville, West Virginia, off Rte. 219. Cabins available late April to early December. Rates: range from $35 for the first night, to $135 per week. Cash, checks, Visa, and MasterCard accepted. Reservations taken up to one year in advance from West Virginia residents, ten months in advance from nonresidents. Cabins rented only for full weeks in summer.

LOST RIVER STATE PARK
MATHIAS, WV 26812
(800) 642-9058 (in-state calls)
(800) 624-8632 (calls from neighboring states)
(304) 897-5372 (all other calls)

Originally part of the massive holdings of Thomas Lord Fairfax, the Lost River area of eastern West Virginia was granted to successful military leaders after the revolutionary war. "Light Horse Harry" Lee acquired the property in this way, and built a cabin here, which is now preserved as a museum and listed on the National Register of Historic Places.

Harry's son, Charles Carter Lee, who inherited the land, had cabins and a large boardinghouse constructed to accommodate those who came for the widely publicized sulphur-spring waters. After several intermediate owners, the Carr family took over, enlarging and remodeling the resort at what came to be known as Lee White Sulphur

Springs. This era ended abruptly in 1910, however, when fire destroyed the facility.

Visitors today choose from nine deluxe and fifteen standard cabins, all tucked away in a tranquil woods. Standard cabins are of log construction, while the more modern deluxe units have wood-sided walls, contemporary furnishings, and forced-air furnaces. All of Lost River's cabins include natural stone fireplaces, baths with tile showers, and up-to-date kitchens.

One of the park's many trails leads to Cranny Crow overlook, site of an impressive view of the region's highlands. Another popular Lost River pastime is trail riding, and horses are available at the stables. A spacious swimming pool, tennis, archery, and horseshoes complete the park's recreation options.

Lost River State Park is four miles west of Mathias, West Virginia, off Rte. 259. Standard cabins available late April to late October, deluxe cabins rented late March to mid-December. Rates: range from $42 to $81 for the first night, to $162 to $386 per week. Cash, checks, Visa, and MasterCard accepted. Reservations taken up to one year in advance from West Virginia residents, ten months in advance from nonresidents. Cabins rented only for full weeks in summer.

NORTH BEND STATE PARK
CAIRO, WV 26337
(800) 642-9058 (in-state calls)
(800) 624-8632 (calls from neighboring states)
(304) 643-2931 (all other calls)

Named for a horseshoe curve on the north fork of the Hughes River, North Bend State Park encompasses fishing streams, hiking trails, abundant wildlife, and distinctive accommodations in its 1405 pastoral acres. North Bend Lodge spreads across a ridge above the picturesque river valley. The lodge has thirty guest rooms, each of which has a bath, two double beds, air conditioning, color television, and a telephone. After an evening meal in the lodge's dining room, you can retire to either of two peaceful patios for quiet conversation or to enjoy the setting sun.

North Bend's eight deluxe cabins, recent additions here, are constructed of solid cedar logs and have wood shingle roofs. Each cabin has a free-standing or a stone fireplace, a modern kitchen, electric heat, wall-to-wall carpeting, and two or three bedrooms.

This west-central West Virginia park offers a wealth of recreation, including tennis courts, miniature golf, and playgrounds. A spacious swimming pool operates during the summer, and — thanks to the help of many volunteers — a superb hiking trail for the handicapped and a playground for the blind and other special-needs guests have been assembled.

North Bend State Park is five miles east of Cairo, West Virginia, off Rte. 31. Lodge and cabins open year-round. Rates: lodge, $28 to $37 per night for two people; cabins, range from $63 to $86 for the first night, to $326 to $391 per week. Cash, checks, Visa, and MasterCard accepted. Reservations taken up to one year in advance from West Virginia residents, ten months in advance from nonresidents. Cabins rented only for full weeks in summer.

PIPESTEM RESORT STATE PARK
PIPESTEM, WV 25979
(800) 642-9058 *(in-state calls)*
(800) 624-8632 *(calls from neighboring states)*
(304) 466-1800 *(all other calls)*

Pipestem Lodge overlooks a sweeping bend in the Bluestone River Gorge of southern West Virginia. Mountain Creek Lodge is a unique getaway set at the bottom of a thousand-foot-deep canyon, accessible only via aerial tramway. A third lodging option is Pipestem's twenty-five deluxe cabins, built of wood and fieldstone. These cabins come in two-, three-, and four-bedroom versions, some with second-story decks for admiring the mountain scenery. All have electric heat, televisions, and wood-burning fireplaces.

Popular activities at Pipestem include golf, archery, horseback riding, swimming in the indoor and outdoor pools, and tennis on lighted courts. Golfers can choose between two fine courses: an eighteen-hole delight with large greens and wooded fairways, which follows Bluestone

Gorge, and a nine-hole "executive" course near the Olympic-size pool.

Winter sports here include cross-country skiing and downhill sledding. At the Visitor Center, mountain artists demonstrate their skills and sell their wares. Plays, concerts, musical revues, and the like are presented at the park's amphitheater, which clings to a wooded hillside. Pipestem also has a supper club and two dining rooms.

Pipestem Resort State Park is four miles south of Hinton, West Virginia, on Rte. 20. Cabins and Pipestem Lodge open year-round, Mountain Creek Lodge open April through October. Rates: cabins, range from $63 to $97 for the first night, to $263 to $467 per week; lodges, $33 to $46 per night for two people. Cash, checks, Visa, and MasterCard accepted. Reservations taken up to one year in advance from West Virginia residents, ten months in advance from nonresidents. Cabins rented only for full weeks in summer.

SENECA STATE FOREST
ROUTE 1, BOX 140
DUNMORE, WV 24934
(800) 642-9058 (in-state calls)
(800) 624-8632 (calls from neighboring states)
(304) 799-6213 (all other calls)

Four-acre Seneca Lake, lined with trees and stocked with trout, bears the name of an Indian tribe that once lived here. Seneca State Forest, the oldest state forest in West Virginia, lies in Pocahontas County along the soothing Greenbrier River, near the Virginia border. The Greenbrier surprises anglers with a variety of fish, including bass, trout, and pike. Hikers roam the countless trails and paths in this peaceful, 11,684-acre preserve. For a unique look at the gorgeous countryside, take a trip on the nearby Cass Scenic Railroad.

Seneca's seven log cabins approximate a pioneer existence, with wood cooking stoves and fireplaces, gas refrigerators, and gas lamps. Well water is nearby, as are the latrines.

Seneca State Forest is four miles south of Dunmore, West Virginia, off Rte. 28. Cabins available late April to *early December. Rates: range from $35 to $55 for the first night, to $135 to $215 per week. Cash, checks, Visa, and MasterCard accepted. Reservations taken up to one year in advance from West Virginia residents, ten months in advance from nonresidents. Cabins rented only for full weeks in summer.*

TWIN FALLS STATE PARK
P.O. BOX 1023
MULLENS, WV 25882
(800) 642-9058 *(in-state calls)*
(800) 624-8632 *(calls from neighboring states)*
(304) 294-4000 *(all other calls)*

From the heavily forested roadway leading into the park, to the splendid falls for which it is named, to a rocky overlook along Cliffside Trail, Twin Falls State Park startles with its beauty. Twin Falls Lodge rests on one of the highest points in these southwestern West Virginia highlands, affording a commanding view of the golf course and swimming pool. Most of the guest rooms in this brick structure have outdoor balconies, and all have air conditioning, color televisions, telephones, and private baths.

Deep woods separate this park's thirteen deluxe cabins, which feature handsome wood-paneled walls, stone fireplaces, electric heat, and color televisions. Up-to-date bathrooms and kitchens complete the accommodations.

It's just a short hike up one of the nature trails to an eighteen-hole golf course and clubhouse. From there, it's not far to tennis courts, an archery range, and playground facilities. The pioneer homestead at Twin Falls dates from the early 1800s; it has been painstakingly restored on Bower's Ridge.

Twin Falls State Park is seven miles north of Pineville, West Virginia, on Rte. 97. Cabins and lodge open year-round. Rates: cabins, range from $63 to $91 for the first night, to $304 to $411 per week. Cash, checks, Visa, and MasterCard accepted. Reservations taken up to one year in advance from West Virginia residents, ten months in advance from nonresidents. Cabins rented only for full weeks in summer.

TYGART LAKE STATE PARK
ROUTE 1, BOX 260
GRAFTON, WV 26354
(800) 642-9058 (in-state calls)
(800) 624-8632 (calls from neighboring states)
(304) 265-2320 (lodge)
(304) 265-3383 (park office)

Tygart Lake, thirteen miles long, undulates through wooded valleys in northern West Virginia. Created by the Army Corps of Engineers in the 1930s to control flooding, this lake's clear waters are ideal for boating, fishing, swimming, and scuba diving. Tygart Lake State Park, fronting the lake's north shore, has a complete marina that rents ski and fishing boats, sells fuel and supplies, and has launching ramps.

Tygart Lake Lodge perches on a promontory overlooking the lake. Its twenty wood-paneled guest rooms feature double beds, color televisions, telephones, and air conditioning. Its spacious restaurant rewards diners with splendid lake views.

About three miles south of the lodge, Tygart's ten deluxe cabins are just around a bend from a swimming beach. These cabins come in one-, two-, and three-bedroom floor plans, and all have native wood walls, stone fireplaces, and electric kitchens.

Tygart Lake State Park is five miles south of Grafton, West Virginia, on Rte. 119. Lodge open Easter through October, cabins available late March to mid-December. Rates: lodge, $37 per night for two people; cabins, range from $47 to $69 for the first night, to $222 to $349 per week. Cash, checks, Visa, and Mastercard accepted. Reservations taken up to one year in advance from West Virginia residents, ten months in advance from nonresidents. Cabins rented only for full weeks in summer.

Cabin, Watoga State Park, West Virginia

WATOGA STATE PARK
STAR ROUTE 1, BOX 252
MARLINTON, WV 24954
(800) 642-9058 *(in-state calls)*
(800) 624-8632 *(calls from neighboring states)*
(304) 799-4087 *(all other calls)*

First and largest of all the West Virginia state parks, Watoga is a sprawling verdant woodland in the Appalachian highlands, along the state's Virginia border. Embracing 10,057 acres of mountainous terrain, the park teems with wildlife, including raccoon, wild turkey, quail, rabbit, grouse, woodchuck, and, on occasion, a black bear or two.

Watoga's name comes from the Cherokee word *watauga*, which means "river of islands." Indians gave this name to the Greenbrier River, which forms several miles of the park's boundary, because its wide, shallow waters are broken by many sandbars and islands.

The boathouse at Watoga's eleven-acre lake rents paddleboats and rowboats. On the lake, you can relax in cool breezes or drop in a line for some warm-water fishing. The Greenbrier also attracts anglers, as do the trout in Laurel Run, which is six miles from the administration building. The administration building holds a restaurant and a small grocery.

Hiking trails climb Watoga's wooded hillsides, ranging in length from a brief path by the lake to six miles of trail through Brooks Memorial Arboretum, a four-hundred-acre natural showcase. Trail riders saddle up at the stables.

Eight deluxe two-bedroom cabins and twenty-five standard cabins shelter overnight guests. The deluxe cabins feature frame construction, rich paneling, forced-air furnaces, and stone fireplaces. Constructed for the most part of logs, the standard cabins also offer stone fireplaces; both styles have complete kitchens.

Watoga State Park is seventeen miles south of Marlinton, West Virginia, off Rte. 219. Deluxe cabins available late March to mid-December, standard cabins rented late April to late October. Rates: range from $42 to $81 for the first night, to $162 to $331 per week. Cash, checks, Visa, and MasterCard accepted. Reservations taken up to one year in advance from West Virginia residents, ten months in advance from nonresidents. Cabins rented only for full weeks in summer.

$\mathcal{T}he$
MIDWEST

ILLINOIS
1. Giant City State Park
2. Illinois Beach State Park
3. Pere Marquette State Park

4. White Pines Forest State Park

INDIANA
5. Brown County State Park
6. Chain O' Lakes State Park
7. Clifty Falls State Park
8. Lincoln State Park
9. McCormick's Creek State Park
10. Pokagon State Park

11. Potato Creek State Recreation Area
12. Shakamak State Park
13. Spring Mill State Park
14. Turkey Run State Park
15. Whitewater Memorial State Park

IOWA
16. Backbone State Park
17. Lacey-Keosauqua State Park
18. Lake of Three Fires State Park

19. Lake Wapello State Park
20. Palisades-Kepler State Park
21. Springbrook State Park

MICHIGAN
22. Isle Royale National Park
23. Porcupine Mountains Wilderness State Park

24. Wilderness State Park

MINNESOTA
25. Voyageurs National Park

26. Itasca State Park

MISSOURI
27. Ozark National Scenic Riverways
28. Bennett Spring State Park
29. Big Lake State Park
30. Lake Wappapello State Park
31. Meramec State Park
32. Montauk State Park

33. Roaring River State Park
34. Sam A. Baker State Park
35. Stockton State Park
36. Thousand Hills State Park
37. Wakonda State Park
38. Washington State Park

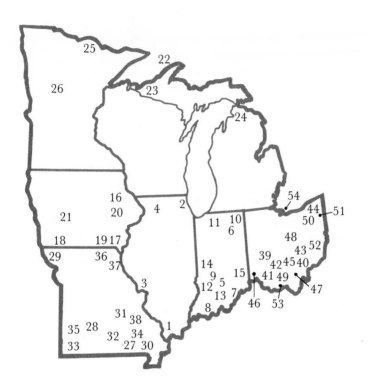

OHIO

39. Buck Creek State Park
40. Burr Oak State Park
41. Cowan Lake State Park
42. Deer Creek State Park
43. Dillon State Park
44. Geneva State Park
45. Hocking Hills State Park
46. Hueston Woods State Park
47. Lake Hope State Park
48. Mohican State Park
49. Pike Lake State Park
50. Punderson State Park
51. Pymatuning State Park
52. Salt Fork State Park
53. Shawnee State Park
54. South Bass Island State Park

Illinois

STATE PARK INFORMATION:
ILLINOIS DEPARTMENT OF CONSERVATION
524 SOUTH SECOND STREET
LINCOLN TOWER PLAZA
SPRINGFIELD, IL 62706
(217) 782-6752

TOURISM INFORMATION:
ILLINOIS OFFICE OF TOURISM
DEPARTMENT OF COMMERCE AND COMMUNITY
  AFFAIRS
620 EAST ADAMS STREET
SPRINGFIELD, IL 62701
(217) 782-7139

STATE BIRD: *Cardinal*
STATE MAMMAL: *White-tailed Deer*
STATE TREE: *White Oak*
STATE FLOWER: *Violet*

GIANT CITY STATE PARK
RR 1
MAKANDA, IL 62958
(618) 457-4836 (park office)
(618) 457-4921 (lodge and cabins)

At the southernmost tip of this 3694-acre park is Giant City Lodge, massive in appearance and built of multihued stone enhanced by log balconies. A spacious lounge, colorfully decorated in an Indian motif, a large dining room, and a snack bar all await visitors. Nearby stand a dozen cabins, whose rustic exteriors belie their completely modern interiors. These forty-year-old, one-room cabins sleep up to four people and have heating, air conditioning, color televisions, and carpeting, but no kitchens.

Giant City State Park is a portion of the Shawnee National Forest, in southern Illinois. A group of huge sandstone blocks, to which the name "Giant City" has been given, intrigues the casual observer here. These rock masses have separated from an adjacent parent ledge.

One bizarre stone feature is man-made. Called Stone Fort, it is the work of an unknown ancient people. Located atop an eighty-foot sandstone cliff, the fort consists of a great wall of loose stone that partially encloses several acres. This structure may have served as a defensive fortification or been used for ceremonial purposes. Artifacts discovered here date from 600 to 900 A.D.

In spring, Giant City's forests are tinted with redbud, shadbush, wahoo, Hercules'-club, and flowering dogwood; throughout the year they are enhanced by the presence of tulip tree, red maple, sweet gum, tupelo, cucumber, and winged elm. Great peach and apple orchards, adjacent to the park, bloom in splendor. Come evening, the eerie calls of the whippoorwill and its southern cousin, the chuckwill's-widow, waft through peaceful valleys. Visible from the lodge and particularly impressive when lighted at night is the Alto Pass Cross, at the summit of Bald Knob Mountain.

Little Grassy Lake invites boat fishing and provides launching ramps near Giant City State Park. An eighteen-hundred-foot unpaved landing strip assists those arriving by air.

Giant City State Park is twelve miles south of Carbondale, Illinois, off Rte. 51. Cabins available March to late November. Rates: $32 per night for two people. Cash, checks, Visa, and MasterCard accepted. Reservations recommended six months in advance.

ILLINOIS BEACH STATE PARK
LAKEFRONT
ZION, IL 60099
(312) 662-4811

ILLINOIS BEACH RESORT
LAKEFRONT
ZION, IL 60099
(800) HOL-IDAY
(312) 249-2100

Early risers here admire sunrises that break over the placid waters of Lake Michigan. Four miles of beach, large expanses of marsh and prairie vegetation, abundant wildlife, migratory birds, and shifting dunes combine to make this park, which stretches along the lake from Waukegan to the Wisconsin state line, most enjoyable. Scrub-oak woodland, dominated by black oak, occupies some of the sandy ridges. Large wetlands, punctuated by bulrushes, occur in poorly draining areas in the western dunes, where cattails form nearly solid stands.

A unique feature of the park is the Dead River, a sluggish stream that carries runoff from surrounding uplands. During much of the year, the mouth of the river is blocked by a sandbar built up by storm waves on the lake, forming an elongated pond. When a rainstorm forces the runoff water high enough, it breaks through the sandbar, draining nearby marshes. Northern pike breed in the wet meadows along Dead River; lake, rainbow, and German brown trout, as well as coho and Chinook salmon, spawn in the river.

Swimming, sunbathing, fishing, and hiking are the major activities at Illinois Beach State Park. The shore of Lake Michigan marks a natural migration route for many bird species, such as ducks, geese, gulls, and occasionally a bald eagle, osprey, or peregrine falcon. Diving ducks splash into the late in winter, and great heron, great blue heron, sora, and redwinged blackbird congregate in the marshes.

Holiday Inn's thirty-year-old Illinois Beach Resort features ninety-six modern guest rooms in a sandstone-and-glass structure. This lakefront resort has a heated indoor swimming pool, a dining room, a whirlpool, and a sauna. The lobby's circular fireplace attracts winter guests, who warm up after an invogorating walk on the beach or a cross-country ski trip.

Illinois Beach State Park is on the shores of Lake Michigan in Zion, Illinois. Lodge open year-round. Rates: $42 to $71 per night. Cash, checks, Visa, MasterCard, and American Express accepted. Reservations taken up to fifty weeks in advance, recommended one month in advance for summer.

Lodge, Pere Marquette State Park, Illinois

PERE MARQUETTE STATE PARK
P.O. Box 158
GRAFTON, IL 62037
(618) 786-3323 *(park office)*
(618) 786-3351 *(lodge and cottages)*

This eight-thousand-acre park follows wooded bluffs along the Illinois River, five miles from its confluence with the powerful Mississippi. Visitors flock to southwestern Illinois each October to admire the splendid autumn foliage and to drive the spectacular Great River Road, which snakes past the bluffs and by the Mississippi. Pere Marquette's four prominent hollows are ravines cut into an elevated plain.

About 200 million years ago, what is now Illinois was lifted from the sea for the last time. Giant dinosaurs flourished, and earth movements dislocated great sheets of rock, producing the Lincoln fold. Archeological sites here indicate the presence of ancient man, who produced large leaf-shaped arrowheads and coarse, heavy pottery at approximately 900 A.D.

The first Europeans to arrive were explorers Father Jacques Marquette and Louis Joliet, who reached Illinois in the spring of 1673 on an expedition along the Mississippi River in search of a passage to the Pacific Ocean. A large white cross marks the spot where these two famous adventurers landed.

Visitors today discover comfortable accommodations in either a fifty-year-old lodge, constructed by the Civilian Conservation Corps of colorful native stone and hand-hewn timbers, or in one of the rock, log, or frame cottages that nestle on a hillside behind the lodge. The eighteen lodge rooms and twenty-nine cottage rooms sleep from two to four people apiece, in heated and air-conditioned comfort. Neither cottages nor lodge rooms have kitchens, but the lodge's dining room (which has dark, exposed beams, hardwood floors, and a stone fireplace) fills that void with everything from country breakfasts to steak, seafood, and specialty dinners. After a meal, you can relax in the deep-sinking chairs and couches in the lounge in front of a massive rock fireplace that weighs more than seven hundred tons.

Lodge and cottage guests swim in a spacious pool. To explore the hilly woodlands, hike Marquette's trails or sign up for horseback riding at the stables. Water sports prevail on the Illinois River, where docks and launching ramps aid fishermen and pleasure boaters.

Pere Marquette State Park is five miles north of Grafton, Illinois, on Rte. 100. Lodge and cottages open year-round. Rates: $31 to $33 per night for two people. Cash and checks accepted. Reservations recommended six to eight weeks in advance for August through October.

In the heart of northwest Illinois's Black Hawk country, this park is rich in historic associations with the brave warrior who resisted for so long the efforts of the white man to drive his people from their beloved Rock River Valley. In one important engagement in 1832, Black Hawk and his braves completely routed poorly disciplined volunteers under the command of Governor John Reynolds. Eventually, however, the Indians were forced from Rock River, and Black Hawk was sent into exile in the custody of his hated rival Keokuk.

Early Ogle County settlers discovered a forest of virgin white pine along the east bank of Pine Creek. Indians valued the tree for its many medicinal uses. The inner bark aided in the treatment of many lung ailments, and long before Turkish baths became popular, the Indian used pine twigs for his sweat bath.

During pioneer days, the blacktop road that today forms the southern boundary of this 385-acre park was the old Chicago-Iowa trail; for years it was the principal east-west route across this slice of Illinois.

Moss-covered cliffs, decorated with trailing vines, share the park with many hardwoods, such as maple, elm, ash, oak, basswood, and hickory. Red squirrels, raccoons, opossums, and chipmunks inhabit this territory, along with pine finches, pine warblers, and a host of wintering birds.

White Pines Forest's lodge houses a lounge in one wing (with colorful Indian artwork), and an attractive dining room in the other. One-bedroom, two-bedroom, and four-bedroom cabins accommodate from two to eight guests, and all have private baths. These sleeping cabins, which form a semicircle near Whispering Pine Trail, have no kitchen facilities.

Because of turbulent water in rainy weather, fords rather than bridges cross Pine Creek and Spring Creek. On a bluff twelve miles northeast of the park is Lorado

Taft's notable statue of an American Indian: a stern-visaged warrior peering out across the Rock River Valley.

White Pines Forest State Park is twelve miles north of Dixon, Illinois, off Rte. 2. Cabins available April through November. Rates: $20 to $112 per night. Cash, Visa, and MasterCard accepted.

Indiana

~~~~~

State Park Information:
Indiana Department of Natural Resources
Division of State Parks
Room 616, State Office Building
Indianapolis, IN 46204
(800) 622-4931 (in-state calls)
(317) 232-4124 (out-of-state calls)

Tourism Information:
Indiana Department of Commerce
Division of Tourism
One North Capitol Avenue, Suite 700
Indianapolis, IN 46204
(800) 622-4464 (in-state calls)
(800) 858-8073 (calls from neighboring states)
(317) 232-8860 (all other calls)

State Bird: *Cardinal*
State Tree: *Tulip Tree*
State Flower: *Peony*

BROWN COUNTY STATE PARK
NASHVILLE, IN 47448
(812) 988-6406 (park office)
(812) 988-4418 (cabins and lodge)

Indiana's largest and most popular state park — Brown County State Park — attracts visitors from all over the United States. This southern Indiana preserve consists of more than fifteen thousand acres of steep, forested hills. During the 1930s, the Civilian Conservation Corps planted black locust, black walnut, pine, and spruce trees, and built everything from shelters, picnic tables, roads, and trails to a pair of log lookout towers and Ogle Lake. All the lumber and sandstone used for these structures came from a forest and quarry near the park's Five Points — the junction of the five ridges.

The north entrance to the park crosses Salt Creek by means of a covered bridge, said to be the oldest timber bridge in Indiana. From the entrance, visitors drive to numerous breathtaking overlooks, which reveal the hills, the extensive woodlands, and their veil of soft blue haze, reminiscent of the Smokies or Shenandoah Valley.

More than ten miles of hiking trails drift through the tranquil woods, across quiet ridges, into deep ravines, and around glistening lakes. Anglers can take on bass in both Ogle Lake and Strahl Lake, while swimmers enjoy an Olympic-size pool.

Brown County's deluxe accommodations include the sixteen-room Abe Martin Lodge, built of stone in 1932, and its accompanying fifty-eight sleeping cabins, plus twenty contemporary two-story cabins. The lodge dining room's daily offerings include such favorites as fried chicken and homemade cobbler. While the sleeping cabins (no kitchens) are part of the lodge complex, the two-story cabins rest on densely wooded Skunk Ridge. Each has two bedrooms, modern kitchen and bath, a living room, and a spacious, shaded deck, creating an idyllic woodland retreat.

Nearby Nashville, Indiana, lures weekend crowds year-round with its craft and antique shops, art galleries, and fine restaurants. Nashville and Brown County are particularly popular for "foliage weekends" in October.

Brown County State Park is just south of Nashville, Indiana, on Rtes. 46 and 135. Lodge and cabins available year-round. Rates: lodge rooms and sleeping cabins, $24 to $30 per night; two-story cabins, $45 per night, $270 per week. Cash, checks, Visa, and MasterCard accepted.

CHAIN O' LAKES STATE PARK
ROUTE 2, BOX 54
ALBION, IN 46701
(219) 636-2654

In an area of northeast Indiana once inhabited by Miami Indians, Chain O' Lakes State Park encompasses eleven natural lakes within its 2678 acres. These lakes, known as kettle lakes, were formed by the last glaciers to leave the area some ten thousand years ago. Churning meltwaters from huge blocks of ice carved out these depressions in the landscape and cut the channels that to this day connect eight of the lakes.

Indians once maintained a village of approximately thirty bark wigwams on the north shore of what is now called Bowen Lake. The lake bears the name of William Bowen, one of the first white settlers here, who arrived in the 1830s and built a home on the lakeshore in 1840.

Bowen's residence is now just a memory, but park visitors will find eighteen two-bedroom cabins providing overnight accommodations. Set near the shore of Long Lake and close to its fishing pier, the cabins sleep up to six people apiece. A fireplace-style wood-burning stove heats each cabin, and a handy pass-through window lets you serve food from the kitchen out to a large screened porch, where there are a picnic table and porch swing. The cabins' balconies overlook the heavily wooded south shore of Long Lake, and their rough-sawed diagonal siding blends subtly with the surrounding terrain.

In addition to a wood-chipped trail from the cabins to the fishing pier, twelve miles of hiking trails lead visitors past swamps, fields, hills, and of course the lakes. Fishermen try their luck for bass and bluegills in the clear waters, and during summer months, swimmers take advantage of the beach and bathhouse. Boats and canoes can be rented. Come winter, ice fishing, ice skating, sledding, and cross-country skiing are popular, and rental cross-country gear is available.

Chain O' Lakes State Park is five miles southeast of Albion, Indiana, off Rte. 33. Cabins available April through October. Rates: $35 per night, $210 per week. Cash and checks accepted. Reservations taken up to one year in advance. Cabins rented only for full weeks in summer; weekend rentals must include both Friday and Saturday nights.

CLIFTY FALLS STATE PARK
MADISON, IN 47250
(812) 273-5495 (park office)
(812) 265-4135 (Clifty Inn)

From bluffs above the Ohio River to the misty plunge basin of Clifty Falls, this southeast Indiana park offers soothing natural settings. In sharp contrast to scenes of long ago, when huge boulders rumbled down from the rim to the canyon floor, wild flowers, ferns, and mosses now flourish on the slopes in peaceful silence. On upland fields, white-tailed deer, red and gray fox, and bobwhite quail can be spotted, and songbirds share the skies with vultures soaring on six-foot wings. The historic river town of Madison, Indiana (known for its well-maintained, Federal-style antebellum homes) and the Ohio River make up the panorama seen from Clifty's lookout tower.

The deeply cut gorges, sheer rock walls, and five major waterfalls of Clifty Falls State Park have been compared with the scenery in the Swiss Alps. In fact, both the mountains there and the bedrock exposures here were sculpted by the last Ice Age. Clifty's shales and limestones are some 425 million years old, which makes them the most ancient exposures in Indiana. The disintegrating cliffs attract a steady stream of paleontologists, who study the abundant fossil remains of marine life interred in the rock.

Clifty Falls's ten hiking trails stretch from the rugged canyon and craggy ridges to old piers and trestle abutments from a section of the Madison and Indianapolis Railroad — a section started in 1853, but never completed. The trails also lead to majestic waterfalls, such as Clifty

Falls, where Clifty Creek plummets more than seventy feet. As it slips through the canyon, it quickly descends another 250 feet before spilling into the Ohio River.

Overlooking the river, Clifty Inn has seventy-two guest rooms, a full-service dining room, an outdoor swimming pool, and tennis courts. The inn, partially destroyed by a tornado in 1974, has been completely rebuilt and re-modeled. Adjacent to the inn at the park's nature center, staff members conduct daily activities in summertime, including hikes, nature talks, slide shows, and campfires.

Clifty Falls State Park is just west of Madison, Indiana, on Rte. 56. Clifty Inn is open year-round. Rates: $30 to $32 per night. Cash, checks, Visa, and MasterCard accepted.

LINCOLN STATE PARK
BOX 216
LINCOLN CITY, IN 47552
(812) 937-4710

Indiana, as well as Kentucky and Illinois, can rightfully lay claim to having contributed to the development of Abraham Lincoln, who spent fourteen of his formative years in the Hoosier state. Adjacent to this 1747-acre, southern Indiana state park is the Lincoln Boyhood National Memorial, operated by the National Park Service. Within the park stands Little Pigeon Primitive Baptist Church, built on the site of an early church where the Lincoln family worshipped. In the churchyard lie the graves of Sarah Lincoln Grigsby, Abraham's only sister, and other pioneer settlers.

Lincoln State Park offers recreation as well as history, and the fun is centered at Lincoln Lake. This eighty-five-acre, man-made lake has earned a reputation as a "good fishing" lake, as it has been stocked with bass, bluegill, and other game fish. Rowboats can be rented and privately owned boats can be launched (electric motors only) at Lincoln Lake. During summer, swimmers and sunbathers flock to the beach on the lake's north shore.

Four hiking trails traverse Lincoln's landscape, passing the site of Noah Gordon's mill, Sarah Lincoln Grigsby's home, and a second, smaller lake — Weber Lake. For a bird's-eye view of the wooded terrain, you can climb Lincoln State Park's fire tower.

Ten modern cabins rest on the east side of Lincoln Lake, each with room to sleep up to six people. The cabins have full kitchens, baths with showers, and gas heat.

Lincoln State Park is on Rte. 162 at Lincoln City, Indiana. Cabins available April through November. Rates: $18 per day, $108 per week. Cash and checks accepted. Reservations taken up to one year in advance.

McCormick's Creek State Park
Route 1, Box 72
Spencer, IN 47460
(812) 829-2235 (park office)
(812) 829-4881 (Canyon Inn and cabins)

Long before pioneers arrived at the area they would call McCormick's Creek, Miami Indians roamed this land. They camped along the White River, which cuts across the western edge of today's park, but they did not inhabit the steep canyons and ravines along McCormick's Creek; the terrain was far too rugged. Instead, it became their hunting grounds, yielding deer, squirrel, grouse, and fish from its deep woods and clear streams.

In 1820 the first white settler, John McCormick, moved here from West Virginia and homesteaded nearly one hundred acres along the canyon, by a waterfall. Others followed, cutting timber and grazing livestock on the steep slopes and farming small patches of flat upland ground. Still others built sawmills and gristmills on the creek, though low water levels kept these endeavors from becoming profitable.

A turning point in the history of this part of west-central Indiana came in 1880, when Dr. Frederick Denkewalter purchased much of the canyon. Convinced that the splendid scenery could be therapeutic, he constructed a sanitarium here, a white-sided structure with expansive porches on every side. The state of Indiana acquired the land after Denkewalter's death in 1915, and Canyon Inn opened for business in the old sanitarium building. Though remodeled and expanded substantially since then, the inn today rests on the original foundation of Denke-walter's facility.

Canyon Inn guests find themselves pampered, with seventy-nine hotel rooms, a spacious dining room, a swimming pool, and a recreation center featuring racquet-ball, volleyball, badminton, shuffleboard, and the like. For those seeking more rustic lodging, there are McCormick's Creek's fourteen cabins. Located in the southwest corner of the park near a splendid overlook, these cabins sleep up to six people each and have full kitchens and gas heat.

Numerous hiking trails, ranging from easy to rigorous, follow the creek and canyon through Wolf Cave Nature Preserve to Wolf Cave. Trail rides commence at the stables, and tennis courts are also available.

McCormick's Creek State Park is two miles southeast of Spencer, Indiana, on Rte. 46. Cabins available April through October; Canyon Inn open year-round. Rates: cabins, $15 per night, $90 per week; inn, $24 to $30 per night. Cash, checks, Visa, and MasterCard accepted. Reservations taken up to one year in advance.

POKAGON STATE PARK
ROUTE 2
ANGOLA, IN 46703
(219) 833-2012 *(park office)*
(219) 833-1077 *(cabins and Potawatomi Inn)*

On the shores of Lake James and Snow Lake, amid the gentle hills in northeast Indiana's lake country, Pokagon State Park supplies recreation for all seasons. Set in an area ruled by Potawatomi Indians for decades, the park takes its name from one of their famous chiefs. By treaty, Chief Pokagon transferred to the United States govern-ment one million acres, including the present site of Chicago, at a price of three cents per acre.

During warm weather, visitors can swim the waters of Lake James from a beach on the upper basin, or rent a boat for a lake cruise. Both lakes teem with bass, bluegill, walleye, crappie, catfish, and northern pike, which makes them favorites with anglers. Boat-launching ramps are located just outside the park.

After swimming or fishing, perhaps you're ready for a set or two of tennis, or to saddle a horse for a trail ride. There's also hiking: Pokagon's trails take you past varied scenery, such as marshland, deep hardwood forests, pinewoods, and sandhills. One path borders Lake James, where waterfowl often can be observed, and leads to a wildlife exhibit.

In winter, sledding, ice-skating, ice fishing, and cross-country skiing are popular. Pokagon is the only Indiana state park with a refrigerated toboggan slide, a twin-run downhill course some eighteen hundred feet long.

Pokagon's Potawatomi Inn features such comforts as an indoor swimming pool, sauna, and whirlpool, along with eighty guest rooms and a complete dining facility. The park's sixteen cabins have a view of Lake James, and are situated near the toboggan run. These sleeping cabins (no kitchens) accommodate up to four people each.

Pokagon State Park is five miles north of Angola, Indiana, on Rte. 27. Cabins and inn open year-round. Rates: cabins, $30 per night, $180 per week; inn, $24 to $30 per night. Cash, checks, Visa, and MasterCard accepted.

POTATO CREEK STATE RECREATION AREA
25601 STATE ROAD 4
NORTH LIBERTY, IN 46554
(219) 656-8186

A fifty-year-old dream became reality on June 6, 1977, at the dedication of Potato Creek State Recreation Area. After half a century of debate over the feasibiilty of the park, which was the brainchild of self-taught naturalist Darcy Worster, Potato Creek now offers a wide range of recreational attractions.

Worster Lake lures fishermen with bass, bluegill, crappie, channel catfish, and an occasional brown trout. Swimmers enjoy an eleven-hundred-foot beach, complete with snack bar and bathhouse. Rental boats and canoes await park guests, and a boat-launching ramp serves private sail and powered craft (electric motors only).

A three-mile bicycle trail (for which bikes may be

rented) follows the lakeshore and wanders through open fields and peaceful woodlands, affording excellent opportunities to observe birds, flowers, and wildlife. One of Potato Creek's hiking trails ends at Swamp Rose Nature Preserve, where an old lake is slowly (over the course of hundreds of years) becoming a wetland.

Cross-country skiing enthusiasts flock here during winter months (rental gear is available), while ice skaters glide across frozen Worster Lake. Deer, fox, hawks, and other wildlife accent the frigid landscape.

Just off the beach trail north of the lake, Potato Creek's four relatively new cabins sleep up to eight people apiece. Each has two bedrooms, a bath with shower, a kitchen, a dining area, and a screened porch.

Potato Creek State Recreation Area is three miles east of North Liberty, Indiana, on Rte. 4. Cabins available year-round. Rates: $35 per night, $210 per week. Cash and checks accepted. Reservations taken up to one year in advance. Cabins rented only for full weeks in summer; weekend rentals must be for both Friday and Saturday nights, in April, May, September, and October.

SHAKAMAK STATE PARK
ROUTE 2
JASONVILLE, IN 47438
(812) 665-2158

Shakamak owes its name to the Kickapoo Indians, who played a prominent role in this region's history through the War of 1812, when they aided Chief Tecumseh's efforts against the United States. A nearby river was dubbed "Shakamak" by the Indians, which means "river of long fish" — a reference to an Indian delicacy, the American eel.

The early non-Indian inhabitants of southwest Indiana extracted coal from shaft mines, farmed the rich Wabash Valley, and operated mills and brick plants. Brick, plentiful when this park was established in 1929, is evident in many of Shakamak's structures. Civilian Conservation Corps workers developed much of the park in the 1930s, planting trees, constructing erosion-control systems, and erecting buildings.

Shakamak's three lakes, which total more than four hundred acres, dominate the park and its activities. Stocked with assorted game fish, the lakes attract anglers ready to try their luck. Rowboats and paddleboats can be rented, and boat-launching ramps assist those with their own craft (only electric motors permitted). A sandy beach pleases swimmers and sunbathers, while tennis fans can take advantage of two double courts.

Visitors can pick up a horse at Shakamak's stables and head for miles of bridle trails, or take a hike along the lakefront, through oak and pine forests, and past an abandoned coal mine. Deer, raccoon, red fox, and squirrels can frequently be seen along the trails, as can cardinals, nuthatches, bluejays, redheaded woodpeckers, and a variety of waterfowl.

The park's twenty-nine cabins line the shore of a long, narrow inlet on Lake Shakamak. Some are equipped with private baths, while others share a community bathhouse. These cheerful cabins sleep from four to nine people apiece, and come equipped with electric ranges and refrigerators and wood-burning stoves.

Shakamak State Park is just west of Jasonville, Indiana, on Rte. 48. Cabins available April through October. Rates: $13 to $15 per night, $78 to $90 per week. Cash and checks accepted. Reservations taken up to one year in advance. Cabins rented only for full weeks in summer.

SPRING MILL STATE PARK
Box 376
MITCHELL, IN 47446
(812) 849-4129 *(park office)*
(812) 849-4081 *(Spring Mill Inn)*

A reconstructed pioneer village and numerous caves distinguish this southern Indiana park, as does a sixty-seven-acre stand of virgin timber. It's one of the few remaining tracts of old-growth hardwood left in the state, although this type of forest once blanketed most of Indiana. The largest trees in this virgin stand are the tulip trees, but the most common are splendid white oaks.

Spring Mill has two major cave systems, and the waters flowing from these caves drain into Spring Mill Lake, a thirty-acre body of water popular for fishing and boating. The Twin-Bronson-Donaldson cave system is famous for its large population of blind northern cave fish. Water from the Hamer cave system powers the park's gristmill, which is the centerpiece of a pioneer village.

In 1817 the wealthy Bullitt brothers, known as the "lords of Louisville, Kentucky," constructed the three-story mill out of locally quarried limestone and area timber. The Bullitts sold the mill to two young brothers, the Hamers, in 1832, and the community flourished. But when the railroad bypassed the town in the late 1800s, its fate was sealed. The homes of Tom and Hugh Hamer stand with a dozen other historic buildings in the pioneer village, including an early tavern, a distillery, and a post office.

After walking through the village, visitors can take a guided boat or hiking tour of Spring Mill's caves, unique formations that have been designated National Natural Landmarks by the federal government. Trail rides and hayrides depart from the Saddle Barn, or you can hike the park's six miles of trails on foot.

Spring Mill Inn boasts quality accommodations in seventy-five guest rooms and an attractive dining room. Amenities here include an indoor-outdoor swimming pool and conference facilities. Each summer the inn hosts the Spring Mill Summer Stock Theater, which stages plays and musicals on weekends. Another Spring Mill attraction is the memorial to Indiana native Gus Grissom, one of the seven original astronauts. On display are his space suit, the "Molly Brown" Gemini space capsule, and a photo montage that chronicles his career.

Spring Mill State Park is six miles east of Mitchell, Indiana, on Rte. 60. Spring Mill Inn is open year-round. Rates: $24 to $30 per night. Cash, checks, Visa, and MasterCard accepted.

TURKEY RUN STATE PARK
MARSHALL, IN 47859
(317) 597-2635 *(park office)*
(317) 597-2211 *(inn and cabins)*

Originally built in 1917 as Turkey Run Hotel, the inn at Turkey Run State Park today offers fifty-one guest rooms, a cozy dining room, an outdoor swimming pool, and tennis courts. Nearby are twenty-one sleeping cabins (no kitchens). The electrically heated cabins sleep up to four people each, and both the inn and the cabins are fully air-conditioned.

Mansfield sandstone forms Turkey Run's cliffs, which were gouged by the action of glacial meltwaters. Turkey Run's trails follow the edges of the cliffs, past sheer walls, stands of sycamores, and huge black walnut trees, and through virgin hemlocks. One trail leads hikers by an old quarry and coal mine to the Lusk home and mill site. After acquiring land here in 1821, Captain Lusk constructed a gristmill that was completed in 1826. Another historic building at Turkey Run State Park is the log-cabin museum at Sunset Point, built in 1848. Its large tulip logs serve as a reminder of the vast tulip forests that supplied America's early builders.

If you tire of hiking the steep trails, horses stand ready at the park's stable to explore the thick forests and rugged ravines. Or, for a change of pace, you can toss in a line along rushing Sugar Creek for a chance at bass and bluegill. Two picturesque covered bridges span the creek. Bicycles can be rented in the park.

Turkey Run State Park is two miles east of Rte. 41 on Rte. 47, near Marshall, Indiana. Inn and cabins open year-round. Rates: inn, $24 to $30 per night; cabins, $30 per night, $180 per week. Cash, checks, Visa, and Master-Card accepted.

WHITEWATER MEMORIAL STATE PARK
ROUTE 2
LIBERTY, IN 47353
(317) 458-5565

Whitewater Memorial State Park, located in eastern Indiana, is dedicated to the men and women who served in World War II. Its focal point is a two-hundred-acre lake with a boat-launching ramp (only electric motors permitted), rowboat and paddleboat rentals, fishing for bass, bluegills, and other game fish, and swimming on a fine beach. Bicycle rentals and saddle horses offer visitors several relaxing ways of viewing Whitewater's 1710 acres, as do eight miles of hiking trails.

One trail leads through fields and pine plantings to a bluff behind the lake's dam, then drops down to the bottom of the spillway before rising back up to the boat dock. Another of Whitewater's six trails follows Silver Creek to the point where it pours into the lake, while a third snakes through a lush climax forest to an overlook of the Whitewater River valley and Brookville Reservoir, which borders the park.

Whitewater's four modern cabins are clustered in the park's southwest corner, with a view of the reservoir. These cabins sleep from six to eight people apiece, and have electric heat and wood-burning stoves. Each comes equipped with a full kitchen and a bath with shower.

Whitewater Memorial State Park is three miles south of Liberty, Indiana, on Rte. 101. Cabins available year-round. Rates: $35 per night, $210 per week. Cash and checks accepted. Cabins rented only for full weeks in summer; weekend rentals in April, May, September, and October must include both Friday and Saturday nights.

Iowa

STATE PARK INFORMATION:
IOWA CONSERVATION COMMISSION
WALLACE STATE OFFICE BUILDING
DES MOINES, IA 50319
(515) 281-5145

TOURISM INFORMATION:
IOWA DEVELOPMENT COMMISSION
CAPITOL PLAZA
600 EAST COURT AVENUE
DES MOINES, IA 50319
(515) 281-3251

STATE BIRD: *Eastern Goldfinch*
STATE TREE: *Oak*
STATE FLOWER: *Wild Rose*

BACKBONE STATE PARK
RR 1
DUNDEE, IA 52038
(319) 924-2527

Backbone State Park takes its name from a high, rocky ridge that bumps along for a quarter of a mile, closely resembling a huge backbone, with boulders and humps of stone forming its "vertebrae." Formerly called the "devil's backbone," this intriguing formation is bounded by the Maquoketa River, which flows southeast along the rock ledge, cuts through a saddle, and turns and flows in the opposite direction.

Densely vegetated, the backbone supports fine stands of tall trees here on the highest ground in northeast Iowa. Wind-blown pines reminiscent of California's famed Cypress Point trees jut over cliffs, and mountain climbers revel at Backbone's precipitous drops, rocky staircases, and numerous caverns. Legend has it that hiding places in the craggy rock formations once sheltered train and bank robbers, cattle rustlers, and horse thieves on the run.

Richmond Springs gushes two thousand gallons of water per minute, which feed Backbone's three trout streams. Fishing is also popular at an eighty-five-acre lake, where bass, carp, bullhead, and crappie await anglers. Visitors swim along Backbone's beach, rent rowboats, canoes, and paddleboats, or launch their own craft from the boat ramp (only electric motors permitted). The park's thirteen miles of hiking trails and twenty miles of snowmobile paths ramble through thick forests of hickory, oak, walnut, aspen, poplar, and pine.

Set on a cliff above the lake's eastern shore, Backbone's eighteen cabins, half a century old, can each sleep four people on a double bed and a sofa bed. Each cabin has a refrigerator, gas stove, and bath with shower. Built by the Civilian Conservation Corps in 1933, these cabins do not have heating or air conditioning, but do come with out-door picnic tables and fire rings.

Backbone State Park is two miles north of Dundee, Iowa, on Rte. 69. Cabins available mid-May through mid-September. Rates: $20 per night, $100 per week. Cash and *checks accepted. Reservations taken starting in January for full-week rentals; cabins also rented for less than a week on a first-come, first-served basis, if not reserved.*

LACEY-KEOSAUQUA STATE PARK
P.O. Box 398
KEOSAUQUA, IA 52565
(319) 293-3502

Lacey-Keosauqua's six fifty-year-old cabins, built of wood, perch on a hilltop in a sea of oaks. Each of these one-room cabins features a double bed, a davenport that forms a double bed, a bath with shower, a full kitchen, and a picnic table.

The great horseshoe bend of the Des Moines River, extending for two miles along the park's northern boundary, can be viewed from numerous overlooks in this 1653-acre park. Ancient Indians once inhabited these tree-covered slopes, limestone gorges, cliffs, and open meadows. More recently, many Van Buren County residents remember the woodsmen who resided on the southern slope of one of the ridges, eking out a living by cutting and selling timber. Ruins of their cabins can be found by hikers who explore this southeastern Iowa park's more than twenty-five miles of trails.

The remnants of dams, locks, old steamboat landings, and mills in nearby Keosauqua and Bentonsport recall the nineteenth century, when the Des Moines River served as a highway to the interior of Iowa. Ely's Ford, on the north side of the park, was the river crossing for the Mormon Trail, which was used by pioneers heading north before any bridges spanned the Des Moines.

Shrouded by oak, walnut, hickory, ash, and cedar woodlands inhabited by white-tailed deer, raccoon, opossum, red fox, and an occasional wild turkey is Lacey-Keosauqua's placid thirty-acre lake. Popular for swimming, boating (electric motors only), and fishing, this small lake teems with bluegill, bass, and catfish. Anglers shift to the Des Moines River for catches of perch, channel catfish, and carp. Snowmobilers power along the hilly trails in winter.

Lacey-Keosauqua State Park is just south of Rte. 1 in

Keosauqua, Iowa. Cabins available May through mid-October. Rates: $20 per night, $100 per week. Cash and checks accepted. Reservations taken starting in January for full-week rentals; cabins also rented for less than a week on a first-come, first-served basis, if not reserved.

LAKE OF THREE FIRES STATE PARK
RR 4
BEDFORD, IA 50833
(712) 523-2700

The blue waters of Lake of Three Fires cover more than eighty-six acres in area, and extend more than a mile in length, twisting into secluded inlets that are ideal for fishing and boating. A sandy beach with diving boards, a bathhouse, and a snack bar invites swimmers and sunbathers. Three launching ramps serve those who bring their boats (electric trolling motors permitted), and boats can also be rented. Typical Lake of Three Fires catches include bass, catfish, bullhead, bluegill, crappie, and tiger muskie, some of which measure thirty inches in length.

Almost 650 acres of rolling, southern Iowa parkland ring the man-made lake; they are forested with virgin oak, hickory, and walnut, and are ideal for hiking, bird-watching, and photography. Bridle and hiking trails skirt the hills and trace the lakeshore.

When Indians roamed Iowa's prairies, great council meetings were held here, in the center of a favorite hunting grounds. Runners alerted the various tribes to watch for smoke from three fires that would designate the exact location of the powwow. The fires blazed atop the highest hill, visible from all directions, and a hilltop just outside the park is believed to have been used many times to bring together the tribes.

Lake of Three Fires's six wooden cabins hug a hillside along the lakeshore, shaded by tall trees. Knotty pine trims the interior walls of these one-room cabins, each of which sleeps up to four people. Constructed in the mid-1930s by the Civilian Conservation Corps, the cabins feature full kitchens and outdoor picnic tables and fire rings. While they do have indoor plumbing and bathrooms, showers are located in a nearby camping area.

Lake of Three Fires State Park is three miles north of Bedford, Iowa, on Rte. 19. Cabins available May through September. Rates: $15 per night, $80 per week. Cash and checks accepted. Reservations for full-week rentals taken starting in January, and are recommended three or four months in advance. Cabins rented for less than a week on a first-come, first-served basis, if not reserved.

LAKE WAPELLO STATE PARK
ROUTE 1
DRAKESVILLE, IA 52552
(515) 722-3371

Heavily draped in oaks, along with walnut, elm, and ash trees, southeastern Iowa's Lake Wapello State Park presents 1150 acres of secluded parkland and a 287-acre, clear-water lake. Visitors utilize the many picnic areas, both grassy and shaded, with Smith Knoll and its unusual stone shelter being a favorite. The view from Smith Knoll is exceptional anytime, but at night, when lights along the beach cast dancing reflections on Lake Wapello's placid waters, it is exquisite.

A seven-mile trail slips by the shore of the lake, past a swimming beach, launching ramps, and rental boats. Bass, crappie, catfish, bullheads, and bluegills abound in Lake Wapello, as is evidenced by the smiling faces of anglers displayed in photographs on the boathouse walls.

Lake Wapello State Park's thirteen cabins rest on ten acres on the west side of the lake, near Wolf Hollow. Each sleeps up to four people, on a double bed and a sofa bed, and has a fully equipped kitchen. Six of these modern cabins were constructed in 1977, and the remainder were remodeled a year earlier. Outside each cabin sits a picnic table and a barbecue grill, perfect for a summer cookout.

Lake Wapello State Park is six miles west of Drakesville, Iowa, on Rte. 273. Cabins available mid-May through September. Rates: $20 per night, $100 per week. Cash and checks accepted. Reservations taken starting in January for full-week rentals; cabins also rented for less than a week on a first-come, first-served basis, if not reserved.

PALISADES-KEPLER STATE PARK
RR 2
MT. VERNON, IA 52314
(319) 895-6039

From its lookout tower, one of Palisades-Kepler's most prominent structures, visitors discover a splendid view of the undulating Cedar River, the upland woods, and the vertical cliffs of the Palisades region. In the late 1890s, James Sherman Minott acquired 160 acres of timberland here. He then built a spacious inn, opened a boat livery, and sold lots for private summer cottages (at prices from $20 to $71). Noted American poet Carl Sandburg visited the Palisades annually, joining professors and students from nearby Cornell College for spring rambles through the parkland during the 1920s and 1930s.

Palisades-Kepler profited greatly from the Civilian Conservation Corps, which established Company 2722 here on July 5, 1934. The 210 CCC men, ages eighteen to twenty-five, built macadamized roads, hiking trails, a two-story lodge, and the stone portals at the park's entrance.

Palisades-Kepler State Park today encompasses 956 acres along the Cedar River in eastern Iowa's Linn County. Deep ravines, stately hardwood forests, and abundant wildlife and wild flowers combine to create diverse natural beauty. A mammoth's molar found here speaks of the distant past, and exposed rocks along the river contain fossil links to millions of years of history. Relics and mounds remind today's visitors that this was once a favorite haunt of Indians.

Anglers fish both above and below the dam for just about any type of fish native to Iowa, with channel and flathead catfish being the most sought-after species. Launching ramps serve those who have pulled in their boats.

Palisades-Kepler's four twenty-year-old cabins occupy a wooded section of the park along 150-foot-high cliffs, not far from the river. Each cabin sleeps up to four people and has a full kitchen and an outdoor picnic table and barbecue grill.

Palisades-Kepler State Park is ten miles east of Cedar

Rapids, Iowa, off Rte. 30. Cabins available mid-May to mid-September. Rates: $20 per night, $100 per week. Cash and checks accepted. Reservations for full-week rentals taken starting in January; cabins also rented for less than a week on a first-come, first-served basis, if not reserved.

SPRINGBROOK STATE PARK
ROUTE 1
GUTHRIE CENTER, IA 50115
(515) 747-3591

Crappie, largemouth bass, bluegill, bullheads, and catfish draw fishermen to the clear blue waters of Springbrook's modest lake during warm weather, and ice fishing attracts anglers in colder months. Boat-launching ramps extend into the lake's waters, and rental boats, bait, and refreshments can be obtained at the lakefront. Hemmed in by 740 acres of forested hills, this lake has a sandy beach for swimmers and a nearby bathhouse. Once called King Park, this delightful park one hour west of Des Moines was renamed in tribute to the gurgling spring-fed brook that created and still feeds the lake.

Countless species of native and migratory birds visit this sanctuary, as do such larger animals as deer and rabbits. Hikers and nature lovers savor the numerous hiking and snowmobile trails, including a popular jaunt that circles the lake.

Springbrook's six wooden cabins, constructed by the Civilian Conservation Corps in the 1930s, each accommodate up to four people on a double bed and a fold-out couch. Set in a semicircle in the woods just west of the lake, these one-room cabins come with fully equipped kitchens and indoor bathrooms, but no showers. Each has an outdoor picnic table.

Springbrook State Park is seven miles north of Guthrie Center, Iowa, on Rte. 384. Cabins available May through September. Rates: $15 per night, $80 per week. Cash and checks accepted. Reservations for full-week rentals taken starting in January, and are recommended three or four months in advance. Cabins also rented for less than a week on a first-come, first-served basis, if not reserved.

Michigan

State Park Information:
Michigan Department of Natural Resources
Parks Division
Box 30028
Lansing, MI 48909
(517) 373-1270

Tourism Information:
Michigan Travel Bureau
Box 30226
Lansing, MI 48909
(800) 292-2520 (in-state calls)
(800) 248-5700 (out-of-state calls)

State Bird: *Robin*
State Mammal: *Wolverine*
State Tree: *White Pine*
State Flower: *Apple Blossom*
State Fish: *Trout*

Lodge, Isle Royale National Park, Michigan

Isle Royale National Park
87 North Ripley Street
Houghton, MI 49931
(906) 482-3310

Rock Harbor Lodge (summer address)
National Park Concessions, Inc.
P.O. Box 405
Houghton, MI 49931
(906) 337-4993

Rock Harbor Lodge (winter address)
National Park Concessions, Inc.
Mammoth Cave, KY 42259
(502) 773-2191

In Lake Superior's northwest corner lies a wilderness island, a roadless land of wild creatures, unspoiled forests, untamed lakes and streams, and rugged shores that is accessible only by boat or floatplane. Forty-five miles long and nine miles wide, Isle Royale is some sixty miles offshore of Michigan's Upper Peninsula, almost in Canadian waters. The absence of roads, automobiles, and telephones enhances the silence and tranquility of this 210-square-mile preserve, which long ago was the site of much activity. Indians of this area mined copper here for a thousand years, beginning in 2000 B.C. Using hand-held cobbles, they hammered out chunks of pure copper from the hard bedrock.

Some 80 percent of this national park is under water, in the form of shallow, warm ponds, streams, and rivers and deep, cold Lake Superior. Though commercial fishing declined here long ago, sportfishing has filled the gap: lake, brook, and rainbow trout, northern pike, walleye, and yellow perch are the most sought-after catches. Wolves, moose, and beavers inhabit the island's forests, maintaining a delicate balance of predators and prey.

Isle Royale's walking and boat tours stop by such sites as Rock Harbor Lighthouse, built in 1855, and Edisen Fishery, established in 1890. On Passage Island, visitors hike a mile through a primeval forest of thick balsam fir, devil's club, and moss.

The sound of water lapping against rocky shores lulls visitors to sleep in Rock Harbor Lodge's sixty guest rooms. A log dining room offers full meal service and will even prepare your just-caught lake trout. On a nearby birch-covered ridge overlooking Tobin Harbor, twenty frame cabins accommodate up to four people apiece. Each has electric heat and a complete kitchen.

Isle Royale National Park's cabins available mid-May to mid-September, lodge open mid-June to early September. Rates: cabins, $57 per night for two people; lodge, $98 per night for two people, including three meals daily. Cash, checks, Visa, and MasterCard accepted. Reservations taken up to one year in advance, recommended two to three months in advance for July and August.

PORCUPINE MOUNTAINS WILDERNESS STATE PARK
RR 2, M-107
ONTONAGON, MI 49953
(906) 885-5798

This fifty-eight-thousand-acre state park encompasses towering stands of virgin forest, four secluded lakes, and miles of wild rivers and streams on the western edge of Michigan's Upper Peninsula. Hikers following its eighty-five miles of trails encounter many steep grades and stream crossings. Little Carp River Trail passes turbulent rapids and inspiring waterfalls along Little Carp River, while

Lake Superior Trail traces the shoreline of the greatest of the Great Lakes. Escarpment Trail skirts an imposing cliff and Cloud Peak before reaching Cuyahoga Peak, where you will discover striking rock formations and vistas of Lake of the Clouds far below.

In a torrent of foaming, swirling water, Presque Isle River rushes through narrow, precipitous gorges and over a series of waterfalls and rapids before tumbling into Lake Superior. Anglers seeking salmon and lake and rainbow trout test their skills at the mouths of the many streams that empty into the lake.

Eight of Porcupine's cabins have four bunks, while the cabin at Mirror Lake has eight bunks; all are accessible only by foot. Each of these rustic cabins has a wood-burning cooking stove, a sink, a table, benches, and chairs, plus a saw and ax for cutting firewood, but no running water or electricity. Cabins at Lake of the Clouds, Mirror Lake, and Lily Pond offer rowboats.

Deer, coyotes, and black bears make their homes here in the Porcupine Mountains (or "Porkies"), along with many bird species. Beginning, intermediate, and advanced ski runs here attract ski buffs from mid-December through March. At the foot of the ski area stands a large A-frame, which houses a day lodge and a complete ski shop with rentals.

Porcupine Mountains Wilderness State Park is twenty miles west of Ontonagon, Michigan, on Rte. 107. Cabins available mid-April through November. Rates: $20 per night. Checks accepted. Reservations taken starting in January, recommended at least one month in advance.

WILDERNESS STATE PARK
CARP LAKE, MI 49718
(616) 436-5381

Wilderness State Park presents spectacular scenery just fifteen minutes' drive from Mackinaw City and Mackinac Island, an area drenched with eighteenth-century history. Fort Michilimackinac, a French fur-trading post established in 1715, has been rebuilt on its original foundation at Mackinaw City as a museum. Control of the fort later fell to the British, who decided at the outbreak of the American Revolution to relocate it to strategically superior Mackinac Island. In addition to the restored Fort Mackinac, the island holds an internationally acclaimed resort — the Grand Hotel — and fine shops and restaurants.

Situated at the extreme northern tip of Michigan's Lower Peninsula, Wilderness encompasses enormous evergreen forests and miles of shoreline on Lake Michigan and Sturgeon Bay. Two small islands, Waugoshance Island and Crane Island, jut off the park's Waugoshance Point.

Wilderness Park's four log cabins are scattered over its seventy-five hundred acres. Two of them — Station Point Cabin and Nebo Trail Cabin — face Lake Michigan, while Waugoshance Cabin looks out across a narrow strait to Waugoshance Island, and Sturgeon Bay Cabin fronts that body of water. All cabins can be reached by road during the summer except Waugoshance, which is accessible by foot or by boat. During winter, visitors must journey to the cabins by snowmobile or snowshoe.

Wilderness State Park's cabins come equipped with bunks and mattresses, stone fireplaces, and small cooking / heating stoves, but no electricity or running water. Guests should bring gas lanterns, and an ax for splitting firewood, and in summer a portable camp stove is recommended for cooking.

Summer activities here include hiking the miles of trails and swimming at lakefront beaches. White-tailed deer, ruffed grouse, waterfowl, and an occasional black bear entice hunters, while the shoreline at Waugoshance Point provides some of the finest smallmouth-bass fishing in Michigan.

Wilderness State Park is eight miles west of Mackinaw City, Michigan, on Rte. 81. Cabins available year-round. Rates: $20 per night. Cash and checks accepted. Reservations taken starting in January for the coming year.

Minnesota

~~~

STATE PARK INFORMATION:
MINNESOTA DEPARTMENT OF NATURAL RESOURCES
DIVISION OF PARKS AND RECREATION
BOX 39, CENTENNIAL OFFICE BUILDING
SAINT PAUL, MN 55155
(800) 652-9747 (in-state calls)
(800) 328-1461 (out-of-state calls)

TOURISM INFORMATION:
MINNESOTA TOURIST INFORMATION CENTER
240 BREMER BUILDING
419 NORTH ROBERT STREET
SAINT PAUL, MN 55101
(800) 652-9747 (in-state calls)
(800) 328-1461 (out-of-state calls)

STATE BIRD: *Common Loon*
STATE TREE: *Norway Pine*
STATE FLOWER: *Showy Pink and White Lady's Slipper*
STATE FISH: *Walleye*

VOYAGEURS NATIONAL PARK
P.O. Box 50
INTERNATIONAL FALLS, MN 56649
(218) 283-9821

WHISPERING PINES OF KABETOGAMA
P.O. Box Q
ORR, MN 55771
(218) 374-3321

KETTLE FALLS HOTEL
P.O. Box 1272
INTERNATIONAL FALLS, MN 56649
(218) 286-5685

Water dominates Voyageurs National Park. More than thirty lakes — some large, some small — fill the glacier-carved basins in this vast wilderness along the Canadian border. Between these lakes (brimming with walleye, great northern pike, crappie, bass, and perch) and the park's rocky knobs and wooded ridges extend bogs, marshes, and beaver ponds. Upon arriving at one of Voyageurs's four entry points, you abandon your car and travel a chain of lakes past hundreds of islands by boat, much as French-Canadian voyageurs did during the heyday of the fur trade, in the late eighteenth and early nineteenth centuries.

Fishing, skiing, boating, and swimming are popular during Voyageurs's relatively short summers; in winter, deep snow blankets invite cross-country skiing and snowshoeing. Osprey, eagle, and great blue heron nest here, while moose, bear, coyote, and rare eastern timber wolves wander the thick northern forests.

Engulfed by tall pines, birches, and maples on the narrows between Kabetogama and Namakan lakes, Whispering Pines resort has twelve cabins, and a lodge with snack bar, game room, and fireplace. Constructed of log siding, with interiors of knotty pine, cedar, and mahogany, the cabins sleep up to six people in one, two, or three bedrooms and have full kitchens and baths with showers. Whispering Pines rents boats, or you can bring your own and use the resort's launching ramp.

Whispering Pines of Kabetogama is on Ash River Trail near the park's main entrance, twenty-five miles south of

International Falls, Minnesota, via Rte. 53. Cabins available mid-May to mid-October. Rates: $210 to $330 per week. Cash and checks accepted. Reservations taken for full-week rentals only, recommended six months in advance for May and June.

Built as a resting place for lumberjacks in 1913, Kettle Falls Hotel takes its name from a nearby waterfall that has worn rock into the shape of a huge kettle. Today's visitors come by boat or plane to stay in the hotel's guest rooms or in four cabins. The hotel dining room retains much of its appearance in the early 1900s — sprawling wooden floors still bear the spike marks of loggers' boots. The modern, three-room cabins sleep up to six people apiece and have running water, fully equipped kitchens, and electricity. A bathhouse is nearby. Kettle Falls rents boats and motors, and for a fee, provides boat transportation from the park entrance.

Kettle Falls Hotel is on a peninsula separating Rainy Lake and Namakan Lake in Voyageurs National Park. Cabins and hotel open mid-May to late September. Rates: cabins, $185 to $225 per week; hotel, $48 per night per person, including all meals. Reservations taken up to six months in advance, recommended that early for May and June.

Itasca State Park
Lake Itasca, MN 56460
(218) 266-3656

Eight thousand years ago, Indian hunters pursuing wild game arrived in this part of north-central Minnesota. They ambushed bison, deer, and moose at watering sites, slaying them with flint-tipped spears. After processing the hides and meat, the Indians discarded the bones and worn stone implements in Lake Itasca. Sediment subsequently covered these items, preserving them for future discovery by archaeologists and anthropologists.

For hundreds of years after white men came to Minnesota, Lake Itasca went unrecognized as the source of America's great river — the Mississippi. Though other explorers claimed they had found the source of the Mississippi at sites in Canada and Minnesota, Henry Rowe

Douglas Lodge, Itasca State Park, Minnesota

Schoolcraft, guided by Ojibwe Indian Chief Ozawindib, arrived on Lake Itasca's eastern shore on July 13, 1832, and made the first official recognition of the source. Ozawindib had taken Schoolcraft directly to Lake Itasca, knowing that the infant Mississippi flows north before turning south.

Today, giant Norway (red) pines — some of them three hundred years old — form a distinctive visual signature at this thirty-two-thousand-acre wildlife preserve, site of more than one hundred lakes and streams. Created by the retreat of the last continental glacier, Itasca has sustained — in its bison kill site and Indian burial mounds — a record of early man stretching back some eight millennia.

Beaver, deer, otter, bear, and raccoon abound here, and an occasional bald eagle can be spotted from the park's hiking trails. Lake Itasca satisfies anglers with catches of panfish, walleye, and northerns, and has a marina with rental boats and launching ramps.

Tall pines and deciduous trees shade the accommodations at Douglas Lodge, along a charming lakeshore. They range from suites in the log lodge, built in 1905; to one-, two-, and three-bedroom cabins, some with fireplaces and screened porches; to eighteen modern motel rooms at Nicollet Court. Douglas Lodge serves three meals daily in its dining room, whose large windows look out on the lake.

Itasca State Park is twenty-two miles north of Park Rapids, Minnesota, on Rte. 71. Lodging available late May through mid-October. Rates: $20 to $34 per night for two people. Cash and checks accepted. Reservations taken starting in April for the coming year, recommended two to four months in advance.

Missouri

STATE PARK INFORMATION:
MISSOURI DEPARTMENT OF NATURAL RESOURCES
DIVISION OF PARKS AND HISTORIC PRESERVATION
P.O. BOX 176
JEFFERSON CITY, MO 65102
(314) 751-3443

TOURISM INFORMATION:
MISSOURI DIVISION OF TOURISM
TRUMAN STATE OFFICE BUILDING
P.O. BOX 1055
JEFFERSON CITY, MO 65102
(314) 751-4133

STATE BIRD: *Bluebird*
STATE TREE: *Flowering Dogwood*
STATE FLOWER: *Hawthorn*

Cabin, Ozark National Scenic Riverways, Missouri

OZARK NATIONAL SCENIC
  RIVERWAYS
Box 490
VAN BUREN, MO 63965
(314) 323-4236

BIG SPRING MANAGEMENT
  COMPANY (CABINS)
P.O. Box 602
VAN BUREN, MO 63965
(314) 323-4423

Flanked by the large oaks and white pines of the Mark Twain National Forest, Ozark National Scenic Riverways tracks the Current and Jacks Fork rivers for 140 miles through the Ozark foothills of southeastern Missouri. The sixty-five thousand acres of the Riverways have well-deserved reputations for unspoiled, unobstructed waters and tree-clad banks. The Current, one of the most popular float streams in the United States, is fed almost entirely by springs, including Big Spring — North America's largest — which spurts out 275 million gallons of water daily. A vast network of underground streams disgorge their cool, clear load at this outlet.

Canoe liveries rent everything needed for a jaunt down the rivers, and swimmers enjoy the waters all along their lengths. Hiking trails allow walkers to appreciate waves of wild flowers, dogwood, and redbud trees, and perhaps to steal a peek at the resident deer, raccoon, and wild turkey. Fishing, tubing, and scuba diving also rate highly here.

Drifting with the current, you're likely to pass Tan Vat Hole, where early settlers soaked animal hides in a "tan vat" of tannic acid, converting them into leather. Canoeists slip through Cave Spring, and great fishing awaits at Rock House Cave. Just past Owls Bend, where barred and screech owls perch on a high bluff, visitors stop to enjoy mountain craft demonstrations such as sorghum-making and blacksmithing. At Alley Spring, the gristmill grinds cornmeal in summer and on May, September, and October weekends, while homemade whiskey drips from an old-fashioned still.

Fourteen fifty-year-old rock and frame cabins with knotty pine interiors sprinkle the woods on the east bank of Big Spring's flow. These one- and two-bedroom cabins sleep up to six people apiece, and most have fireplaces, kitchenettes, outdoor barbecue grills, and screened porches with porch swings.

Not far from the cabins, Big Spring Lodge, listed in the National Register of Historic Places, serves fine meals in a magnificent stone structure. Its dining room looks out on the spring branch and a boat dock, where river tours depart on a twenty-four-foot, flat-bottomed boat.

Big Spring Lodge is four miles south of Van Buren, Missouri, on Rte. 103. Cabins available April through October. Rates: $22 to $35 per night. Cash and checks accepted. Reservations recommended two to three months in advance. Two-night minimum rental on weekends, three nights on holiday weekends.

BENNETT SPRING STATE PARK
LEBANON, MO 65536
(417) 532-4338 *(park office)*
(417) 532-4307 *(cabin reservations)*

The sparkling waters of Bennett Spring have fascinated travelers through the west-central Missouri hills for thousands of years. The Indians who first inhabited this green valley referred to the spring, which daily pours one hundred million gallons of water into the Niangua River, as the "eye of the earth."

In the mid-1800s, pioneers built gristmills powered by the spring waters, and none was more successful than that established by this park's namesake, Peter Bennett. Farmers often camped here for three or four days, fishing, hunting, and munching from open barrels of soda crackers, sauerkraut, and dill pickles at the mill store while waiting their turn at the mill's grinding stones. Although Bennett Spring's chilled waters lured anglers for decades before the state of Missouri acquired this property in 1924, their sport has been enhanced by a trout hatchery now located in Bennett Spring State Park.

Forests of oak and hickory cover the Ozark ridges here, while redbuds, dogwoods, and Missouri wild flowers provide an understory of contrasting spring colors. Beaver, deer, wild turkey, and blue heron inhabit this 1240-acre park year-round, and golden and bald eagles can sometimes be spotted in winter.

In addition to fine trout fishing during the March-October season, winter angling is permitted under a catch-and-release program. Visitors can also swim in a large, modern pool, or rent a canoe for a trip down the Niangua River. The community of Lebanon sponsors a three-day festival each summer known as Hillbilly Days, featuring arts and crafts demonstrations and such Ozark customs as square dancing and fiddling.

Bennett Spring's eighty-two cabins dot the landscape throughout the park. They have from one to three bedrooms, some have kitchens, and they range in age from one to forty years. The park's dining lodge serves meals daily during trout season.

Bennett Spring State Park is twelve miles northwest of Lebanon, Missouri, on Rte. 64. Cabins available March through October. Rates: $18 to $52 per night. Cash, checks, Visa, and MasterCard accepted. Reservations taken up to nine months in advance. Two-night minimum rental for cabins with kitchens.

BIG LAKE STATE PARK
BIGELOW, MO 64425
(816) 442-3770 (park office)
(816) 442-5683 (cabin and motel reservations)

Northwestern Missouri's Big Lake State Park, acquired by the state in 1932, lies on the eastern shore of a 625-acre natural oxbow lake that was once part of the Missouri River. Scattered sugar maple, green ash, black willow, and sycamore trees highlight this subtly rolling floodplain, home of a rare species of bulrush and (infrequent in Missouri) the western hognose snake.

Big Lake offers swimming and boating, and it's stocked with catfish, carp, crappie, bass, and bluegill for fishermen. Other park facilities include a sizable swimming pool and numerous picnic areas.

Overnight guests at Big Lake choose from a twenty-two-room motel and eight cabins, all of which stand in a grassy area along the lake. These accommodations are heated, air-conditioned, and completely furnished, and the cabins feature kitchens with all cooking gear. A restaurant serves cabin and motel guests, as well as day visitors to the park.

Nearby attractions include Watkins Mill State Historic Site, where numerous nineteenth-century buildings stand, including a woolen mill with its machinery still intact. There is also a wildlife refuge near Big Lake: Squaw Creek National Wildlife Refuge.

Big Lake State Park is eleven miles west of Mound City, Missouri, on Rtes. 111 and 159. Cabins and motel rooms available mid-April through late December. Rates: $20 to $36 per night. Cash, Visa, and MasterCard accepted. Reservations taken starting in January for coming season; recommended three to six months in advance for summer, weekends, and duck- and goose-hunting seasons.

LAKE WAPPAPELLO STATE PARK
ROUTE 2, BOX 46
WILLIAMSVILLE, MO 63967
(314) 297-3232 (park office)
(314) 297-3247 (cabin reservations)

Lake Wappapello presents some of the finest fishing in southeastern Missouri, with bass, bluegill, crappie, and catfish the principal attractions. This eighty-six-hundred-acre lake delights swimmers, and Lake Wappapello's marina rents boats for fishing and cruising.

Set at the southern end of the lake, on Allison's Peninsula, Lake Wappapello State Park lies in a transitional zone between the Ozarks and the southeastern lowlands. Black oak, northern and southern red oak, dogwood, scarlet, mockernut hickory, and an unusual stand of American beech flourish on the rugged hillsides, while sweet gum, yellow poplar, river birch, and sycamore thrive in the bottomlands of the Saint Francois River floodplain. Miles of hiking trails cross these unique vegetation zones.

Not far from the marina and a picnic area, Lake Wappapello's eight two-bedroom cabins face the lakeshore under scattered oaks. These modern cabins sleep from two to six people apiece, are heated and air-conditioned, and have full kitchens.

Lake Wappapello State Park is fifteen miles northeast of Poplar Bluff, Missouri, on Rte. 172. Cabins available April through October. Rates: $24 to $60 per night. Cash and checks accepted. Reservations taken starting in January for coming season, recommended three to four weeks in advance for summer. Two-night minimum rental on weekends.

MERAMEC STATE PARK
P.O. BOX 57
SULLIVAN, MO 63080
(314) 468-6072 (park office)
(314) 468-6519 (cabin reservations)

The soothing Meramec River threads through grassy valleys and rough timbered hills — steep slopes that contain mature oak and hickory forests above, and twenty-two caves below. Legend has it that an enterprising Missouri governor of the 1860s attempted to hold his inaugural ball in a large chamber in Fisher Cave, but smoke and overcrowding drove away most of the guests. This eastern Missouri park boasts unusual geological attractions, including sinkholes, dolomite cliffs, and gushing springs, and some 460 of its 6489 acres constitute the largest undisturbed Ozark chert forest in Missouri.

Spearpoints, arrowheads, pottery, ax heads, and other artifacts unearthed here suggest an extended presence of ancient Indian hunters, followed by Osages, Delawares, and Shawnees. French miners prospecting for lead followed the Spanish adventurerers who were the first whites to explore this section of the "cave state." About 1800, Daniel Boone led an expedition of hunters and prospectors along the Meramec River.

Float trips ranging from several hours on the Meramec to camping overnights delight visitors, and canoe rentals are available. Anglers pursue the Meramec's bass, catfish, and perch, while swimmers relax in its cool waters. More than ten miles of hiking trails amble through white oak, black oak, shagbark hickory, and flowering dogwood.

Meramec's seventeen cabins, scattered across a hillside, have one, two, three, or five bedrooms, and sleep from two to fourteen people apiece. All feature kitchens, heating, and air conditioning, and some have wood exteriors and large stone fireplaces. The park's rock-and-timber lodge serves up home-cooked meals and Ozark hospitality.

Meramec State Park is four miles east of Sullivan, Missouri, on Rte. 185. Cabins available April through October. Rates: $24 to $76 per night. Cash and checks accepted. Reservations taken starting in January for the coming season, recommended two months in advance. Two-night minimum rental on weekends.

MONTAUK STATE PARK
ROUTE 5, BOX 278
SALEM, MO 65560
(314) 548-2525 (park office)
(314) 548-2434 (cabin and motel reservations)

The splendor of the Ozark highlands and the steady flow of gushing springs first attracted settlers to this area of south-central Missouri in the early 1800s. The pioneer village of Montauk was named by travelers homesick for a Long Island town of the same name. Four mills served the community, including an 1896-vintage gristmill that still stands in the park, awaiting restoration.

The Current River, widely known as one of the Midwest's best canoeing streams, takes its headwaters from seven Montauk springs that pour out forty-three million gallons of water daily. The Current and the Jacks Fork have been designated National Scenic Riverways by the National Park Service. Nearby canoe liveries rent all needed gear for river running, and the northernmost canoe access to the Current, Inman Hollow, is just south of this state park.

Montauk's twenty-six cabins feature heating, air conditioning, and baths with showers, and many have full kitchens. Additional accommodations can be found in a sixteen-unit motel. Montauk's lodge has a dining room and sells groceries and fishing supplies. Rental bicycles are also available in the park.

Montauk State Park contains a trout hatchery that stocks the Current River daily from March through October. The Current's fast-flowing, spring-fed waters make it an ideal habitat for rainbow trout. Pine, oak, and hickory flourish on the slopes of the Ozarks, while sycamore, cottonwood, and birch prefer low-lying areas. Rock outcrops of dolomite protrude from bluffs along the curling river.

Montauk State Park is twenty miles southwest of Salem, Missouri, on Rte. 119. Cabins and motel rooms available March through October. Rates: cabins, $20 to $48 per night; motel rooms, $25 to $34 per night. Cash, checks,

Visa, and MasterCard accepted. Reservations taken starting in January for the coming season, recommended three or four months in advance for weekends. Two-night minimum rental on weekends.

ROARING RIVER STATE PARK
P.O. Box D
CASSVILLE, MO 65265
(417) 847-2539 *(park office)*
(417) 847-2330 *(cabin and motel reservations)*

Roaring River State Park comprises chert-covered ridges that rise more than a thousand feet and deep hollows, such as Ketchum Hollow, where spicebush and butternut grow and placid pools attract rare gray-bellied salamanders. On some ridges, the unique Ozark chinquapin persists next to more typical hardwoods and cedars. One of the most densely forested regions of the Ozarks, Roaring River teems with wildlife, including bobcats and black bear. In winter, bald eagles soar above the Roaring River valley. The tranquil hollows and narrow ridges here in southwestern Missouri served as Indian hunting grounds for generations: as late as the 1830s, Indians camped along Roaring River.

During trout season, the state of Missouri stocks the waters of the river daily, making this a premiere location for fishing. Ten miles of hiking trails twist through the parkland, past a waterfall that (during much of the year) pours from a mountainside into Roaring River Spring. Swimmers take advantage of a large outdoor pool.

Overnight guests choose from twenty-nine cabins and a three-story, twenty-three-room motel. The cabins sleep from two to twelve people and have both heating and air conditioning. Some feature full kitchens and fireplaces, and all stand in scenic wooded or riverbank locations. A restaurant not far from the modern motel serves homemade pies and biscuits, and mountain specialties.

Roaring River State Park is seven miles south of Cassville, Missouri, on Rte. 112. Cabins and motel rooms available March through October. Rates: cabins, $18 to

$44 per night; motel rooms, $20 to $30 per night. Cash and checks accepted. Reservations taken starting in January for the coming season; recommended three to four months in advance for summer and weekends.

SAM A. BAKER STATE PARK
PATTERSON, MO 63956
(314) 856-4411 (park office)
(314) 856-4223 (cabin reservations)

Sam A. Baker State Park, one of the oldest parks in Missouri, lies in one of the oldest mountain regions in North America — the Saint Francois Mountains, in the southeastern part of the state. High, conical, domelike hills and outcroppings of ancient igneous rock characterize this range, which hosts forests of mixed hardwood and pine.

For thousands of years, white oaks, black oaks, and other native species on Mudlick Mountain have been subjected to lightning, wind, and ice, resulting in a bizarre array of growth. Many of the summit's trees have stunted trunks, knobby scars, and perhaps a single limb. Ice storms have left most unusual shapes: trees so stripped of limbs that they resemble telephone poles with bushlike appendages sprouting from them.

The Saint Francois River and Big Creek, a crystal clear, rocky-bottomed tributary, form Sam A. Baker's eastern boundary. They offer swimming and fishing for bluegill, bass, crappie, sunfish, buffalo, and carp. Canoeists float down Big Creek in spring and early summer, while liveries put in rental canoes on the Saint Francois year-round.

Civilian Conservation Corps workers built Baker's nineteen cabins in the 1930s, between an oak and hickory forest and the banks of Saint Francois River. The cabins sleep from two to six people and have heating and air conditioning. Twelve feature complete kitchens, and some have wood-burning fireplaces.

Sam A. Baker State Park is three miles north of Patterson, Missouri, on Rte. 143. Cabins available mid-April through October. Rates: $20 to $65 per night. Cash, Visa, *and MasterCard accepted. Reservations taken starting in January for the coming season; recommended three to four months in advance for summer and weekends.*

STOCKTON STATE PARK
Box 97
DADEVILLE, MO 65636
(417) 276-4259 *(park office)*
(417) 276-5329 *(motel reservations)*

Stockton State Park lies on a peninsula jutting northward between the Big and Little Sac arms of the sparkling blue Stockton Reservoir, in southwestern Missouri. When the U.S. Army Corps of Engineers constructed Stockton Dam on the Sac River, they created this twenty-five-thousand-acre lake. A dependable southwesterly breeze makes the lake a favorite with sailors, while its stocked bass, crappie, walleye, catfish, pike, and bluegill thrill anglers.

Stockton rests atop Missouri's Ozark plateau, and its second-growth woods of white oak, post oak, black hickory, and chinquapin oak form a habitat for deer, turkeys, and numerous bird species. Two launching ramps and a marina serve boaters, and public swimming beaches are nearby.

Not far from the marina and a dining lodge, Stockton's eleven-room motel provides overnight accommodations. Each room sleeps from two to six people and is heated and air-conditioned.

Stockton State Park is five miles southeast of Stockton, Missouri, on Rte. 215. Motel open mid-April through October. Rates: $20 to $54 per night. Cash, Visa, and MasterCard accepted. Reservations taken starting in January, recommended three to four months in advance for summer.

THOUSAND HILLS STATE PARK
ROUTE 3
KIRKSVILLE, MO 63501
(816) 665-6995 (park office)
(816) 665-7119 (cabin reservations)

Archaeologists believe that the Indians who inhabited Missouri between 1000 and 1600 A.D. used Thousand Hills as a ceremonial ground. The rock carvings, or petroglyphs, they left behind include thunderbirds, sunbursts, and crosses, symbols of a religion that had been introduced to them by Indians of the Middle-Mississippi Cultural Tradition.

Set in the green hills of northern Missouri, Thousand Hills State Park edges 573-acre Forest Lake, which is popular for swimming, motorboating (ninety horsepower maximum), sailing, waterskiing, and paddleboating. Well-stocked with crappie, largemouth bass, bluegill, channel catfish, northerns, and walleye, Forest Lake also lures anglers.

Thousand Hills occupies an upland area along a drainage divide: lands west of the park drain into the Missouri River, those to the east feed the Mississippi. Second-growth stands of white oak, northern red oak, and shag-bark hickory loom over an understory of ironwood, mulberry, and redbud in most of the park; American elm, swamp white oak, silver maple, cottonwood, and syca-more populate the bottomland along the Cheriton River. Thousand Hills hosts a rare native grove of big-toothed aspen, which is usually found much farther north.

Thousand Hills's five duplex cabins face the lakeshore in a grassy meadow, not far from a dining lodge and marina. These modern cabins sleep from two to six people and feature full kitchens, heating, air conditioning, and patios with picnic tables and barbecue grills.

Thousand Hills State Park is four miles west of Kirksville, Missouri, on Rtes. 6 and 157. Cabins available mid-April through October. Rates: $30 to $45 per night. Cash, Visa, and MasterCard accepted. Reservations taken starting in January for the coming season, recommended three to four months in advance.

WAKONDA STATE PARK
RR 1, BOX 242
LA GRANGE, MO 63448
(314) 655-2280 *(park office)*
(314) 655-4827 *(cabin reservations)*

Just twenty-seven miles from Mark Twain's boyhood home in Hannibal, Missouri, and two miles from the Mississippi River, Wakonda State Park occupies 273 acres of lakes, patches of trees, and sandy soil in the mighty river's floodplain. Cottonwood, sycamore, black locust, elm mulberry, willow, and cedar trees shade this long, narrow park, where water sports prevail.

To the west rise bluffs overlooking the Mississippi, which offer wondrous views each evening at sunset. Sioux Indians believed their Great Spirit resided at the junction of the Wyaconda and Mississippi rivers, some three miles from the park. Rental canoes now provide modern-day explorers with a glimpse of the Wyaconda, a little-known scenic waterway. The proximity of the Mississippi, Hannibal, and Twain's birthplace in Stoutsville, forty miles away, gives a nostalgic charm to Wakonda State Park. Not so many years ago the blast of steamboat whistles and splash of paddleboards could be heard on the great river.

Wakonda Lake, the bigger of two lakes here, has seventy-five acres of water teeming with crappie, catfish, carp, bass, and bluegill, and the largest natural sand beach in the Missouri state park system. Fishermen cast from the shore or from boats (rentals available) on this quiet lake, which allows motorboats of no more than ten horsepower. The vast beach has room for volleyball, tetherball, horseshoes, and badminton, and paddleboats and inner tubes can be rented.

Wakonda's seven wood-frame duplex cabins (fourteen units) sleep four people in each unit, on double beds and sofa beds. Each unit has a full kitchen and an outdoor barbecue grill and picnic table. Heated and air-conditioned, these two-room cabin units face the lake at the extreme southern end of the park.

Wakonda State Park is three miles south of La Grange,

Missouri, off Rte. 61. Cabins available mid-April through October. Rates: $25 to $52 per night. Cash and checks accepted. Reservations taken starting in January for the coming season, recommended two months in advance for summer. Two-night minimum rental in summer.

WASHINGTON STATE PARK
ROUTE 2
DeSOTO, MO 63020
(314) 586-2995 *(park office)*
(314) 586-6696, 438-4106 *(cabin reservations)*

Big River, a tributary of the Meramec River, forms the northern boundary of Washington State Park in eastern Missouri. Rock carvings at the southern edge of the park give clues to the people who inhabited this steep terrain between 1000 and 1600 A.D. Ancient Indians probably etched these symbols into the dolomite rock, for religious or ceremonial purposes.

The Washington Hardwoods Forest, located along the Big River bluffs near a campground, is quite different from the dry woods throughout the rest of the park. This towering forest sprouted from deep accumulations of decomposed vegetation and weathered limestone boulders that had tumbled down from bluffs above. The fertile, rocky soil — called talus — supports a rich carpet of ferns and wild flowers, along with a small understory tree, bladdernut. The mature, hundred-foot-high trees in Washington Hardwoods Forest range from Kentucky coffees to sugar maples and slippery elms.

Washington State Park is known for its beautiful limestone glades, which are rocky openings in the forest. Unusual cone-shaped red cedars populate the glades, as do prairie grasses and such wild flowers as evening primrose and Fremont's leather flower.

Eight rustic cabins sleep from two to six people apiece in a wooded area near Big River. Some of these one- and two-bedroom cabins have fireplaces, and all are equipped with kitchen appliances, heating, and air conditioning.

Swimming and fishing are favorite activities in Big River, and the park offers a modern swimming pool as well. Many visitors rent canoes and inner tubes for a leisurely drift downriver. Fine meals are available at Washington's stone dining lodge.

Washington State Park is fourteen miles northeast of Potosi, Missouri, on Rte. 21. Cabins available mid-April through October. Rates: $28 to 40 per night. Cash, Visa, and MasterCard accepted. Reservations taken starting in January for the coming season, recommended three to four months in advance.

Ohio

~~~~

STATE PARK INFORMATION:
OHIO DEPARTMENT OF NATURAL RESOURCES
DIVISION OF PARKS AND RECREATION
FOUNTAIN SQUARE
COLUMBUS, OH 43224
(614) 265-7000

TOURISM INFORMATION:
OHIO DEPARTMENT OF DEVELOPMENT
OFFICE OF TRAVEL AND TOURISM
P.O. 1001
COLUMBUS, OH 43216
(800) 282-5393

STATE BIRD: *Cardinal*
STATE TREE: *Ohio Buckeye*
STATE FLOWER: *Scarlet Carnation*

Legendary frontiersman Simon Kenton once lived in this region and his wife gets credit for the name "Springfield," inspired by the many springs welling from broad meadows. A remnant of a natural wet meadow is preserved at Buck Creek State Park, site of rare botanical wonders. Buck Creek's northernmost region is an excellent place to observe waterfowl: the shallow waters annually attract thousands of migrating ducks. Uncommon open-ground songbirds can also be spotted, including dickcissels, bobolinks, and henslow sparrows.

The relatively new Buck Creek State Park lies in Ohio's fertile western plain. A twenty-four-hundred-foot sand beach awaits swimmers and sunbathers at the 2120-acre Clarence J. Brown Lake, which is also popular for fishing, boating, and waterskiing. A four-lane launching ramp serves boaters, and the park recently opened a 211-slip marina.

Buck Creek's twenty-six cabins are also recent additions, part of a five-million-dollar improvement package completed at this 4030-acre park in 1981. These deluxe two-bedroom cabins sleep up to six people apiece and have electric heat and kitchen appliances, screened porches, and baths with showers.

On the lake's west shore, the Clark County Historical Society maintains historic Crabill House, a fine example of a very early brick farmhouse. Nearby attractions include Clifton Gorge Nature Preserve, designated a National Natural Landmark by the National Park Service, and the United States Air Force Museum. Within some 160,000 feet of hangar space, this museum comprehensively chronicles the history of flight and milestones in aviation. Spads, Camels, Spitfires, Mustangs, B-29s, a Wright Brothers original, and an Apollo space capsule are only a sampling of the more than 130 aircraft and missiles displayed.

Buck Creek State Park is four miles east of Springfield, Ohio, on Rte. 4. Cabins available year-round. Rates: from

$48 for one night to $198 per week. Cash and checks accepted. Reservations taken up to one year in advance. Cabins rented only for full weeks in summer.

BURR OAK STATE PARK
ROUTE 2, BOX 128
GLOUSTER, OH 45732
(800) 282-7275 *(in-state cabin and lodge reservations)*
(614) 767-2112 *(all other calls)*

Burr Oak's 3256 acres of woodland abound with wildlife, including white-tailed deer, ruffed grouse, and box turtles. Along the shore of Lake Burr Oak, a skinny reservoir in the shape of a crooked tree branch, quiet observers might see an industrious beaver, a multicolored wood duck, or the splash of feeding bass. Rock outcrops in all sizes and shapes are evident here, including several caves. Overhead tower magnificent oaks and hickories.

Come spring in the southern Ohio hill country, wild flowers burst into bloom: orchids, trilliums, jack-in-the-pulpits, lilies, and violets all show their best. In fall, the woods blaze with deep reds, brilliant yellows, and burnt oranges. Hikers discover these sights and more on miles of trails, including a twenty-nine-mile backpack trail.

Burr Oak Lake boasts of largemouth bass, crappie, bluegill, and catfish. The park's marina rents pontoon boats, fishing boats, canoes, rowboats, sailboats, and paddleboats, while privately owned craft use its four launching areas (maximum of ten horsepower permitted). Scuba divers also flock to the lake's pristine waters, which flow from Sunday Creek.

Constructed of rough timber and stone, Burr Oak's sixty-room lodge blends into a hillside, circled by tall trees. This modern facility has an indoor-outdoor pool, a dining room, tennis courts, and rental bicycles. Nearby, thirty two-bedroom frame cabins stand in meadows or under trees. Each cabin sleeps up to six people and has electric heat, a full kitchen, a comfortable living area, a bath with shower, and a cool screened porch.

Burr Oak State Park is five miles northeast of Glouster, Ohio, on Rte. 78. Cabins and lodge open year-round. Rates: cabins, from $75 for one night to $298 per week;

lodge, $49 per night for two people; reduced in winter. Cash, checks, and MasterCard accepted. Reservations taken up to one year in advance, recommended that early for summer. Cabins rented only for full weeks in summer.

COWAN LAKE STATE PARK
729 BEACHWOOD ROAD
WILMINGTON, OH 45177
(513) 289-2105

When the wind picks up on warm days in southwestern Ohio, many a sailor heads for Cowan Lake. This charming, seven-hundred-acre lake, replete with coves and inlets, offers ideal sailing to and around Austin Island, thanks in part to a ten-horsepower limit on powerboats. At the marina, canoes, rowboats, pontoon boats, fishing boats, and sailboats wait to be rented, and launching ramps are available. Just west of the marina, the swimming beach has a complete bathhouse and snack bar. Anglers pull fine catches of muskie, crappie, largemouth bass, catfish, and bluegill from Cowan Lake.

Clinton County's first settler, William Smalley, cleared land for his home along Cowan Creek in 1797. Smalley, twice captured by Indians, had fought against the Ottawas as a soldier under General "Mad Anthony" Wayne.

No doubt Smalley and other pioneers roamed the land that now constitutes 1775-acre Cowan Lake State Park. Today, Lotus Cove Trail offers hikers a boardwalk view of an American lotus (water lily) colony, while Emerald Woods Trail threads a mature beech forest. In cold weather, iceboating, ice-skating, ice fishing, and cross-country skiing predominate.

Graceful trees ring Cowan's twenty-seven two-bedroom cabins, which line the north lakeshore. These wood-sided cabins accommodate up to six people apiece. They feature baths with showers, complete kitchens, electric heat, screened porches, and outdoor barbecue grills.

For a change of scenery, you can take a day trip to the historic towns of Lebanon and Waynesville. Lebanon offers dining and overnight quarters at the Golden Lamb, a four-story hotel built in 1815, and tours of an exquisite Greek Revival mansion called Glendower. Waynesville deserves mention for its profusion of antique dealers — more than thirty individual shops and several consignment warehouses.

Cowan Lake State Park is five miles south of Wilmington, Ohio, on Rte. 350. Cabins available year-round. Rates: from $48 for one night to $198 per week. Cash and checks accepted. Reservations taken up to one year in advance. Cabins rented only for full weeks in summer.

DEER CREEK STATE PARK
20635 WATERLOO ROAD
MOUNT STERLING, OH 43143
(800) 282-7275 *(in-state cabin and lodge reservations)*
(614) 869-3124 *(all other calls)*

In south-central Ohio, you can spend a night or a week in President Warren G. Harding's favorite retreat — a one-and-a-half-story, deluxe lake house known facetiously as the "shack." Whether the cabin was the site of political intrigue or merely a refuge for the president's entourage is not known, but it's likely that it hosted strategy sessions regarding the scandals that rocked the Harding administration, including the infamous Teapot Dome affair.

The state of Ohio spent more than $70,000 renovating and furnishing the cabin in 1972, when it was rescued from being razed. New cedar siding covers the exterior walls, and the roof now has cedar shingles. An original stone fireplace was repaired, and massive wooden beams were refinished. Oak floors and red-oak paneling highlight the interior, and the kitchen features electric appliances, including a dishwasher. Harding Cabin, heated and air-conditioned, sleeps up to seven people in three bedrooms. A fifty-foot rear porch overlooks Deer Creek Lake.

Other accommodations at Deer Creek State Park include a 110-room lodge and twenty-five two-bedroom cabins, all constructed in 1981. Perched on a hill above the lake, the lodge has a craggy limestone-and-cedar exterior, and an interior with cathedral ceilings, exposed beams, and plenty of wood trim. Lodge facilities range from indoor and outdoor pools to tennis courts and an eighteen-hole golf course.

Deer Creek's frame cabins, which trace the shore of the 1277-acre lake, sleep up to six people apiece. These deluxe cabins have full kitchens, baths with showers, and screened porches.

A seventeen-hundred-foot sandy beach and boat-launching ramps serve water-lovers, and Deer Creek's marina rents rowboats, canoes, ski boats, sailboats, and pontoon boats. Anglers wet a line in the lake for largemouth, smallmouth, and white bass, bluegill, crappie, and catfish, while walleye and muskie lurk in the tailwaters below the dam.

Deer Creek State Park is five miles south of Mount Sterling, Ohio, on Rte. 207. Cabins and lodge open year-round. Rates: Harding Cabin, from $75 for one night to $375 per week; two-bedroom cabins, from $79 for one night to $315 per week; lodge rooms, $62 per night for two people. Rates reduced in winter. Cash, checks, Visa, and MasterCard accepted. Reservations taken up to one year in advance. Harding Cabin rented only for full weeks in summer.

DILLON STATE PARK
5265 DILLON HILLS DRIVE
P.O. Box 126
NASHPORT, OH 43830
(614) 453-4377

Weapons aficionados fancy Dillon State Park, home of a complete firearms complex. This modern facility includes lighted trap and skeet fields, a hundred-yard rifle range, and a twenty-five-yard pistol range. A heated building houses a thirty-foot small-bore range, and a four-hundred-foot archery field is nearby.

Moses Dillon, for whom this park is named, purchased land here in 1803. This industrious and farsighted early American built and operated a local iron foundry, established the village of Dillon Falls, and dammed the Licking River to provide waterpower for the community. Mr. Dillon's primary claim to fame, however, remains the design and construction of the famous "Y" bridge in nearby Zanesville, Ohio.

Dillon State Park's 7548 acres rim the 1660-acre Dillon

Reservoir, and also subsume the swampland that adjoins the lakeshore. A sandy beach with bathhouse pleases swimmers. Having no horsepower limits, the reservoir attracts large numbers of ski boats and speedboats, but sailors and fishermen don't mind; part of the lake is a "no wake" zone. Anglers reel in largemouth and small-mouth bass, muskie, bluegill, crappie, and catfish. Dillon's hiking trails crest unglaciated ridges, which are the site of sledding and skiing in winter.

Overlooking the reservoir's north shore from a thick woods, Dillon's twenty-nine wood cabins each accommodate up to six people in two bedrooms. Each has a bath with shower, a kitchen, a living area, and a screened porch.

Dillon State Park is seven miles northeast of Zanesville, Ohio, on Rte. 146. Cabins available year-round. Rates: from $48 for one night to $198 per week. Cash and checks accepted. Reservations taken up to one year in advance. Cabins rented only for full weeks in summer.

GENEVA STATE PARK
ROUTE 1, BOX 429
GENEVA, OH 44041
(216) 466-8400

Geneva's twelve frame cabins, built in the mid-1960s, form a semicircle facing Lake Erie. Picnic tables and mature trees stand near these cabins, but each screened porch retains an unobstructed view of the shoreline and lake waters. Each cabin has three bedrooms, a kitchen, a dinette, a bath with shower, and a fireplace.

Recreation in this 698-acre park ranges from swimming along its two and a half miles of Lake Erie beach to hiking its five miles of trails. Boat ramps provide access to Lake Erie for fishermen, skiers, pleasure boaters, and sailors. Those who appreciate outstanding natural areas will want to explore the freshwater marshes and estuaries at Geneva. Rows of silver maples and virgin oaks over-look the lake and shade a pleasant picnic area.

Located in the northeastern part of the state, in Ohio's snow belt, Geneva is an excellent base for snowmobiling on designated trails and for cross-country skiing. Hunting for deer, rabbit, duck, and pheasant is permitted in season. Nearby attractions include the Ashtabula Harbor area, where twenty-six buildings have been listed on the National Register of Historic Places. Once a booming shipping center, Ashtabula now features charming shops and restaurants in hundred-year-old buildings along Bridge Street.

Geneva State Park is ten miles west of Ashtabula, Ohio, on Rte. 534. Cabins available from May through September. Rates: from $40 for one night to $166 per week. Cash and checks accepted. Reservations taken up to one year in advance. Cabins rented only for full weeks in summer.

HOCKING HILLS STATE PARK
20160 ROUTE 664
LOGAN, OH 43138
(614) 385-6841

Thick deciduous and coniferous forests overlie thousands of hilly acres in southeastern Ohio, but it's the fascinating limestone and shale formations at Hocking Hills State Park that truly distinguish it. Primitive man may have sought shelter in caves, cliffs, and recesses here as long as seven thousand years ago; pottery fragments positively confirm the presence of Adena Indians sometime between the birth of Christ and 800 A.D. European settlers finally stumbled onto the magnificent forests in the 1790s.

Visitors hike varied trails to six major rock formations, ranging from Cedar Falls — a serene waterfall near a dense hemlock stand that early settlers mistook for cedar — to the Rock House, a massive cavern walled in stone except for "windows" that afford a view of the adjacent woodlands.

A deep gorge runs along Old Man's Cave, named for a hermit who was so awed by its beauty that he decided to live out his days at the cave. Water churning through the gorge tumbles over two waterfalls and into a large pothole called the Devil's Bathtub. Hundreds of years of erosion have produced another outstanding recess known as Ash Cave — this seven-hundred-foot-long, horseshoe-shaped ledge creates a recess one hundred feet deep.

Hocking Hills State Park's forty deluxe cabins perch on a pine ridge overlooking a dining lodge. Each of these two-bedroom cabins sleeps up to six people, and is equipped with gas heat, an electric kitchen, a bath with shower, and a screened porch.

Bridle paths traverse this nineteen-hundred-acre park and adjoining state forest, and several riding stables are nearby. Seventeen-acre Rose Lake satisfies anglers, while swimmers take a dip in a pool next to the dining lodge.

Hocking Hills State Park is fourteen miles southwest of Logan, Ohio, on Rte. 664. Cabins available year-round. Rates: from $48 for one night to $198 per week; reduced in winter. Cash and checks accepted. Reservations taken up to one year in advance, recommended that early for summer and October. Cabins rented only for full weeks in summer.

HUESTON WOODS STATE PARK
ROUTE 1
COLLEGE CORNER, OH 45003
(800) 282-7275 *(in-state cabin and lodge reservations)*
(513) 523-6347 *(all other calls)*

Matthew Hueston, while serving with General "Mad Anthony" Wayne in the 1790s, observed fertile soil in southwestern Ohio, and he later purchased land here. Apparently an early conservationist, he preserved a section of virgin forest, as did his descendants. Big Woods, as this National Natural Landmark is called, has a lofty canopy typical of the wilderness forest that covered this continent from the Appalachian Mountains to the Great Plains nearly two hundred years ago. As settlers trudged west, they perceived that forest of towering oaks, hickories, beeches, maples, tulip trees, walnuts, elms, gums, and ashes — many exceeding 150 feet in height — as both a magnificent sight and an awesome challenge. Today, barely two thousand acres of that original wilderness remain in Ohio, and two hundred of those acres are in Big Woods.

Hueston Woods's contemporary lodge features A-frame construction of wood and stone. Lodge amenities include a dining room, indoor and outdoor swimming pools, tennis, volleyball, and shuffleboard courts, and rental bicycles. Other accommodations here consist of wooden one- and two-bedroom cabins. The thirty-four smaller cabins sleep up to four people in single bedroom / living areas, and have baths and kitchenettes. The twenty-five deluxe two-bedroom models, some of which front Acton Lake, sleep up to six people and offer baths, kitchens, living areas, and screened porches.

A modern marina rents boats and motors (maximum ten horsepower permitted on the lake) and has rental dock space and launching ramps. Fishermen find bass, crappie, bluegills, walleyes, and catfish stocked in Acton Lake's water, while golf enthusiasts enjoy an eighteen-hole course. At the nature center, small native animals can be viewed indoors. Larger wildlife live in outdoor areas, such as a flight cage inhabited by birds of prey and a pen full of white-tailed deer.

Hueston Woods State Park is five miles northwest of Oxford, Ohio, on Rtes. 732 and 177. Lodge and large cabins open year-round, small cabins available April through October. Rates: cabins, from $51 to $75 for one night to $225 to $298 per week; lodge, $62 per night for two people; all rates reduced in winter. Cash, checks, Visa, and MasterCard accepted. Reservations taken up to one year in advance, recommended three to six months in advance for summer. Cabins rented only for full weeks in summer.

LAKE HOPE STATE PARK
ZALESKI, OH 45698
(614) 596-5253

Lake Hope State Park lies entirely within 25,937-acre Zaleski State Forest, a landscape of steep gorges and narrow ridges in southeastern Ohio's Raccoon Creek valley. Prehistoric Mound Builders first inhabited this terrain, followed by Wyandot Indians, and white settlers arrived on the scene in 1798.

Coal and iron ore were keys to more recent history around Lake Hope, which was part of a hundred-mile-long, thirty-mile-wide belt of southern Ohio and northern

Kentucky known as the Hanging Rock Iron Region. Eighty charcoal furnaces produced iron for the Industrial Revolution from 1818 to 1916, cranking out ingots used to manufacture railroads, heavy machinery, and farm equipment. Hope Furnace and the many abandoned mine shafts in the park give silent witness to that era.

This 3103-acre park features a cool, 120-acre lake with a large swimming beach, bathhouse, and rowboats and canoes for rent. Bluegill and catfish teem in the lake, where electric motors up to four horsepower are permitted. Hikers follow Hope Furnace Trail along the lake's west shore, or Peninsula Trail up hills that harbor a delicate assemblage of shrubs and wild flowers. The yellow lady's slipper, one of the rarest and most showy orchids, blooms in secluded hollows.

Lake Hope State Park has the widest variety of cabins in Ohio, including deluxe two-bedroom cabins, standard two-bedroom cabins, and one- to four-bedroom sleeping cabins. The twenty-five deluxe cabins feature electric heat, baths, kitchens, and screened porches. Fireplaces add charm to twenty-one standard cabins, which have complete kitchens and baths. Lake Hope's twenty-three sleeping cabins also contain wood-burning fireplaces, baths, and refrigerators, but have limited cooking facilities. All Lake Hope cabins linger in a peaceful, wooded section of the park. A dining lodge serves meals from May through October, and Laurel Lodge, a group lodge capable of sleeping twenty-eight people, can also be rented.

Lake Hope State Park is five miles north of Zaleski, Ohio, on Rte. 278. Deluxe and sleeping cabins available year-round, standard cabins available April through October. Rates: from $32 to $48 for one night to $140 to $198 per week. Cash and checks accepted. Reservations taken up to one year in advance. Deluxe and standard cabins rented only for full weeks in summer.

MOHICAN STATE PARK CABINS
P.O. Box 22
LOUDONVILLE, OH 44842
(419) 994-4290

MOHICAN STATE PARK LODGE
ROUTE 2
PERRYSVILLE, OH 44864
(800) 472-6700 (*in-state calls*)
(419) 938-5411 (*all other calls*)

The steep hills, deep forests, and swift rivers in this area so captivated author Louis Bromfield that he remarked, "I live on the edge of paradise." Indeed, the Pulitzer Prize–winning Bromfield established a working farm bordering Mohican Country, where white pines flourish along ridges and hemlocks fill hollows and gorges. Not far from Mohican State Park, Bromfield's 640-acre farm, Malabar, and his rambling home are now open to visitors, who are intrigued to learn that Humphrey Bogart and Lauren Bacall were married in the center hallway in 1945.

The setting of Mohican's twenty-five two-bedroom cabins may be the most picturesque of any state park in Ohio. They line the bank of Clear Fork Creek, a favorite with rafting and canoeing enthusiasts. During warm months, significant numbers of them will drift by on the creek's lazy current.

These wooden cabins sleep six and have complete kitchens, baths, and screened porches. Down the road from the cabins, on a bluff above Pleasant Hill Lake, rests the stone, timber, and glass Mohican Lodge. Built in the 1970s, this dazzling structure features ninety-six guest rooms, an outdoor pool, an indoor pool, two tennis courts, and a private boat dock. Visitors enjoy meals in the spacious dining room, or take part in a poolside barbecue.

Clear Fork Creek and Black Fork River, both of which are populated with canoe liveries, form the Mohican River, noted for its trout and smallmouth bass. Boat-launching ramps serve Pleasant Hill Lake, which has plenty of largemouth bass, carp, crappie, catfish, perch, and bluegill, and is also a favorite with skiers and sailors. Hikers and horseback riders favor Clear Fork Gorge and a virgin pine forest, both designated as National Natural Landmarks.

Mohican State Park is just south of Loudonville, Ohio, on Rte. 3. Cabins and lodge open year-round. Rates: cabins, from $48 for one night to $198 per week; lodge, $58 per night for two people. Cash and checks accepted for cabins; those forms of payment plus Visa, Master-Card, and American Express at the lodge. Reservations taken up to one year in advance; recommended that early for cabins in summer. Cabins rented only for full weeks in summer.

PIKE LAKE STATE PARK
1847 PIKE LAKE ROAD
BAINBRIDGE, OH 45612
(614) 493-2212

Three million men, ages seventeen to twenty-three, served in the Civilian Conservation Corps in the 1930s and 1940s, developing America's natural resources — our forests, soil, and water. The CCC built Pike Lake, a pastoral, thirteen-acre lake bordered by rising hills, and planted hundreds of pines in this six-hundred-acre park in southwestern Ohio. These days, Pike Lake's very clear waters entice swimmers, scuba divers, and anglers, who pitch in a line for largemouth bass, channel catfish, bull-head, bluegill, crappie, blue catfish, and shovelhead.

A sand beach with diving boards delights swimmers, and rowboats, paddleboats, and canoes can be rented. (Electric motors of up to four horsepower are permitted on Pike Lake.) Three hiking trails course through pine groves, open meadows, and past the lake, presenting diverse habitats for bird-watchers. Game birds, such as ring-necked pheasant, wild turkey, and ruffed grouse, also inhabit the park and the adjoining state forest.

Pike Lake's twenty-five wooden cabins line a road that rises up from the lake, set in a serene forest. Twelve deluxe, two-bedroom cabins sleep up to six people apiece and have electric kitchens, screened porches, and baths with showers. The fifty-year-old, one-bedroom cabins, which also accommodate up to six, have baths and full kitchens as well.

A third lodging option here is a two-story group lodge with a lake view. This CCC-era building has a dormitory-style sleeping area upstairs and two bedrooms, a dining room, a kitchen, and two bathrooms downstairs. The group lodge sleeps up to twenty guests.

Pike Lake State Park is five miles northwest of Morgantown, Ohio, off Rte. 124. Two-bedroom cabins available year-round, one-bedroom units April through October. Rates: from $36 to $48 for one night to $156 to $198 per week. Cash and checks accepted. Reservations taken up to one year in advance, recommended three to six months in advance for summer. Cabins rented only for full weeks in summer.

Manor House, Punderson State Park, Ohio

PUNDERSON STATE PARK
P.O. BOX 338
NEWBURY, OH 44065
(216) 564-9144

Punderson has become Ohio's premier winter-sports park. A unique sports chalet atop a large sledding hill offers enthusiasts a warming fire and refreshments. Skating, snowmobiling, sledding, hiking, and cross-country skiing are all at their best here in northeastern Ohio.

One of Ohio's few natural lakes, Punderson Lake was formed during the ice ages when a glacier scoured a deep depression in the landscape. That water-filled depression now facilitates swimming along a beach; fishing for sunfish, largemouth and smallmouth bass, and trout; and boating (electric motors up to four horsepower permitted).

Lemuel Punderson, who once owned the property that is now the park, operated a gristmill and a distillery here. At the turn of the century, an amusement park on this site entertained families from nearby Cleveland. In 1929, work began on a Tudor-style manor house that today serves as the park lodge. Never completed by the original builder, the lodge was acquired by the state in the 1950s.

Recently renovated, Punderson Lodge holds thirty-two guest rooms, each distinctive and homey. It reflects the elegance of English country living, and has a reputation for fine cuisine. Other amenities include an outdoor swimming pool and nearby volleyball and shuffleboard courts.

Punderson's twenty-six two-bedroom, frame cabins rim a broad, circular road near the tip of the lake. Each sleeps six, and has electric heat and appliances and a screened porch.

Three tennis courts and an eighteen-hole golf course round out the park's facilities. Nearby attractions include an Amish settlement and Swiss cheese factory in Middlefield, Ohio, a restored eighteenth-century village in Burton, Ohio, and world-renowned Holden Arboretum — two thousand acres brimming with six thousand trees, shrubs, and vines from all over the globe.

Punderson State Park is three miles east of Newbury, Ohio, on Rte. 87. Cabins and lodge open year-round. Rates: cabins, from $76 for one night to $298 per week; lodge, $54 to $65 per night for two people; reduced in winter. Cash, checks, Visa, MasterCard accepted. Reservations taken up to one year in advance, recommended three to six months in advance for summer. Cabins rented only for full weeks in summer.

PYMATUNING STATE PARK
ROUTE 1
ANDOVER, OH 44003
(216) 293-6329

Spectacular walleye fishing has made Pymatuning Lake famous, as ten-pound catches are common. Anglers also reel in white bass, yellow perch, catfish, bluegill, and crappie from this enormous, 14,650-acre lake, which laps some seventy-seven miles of shoreline along the Ohio-Pennsylvania border.

Other popular pastimes at this lake include swimming at a thousand-foot sand beach, and such winter sports as ice-skating and ice fishing. Boat-launching ramps edge into the water at five locations around the lake, which has a ten-horsepower limit. Fishing boats and canoes are available for rent.

Once a vast swamp with floating bogs, this terrain attracted Erie Indians who sought its fish and game. Early white settlers, however, steered clear of Pymatuning Swamp because of the dangerous footing and almost impenetrable vegetation. The dam that created Pymatuning Lake, built in Pennsylvania in 1933, regulates the flow of the Shenango and Beaver rivers.

Pymatuning's fifty-two wood-sided cabins, which sprinkle the forest, come in one- and two-bedroom floor plans. The older, one-bedroom cabins sleep up to four people on double beds and fold-out couches, and have baths and kitchenettes. The two-bedroom units accommodate up to six people, and have full kitchens and baths with showers.

Pymatuning State Park is two miles southeast of Andover, Ohio, on Rte. 85. Two-bedroom cabins available year-round, one-bedroom units available April through October. Rates: from $36 to $48 for one night to $156 to $198 per week. Cash and checks accepted. Reservations taken up to one year in advance. Cabins rented only for full weeks in summer.

SALT FORK STATE PARK
P.O. Box 672
CAMBRIDGE, OH 43725
(800) 282-7275 (in-state cabin and lodge reservations)
(614) 439-2751 (all other calls)

Site of the northernmost Civil War skirmish, Salt Fork State Park comprises 20,156 rolling acres of graceful meadows and rich woodlots in east-central Ohio. Its long, undulating lake with dozens of coves and inlets has seventy-four miles of shoreline ready to be explored, as well as three swimming beaches, and waters teeming with largemouth bass, crappie, bluegill, walleye, and muskellunge. Rent a paddleboat, rowboat, canoe, ski boat, pontoon boat, or sailboat at the 368-slip marina, or launch your own craft at the boat ramps.

Salt Fork's imposing 148-room lodge has comfortable guest rooms with knotty-pine interiors, full dining facilities, indoor and outdoor pools, tennis courts, rental bicycles, and a putting green. This stone, timber, and brick lodge features a limestone fireplace, whose chimney stretches eighty-six feet into the air, a sauna, and a game room.

Constructed of natural wood siding, Salt Fork's fifty-four cabins occupy pleasant, shaded sites, some right on the lakefront. Enhanced by private boat-launching and swimming areas, the cabins sleep up to six people in two bedrooms. Each has a fully equipped kitchen, a bath with shower, a screened porch, and electric heat.

For an outstanding view of the eastern Ohio landscape, you can climb the hundred-foot fire tower or rent a horse at the stables. Golfers will be challenged by an eighteen-hole course; cold-weather visitors may want to try sledding, ice-skating, or ice fishing.

Salt Fork State Park is eight miles northeast of Cambridge, Ohio, off Rte. 22. Cabins and lodge open year-round. Rates: cabins, from $79 for one night to $315 per week; lodge, $62 per night for two people; reduced in winter. Cash, checks, Visa, and MasterCard accepted. Reservations taken up to one year in advance. Cabins rented only for full weeks in summer.

SHAWNEE STATE PARK
P.O. Box 98
FRIENDSHIP, OH 45630
(800) 282-7275 *(in-state cabin and lodge reservations)*
(614) 858-6621 *(all other calls)*

Bordering the sweeping Ohio River in the Appalachian foothills of southern Ohio, Shawnee State Park rests in the fifty-eight-thousand-acre Shawnee State Forest. Ridge upon ridge rolls toward the horizon in a seemingly endless expanse of woodland. Known as the "Little Smokies of Ohio," this invigorating terrain offers a host of wild flowers, including rare types of orchids. Scattered mists arising from densely forested hills are reminiscent of the southern Appalachians.

The park and state forest hold more than 130 miles of paved roads, not to mention miles of hiking, bridle, and backpacking trails. Visitors flock here each October, when slopes blaze with fiery reds, brilliant yellows, and vibrant oranges.

Shawnee's two small lakes, Turkey Creek Lake and Roosevelt Lake, both have sandy swimming beaches. Sailboats, canoes, rowboats, and electrically powered boats are permitted on the lakes, where a Trout Derby is held each spring.

Stepping into Shawnee Lodge, you're greeted by a huge stone fireplace and a breathtaking view of Turkey Creek Lake. Guest rooms here feature rich wood walls, and indoor and outdoor swimming pools, game courts, and a dining room complete this cheerful facility.

Shawnee's twenty-five wooden cabins are well isolated from the rest of the park, in a peaceful woods. These cabins have two bedrooms, complete kitchens, living and dining areas, baths with showers, and screened porches.

Shawnee State Park is twelve miles northwest of Portsmouth, Ohio, on Rte. 125. Cabins and lodge open year-round. Rates: cabins, from $75 for one night to $298 per week; lodge, $52 per night for two people; reduced in winter. Cash, checks, Visa, and MasterCard accepted. Reservations taken up to a year in advance, recommended that early for summer cabin rentals. Cabins rented only for full weeks in summer.

SOUTH BASS ISLAND STATE PARK
c/o CATAWBA ISLAND STATE PARK
4049 EAST MOORES DOCK ROAD
PORT CLINTON, OH 43452
(419) 797-4530

During the War of 1812, the fleet of Commodore Oliver H. Perry put in at South Bass Island before defeating the British in the Battle of Lake Erie. After the battle, Perry reported to General Harrison, "We have met the enemy, and they are ours."

Today a 352-foot granite column — the world's largest Doric column — on the north side of the island commemorates Perry's victory on September 10, 1813. From the monument's peak, visitors gaze at the large harbor at Put-in-Bay, crowded with power and sailing craft, and at the popular resort community. Daily ferries transport cars and passengers to South Bass to explore Perry's Cave, Heineman's Winery, and countless shops and restaurants.

South Bass Island State Park occupies the island's southern tip and incorporates the site of the once-famous Victory Hotel. At one time the largest hotel in America, the Victory was destroyed by fire in 1919. Its remains are still visible in the park.

South Bass has perhaps the most unusual lodging in the Ohio park system: the "cabent." A cross between a cabin and a tent, this hexagonal structure rests above the ground on wooden beams, and has wooden framing and a fabric roof. The cabent's base is approximately twenty-three feet square, and its roof is eighteen feet high at its peak. This two-bedroom unit sleeps up to six people, and features a bath with shower and a kitchenette.

The pier adjoining this park assists fishermen in landing Lake Erie bass, perch, crappie, and bluegill, while launching ramps serve those who have brought their boats. Ice fishing and ice-skating rate highly here in winter.

South Bass Island State Park is on the southern edge of South Bass Island, in Lake Erie. Cabent available May through September. Rates: from $30 for one night to $150 per week. Cash and checks accepted. Contact the park office in January for information on the lottery that determines cabent reservations.

The
MIDSOUTH

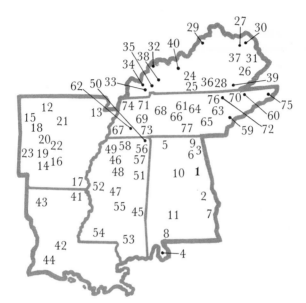

Alabama

STATE PARK INFORMATION:
ALABAMA DIVISION OF STATE PARKS
64 NORTH UNION STREET
MONTGOMERY, AL 36130
(800) 252-7275 (in-state calls)
(205) 261-3333 (out-of-state calls)

TOURISM INFORMATION:
ALABAMA BUREAU OF TOURISM AND TRAVEL
532 SOUTH PERRY STREET
MONTGOMERY, AL 36130
(800) 392-8096 (in-state calls)
(800) 252-2262 (out-of-state calls)

STATE BIRD: *Yellowhammer*
STATE TREE: *Southern Pine*
STATE FLOWER: *Camellia*
STATE FISH: *Tarpon*

CHEAHA STATE PARK
ROUTE 3, BOX 79-A
LINEVILLE, AL 36266
(800) 252-7275 *(in-state reservations)*
(205) 261-3333 *(out-of-state reservations)*
(205) 488-5111 *(park office)*

Capping Cheaha Mountain, the highest summit in the state, this eastern Alabama park embraces 2719 wooded acres at the southern end of the Appalachian chain. The 200,000-acre Talladega National Forest completely encircles Cheaha, which attracts rock climbers and rappelers to its many sheer cliffs. Deer, wild turkey, raccoons, opossums, and even bobcats can be spotted in the area, along with beavers and large turtles around Lake Cheaha. Virginia pine dominate the forests, which are highlighted by southern red oaks and chestnut oaks. Springtime blooms of wild hydrangea and mountain laurel delight those who appreciate their subtle beauty.

Cheaha's hiking trails range from short jaunts to a sixty-four-mile backpacking path. Swimmers and anglers share Lake Cheaha, where fishing boats and paddleboats can also be rented.

Cabin guests choose from Civilian Conservation Corps–era stone cabins and five modern A-frame chalets with spacious decks. The fifty-year-old stone cabins sleep from two to eight people, while the chalets accommodate up to six in two bedrooms. All of these units come equipped with heating, air conditioning, and full kitchens. Fireplaces add charm and warmth to the cabins and chalets.

Surrounded by trees and not far from a cliff-top vista, Cheaha's rock-walled lodge has thirty guest rooms, which sleep up to four people. Heated and air-conditioned, the lodge is within easy walking distance of the park's swimming pool, restaurant, and store, plus numerous hiking trails. Visitors to Cheaha can also travel to Talledega Motor Speedway — some twenty miles away — home of the Winston 500 and Talladega 500 auto races, and to the nearby Anniston Museum of Natural History.

Cheaha State Park is seventeen miles northwest of Lineville, Alabama, on Rte. 49. Cabins and lodge open year-round. Rates: cabins, $37 to $53 per night, $210 to

$318 per week; lodge, $35 to $39 per night for two people. Cash, checks, Visa, MasterCard, and American Express accepted. Reservations taken up to a year in advance, recommended two to four months in advance for weekends. Cabins rented for a minimum of two nights, May through August and fall weekends; three-night minimum on holiday weekends.

CHEWACLA STATE PARK
P.O. Box 447
AUBURN, AL 36831
(800) 252-7275 (in-state reservations)
(205) 261-3333 (out-of-state reservations)
(205) 887-5621 (park office)

Step out of your stone cabin at eastern Alabama's Chewacla State Park, and you'll find a barbecue grill and picnic table, plus a fishing boat ready to be pushed into a twenty-six-acre lake. Densely wooded with oak, hickory, pine, poplar, sweet gum, and elm, this 696-acre state park lies on the fall line separating the Piedmont Plateau from the Lower Coastal Plain. Take a drive or bicycle ride on Murphy Drive, lined with dogwoods, cherries, violets, and other wild flowers, to the top of the mountain. There hiking trails branch off into the woods, several converging at a soothing waterfall.

Popular with college students and faculty at nearby Auburn University, Chewacla was developed in the 1930s by the Civilian Conservation Corps—it's one of Alabama's original state parks. Noted for its varied terrain and unique rock formations, this park offers swimming in Chewacla Lake and fishing for bass, bream, crappie, catfish, shellcracker, and bluegill in both the lake and Chewacla Creek. Rowboats, canoes, fishing boats, and paddleboats can be rented at the lakefront, and tennis courts are nearby.

Chewacla's five stone cabins, dating from CCC days, sleep four to six people. The smaller cabins feature single living / dining / sleeping rooms, with adjoining baths and kitchenettes. The larger cabins come similarly equipped, except that they have separate bedrooms. One cabin features a fireplace, three have open-beamed cathedral ceilings, and all are heated and air-conditioned. Lawns of Bermuda grass and splendid woods full of birds and squirrels trim the secluded cabin area.

Halfway between the dam that impounds Chewacla Lake and the confluence of Moore's Mill Creek and Chewacla Creek stand the remains of Wright's Mill, built in 1840 and operated for more than sixty years. Grinding corn and wheat for area farmers, William Wilmot Wright's gristmill sparked economic development in the county, as did the cotton gin and sawmill once located a half-mile up creek from Wright's.

Chewacla State Park is three miles south of Auburn, Alabama, off Rte. 29. Cabins available year-round. Rates: $30 to $38 per night, $180 to $228 per week for two people. Cash, checks, Visa, and Mastercard accepted. Reservations taken starting in January for coming year, and are recommended that early for Auburn University home-football-game weekends. Cabins rented a minimum of two nights on weekends; three-night minimum on holiday weekends.

DeSoto State Park
Route 1, Box 210
Fort Payne, AL 35967
(800) 252-7275 *(in-state reservations)*
(205) 845-5380 *(out-of-state reservations)*
(205) 845-0051 *(park office)*

Imposing Lookout Mountain stretches into three states — Georgia, Tennessee, and Alabama — and DeSoto State Park straddles the mountain at its geographic center. This thirty-five-mile-long park follows the Little River, an Alabama Wild and Scenic River and the only river in America that flows its entire length on a mountaintop. The park reaches from DeSoto Falls, a spectacular 120-foot waterfall, to the mouth of Little River Canyon, the deepest canyon east of the Rocky Mountains.

Near DeSoto Falls, Little River drops over a small dam built in the 1930s to generate electricity. The river then cascades over massive rock formations before plunging into a canyon basin. This stunning pool of deep green water lies surrounded by steep cliffs dotted with rhodo-

Chalet, DeSoto State Park, Alabama

dendron and azalea. Up above, the stone dam forms a small lake, popular for fishing and swimming.

Scattered for more than a mile along the west fork of the river, DeSoto's twenty-three cabins include twelve CCC-era log cabins and eleven modern chalets. Original handmade furniture fills the log cabins, which sleep from four to ten people. The wood chalets accommodate up to six in downstairs bedrooms and upstairs lofts with skylights. All DeSoto units have screened porches, heating, and air conditioning, and most have fireplaces.

DeSoto State Park lodge's new exterior has been uniquely constructed around the original stone building, so interior stone walls, beamed ceilings, and a giant fireplace have been preserved. The lodge's twenty-five guest rooms, tucked away in a modern building adjacent to the lodge, look out on the woods and a stream, and down the hillside to Little River.

DeSoto State Park is eight miles northeast of Fort Payne, Alabama, on Rte. 89. Cabins and lodge open year-round. Rates: cabins, $37 to $53 per night, $222 to $252 per week; lodge, $35 to $39 per night, $210 to $234 per week, for two people. Cash, checks, Visa, MasterCard,

*and American Express accepted. Reservations taken up to
one year in advance, recommended one to two months
in advance for May through October. Cabins rented a
minimum of two nights, May through August and fall
weekends; three-night minimum on holiday weekends.*

GULF STATE PARK
ROUTE 2, BOX 9
GULF SHORES, AL 36542
(800) 252-7275 *(in-state reservations)*
(205) 968-7544 *(out-of-state cabin reservations)*
(205) 968-7531 *(out-of-state lodge reservations)*

Pure white sand beaches and the blue-green waters of the
Gulf of Mexico beckon at this resort park. The expansive
beach consists of rolling dunes that reach thirty feet in
height and harbor plant life such as sea oats, panic grass,
and golden aster. Many species of birds winter here —
brown pelicans, herring gulls, caspian and royal terns,
plus hawks and ducks. Year-round residents include king-
fishers, quail, mourning doves, owls, and woodpeckers.
Back on the ground, you might cross paths with a raccoon, fox, bear, otter, deer, bobcat, or even an alligator.

In addition to fronting the gulf, this park holds three
freshwater lakes connected by canals. Trees populate the
area around the lakes, with pines, live oaks, magnolias,
and sweetbays prevalent.

The 144 guest rooms in the contemporary lodge face
the gulf, with individual patios and direct beach access.
This concrete structure also has a cocktail lounge overlooking an Olympic pool and the gulf, and a restaurant
featuring seafood specialties.

Gulf State Park's twenty-one cabins line the north
shore of Lake Shelby — some right on the lakefront, while
others blend into a forest of oaks and pines. The modern
cabins stand on stilts twelve feet above the ground and
sleep from six to eight people, while the fifty-year-old
wood cabins sleep from four to eight.

Swimming and sunbathing along the gulf are obvious
attractions here, and an 825-foot fishing pier juts out
over the salt water, giving anglers a shot at gulf tarpon and

flounder, among others. Bass, bream, crappie, and catfish abound in the freshwater lakes, along with redfish and mullet. Swimming, waterskiing, and sailing are also popular on the lakes, while landlubbers enjoy an eighteen-hole golf course and tennis courts.

Gulf State Park is on Rte. 182 in Gulf Shores, Alabama. Cabins and lodge open year-round. Rates: cabins, $30 to $54 per night, $180 to $324 per week; lodge, $67 to $75 per night, $240 to $450 per week for two people. Cash, Visa, and MasterCard accepted. Reservations taken starting in January for the coming year, recommended that early for April through September rentals.

JOE WHEELER STATE PARK
ROUTE 4, BOX 369A
ROGERSVILLE, AL 35652
(800) 252-7275 (in-state reservations)
(205) 685-3306 (out-of-state cabin reservations)
(205) 247-5461 (out-of-state lodge reservations)
(205) 247-5466 (park office)

This entire complex — 2550 acres of parkland in three separate areas of northern Alabama — bears the name of General Joseph Wheeler, who led Confederate troops during the Civil War and American forces in the Spanish American War. The park adjoins Wheeler Dam, which, along with Wilson Dam and Pickwick Landing Dam, eliminated the famous Muscle Shoals, which once barred navigation on the Tennessee River.

The seventy-five-room stone-and-redwood Wheeler Lodge serves as the hub of one of the park's three areas, with boating, golf, tennis, and swimming nearby. This modern three-story lodge has a marina, a swimming pool, and rooms and suites overlooking Wheeler Lake. Dock space at the lodge allows visiting boaters to stop for a meal at the popular restaurant. Fishing boats, sailboats, canoes, and bicycles can be rented at the marina.

Wheeler Lake boasts an abundance of fish, including bream, half a dozen types of bass, jack salmon, crappie, and catfish. A public beach on the lake draws swimmers and sunbathers.

Across the seventy-two-foot-high Wheeler Dam, one of nine mainstream Tennessee Valley Authority (TVA) dams on the Tennessee River, are the park's twenty-two cabins. The brick units command a fine view of the river, while the wooden cabins occupy a quiet forest of pine, black walnut, cedar, dogwood, black locust, and oak. All feature full kitchens, heating, and air conditioning, and they range in size from two to four bedrooms. Most have screened porches, outdoor barbecue grills, and picnic tables.

Joe Wheeler State Park is twenty-five miles west of Athens, Alabama, on Rte. 72. Cabins and lodge open year-round. Rates: cabins, $30 to $45 per night, $180 to $270 per week; lodge, $39 to $46 per night, $234 to $276 per week, for two people. Cash, Visa, and MasterCard accepted. Reservations taken starting in January for the coming year, recommended three to six months in advance for summer. Two-night minimum rental on weekends.

LAKE GUNTERSVILLE STATE PARK
STAR ROUTE 63, BOX 224
GUNTERSVILLE, AL 35976
(800) 252-7275 *(in-state reservations)*
(205) 261-3333 *(out-of-state reservations)*
(205) 582-3666 *(park office)*
(205) 582-2061 *(lodge and convention center)*

Twenty miles of hiking trails lace this park, generally following paths established by Cherokee Indians and early white settlers. In fact, this area has a history of peaceful cohabitation by whites and Indians, who lived here side by side, frequently intermarrying. One of those early settlers, Welsh trader John Gunter, married the daughter of a Cherokee chief in the 1780s and was the great-grandfather of American humorist Will Rogers.

Situated in the Tennessee Valley in northern Alabama on the vast, 66,470-acre Guntersville reservoir, this park ranges over 5559 acres of ridgetops and meadows. Guntersville's one hundred-room resort lodge features luxury accommodations, a full-service dining room, a swimming pool, two lighted tennis courts, a sauna, and a heliport.

Other accommodations at the park include eighteen chalets and sixteen lakeview cottages, all modern in design and construction. The chalets, poised on a mountaintop near the lodge, sleep up to six people in two bedrooms, and have baths, efficiency kitchens, sun decks, and living rooms with fireplaces. At the water's edge, the lakeview cottages sleep up to eight people in two bedrooms, and each has two baths, a kitchen, and a deck.

Fishing, boating, skiing, and swimming complement the fine lodgings at Lake Guntersville, as do tennis, hiking, and golf. Boat launching ramps and a sandy beach lead into the lake's shimmering waters, waters renowned for outstanding bass fishing. Anglers also reel in superior catches of bream, shellcracker, crappie, and catfish, while sailors savor brisk winds that gust across the reservoir's broad expanses. Back on shore, deer, fox, raccoon, wild turkey, and eagles inhabit forests of sweet gum, yellow poplar, pine, white oak, huckleberry, sassafras, and chestnut.

Lake Guntersville State Park is six miles northeast of Guntersville, Alabama, off Rte. 227. Cabins and lodge open year-round. Rates: cabins, $70 to $80 per night; lodge, $37 to $41 per night. Cash, Visa, and MasterCard accepted. Lakeview cottages rented a minimum of two nights.

LAKEPOINT RESORT STATE PARK
ROUTE 2, BOX 94
EUFAULA, AL 36027
(800) 252-7275 (in-state reservations)
(205) 687-8011 (out-of-state reservations)
(205) 687-6676 (park office)

Water sports — swimming, sailing, waterskiing — dominate this 1220-acre park, which hugs the Alabama-Georgia state line in southeast Alabama. Regarded as one of the best bass fishing lakes in the United States, Lake Eufaula stretches some 85 miles along the Chattahoochee River, creating 640 miles of shoreline. Lakepoint's marina provides fishing gear, bait, marine fuel, and rental fishing boats, plus slip space and launching ramps.

Equestrians will want to saddle up at the stables for a

trial ride through woods of pine, oak, hickory, dogwood, sweet gum, and sassafras. While hiking or riding the trails, it's not unusual to observe deer, raccoons, rabbits, and even an occasional Canada goose. Lakepoint also features an eighteen-hole golf course with pro shop, and tennis courts. The park adjoins the Eufaula National Wildlife Refuge — an 11,160-acre preserve for threatened and endangered species, such as American alligators and southern bald eagles.

The park's fifteen two-bedroom cabins and seven duplex cabins sleep six and twelve, respectively. Modern units constructed of wood, all are heated and air-conditioned, and the two-bedroom models have fireplaces. The four-bedroom duplex cabins contain dual living areas, baths, and kitchen — ideal for two families vacationing together.

Lakepoint's rock, wood, and glass 101-room lodge features a high-ceilinged lobby trimmed with countless indoor plants. In addition to its suites and guest rooms, the lodge has both indoor and outdoor pools, and tennis courts and a boat dock are close by.

Nearby attractions include the historic town of Eufaula, Alabama, site of exquisite examples of Greek Revival, Victorian, Italianate, and Neo-Classical Revival architecture. Across the Georgia state line stands Westville, a restored 1850s village where craftspeople preserve pioneer traditions by making quilts, soap, pottery, and candles.

Lakepoint Resort State Park is six miles north of Eufaula, Alabama, on Rte. 431. Cabins and lodge open year-round. Rates: cabins, $53 to $89 per night, $318 to $534 per week; lodge, $39 to $46 per night, $234 to $276 per week. Cash, checks, Visa, MasterCard, and American Express accepted. Reservations taken up to one year in advance, recommended six months in advance for summer. Two-night minimum cabin rental, May through August and fall weekends; three-night minimum on holiday weekends.

LITTLE RIVER STATE PARK
ROUTE 2, BOX 77
ATMORE, AL 36502
(800) 252-7275 (in-state reservations)
(205) 261-3333 (out-of-state cabin reservations)
(205) 862-2511 (park office)

Beneath towering pines in southern Alabama, this 960-acre park offers two forty-five-year-old wood cabins, each with a view of a twenty-five-acre lake. These cabins, set about one hundred yards apart, have four rooms, including two bedrooms, and sleep up to four people apiece. Each contains a stove, a refrigerator, electric heat, and air conditioning, and one has a screened breezeway.

Covered with pine and hardwood timber on gently rolling hills, Little River State Park resembles a beautiful garden each spring, when a profusion of dogwoods and wild flowers blossom. Little River, actually a modest creek, dips through the park, providing drinking water for the wildlife that inhabits this acreage. Hiking the old logging roads, you might encounter deer, raccoons, opossums, turkey, quail, or duck, among others.

Stocked with bream, catfish, and bass, the lake lures anglers to its tranquil shoreline, while swimmers and sunbathers relax along the beach. Rental boats, picnic shelters with tables and grills, and a primitive camping area complete Little River's facilities.

Little River State Park is seventeen miles north of Atmore, Alabama, on Rte. 21. Cabins available year-round. Rates: $90 per week. Cabins only rented for full weeks. Cash and checks accepted. Reservations taken starting in January for the coming year, recommended one to two months in advance for May through September.

MONTE SANO STATE PARK
5105 NOLEN AVENUE
HUNTSVILLE, AL 35801
(800) 252-7275 (in-state reservations)
(205) 261-3333 (out-of-state reservations)
(205) 534-3757 (park office)

Your first stop while exploring White Trail in this northeastern Alabama state park is a forest stream, where the footprints of raccoons, opossums, skunks, squirrels, and birds can often be examined. Next you come across charts and illustrations demonstrating techniques for tapping sap from sugar maple trees — sap that boils into pure maple syrup. Then you come face to trunk with a sassafras tree, which has been used for generations to make tea and spicy jellies. Other stops along this trail include a comparison of three types of oak trees, a look at a wild carrot patch, and a unique ecological habitat — a swamp.

White Trail is just one of many paths in this 2140-acre park in the foothills above Huntsville, Alabama. While on these trails, hikers may venture past Panther's Knob, Teakettle Cave, O'Shaughnessy Point, and Hawk's View.

Monte Sano's fourteen cabins line a bluff ridge on Monte Sano Mountain. Civilian Conservation Corps workers constructed these log-and-stone cabins in the mid-1930s, and each sleeps up to four people. These rough one-room structures feature stone fireplaces, electric lights and kitchen appliances, and heating and air conditioning. CCC workers handcrafted all of the furniture found in these cabins. Each has an outdoor barbecue grill and picnic table, and some come with screened porches.

Other attractions at hand include the Old Tavern, located near the park entrance and awaiting restoration, and Alabama's Space and Rocket Center, some ten miles west of the park. Monte Sano's rare chittamwood tree, according to some biblical interpretations, is the same type of wood used by Moses to build the Ark of the Covenant.

Monte Sano State Park is seven miles east of Huntsville, Alabama, off Rte. 72. Cabins available year-round. Rates: $30 per night, $180 per week, for two people. Cash, Visa, and MasterCard accepted. Reservations taken starting in January for the coming year, recommended three months in advance. Two-night minimum rental, May through August and fall weekends; three-night minimum on holiday weekends.

OAK MOUNTAIN STATE PARK
P.O. Box 278
PELHAM, AL 35124
(800) 252-7275 *(in-state reservations)*
(205) 663-6783, 663-6771 *(out-of-state reservations)*

Once an area popular with central Alabama moon-shiners, Oak Mountain State Park's 9940 acres nestle in a valley between Appalachian peaks. Double Oak Mountain and Johnson Mountain are the highest summits in the park, and they join four lakes, several streams, and a lovely waterfall — Peavine Falls — to create an outstanding natural setting for exploration and relaxation.

Anglers drop their lines in two eighty-five-acre fishing lakes stocked with bass, bream, and catfish. Swimmers frolic in their own seventy-four-acre lake with sandy beach, where canoes and paddleboats can be rented. Oak Mountain's other facilities include lighted tennis courts and an eighteen-hole golf course with pro shop and rentals.

The park's ten two-bedroom cabins line the shore of five-acre Lake Tranquility, among pine thickets and majestic oaks and near Foothills Trail. These ten-year-old cabins sleep up to eight people, and have central air conditioning and screened porches. Each comes equipped with a kitchen, bath, living room, and dining area.

One unique feature here in Alabama's largest state park is the motocross racetrack, site of monthly, sanctioned bicycle races in summer. Nearby attractions include the Tannehill Historic Site, a restored iron works near Bessemer, Alabama.

Oak Mountain State Park is fifteen miles south of Birmingham, Alabama, off I-65. Cabins available year-round. Rates: $50 per night, $295 per week. Cash, in-state checks, Visa, and MasterCard accepted. Reservations taken up to a year in advance, recommended at least one month in advance. Three-night minimum rental on holiday weekends.

ROLAND COOPER STATE PARK
P.O. Box 301
CAMDEN, AL 36726
(800) 252-7275 (in-state reservations)
(205) 682-4838 (out-of-state reservations)

Rolling along the twenty-two-thousand-acre Dannelly Reservoir, this two-hundred-acre south-central Alabama park boasts of tall pines in one of the state's most scenic areas. Deer, raccoons, rabbits, and squirrels abound in thick woodlands that line Roland Cooper's nine-hole championship golf course — noted for its velvet-smooth Bermuda greens. Boating enthusiasts take advantage of launching ramps on the reservoir, which teems with bass, crappie, bream, and catfish. For a soothing tour of the peaceful forest, rent a bicycle at the park office.

Cooper's five twelve-year-old cabins feature two bedrooms, full kitchens with utensils, and central heating and air conditioning. Each unit sleeps up to six people on two double beds and a sofa bed, and each has an outdoor barbecue grill and porch. Mammoth pines blanket the cabin area.

Roland Cooper State Park is six miles north of Camden, Alabama, on Rte. 41. Cabins available year-round. Rates: $51 per night, $306 per week. Cash, checks, Visa, and MasterCard accepted. Reservations recommended one month in advance for spring and summer. Two-night minimum rental on weekends, three-night minimum on holiday weekends.

Arkansas

STATE PARK INFORMATION:
ARKANSAS DEPARTMENT OF PARKS AND TOURISM
STATE PARKS DIVISION
ONE CAPITOL MALL
LITTLE ROCK, AR 72201
(501) 371-1191

TOURISM INFORMATION:
ARKANSAS DEPARTMENT OF PARKS AND TOURISM
TOURISM DIVISION
ONE CAPITOL MALL
LITTLE ROCK, AR 72201
(800) 482-8999 (in-state calls)
(800) 643-8383 (out-of-state calls)

STATE BIRD: *Mockingbird*
STATE TREE: *Pine*
STATE FLOWER: *Apple Blossom*

BUFFALO NATIONAL RIVER
P.O. Box 1173
HARRISON, AR 72601
(501) 741-5443

BUFFALO POINT CONCESSION
(CABINS)
ROUTE A, Box 214-A
YELLVILLE, AR 72687
(501) 449-6206

Canoeists and floaters have long treasured Buffalo River for its breathtaking views; endless picturesque scenes presided over by massive sandstone and limestone bluffs. Repeating patterns of pools and swift charges on the upper Buffalo give way to quiet waters on its lower reaches. It comes as a surprise that a river so closely surrounded by civilization could so thoroughly escape impoundment, impairment, and change, yet it flows today as it always has.

Buffalo National River, deep in the Ozarks, offers more than 120 miles of river wilderness in northwest Arkansas. With eight hundred to a thousand flowering plants, the Buffalo Valley enjoys a long growing season. It begins in January's warmer days, when witch hazel blooms, and runs until late fall, when white Indian pipes appear. Delicate fernfalls spill like soft green fireworks from the faces of moist bluffs above the river, a special gift for floaters.

The Buffalo River bluffs, attaining heights of up to five hundred feet, are the highest in the Ozarks. They represent stacks of ancient seabeds, eons of slow sedimentation. The river tumbles down nineteen hundred feet over its course, ending at four hundred feet above sea level when it joins the White River. Hemmed-in Hollow, one of many scenic side canyons, dramatizes this drop — its two-hundred-foot free-leaping waterfall is the tallest of its kind between the Appalachians and the Rockies.

Many nearby rivers have been altered by dams, but the Buffalo provides productive, free-flowing bass waters, where largemouth and smallmouth mingle with catfish and panfish. Numerous canoe liveries service the river, renting canoes and gear at a variety of locations along the banks.

Buffalo Point Concession has modern duplex and rustic single cabins along the eastern leg of the river, south of

Yellville, Arkansas. The duplex cabins have decks and electric heat, while the single cabins are warmed by wood-burning fireplaces and have screened porches. Both types come equipped with electric kitchens, baths and showers, and air conditioning, and sleep up to six people.

Buffalo Point Concession is seventeen miles south of Yellville, Arkansas, off Rte. 14. Cabins available April through November. Rates: $37 per night for two people. Cash, Visa, and MasterCard accepted.

CROWLEY'S RIDGE STATE PARK
P.O. Box 97
WALCOTT, AR 72474
(501) 573-6751

A narrow band of gently rolling hills rises abruptly above the delta region of eastern Arkansas's Crowley's Ridge. Extending nearly two hundred miles through Missouri and Arkansas, this unique natural feature, consisting of some half million acres, was formed just prior to the last Ice Age, when the Mississippi and Ohio river systems cut vast trenches in the great plain covering this region. The "island" left behind when the two rivers retreated to the east became Crowley's Ridge.

Crowley's Ridge State Park occupies the former estate of Benjamin Crowley, whose family settled here in the early 1800s, building a vast plantation at the site of a gushing spring. In spring, wild flowers such as Solomon's seal, wild petunia, white milkweed, wild sunflower, and wild rose color the forest floor, while autumn sets the hardwood forest ablaze with crimson and gold.

The park's two duplex cabins (four units) feature modern concrete-block construction, and rear walls of glass to expose the scenery. Quietly circled by pines, the cabins stand in a low-traffic section of the park within easy walking distance of a small, five-acre swimming lake. Each unit has a bedroom with two double beds and a completely equipped kitchen. Heating and air conditioning provide year-round comfort, and outdoor picnic tables and barbecue grills sit just behind these twenty-year-old structures.

In addition to its swimming lake, Crowley's Ridge also has a thirty-acre fishing lake loaded with channel catfish, largemouth bass, crappie, and bream (only electric motors permitted on this lake). Nearby 350-acre Lake Frierson is also a favorite with anglers, and gas motors up to ten horsepower are allowed on this larger lake.

Crowley's Ridge State Park is eleven miles west of Paragould, Arkansas, on Rte. 168. Cabins available year-round. Rates: $22 per night for two people. Cash and checks accepted. Reservations taken starting in January for April through October, recommended two months in advance for May through September.

DeGray State Park	DeGray State Park Lodge
Route 1, Box 144	P.O. Box 375
Bismarck, AR 71929	Arkadelphia, AR 71923
(501) 865-4501	(501) 865-4591

The earliest known inhabitants of the Caddo River Valley were the Caddo Indians, a tribe of hunters and farmers pushed westward by incoming white settlers. In the early 1900s, extensive logging took place in this valley, and clear-cutting devastated the area. Since then, second-growth cover has reforested the parkland.

DeGray State Park nestles the shores of the clear blue, 13,800-acre DeGray Lake, situated among tall pines and majestic hardwoods in the Ouachita Mountains of west-central Arkansas. The park's terrain consists of numerous "hogback" ridges and seasonal streams, and, except for an eighteen-hole golf course, it is heavily wooded.

DeGray Lodge, situated on a small island and accessible to the shore by a man-made causeway, affords commanding lake views from many of ninety-six guest rooms. Constructed of native stone and handsome woods, the lodge holds a comfortable dining room that serves three meals daily, along with a popular buffet during summer months. Lodge visitors cool off with a swim in a refreshing pool or at one of several lakefront beaches.

DeGray Park's 132-slip marina supplies rental sailboats, fishing boats, and party barges. Anglers try their luck on DeGray Lake for bass, including stripers and fighting hybrid; bream; slab crappie; and many varieties of catfish.

On-land activities in this 938-acre resort park include golf, tennis, and bicycling (rentals available). Park naturalists conduct programs year-round, such as hikes on four trails, interpretive boat trips, snake demonstrations, and hayrides.

DeGray State Park is ten miles northwest of Arkadelphia, Arkansas, on Rte. 7. Lodge open year-round. Rates: $36 to $50 per night for two people. Cash, in-state checks, Visa, MasterCard, and American Express accepted. Reservations taken up to two years in advance, recommended two months in advance for March through November.

DEVIL'S DEN STATE PARK
ROUTE 1, BOX 118
WEST FORK, AR 72774
(501) 761-3325

Deep in the Boston Mountains of northwest Arkansas, along rugged Lee Creek Valley, lies Devil's Den State Park. Hiking trails within these 1700 acres lead through forests of hickory, maple, and oak, wind among crevices, pass by Devil's Den Cave — believed to have been created by a rockslide — and cross high bluffs to spectacular vistas. With almost eight hundred feet of vertical relief between the valley and the mountaintops, hiking these trails can be rigorous.

A clear mountain creek spills its cool waters across the rocky valley floor; its momentum slowed but for a moment by a dam of native stone. Devil's Den's cabins, swimming pool, and restaurant overlook the peaceful lake formed by this dam. Catfish, bream, bass, and perch wait to be pulled from the three-acre lake or from Lee Creek. Park visitors enjoy renting canoes and paddleboats at the lake's dock.

The park's thirteen log-and-stone cabins date from the Civilian Conservation Corps days in the 1930s, and have from one to three bedrooms. CCC workers also constructed all of the cabin's furnishings, though modern conveniences such as air conditioning and heating have been added subsequently. Each cabin features a stone fireplace, a fully equipped kitchen, an outdoor barbecue grill, and a picnic table. Scattered along a densely wooded ridge above Lee Creek, these charming cabins sleep from four to eight people.

Devil's Den State Park is eighteen miles south of West Fork, Arkansas, on Rte. 170. Cabins available year-round. Rates: $35 to $45 per night for two people. Cash and checks accepted. Reservations taken starting in January for April through October.

LAKE CATHERINE STATE PARK
ROUTE 19, Box 360
HOT SPRINGS, AR 71913
(501) 844-4176

Just fifteen miles from the world-famous "Bathhouse Row" spas at Hot Springs National Park, Lake Catherine State Park consists of 2180 acres of splendid lakefront. The park's terrain ranges from hilly to mountainous, and a sixty-year-old second-growth forest overlies its acreage with oak, hickory, pine, sweet gum, and others. Wintering bald eagles occasionally can be spotted along the lake, here in the foothills of the Ouachita Mountains.

Lake Catherine's seventeen cabins line the lakeshore under tall pines and magnificent hardwoods. Each offers a lake view, air conditioning and heating, plus access to the water right out the back door. Five rustic cabins, constructed of split logs by the CCC in the 1930s, have fireplaces and private boat docks. The twelve duplex cabins, eight constructed of concrete block and four of wood, share boat docks for each two units. All Lake Catherine cabins sleep up to six people and have fully equipped kitchens.

In addition to building some of the cabins, the Civilian Conservation Corps also constructed the Nature Cabin adjacent to the swimming beach, where exhibits depict Lake Catherine's natural and cultural heritage. During summer, fishing boats, party barges, canoes, and paddleboats can be rented at the park marina, and a launching ramp is available. Another CCC-era project was the enormous smoker; the park restaurant uses the smoker each summer to barbecue beef and pork for mouthwatering sandwiches and entrees.

Lake Catherine State Park is fifteen miles southeast of Hot Springs, Arkansas, on Rte. 171. Cabins available year-round. Rates: $29 to $36 per night for two people. Cash, checks, Visa, and MasterCard accepted. Reservations taken starting in January for April through October.

LAKE CHICOT STATE PARK
ROUTE 1, BOX 648
LAKE VILLAGE, AR 71653
(501) 265-5480

At about A.D. 1450, the wandering Mississippi River cut through one of its narrow bends, leaving behind an oxbow remnant and Arkansas's largest natural lake. French explorers called this former stretch of the great river Chicot, "stumpy," referring to the many cypress knees in the water. Situated in a grove of wild pecan trees and ringed with cypresses standing literally "up to their knees" in water is Lake Chicot State Park — a slice of Delta country in southeastern Arkansas.

Famous nationwide for fantastic catches of bream, crappie, bass, and catfish, Lake Chicot draws anglers from all over the country to its quiet coves in a bayoulike haven. This park is also a favorite with Arkansas and Mississippi bird-watchers, who slip through the swamps and across high ground to observe orioles, Mississippi kites, and many species of waterfowl.

In the early 1800s a band of pirates roamed this area, robbing and killing innocent settlers along the river. The most notorious member of the gang was John Murrel, whom Mark Twain described in *The Adventures of Tom Sawyer*.

It's quiet and peaceful at Lake Chicot today, and seven duplex cabins (fourteen units) offer overnight accommodations. These units, built of wood and cinder block, come equipped with kitchens, heating, and air conditioning, and they have outdoor picnic tables and barbecue grills. Each sleeps up to six people. Four of the cabins front the lakeshore, and the other three are a short distance from the water.

Lake Chicot's marina rents fishing boats, party barges,

and canoes, and has a boat launching ramp. Not far from the park's picnic area is a twenty-five-meter swimming pool, complete with diving well, wading pool, and bathhouse. Park naturalists conduct guided nature walks, party barge tours of the lake, and johnboat excursions through the cypress swamps.

Lake Chicot State Park is eight miles northeast of Lake Village, Arkansas, on Rte. 144. Cabins available year-round. Rates: $34 per night for two people. Cash and checks accepted. Reservations taken starting in January for April through October.

LAKE FORT SMITH STATE PARK
P.O. Box 4
MOUNTAINBURG, AR 72946
(501) 369-2469

From the splendor of blooming dogwoods and redbuds in springtime to the blaze of bright reds, oranges, and yellows each fall, the stately Boston Mountains soothe the spirit. Guarded by thousands of acres of national forest land, northwest Arkansas's Lake Fort Smith State Park spans a wooded valley in the heart of the Bostons. Lake Fort Smith forms the northern boundary of the park, and its spillway splits the parkland in two.

The park's boat dock offers rental fishing boats, boat motors and canoes, plus a boat-launching ramp, giving anglers and boaters easy access to the lake, which serves as the water supply for area communities. (Swimming and skiing are not allowed.) Swimmers do take advantage of a 640,000-gallon pool — the largest park pool in the state — with separate diving well and wading areas. Two tennis courts, picnic sites, and playground equipment round out Lake Fort Smith's facilities.

Across the spillway from the pool and tennis courts, under oaks, elms, and sweet gums are five rock-and-cedar cabins. Four have one bedroom, while the fifth offers two, and all include heating, air conditioning, and full kitchens. Lake Fort Smith's cabins sleep from four to six people, and each one-bedroom cabin has a native stone fireplace.

Lake Fort Smith State Park is one mile north of Mountainburg, Arkansas, on Rte. 71. Cabins available year-round. Rates: $29 to $34 per night. Cash and checks accepted. Reservations taken starting in January for April through October.

Cabin, Lake Ouachita State Park, Arkansas

LAKE OUACHITA STATE PARK
STAR ROUTE 1, BOX 1160
MOUNTAIN PINE, AR 71956
(501) 767-9366

Built in the late 1970s, this park's five A-frame cabins inhabit a thickly wooded strip of shoreline on Lake Ouachita, in west-central Arkansas. Each has a kitchen, dining area, living room, bath and bedroom downstairs, and a large bedroom with two double beds upstairs. These cabins feature private outdoor barbecue grills and picnic tables, plus heating and air conditioning. After a day on the lake, you can relax on the deck for an afterdinner view of the surrounding mountains softly reflected in Lake Ouachita's shimmering waters.

Stretching westward from Blakely Mountain Dam, Lake Ouachita extends more than fifty miles into the headwaters of the Ouachita River. Recognized as one of Arkansas's finest fishing lakes — bass, crappie, bream, and catfish abound — Lake Ouachita is also stocked with rainbow trout, northern pike, and ocean stripers. Its wide-open waters and quiet lagoons please water-skiers, sailing enthusiasts, canoeists, and scuba divers.

Originally a private resort, this area has attracted countless visitors because of the reputed medicinal quality of the local Three Sisters Springs. The water in each of these natural springs has a unique mineral composition, and to this day people come to fill gallon jugs with pure spring water.

Lake Ouachita's forty-six-slip marina rents fishing boats, party barges, and slip space, plus paddleboats. At Three Sisters Cafe, which operates during summer months, you can order breakfasts, short-order lunches, and snacks.

Hikers wander along Caddo Bend Trail, a four-mile trek through pine and hardwood forests and along the lakeshore. A park naturalist offers guided hikes, party-barge lake tours, and evening slide and film showings. Nearby attractions include Hot Springs National Park and commercial bathhouses, where guests soak in thermal waters, and Oaklawn racetrack, site of some of the South's finest thoroughbred racing.

Lake Ouachita State Park is six miles north of Mountain Pine, Arkansas, on Rte. 227. Cabins available year-round. Rates: $45 per night for two people. Cash, checks, Visa, and MasterCard accepted. Reservations taken starting in January for April through October.

MOUNT NEBO STATE PARK
ROUTE 2, BOX 160-A
DARDANELLE, AR 72834
(501) 229-3655

Mount Nebo, inhabited since pre-Civil War days, has long been a favorite vacation spot. In 1889 a resort hotel, Summit Park Hotel, was constructed here to accommodate travelers who arrived via steamboat on the Arkansas River. Cool mountain temperatures, lush vegetation, abundant wildlife, and breathtaking scenery attracted those early visitors, along with the reported recuperative powers of the orange-colored waters of Darling Springs.

Rising eighteen hundred feet above the valleys of west central Arkansas, imposing Mount Nebo favors today's visitors with a spectacular view of thirty-four-thousand-acre Lake Dardanelle, the Arkansas River, and neighboring ridges of the Ouachita Mountains. Atop this biblically named plateau, fringed by the Ozark National Forest, is Mount Nebo State Park.

In 1933 approximately two hundred men joined a Civilian Conservation Corps camp here, and labored to build roads, cabins, and trails on Mount Nebo. Working two years for a dollar per day, these men carved this park out of the mountain using virtually no machinery.

Ten cabins built by the CCC were remodeled in 1975, and four modern A-frames were added in 1978. Scattered around the mountain, these cabins come equipped with all-electric kitchens and sleep up to six people. Twelve have cozy fireplaces, and all feature heating, air conditioning, and outdoor barbecue grills.

Mount Nebo's thirteen miles of hiking trails trace forests of oak, hickory, and pine. Popular stops along the way include spring-fed Fern Lake, a thundering waterfall, and several caves. You can greet the morning with a dazzling view from Sunrise Point, or enjoy the last light of day from Sunset Point.

Tennis courts and a softball diamond rest at the south end of the mountaintop, while a swimming pool and bathhouse overlook the eastern rim. Bicycle rentals are also available. Fishing, swimming, and boating are popular on nearby Lake Dardanelle; tubing and rafting are preferred activities on area streams and creeks.

Mount Nebo State Park is just west of Dardanelle, Arkansas, on Rte. 155. Cabins available year-round. Rates: $32 to $36 per night. Cash, checks, Visa, and MasterCard accepted. Reservations taken starting in January for April through October.

OZARK FOLK CENTER
P.O. Box 500
MOUNTAIN VIEW, AR 72560
(501) 269-3851 (park office)
(501) 269-3871 (reservations)

Since the early 1960s Americans have journeyed to Mountain View, Arkansas, to attend the annual Arkansas Folk Festival. Out of the festival grew the Ozark Folk Center, which has the unique mission of preserving the Ozark Mountains way of life — its "cabin crafts," its music and dance, its oral history and lore. This complex, which opened in 1973, consists of fifty native-stone-and-cedar buildings constructed on eighty acres of a 915-acre wooded site.

The Ozark Folk Center features a 1043-seat music auditorium, complete with rehearsal rooms, recording facilities, and an indoor-outdoor stage. On scheduled evenings, Stone County musicians perform on dulcimers, Autoharps, banjos, fiddles, guitars, and mandolins. Many of the instruments played by these resident musicians were handmade by local artisans.

During the summer and on selected dates throughout the year, craftspeople demonstrate their skills at the Crafts Forum: quilting, spinning, and wood carving, along with displays of leather work, wheel pottery, basketry, broom-making, and doll-making. The sounds of the blacksmith's anvil and the aroma of smoked turkey and fried pies waft through the exhibit buildings.

The Ozark Folk Center Lodge provides overnight accommodations in thirty hexagon-shaped duplex units. These distinctive structures each feature two double beds, a sitting area, and a private patio looking out on the oak and hickory hillsides, but they have no kitchens. A swimming pool and recreation room serve lodge guests, and the restaurant offers home-style southern recipes such as country ham and redeye gravy, catfish, and chicken and dumplings.

Nearby attractions include Blanchard Springs Cavern, which, when discovered in 1963, was described as the "cave find of the century." White River, nationally recognized for its fine trout fishing, and Buffalo National

River, a favorite with canoeists, both entice significant numbers of visitors.

Ozark Folk Center is two miles north of Mountain View, Arkansas, on Rtes. 5, 9, and 14. Lodge open year-round. Rates: $36 per night for two people. Cash, checks, Visa, and MasterCard accepted. Reservations taken starting in January for April through October.

PETIT JEAN STATE PARK
ROUTE 3, BOX 164
MORRILTON, AR 72110
(501) 727-5441 *(park office)*
(501) 727-5431 *(lodge and cabin reservations)*

The top of Petit Jean Mountain, a horseshoe-shaped mesa measuring approximately nine by fourteen miles, supports a forest of shortleaf pine. Down in the canyons, one finds oak and hickory, though a smattering of sweet gum, juniper, and dogwood grow there as well. The mountaintop is relatively flat, but Petit Jean's three acclaimed hiking trails lead visitors into the canyons, past some marvelous scenery, including a ninety-foot-high waterfall — Cedar Falls.

Petit Jean State Park lies in an unspoiled area between the Ozark and Ouachita mountain ranges, in west-central Arkansas. Situated upon Petit Jean Mountain, the park encompasses some thirty-five hundred acres of woods, ravines, streams, springs, and unique geological formations preserved almost as French explorers found them some three hundred years ago.

When the Civilian Conservation Corps constructed the twenty-four-room Stephen Mather Lodge in 1934, they used local building materials: timber and stone. CCC-era furniture and two huge fireplaces grace the lobby, which has an open, airy atmosphere because of its high ceiling. The lodge's restaurant serves everything from sandwiches to steaks, and has a glass wall facing Cedar Creek Canyon and the Arkansas River Valley beyond.

Just south of the lodge are six duplex cabins. Each cabin has two units, one with a fireplace. These sleeping cabins accommodate up to four people, but have no kitchens. In contrast, the eighteen cabins that rim Cedar

Creek Canyon have full kitchen facilities. All Petit Jean cabins have heating and air conditioning, and most of these CCC-vintage structures have been fully restored.

Fishing on Lake Bailey, softball on the playing field, canoe and paddleboat rentals at the boathouse, tennis, swimming in a modern pool overlooking Cedar Creek Canyon — these are but a sampling of the activities at Petit Jean State Park. Horseback riding takes place just outside the park, and an antique car museum is nearby.

Petit Jean State Park is twenty miles west of Morrilton, Arkansas, on Rte. 154. Cabins available year-round, lodge rooms available March to Thanksgiving. Rates: cabins, $29 to $40 per night; lodge, $24 to $28 per night. Cash, checks, Visa, and MasterCard accepted. Reservations taken starting in January for April through October.

QUEEN WILHELMINA STATE PARK
ROUTE 7, BOX 53A
MENA, AR 71953
(501) 394-2863

Queen Wilhelmina State Park, set atop Rich Mountain in far western Arkansas, offers an unparalleled ecosystem. The Ouachita Mountains are one of a few ranges in the Western Hemisphere that run east-west, rather than north-south, resulting in distinct flora and fauna on its respective slopes. The south slope features shortleaf pine with scattered blackjack, black oak, southern red oak, and black hickory. Many of these trees are gnarled and dwarfed, because of the pruning effect of winter icing and freezing fog, combined with the pressure of prevailing south winds. North-slope trees, such as white oak, northern red oak, black walnut, black locust, basswood, maple, and Ohio buckeye, thrive in the rich soil.

Attracted by cool temperatures atop Rich Mountain, vacationers have flocked here since the nineteenth century. In 1896 the Kansas, Pittsburg and Gulf Railroad built the first lodge on the mountaintop. The railroad, largely Dutch financed, named the resort in honor of Holland's young Queen Wilhelmina. The three-story lodge became known as the "castle in the sky," and a royal suite was set aside for the queen's use in the vain hope that she would pay an official visit to the area.

A new stone lodge was completed in 1975, offering overnight accommodations in thirty-eight guest rooms, each with a spectacular view of the imposing Ouachitas, and a full-service restaurant. The charming lobby features a handsome fireplace, and just outside is an observation deck.

Old Reservoir Trail, a rigorous path on the mountain's south side, leads down to the reservoir that served the original lodge. Spring Trail crosses a mountain spring and a rock glacier. Other attractions include a ride around Rich Mountain on a miniature train, a petting zoo loaded with exotic and native animals, and a miniature golf course. Lake Wilhelmina, a three-hundred-acre reservoir, can be seen in the valley below.

Queen Wilhelmina State Park is thirteen miles northwest of Mena, Arkansas, on Rte. 88. Lodge open yearround. Rates: $40 per night for two people, $47 per night for queen's bedroom with fireplace. Cash, Visa, and MasterCard accepted. Reservations taken starting in January for April through October.

Kentucky

STATE PARK AND TOURISM INFORMATION:
TRAVEL
FRANKFORT, KY 40601
(800) 225-8747 (park information)
(800) 255-7275 (cabin and lodge reservations)
(502) 564-2172 (state park office)

STATE BIRD: *Cardinal*
STATE MAMMAL: *Gray Squirrel*
STATE TREE: *Kentucky Coffee Tree*
STATE FLOWER: *Goldenrod*
STATE FISH: *Kentucky Bass*

MAMMOTH CAVE NATIONAL PARK
MAMMOTH CAVE, KY 42259
(502) 758-2251

NATIONAL PARK CONCESSIONS, INC. (HOTEL, LODGE, AND
  COTTAGES)
MAMMOTH CAVE, KY 42259
(502) 758-2225

Mammoth Indians, their torches blazing, entered these caverns in south-central Kentucky more than 4500 years ago, scouring the miles of corridors for gypsum. In the 1790s and early 1800s, torches gave way to oil lamps carried by settlers who mined nitrates that were used in the production of gunpowder. When the British blockaded American seaports during the War of 1812, Mammoth Cave became the major supplier of nitrates for gunpowder factories in the East.

Like most limestone caverns, Mammoth Cave was formed when subterranean water dissolved porous rock and then receded, leaving dry passageways. Visitors on cave tours stroll through huge rooms, over yawning pits, past leaching vats, and under cascading stone sculptures. Amid stalactites and stalagmites in this, the world's largest network of caves (294 miles of explored passages), are chambers such as the Methodist Church, where two lines of pews mark where worship services took place from 1830 to 1940. In 1876, noted Shakespearean actor Edwin Booth delivered portions of Hamlet's soliloquy at a spot now known as Booth's Amphitheater.

Above ground, steamboats once plied the Green River, which slithers through the fifty-two thousand acres of Kentucky meadows and forests in this national park. You can relive the steamboat era by boarding the sixty-three-foot *Miss Green River II*, for a river view of looming limestone cliffs and woodlands full of deer, beaver, wild turkey, turtles, and numerous species of birds.

Blessed with a variety of overnight accommodations, Mammoth Cave National Park features the brick, two-story Mammoth Cave Hotel, which has thirty-eight guest rooms with private patios overlooking a magnificent ravine. At the edge of a forest rests Sunset Point Motor Lodge, where twenty rooms are enclosed in a structure of wood and stone. For more secluded quarters, Mammoth Cave's ten hotel cottages, set in a peaceful meadow not far from the hotel, and thirty-eight woodland cottages, scattered under tall trees, are available in one-, two-, three-, and four-room floor plans. Although none of the cottages has cooking facilities, the hotel dining room serves southern specialties year-round.

Mammoth Cave National Park is just east of Brownsville, Kentucky, on Rte. 70. Motel and lodge open year-round, cottages available May through October. Rates: hotel and lodge, $31 to $45 per night for two people; cottages, $24 to $31 per night for two people. Cash, checks, Visa, and MasterCard accepted. Reservations taken up to one year in advance, recommended one month in advance for July and August.

BARREN RIVER LAKE STATE RESORT PARK
LUCAS, KY 42156
(800) 225-8747 (park information)
(800) 255-7275 (lodging reservations)
(502) 646-2151 (park office)

Just twenty-five miles south of Mammoth Cave and some sixty-five miles from Nashville's Opryland and other country music attractions, this state park stretches over eighteen hundred acres and fronts ten thousand acres of water — Barren River Lake. The lake's name may be deceptive, for it is hardly barren of fish or recreational opportunities. Anglers applaud excellent catches of white, largemouth, and smallmouth bass, plus channel catfish, bluegill, walleye, and muskie. At the park marina, visitors rent fishing boats and pontoon boats or use the launching ramps and slips available. Swimmers soak up sunshine and relax in Barren River Lake's warm summer waters, along a length of sandy beach. Others take advantage of more than two miles of bicycle paths (for which rental bikes are available), lighted tennis and handball courts, and horseback riding. A nine-hole, regulation course awaits golf enthusiasts.

Barren River's twelve cabins, built of western cedar, have four rooms (including two bedrooms and full kitchens), central air conditioning, and color TV. Each deluxe cabin features a front and a rear porch, an outdoor picnic table and barbecue grill, and a view of the lake.

Also overlooking Barren River Lake is Louie B. Nunn Lodge, a cedar, fifty-one-room facility with high ceilings and rough, exposed beams in its lobby and dining area. Each guest room sleeps up to four people, on two double beds, and has a private balcony.

Barren River Lake State Resort Park is fourteen miles southwest of Glasgow, Kentucky, on Rte. 31E. Cabins and lodge open year-round. Rates: cabins, $85 per night; lodge, $40 to $47 per night for two people. Cash, checks, Visa, MasterCard, and American Express accepted. Reservations taken up to one year in advance, recommended very early for summer.

BUCKHORN LAKE STATE RESORT PARK
BUCKHORN, KY 41721
(800) 225-8747 *(park information)*
(800) 255-7275 *(lodging reservations)*
(606) 398-7510 *(park office)*

Resting along the northern edge of a slice of the Daniel Boone National Forest, Buckhorn Lake State Resort Park is enhanced by the beauty of a twelve-hundred-acre mountain lake. Looking down a grassy hillside onto Buckhorn Lake — an impoundment of the middle fork of the Kentucky River — the park's native-stone-and-wood lodge has thirty-six guest rooms, each accommodating up to four people. From its pleasing lobby and dining area to an outdoor swimming pool and lakefront beach, this twenty-year-old lodge presents everything necessary for a relaxing getaway.

Within view of the lodge floats Buckhorn's marina, complete with rowboats, fishing boats, and pontoon boats available for rental, day slips and launching ramps. Those tempted to throw in a line might bring home a catch of largemouth or smallmouth bass, crappie, bluegill, or channel catfish. Tennis courts, miniature golf, and rental bicycles round out the recreational offerings at Buckhorn Lake.

The spectacular scenery at this park typifies the southeast Kentucky countryside, where mountains and hills hold forests of sycamore, maple, pine, hickory, dogwood, and poplar. The 661,000-acre Daniel Boone National Forest is characterized by steep slopes, narrow valleys, and protruding cliffs. Miles of trails thread both the park and national forest, giving abundant opportunities for bird-watching, wildlife observation, photography, and cross-country skiing — even gathering nuts and berries.

Buckhorn Lake State Resort Park is twenty-three miles northwest of Hazard, Kentucky, on Rte. 28. Lodge open April through October. Rates: $27 to $34 per night for two people. Cash, checks, Visa, MasterCard, and American Express accepted. Reservations taken up to one year in advance, recommended three months in advance for summer.

CARTER CAVES STATE RESORT PARK
ROUTE 2, BOX 1120
OLIVE HILL, KY 41164
(800) 225-8747 *(park information)*
(800) 255-7275 *(lodging reservations)*
(606) 286-4411 *(park office)*

Caves, caves, caves — this northeast Kentucky park has more than twenty caves, and tours are available in six of them. Electric lights illuminate some of the caverns, while others come to life under the glow of a lantern. A thirty-foot-high underground waterfall highlights Cascade Cave, once owned and operated by a local family from Grayson, Kentucky. Legend claims that Simon Kenton, famed Kentucky frontiersman, supervised a mining operation in 1812 at Saltpeter Cave; the saltpeter was a component of the ammunition supposedly used by Kentucky riflemen during the War of 1812. Visitors in summer take flashlight tours of Bat Cave, the winter home of thousands of bats.

After seeing the caves, you can join the park staff for a canoe trip along lush Tygart's Creek, which has a reputation as one of the best muskie-fishing streams in the state. Smoky Mountain Lake, a cool forty-five acres, pleases anglers with bass, catfish, and crappie.

Golfers tee off for nine holes from a hilltop, using rental clubs and carts available at the pro shop. Two swimming pools serve water-lovers, and the park stable has regularly scheduled summer trail rides, including trips to Carter Caves's natural bridges. Water erosion has created these intriguing rock arches and tunnels.

A twenty-eight-room lodge and fifteen cabins provide overnight accommodations for park guests. The cabins, constructed of wood, come in efficiency, one-bedroom, and two-bedroom models, and sleep from six to twelve people apiece. All have full kitchens, heating and air conditioning, screened porches, and outdoor picnic tables and barbecue grills. Carter Caves's thirty-year-old lodge features guest rooms that sleep up to four people, each with a private patio, and a restaurant and game room.

Carter Caves State Resort Park is eight miles north of Olive Hill, Kentucky, on Rte. 182. Cabins and lodge open year-round. Rates: cabins, $47 to $65 per night; lodge, $40 to $47 per night for two people. Cash, checks, Visa, MasterCard, and American Express accepted. Reservations taken up to one year in advance, recommended six to eight months in advance.

CUMBERLAND FALLS STATE RESORT PARK
CORBIN, KY 40701
(800) 225-8747 (park information)
(800) 255-7275 (lodging reservations)
(606) 528-4121 (park office)

Called the "Niagara of the South," Cumberland Falls thunders as it plummets sixty-eight feet into the Cumberland River, creating an awesome spectacle. This marvelous 150-foot-wide waterfall also attracts attention by displaying the only "moonbow" in this hemisphere. On clear nights illuminated by a full moon, a "moonbow" appears at the base of the waterfall as moonlight refracts in the mist billowing up from the river. This phenomenon is particularly colorful on clear winter nights.

When not absorbed by the falls, visitors enjoy hiking the more than twenty-five miles of trails in this southeast Kentucky park and the adjoining Daniel Boone National Forest; fishing for bass, catfish, panfish, and rough fish in the Cumberland River; riding horseback; playing tennis; or swimming in an Olympic-size pool. The park's 1794 acres are blanketed with pine, hemlock, rhododendron, mountain laurel, azalea, beech, tulip, and magnolia trees, as well as oak and hickory. Small streams plunge down cliffs of sandstone and shale, creating scenic sprays against wooded backdrops. Wild river-running trips originate below Cumberland Falls, affording a fabulous ride through gorges and canyons.

DuPont Lodge, constructed in 1942, offers fifty-three guest rooms; its exposed pine and hemlock beams and sandstone fireplace create a warm, comfortable atmosphere. From the lodge's patio, visitors have a commanding view of the Cumberland River some 190 feet below. Other lodging options include twenty-five cabins, which come in efficiency, one-bedroom, and two-bedroom sizes, and the twenty Woodland Rooms — sleeping cabins with no kitchen facilities. Constructed of wood, all cabins are heated and air-conditioned, and some have fireplaces.

Cumberland Falls State Resort Park is eighteen miles west of Corbin, Kentucky, on Rte. 90. Lodging available year-round. Rates: cabins, $47 to $60 per night; Woodland Rooms, $27 to $43 per night for two people; lodge rooms, $70 to $100 per night for up to four people. Cash, checks, Visa, MasterCard, and American Express accepted. Reservations taken up to one year in advance.

GENERAL BUTLER STATE RESORT PARK
P.O. Box 325
CARROLLTON, KY 41008
(800) 225-8747 (park information)
(800) 255-7275 (lodging reservations)
(502) 732-4384 (park office)

General William Orlando Butler distinguished himself at the Battle of New Orleans in the War of 1812. He later served in the Kentucky legislature and the United States Congress, and even was offered the governorship of the new state of Nebraska, an offer he declined. The Butler family prospered on the northern Kentucky land that today constitutes this 809-acre park; the mansion home of Butler's niece, built in 1859, is virtually unchanged in appearance since its construction. Visitors can tour this brick, Federal-style, eight-room residence and inspect its original woodwork, mantels, floors, and stairways. Late

Empire, Regency, and early Victorian pieces, dating from 1810 to 1850, furnish the Butler home.

Chunky stones and western cedar form the exterior of this park's impressive, fifty-seven-room lodge, whose interior spaces are trimmed with rich cedar floors, walls, rafters, and ceilings. The lodge rooms accommodate up to four people, and each has a balcony view of the Ohio Valley. An outdoor swimming pool adjoins the lodge, and the dining room prepares three meals daily.

Clustered in a stand of tall trees, Butler's twenty-three cabins range in size from efficiencies to deluxe three-bedroom structures. Seven of the stone-and-wood cabins feature fireplaces, and all have complete kitchens, televisions, heating, and air conditioning. Four duplex units come in two- or three-bedroom versions, the latter of which offer loft sleeping areas.

Recreation at Butler ranges from fishing, swimming, and boating at a thirty-acre lake (paddleboats and rowboats can be rented) to tennis and golf. During winter, downhill skiing is very popular at the park's ski complex, which includes rope tows, rental equipment, and sophisticated snowmaking machines. A popular day trip is across the border to nearby Madison, Indiana, site of numerous antique shops and historic buildings.

General Butler State Resort Park is two miles south of Carrollton, Kentucky, on Rte. 227. Cabins and lodge open year-round. Rates: cabins, $52 to $100 per night; lodge, $44 per night for two people. Cash, checks, Visa, MasterCard, and American Express accepted. Reservations taken up to one year in advance.

GREENBO LAKE STATE RESORT PARK
P.O. Box 90
GREENUP, KY 41144
(800) 225-8747 *(park information)*
(800) 255-7275 *(lodging reservations)*
(606) 473-7324 *(park office)*

Three streams — Claylick Creek, Buffalo Branch, and Pruitt Fork — spill into 225-acre Greenbo Lake, in a mountain valley in eastern Kentucky. The iron industry flourished here during the 1800s, and by 1850, nineteen blast furnaces operated in Greenup County. The remains of Buffalo Furnace, which produced pig iron from 1818 to 1856, stand at the entrance to this 3330-acre state park.

Named for a noted local poet and author, the thirty-six-room Jesse Stuart Lodge features country furnishings under large beams, within an exterior of Indian stone and cedar. A patio looks down on the lake and out on oak, pine, fir, locust, elm, and hickory forests.

Greenbo's marina, a mile from the lodge, rents rowboats, paddleboats, pontoon boats, canoes, and slip space. Privately owned boats also glide across the lake, where motors of up to 7.5 horsepower are permitted. In 1966, an area fisherman wrestled in a record largemouth bass here — thirteen pounds, eight ounces — and fishing remains a popular pastime. Lodge guests choose between an outdoor swimming pool and a sandy beach tucked between two shady hillsides.

Greenbo has four hiking trails, including the twenty-five-mile Michael Tygart Trail. Tennis courts and a miniature golf course are also present and riding stables are nearby.

Greenbo Lake State Resort Park is eighteen miles north of Grayson, Kentucky, on Rte. 1. Lodge open year-round. Rates: $38 to $46 per night for two people. Cash, checks, Visa, MasterCard, and American Express accepted. Reservations taken up to one year in advance, recommended two to three months in advance for weekends and holidays.

JENNY WILEY STATE RESORT PARK
PRESTONBURG, KY 41653
(800) 225-8747 (park information)
(800) 255-7275 (lodging reservations)
(606) 886-2711 (park office)

Near the heart of the state's coalfields, Jenny Wiley State Resort Park straddles the mountains of eastern Kentucky at Dewey Lake. The park bears the name of a pioneer woman who was captured by Indians in 1787. After enduring a lengthy imprisonment, Jenny escaped one night during a driving rain, swam Big Sandy River at

Harmon Station, and rejoined her husband, Tom Wiley. They lived out their lives not far from this park.

Jenny Wiley State Resort Park edges the narrow, winding, eleven-hundred-acre Dewey Lake, which has eighteen miles of shoreline. Built primarily for flood control, the lake is a haven for water sports such as boating, water-skiing, and fishing. Paddleboats, pontoon boats, and fishing boats can be rented at the park's marina, and slip space and launching ramps are also available. Largemouth and white bass, crappie, catfish, and carp lurk in the pleasing lake waters, while deer, fox, bobcat, mink, duck, and quail roam the wooded hills along the waterfront. Jenny Wiley Summer Theater performs three Broadway musicals outdoors each season. Riding stables, hiking trails, and a golf course round out the park's extensive facilities.

Jenny Wiley's mountaintop lodge has forty-eight guest rooms and one suite, as well as a dining room capable of seating 224 people. This rough-hewn lodge with high wooden beams was built in the early 1960s. Each room features a private balcony.

Under the trees, 150 yards from the lodge and even closer to the lake, stand ten two-bedroom cabins. A little farther down the road are one-bedroom duplex cabins. Both types are made of wood, and have kitchens, heating, and air conditioning. The one-bedroom models sleep up to five people and have small decks with picnic tables and barbecue grills. The larger cabins sleep up to ten people and include screened porches.

Jenny Wiley State Resort Park is east of Prestonburg, Kentucky, off Rte. 23. Cabins and lodge open year-round. Rates: cabins, $54 to $71 per night; lodge, $42 to $46 per night. Cash, checks, Visa, MasterCard, and American Express accepted. Reservations taken up to one year in advance, recommended four to six months in advance for summer.

JOHN JAMES AUDUBON STATE PARK
P.O. Box 576
HENDERSON, KY 42420
(800) 225-8747 (park information)
(800) 255-7275 (lodging reservations)
(502) 826-2247, 826-0586 (park office)

Early in the nineteenth century, John James Audubon studied the birds in a western Kentucky forest near the Ohio River. The fruits of his study were paintings later published as *Birds of America*, which established him as a leading American artist and ornithologist. Original paintings by Audubon and his sons, along with 126 first-edition prints of his works, highlight the museum that serves as the focal point of the 692-acre John James Audubon State Park. Manicured lawns and tall trees create the setting for this classic stone-and-brick museum, which has a hefty turret and intriguing masonry.

Audubon State Park offers a host of recreational activities, as well. Two small lakes reflect the rolling hills and await fishermen seeking bass, bluegill, and catfish. A bathhouse complements the sandy beach at Scenic Lake, and rowboats and paddleboats can be rented there. Adjacent to the swimming area is a tennis court, and several hiking trails open up an adjoining nature preserve that incorporates Wilderness Lake. Golfers negotiate the hilly terrain of an attractive nine-hole course.

Overnight accommodations at Audubon consist of five fifty-year-old cabins, set in a mature stand of trees on Scenic Lake's eastern shore. These dark wood structures have four rooms (one bedroom) and sleep five comfortably. Each has a fireplace, bath with shower, color television, air conditioning, and a small electric heater, plus an outdoor picnic table and barbecue grill.

John James Audubon State Park is one mile north of Henderson, Kentucky, on Rte. 41. Cabins available April through October. Rates: $48 per night for two people. Cash, checks, Visa, MasterCard, and American Express accepted. Reservations taken up to one year in advance.

KENLAKE STATE RESORT PARK
ROUTE 1
HARDIN, KY 42048
(800) 225-8747 (park information)
(800) 255-7275 (lodging reservations)
(502) 474-2211 (park office)

Spinnakers unfurl, masts bend, and fiberglass hulls slice through the waters of Kentucky Lake during the annual Watkins Cup and Governor's Cup sailing regattas, held near this western Kentucky resort park. Bass, channel and blue catfish, bluegill, rockfish, and crappie hit lures and bait in the vast, 128,000-acre lake, while excellent skiing and swimming attract nonanglers.

Kenlake's eighteen hundred acres are largely wooded with maple, oak, evergreen, and dogwood, and also have abundant wild flowers. Deer, rabbits, and raccoons inhabit these forests, and ducks, geese, hawks, doves, and quail frequently can be sighted. Visitors take in the park's natural beauty either by hiking its trails or by renting a horse at the stable.

Just three miles from Kenlake lies the Tennessee Valley Authority's Land Between the Lakes, a 170,000-acre strip between Kentucky Lake and Lake Barkley. Set aside for recreation and wildlife management, Land Between the Lakes features historic buildings, a herd of buffalo, an environmental education center, and a planetarium, plus numerous trails.

Surrounded by some of Kentucky's largest water maples, Kenlake Hotel has forty-eight guest rooms, a dining room, and a gift shop. A swimming pool, tennis court, and shuffleboard court adjoin the hotel, and eight more tennis courts (four indoor) are located at the knoll-top Kenlake Tennis Center. Kenlake's nine-hole golf course is within easy walking distance of the hotel.

The park's thirty-four frame cabins range in size from one-room efficiencies to three-bedroom models. All have heating, air conditioning, telephones, televisions, screened porches, and barbecue grills. Most of these deluxe cabins occupy wooded sites, though five front Kentucky Lake.

Kenlake State Resort Park is one mile southwest of Aurora, Kentucky, on Rte. 68. Cabins and hotel open *year-round. Rates: cabins, $44 to $61 per night; hotel, $37 to $47 per night for two people. Cash, checks, Visa, MasterCard, and American Express accepted. Reservations taken up to one year in advance, recommended six to nine months in advance for May through September.*

KENTUCKY DAM VILLAGE STATE RESORT PARK
P.O. Box 69
GILBERTSVILLE, KY 42044
(800) 225-8747 *(park information)*
(800) 255-7275 *(lodging reservations)*
(502) 362-4271 *(park office)*

Kentucky Dam Village State Resort Park spans twelve hundred acres at the broad northern tip of immense Kentucky Lake. Not surprisingly, water sports dominate the recreation at Kentucky Dam, with fishing, boating, skiing, and swimming all being favorites at this western Kentucky complex. Facilities on the tree-lined lake include a marina, the largest in the Kentucky park system, where paddleboats, fishing boats, houseboats, ski boats, and pontoon boats can be rented.

During warm months, horseback trail rides are an excellent way to scout the level, wooded parkland. Lighted tennis courts and an eighteen-hole golf course complete Kentucky Dam's offerings.

The sixty-nine cabins here feature rough wood exteriors and come in a wide variety of sizes and styles. Shielded by quiet trees, they range from one-bedroom models to fancy executive cabins with two or three bedrooms, custom kitchens, one or two baths, and central air conditioning — some even have attached garages! Screened porches are another amenity of the more elaborate cabins.

About a half-mile from the cabins stands a twenty-year-old timber lodge that faces Kentucky Lake. All guest rooms have lake views from their balconies and patios, plus two double beds and a private bath. The dining room serves regional specialties such as Kentucky Lake catfish and Kentucky-raised trout, both accompanied by hush puppies. Guests can also enjoy a dip in the clear waters of the lodge's swimming pool.

For those wishing to arrive by air, Kentucky Dam

Village has a four-thousand-foot paved and lighted runway. Jet and aviation fuel are available, as is transportation to the lodge and cabins.

Kentucky Dam Village State Resort Park is eleven miles north of Benton, Kentucky, on Rte. 641. Cabins and lodge open year-round. Rates: cabins, $62 to $107 per night; lodge, $43 to $59 per night for two people. Cash, checks, Visa, MasterCard, and American Express accepted. Reservations taken up to one year in advance, recommended six months in advance for summer.

LAKE BARKLEY STATE RESORT PARK
Box 790
CADIZ, KY 42211
(800) 225-8747 *(park information)*
(800) 255-7275 *(lodging reservations)*
(502) 924-1171 *(park office)*

Expansive Lake Barkley — 57,920 acres — covers the traces of prehistoric Indians who roamed the Cumberland River valley centuries ago, Indians as far back as the mastodon hunters who came to North America from Asia. Later, Shawnees lived north of the Cumberland River, which they called the Suwanee, and Cherokees lived south of the Tennessee River, which was known then as the Cherokee. Bountiful game — bear, deer, geese, buffalo, duck, and wild turkey — led the first white settlers to ford the Cumberland in the late 1700s and carve out a home in the western Kentucky wilderness.

Lake Barkley's fir-and-cedar, 120-room lodge rests on a point between Little River Bay and Blue Springs Bay. Its four acres of glass and unique half-circle design translate into spectacular vistas from each room and suite. A baby grand piano and massive fireplace warm a comfortable lounge, cobblestone surrounds an outdoor swimming pool, and a deluxe dining room serves fine meals daily.

Barkley's nine two-bedroom cabins occupy a ridge along Blue Spring Bay, about a mile from the lodge. Constructed of western cedar, these cabins sleep up to six people, and have heating and air conditioning, front and back porches with lounge furniture, and outdoor picnic tables and barbecue grills.

Sustained by the flow of the Cumberland and Little rivers and connected by canal with Kentucky Lake, Lake Barkley provides all manner of water-oriented recreation. A marina rents fishing, skiing, and pontoon boats and has launching ramps and dock space. Fishermen pull in catches of bass, crappie, catfish, and others, while swimmers frolic in the lake.

Barkley's hiking and equestrian trails venture through fields, wetlands, and rolling hills forested with oak, hickory, dogwood, elm, and beech. Other park activities include golf on an eighteen-hole course, tennis on two lighted courts, and trapshooting. Canoeists enjoy the challenge of the nearby Little River. Barkley's forty-eight-hundred-foot paved runway serves private aircraft.

Lake Barkley State Resort Park is seven miles west of Cadiz, Kentucky, on Rte. 68. Lodge and cabins open year-round. Rates: lodge, $40 to $55 per night for two people; cabins, $85 per night. Cash, checks, Visa, MasterCard, and American Express accepted. Reservations taken up to one year in advance, recommended that far in advance for summer.

LAKE CUMBERLAND STATE RESORT PARK
JAMESTOWN, KY 42629
(800) 225-8747 *(park information)*
(800) 255-7275 *(lodging reservations)*
(502) 343-3111 *(park office)*

Dr. Thomas Walker named the Cumberland River in 1750. Looking down from a bluff on the giant, wild artery that few white men had ever seen, Walker was so impressed that he named it in honor of the Duke of Cumberland, son of King George II of England. In 1951, Wolf Creek Dam blocked the flow of the river, creating 101-mile-long Lake Cumberland, which has thirteen hundred miles of shoreline.

Water sports flourish in this three-thousand-acre park in south-central Kentucky, thanks to a boat dock with open and covered slips, and launching ramps. Houseboats, ski boats, fishing boats, and pontoon boats can be rented. Fishermen come to Lake Cumberland to try their skill for

Cabin, Lake Cumberland State Resort Park, Kentucky

largemouth, smallmouth, and Kentucky bass, plus walleye, crappie, bluegill, and rainbow trout. Hikers and horseback riders follow nature trails through oak, beech, and hickory forests, while other visitors enjoy bicycle rentals, tennis courts, swimming pools, and a nine-hole golf course.

Sprinkled along the park peninsula are Lake Cumberland's thirty cabins, available in three distinct styles. Six one-bedroom and fourteen two-bedroom ranch cabins feature air conditioning, electric heat, telephones, and color televisions. Lake Cumberland's most striking units are the ten dark-stained Wildwood Cabins, which have stone fireplaces and porch decks in a contemporary two-story design.

On a bluff at the far northern end of the peninsula sits the forty-eight-room Lure Lodge. From the lobby (with its cozy fireplace), the dining room, or any guest room, you can gaze through the trees at the lake. Guest rooms also provide two double beds, telephones, televisions, and baths with showers.

Lake Cumberland State Resort Park is ten miles south of Jamestown, Kentucky, off Rte. 127. Cabins and lodge open year-round. Rates: cabins, $55 to $65 per night; lodge, $40 to $47 per night for two people. Cash, checks, Visa, MasterCard, and American Express accepted. Reservations taken up to one year in advance, recommended that early for May through September.

NATURAL BRIDGE STATE RESORT PARK
HIGHWAY 11
SLADE, KY 40376
(800) 225-8747 *(park information)*
(800) 255-7275 *(lodging reservations)*
(606) 663-2214 *(park office)*

Northeast Kentucky's Natural Bridge State Park typifies the terrain of this section of the Cumberland Plateau — very rugged sandstone cliffs capping steep ridges. The park lies within Red River Gorge (in the Daniel Boone National Forest), a canyon sliced open by the river's middle fork and numerous other streams. Hundreds of cavelike rock houses, towering rock castles, and intriguing formations dot the landscape, including an abundance of natural arches such as Natural Bridge. This enormous arch — eighty feet long and more than sixty-five feet high — rests at the top of a narrow ridge. Hiking trails lead to Natural Bridge, and a summer chair lift shortens the climb to the magnificent vistas at the top.

Beech, hemlock, white pine, sugar maple, red oak, and tulip trees dominate the thick woodlands here, as they once did throughout the Appalachians. More than 760 species of wild flowers have been identified in the area.

The exterior of the park's Hemlock Lodge consists of native fieldstones, while red-oak paneling warms the interior. The lodge features thirty-five guests rooms, a relaxing lobby with fireplace, and an outdoor swimming pool. Two miles from the lodge on a wooded hillside, the park's ten thirty-year-old cabins have either efficiency or one-bedroom floor plans. Each has a kitchen, a full bath, heating and air conditioning, a screened porch, and a barbecue grill, and two offer wood-burning fireplaces.

Anglers drop their lines into the Red River and forty-acre Mill Creek Lake for bass, sunfish, catfish, crappie, and rainbow trout. Horseback riding is popular in summer, and the park also has two tennis courts.

Natural Bridge State Resort Park is fourteen miles east of Stanton, Kentucky, on Rte. 11. Cabins and lodge open year-round. Rates: cabins, $52 to $55 per night for two people; lodge, $40 to $52 per night for two people. Cash, checks, Visa, MasterCard, and American Express accepted. Reservations taken up to one year in advance, recommended six months in advance for May through October.

PENNYRILE FOREST STATE RESORT PARK
ROUTE 4, BOX 137
DAWSON SPRINGS, KY 42408
(800) 225-8747 *(park information)*
(800) 255-7275 *(lodging reservations)*
(502) 797-3421 *(park office)*

Site of perhaps the most beautiful woods in western Kentucky, Pennyrile Forest State Resort Park contains 435 acres of gently rolling terrain populated by oaks, maples, walnuts, hickories, and evergreens. Set amid a vast, fifteen-thousand-acre state forest, the park surrounds gurgling Cliffty Creek, which feeds Pennyrile Lake. These water sources attract deer, wild turkey, fox, beaver, and waterfowl to the area. While hiking Pennyrile's trails, visitors discover sandstone outcroppings, hilltop overlooks, and a stand of bald cypress trees, not to mention seasonal wild-flower displays and gorgeous autumn colors.

Guests choose among thirteen cabins and a twenty-four-room lodge for their overnight accommodations. Inside the stone-and-timber lodge, a huge fireplace, heavy wood furnishings, and waxed wood floors greet new arrivals. Each guest room sleeps up to four people and has a patio with a view of the fifty-five-acre lake. Other lodge amenities include a dining room, a game room, and a swimming pool.

Pennyrile's frame cabins rest in a wooded section of the park, most of them near the lakefront. These efficiency, one-bedroom, and two-bedroom cabins have full kitchens, baths with showers, and heating and air conditioning. Four of them feature fireplaces, and most have individual boat docks at the lake.

A sandy swimming beach borders Pennyrile Lake, and rowboats and paddleboats can be rented there. During warm months, horseback rides depart from the stable, while tennis enthusiasts use two courts near the cabins. A nine-hole course with pro shop awaits golfers. To fish for some fine bass, crappie, bluegill, and channel catfish, you can drive four miles to Lake Beshear.

Pennyrile Forest State Resort Park is six miles south of Dawson Springs, Kentucky, on Rte. 109. Cabins and lodge open April through October. Rates: cabins, $46 to $55 per night; lodge, $38 to $46 per night for two people. Cash, checks, Visa, MasterCard, and American Express accepted. Reservations taken up to one year in advance, recommended four to six months in advance for summer.

PINE MOUNTAIN STATE RESORT PARK
P.O. Box 610
PINEVILLE, KY 40977
(800) 225-8747 *(park information)*
(800) 255-7275 *(lodging reservations)*
(606) 337-3066 *(park office)*

Pine Mountain borders one of the most significant westward routes in American history — the famed Wilderness Road, which also was strategically important during the Civil War. A list of noteworthy passersby here would include Daniel Boone, George Rogers Clark, and Ulysses S. Grant. Pine Mountain State Resort Park clings to the south side of the mountain in southeast Kentucky, overlooking the picturesque Clear Creek valley.

Pine Mountain's lodge perches on a bluff two-thirds of the way up the mountain; its dining room provides a view of the mountain's crest and the higher peaks of the Log Mountains. The CCC-era lodge, built of native sandstone and chestnut logs, has thirty guest rooms. Each room accommodates up to four people and has a private balcony facing peaceful woods, which include a two-hundred-year-old stand of virgin hemlock. A swimming pool and shuffleboard courts are available to guests, and a nine-hole golf course is nearby.

Pine Mountain Park offers two styles of cabins: fifty-year-old log structures and modern two-bedroom units. Ten one-bedroom log cabins, which sleep up to four people, have stone fireplaces. The ten modern cabins accommodate up to ten people apiece. All cabins come equipped with kitchens and outdoor barbecue grills.

Hiking is rewarding here, as trails wind through pine forest and past exposed ridges. Plants such as mountain laurel, red azalea, pink lady's slipper orchids, and wild blueberries abound. Oaks, hickories, and red maples dominate the upper vegetation, while dogwoods, sourwoods, and serviceberries are frequent understory trees. A favorite hiking destination is Chained Rock, a huge boulder poised menacingly above the town of Pineville. The rumor that the rock needed to be chained to the mountainside finally prompted townspeople to buy and install 137 feet (1.5 tons) of chain, creating notoriety (and perhaps some tourism) for the community.

Pine Mountain State Resort Park is one mile south of Pineville, Kentucky, off Rte. 25E. Two-bedroom cabins available year-round; one-bedroom cabins available mid-March to late December; lodge open year-round. Rates: cabins, $49 to $68 per night; lodge, $42 to $54 per night for two people. Cash, checks, Visa, MasterCard, and American Express accepted. Reservations taken up to one year in advance.

ROUGH RIVER STATE PARK
ROUTE 1
FALLS OF ROUGH, KY 40119
(800) 225-8747 *(park information)*
(800) 255-7275 *(lodging reservations)*
(502) 257-2311 *(park office)*

Settlers arrived in this part of western Kentucky as early as the late 1700s, when George Washington granted land to the Green brothers for their services during the revolutionary war. Together the Greens built a successful farm, store, and mill — a mill that operated more than 140 years. The farm and mill can still be seen today, some eight miles from the park.

A 130-foot-high dam that checks the flow of the undulating Rough River (a tributary of the Green River) created Rough River Lake. Rough River State Park hugs the shore of this 4860-acre lake, which is a fisherman's dream. It teems with largemouth and smallmouth bass, which roam the stump beds, rock banks, and shallow bays, plus crappie, bluegill, channel catfish, walleye, and trout.

Rowboats, motorboats, pontoon boats, and paddleboats can be rented at the park's marina, which also offers slip space, launching ramps, and a nearby sand swimming beach. For a tour of the meandering lake, take one of the cruises offered daily during warmer months on the excursion vessel *Lady of the Lake.* Nonaquatic activities at Rough River include hiking, golf, tennis, volleyball, and archery. Nearby attractions include Mammoth Cave.

Rough River's lodge shares a hilly bend of shoreline with numerous limestone outcroppings. Built of stone and wood, the twenty-year-old lodge has forty guest rooms, each with heating, air conditioning, a private bath, and a patio or balcony. The lodge also features a 209-seat dining room and a swimming pool.

The park's cabins occupy two areas; six are near a twenty-five-hundred-foot paved and lighted airstrip, and nine form a circle near the marina. Each cabin has two bedrooms, a living room, a kitchenette, a bath with shower, and a screened porch. They sleep up to eight people apiece, on four double beds.

Rough River State Park is on Rte. 79 between Leichfield and Hardinsburg, Kentucky. Cabins and lodge open year-round. Rates: cabins, $68 per night for up to four people; lodge, $42 to $49 per night for two people. Cash, checks, Visa, MasterCard, and American Express accepted. Reservations taken up to one year in advance, recommended that early for summer.

Louisiana

STATE PARK INFORMATION:
LOUISIANA OFFICE OF STATE PARKS
P.O. DRAWER 1111
BATON ROUGE, LA 70821
(504) 925-3830

TOURISM INFORMATION:
LOUISIANA OFFICE OF TOURISM
P.O. BOX 44291
BATON ROUGE, LA 70804
(800) 535-8388
(504) 925-3860

STATE BIRD: *Brown Pelican*
STATE TREE: *Bald Cypress*
STATE FLOWER: *Southern Magnolia*

Cabin, Chemin-A-Haut State Park, Louisiana

CHEMIN-A-HAUT STATE PARK
ROUTE 5, BOX 617
BASTROP, LA 71220
(318) 281-5805

Chemin-A-Haut — French for "high road" — takes its name from an old Indian trail once used for seasonal migrations. The ancient tribesmen camped among virgin pines, lulled to sleep by soft sounds of water rippling in the bayou.

This 503-acre park rests on high ground at the junction of two bayous — Bayou Chemin-A-Haut and Bayou Bartholomew — in northeast Louisiana. Deer, squirrels, and rabbits abound in forests of oak and pine, and a nature trail twists through the wooded terrain.

A 1.6-million-dollar construction program in 1980 funded the addition of an Olympic-size swimming pool, a bathhouse, new campsites, and three new cabins, as well as renovation of the park's three rustic cabins. These thirty-year-old cabins, made of wood, sleep up to eight people apiece. Each of the park's six cabins has a private screened porch, a fireplace, a full kitchen, and an outdoor picnic table and barbecue grill. Tall shade trees hang over the cabins, which are both heated and air-conditioned.

Anglers enjoy Chemin-A-Haut's small, man-made lake,

which is stocked with bass, catfish, and bream. Boats can be rented, and swimmers also take advantage of the waters.

About an hour's drive to the southeast is the historic Poverty Point State Commemorative Area. These four hundred acres are the site of an Indian culture that flourished nearly four thousand years ago, the earliest culture yet discovered in the Mississippi Valley. Thousands of artifacts, including arrowheads, spearpoints, cooking balls, and pottery, have been unearthed here, and some are displayed at a recently completed museum. Another worthwhile stop is the nineteen-room plantation home at the Winter Quarters State Commemorative Area — a home General Ulysses S. Grant spared on his march to Vicksburg, using it as his headquarters during the winter before the siege.

Chemin-A-Haut State Park is ten miles north of Bastrop, Louisiana, off Rte. 139. Cabins available year-round. Rates: $25 per night. Cash accepted. Reservations for January through May taken starting in October; reservations for June through December accepted in January, recommended three to four months in advance for summer.

CHICOT STATE PARK
ROUTE 3, BOX 494
VILLE PLATTE, LA 70586
(318) 363-2503

The cool, clear waters of Lake Chicot yield record catches of largemouth bass, crappie, bluegill, and redear sunfish. Visitors at Chicot can use the convenient boathouse, with its rental boats and launching ramps, while swimmers dive into a large pool set on the lakeshore.

Chicot State Park, which covers 6162 acres of rolling hills in southern Louisiana, hems in this fish-rich, two thousand-acre reservoir. An extensive hiking / backpacking trail skirts Lake Chicot, passing primitive campsites along the way.

Chicot offers overnight accommodations in twenty-seven cabins and a small, two-bedroom lodge. Clustered in a wooded section of the park, Chicot's cabins come in two types: rugged, twenty-five-year-old cabins and larger, newer, modular units. Both types have two bedrooms; the older cabins sleep four people, while the ones built in the 1970s sleep up to six. All cabins have full kitchens, heating and air conditioning, and outdoor picnic tables and barbecue grills. The two-bedroom lodge, constructed in the late 1950s, accommodates up to twelve people and has a cozy fireplace.

Louisiana State Arboretum, adjacent to Chicot, displays more than 150 trees and plants native to the state, all labeled for easy identification. Six miles from the park is Ville Platte, Louisiana, home of the annual Louisiana Cotton Festival. Highlights of this October celebration include colorful Cajun "Fais-do-do" street dancing and the grand parade of cotton, climaxed by the internationally acclaimed Tournoi de Ville Platte. Le Tournoi (French for "tournament") is a revival of the "sport of kings," which was introduced by early settlers who are thought to have served in Napoleon's army. Participants, riding horseback, carry long slender lances, which they try to poke through a series of seven small iron rings.

Chicot State Park is six miles north of Ville Platte, Louisiana, on Rte. 3042. Cabins and lodge available year-round. Rates: cabins, $25 to $30 per night; lodge, $50 per night. Cash and checks accepted. Reservations for January through May taken starting in October, for June through December starting in January. Two-night minimum rental on weekends.

LAKE BISTINEAU STATE PARK
P.O. Box 7
DOYLINE, LA 71023
(318) 745-3503

A giant logjam on the Red River in 1800 initially formed Lake Bistineau, by flooding several thousand acres. In 1935, a permanent dam was constructed across Loggy Bayou; it has since been enlarged, giving this reservoir a surface area of almost twenty-seven square miles.

Located in gentle hills in northwest Louisiana, Lake Bistineau State Park harbors 750 acres of pines and hardwoods. At higher elevations, loblolly pine predominates, but as you travel closer to the water's edge, oak, hickory, dogwood, persimmon, sassafras, and pecan take over. Elegant cypress trees draped with Spanish moss line the banks of the lake.

Lake Bistineau serves as the park's focal point, and boating, fishing, and swimming are all popular here. Two launching ramps and rental boats assist those eager to be on the water, while swimmers take advantage of a protected beach and an Olympic-size pool. A favorite with anglers, Lake Bistineau boasts perch, bass, bullhead, bluegill, redear sunfish, and catfish.

Bistineau's thirteen cabins stand apart from the rest of the park, nestled by oaks, pines, and cypresses. The six ten-year-old modular cabins have two bedrooms, baths, screened porches, and kitchenettes, and sleep up to six people apiece. The newer cabins were constructed of wood, and each of these seven cabins has a fireplace. All Lake Bistineau cabins come with heating, air conditioning, and outdoor picnic tables and barbecue grills.

Hikers exploring Lake Bistineau's peaceful trails frequently encounter deer — particularly at dusk — as well as squirrels, bluebirds, cardinals, hummingbirds, nuthatches, and various species of ducks. Fans of thoroughbred racing can visit nearby Louisiana Downs during the racing season (late April through October).

Lake Bistineau State Park is twenty-one miles south of Minden, Louisiana, on Rte. 163. Cabins available year-round. Rates: $30 per night. Cash and checks accepted. Reservations for January through May taken starting in October; for June through December beginning in January, recommended six months in advance for summer. Two-night minimum rental.

SAM HOUSTON JONES STATE PARK
ROUTE 4, BOX 294
LAKE CHARLES, LA 70601
(318) 855-2665

Heavily wooded with pines and hardwoods, Sam Houston Jones State Park's 1087 acres follow the banks of the Houston and Calcasieu rivers and the waters of Indian Bayou. Bald cypress and live oak trees thrive along Sam

Houston Jones's three small lakes, while deer, raccoons, and squirrels dart nimbly over gentle hills here in southwest Louisiana. The hero of the Alamo must have reveled in the beauty here, for legend has it that Sam Houston often visited a lodge on this parkland, the remains of which can still be seen along one of the hiking trails.

Its own bodies of water and its proximity to the Gulf of Mexico make water sports a natural at Sam Houston Jones State Park. A boat-launching ramp on the Calcasieu River gives easy access to riverways, expansive Calcasieu Lake, and, further south, the gulf. Fishermen bring in fine catches of white perch, bass, bream, and catfish. Non-motorized boats can be rented, and water-skiers savor the glassy-calm waters on the rivers. Swimmers travel twelve miles to Lake Charles, the site of a man-made beach. Sam Houston Jones's two primary nature trails are one and three miles in length. Particularly appealing is an old stagecoach road, which hikers use to explore the banks of the meandering Calcasieu River.

Twelve hilltop cabins, six built of redwood and six of concrete blocks, feature kitchens, baths, heating, and air conditioning, and each sleeps up to six people. The concrete-block units have screened porches and a single bedroom, while the newer wood cabins contain two bedrooms.

Sam Houston Jones State Park is twelve miles north of Lake Charles, Louisiana, on Rte. 378. Cabins available year-round. Rates: $30 per night. Cash and checks accepted. Reservations for January through May taken starting in October; for June through December beginning in January; recommended two months in advance for May through September. Two-night minimum rental on weekends.

Mississippi

STATE PARK INFORMATION:
MISSISSIPPI DEPARTMENT OF NATURAL RESOURCES
BUREAU OF RECREATION AND PARKS
P.O. BOX 10600
JACKSON, MS 39209
(601) 961-5014, 961-5240

TOURISM INFORMATION:
MISSISSIPPI DEPARTMENT OF ECONOMIC
    DEVELOPMENT
DIVISION OF TOURISM
P.O. BOX 849
JACKSON, MS 39205
(800) 962-2346 (in-state calls)
(800) 647-2290 (out-of-state calls)

STATE BIRD: *Mockingbird*
STATE MAMMAL: *White-tailed Deer*
STATE TREE: *Magnolia*
STATE FLOWER: *Magnolia*
STATE FISH: *Largemouth Bass*

Cabin, Clarkco State Park, Mississippi

CLARKCO STATE PARK
ROUTE 1, BOX 186
QUITMAN, MS 39355
(601) 776-6651

Clarkco State Park comprises 815 acres of gently tumbling woodlands and a sixty-five-acre freshwater lake in east-central Mississippi. Developed by the Civilian Conservation Corps, the park has been a favorite recreation retreat for Mississippians and others since 1938. Forests of hardwoods and pines overlie the landscape, and blooming dogwoods herald the arrival of spring.

Clarkco's ultramodern lodge, built in 1980, rests at the water's edge and serves as park office, camp store, and the bathhouse for a nearby white-sand swimming beach. Fishing boats, paddleboats, and canoes can be rented year-round, and waterskiing is permitted on specified days (no more than eighty-five-horsepower motors).

Eleven heated and air-conditioned cabins — some rustic, some modern chalets — overlook the lake and accommodate up to eight people apiece. The chalets feature two-story-high walls of glass that present splendid views of the surrounding woods, and each has an outdoor deck. All eleven cabins include full kitchens and baths. Located not far from one of Clarkco's beaches, they also afford private lake piers.

Nonaquatic activities here range from hiking on trails through the stately forest to bicycle riding (rentals available) and picnicking. Tennis enthusiasts can serve and volley on two lighted courts.

Clarkco State Park is twenty miles south of Meridian, Mississippi, off Rte. 45. Cabins available year-round. Rates: $27 to $44 per night, reduced off-season. Cash, checks, Visa, and MasterCard accepted. Reservations taken starting in January for coming year. Three-night minimum reservation during peak months, two nights the rest of the year. Cabins rented for one night if not reserved.

GEORGE PAYNE COSSAR STATE PARK
ROUTE 1
OAKLAND, MS 38948
(601) 623-7356

Eight modern cabins, each capable of sleeping up to four people, line the shores of a peninsula jutting into northern Mississippi's Enid Lake. This park's cabins come equipped with kitchens, baths, heating and air conditioning, screened porches, and fireplaces.

Originally known as Yocona Ridge State Park, George Payne Cossar State Park bears the name of a longtime area legislator. For fishermen, forty-two-square-mile Enid Lake provides some of the best freshwater catches in the Southeast. One delighted angler pulled in the world's largest white crappie here — it weighed in at five pounds, three ounces. Bass, catfish, and bream also abound, and fishing boats can be rented. Swimmers choose from lakefront beaches and an in-ground pool, while skiers glide across the lake's placid waters.

Visitors at Cossar can rent bicycles to tour the countryside, hike its trails through pines and hardwoods, or — in summer — take a guided tour of the Quail Run nature trail. The park restaurant, open all year, specializes in fresh fish dinners.

George Payne Cossar State Park is six miles east of Oakland, Mississippi, off Rte. 32. Cabins available year-round. Rates: $40 per night, reduced off-season. Cash, checks, Visa, and MasterCard accepted. Reservations taken starting in January for coming year. Three-night *minimum reservation during peak months, two nights the rest of the year. Cabins rented for one night if not reserved.*

HOLMES COUNTY STATE PARK
ROUTE 1, BOX 153
DURANT, MS 39063
(601) 653-3351

A brilliant array of red and yellow leaves in autumn, or white dogwood blossoms in spring greet visitors to Holmes County State Park. One of Mississippi's original state parks, it lies almost precisely in the geographic center of the state. Construction began here in 1935, and by 1939 the Civilian Conservation Corps completed the initial phase of the park's development.

Arranged in a semicircle with a view of the larger of the park's two lakes, five CCC-era cabins perch just up a hill from a boat-launching ramp. In addition, three modern duplex cabins (a total of six units) are set back from the lakefront, near an archery range. Each cabin features air conditioning and heating, a kitchenette, and a fireplace.

Thanks to a regular program of lake fertilization, both lakes here offer excellent catches of bass, bream, and catfish. Swimmers and sunbathers enjoy a sand beach, and waterskiing is permitted on specified days. Fishing boats and paddleboats for rent round out Holmes County's water-sports attractions.

Four miles of interpretive nature trails circle the park's smaller lake and trace the shoreline of its larger one. An unusual feature of the park is an indoor roller-skating rink, with snack bar, video games, and pinball machines.

Holmes County State Park is four miles south of Durant, Mississippi, off I-55. Cabins available year-round. Rates: $30 to $44 per night, reduced off-season. Cash, checks, Visa, and MasterCard accepted. Reservations taken starting in January for coming year. Three-night minimum reservation during peak months, two nights the rest of the year. Cabins rented for one night if not reserved.

HUGH WHITE STATE PARK
P.O. Box 725
GRENADA, MS 38901
(601) 226-4934

Northern Mississippi's Hugh White State Park, named for a former Mississippi governor, fronts the enormous, sixty-four-thousand-acre Grenada Lake, which was created by damming the Yalobusha River. Hugh White occupies three peninsulas along the southwest corner of the Grenada reservoir.

The lake delights water-skiers, and boat-launching ramps dot the shoreline. Hugh White's marina sells marine fuel and supplies at Grenada Landing in the summer. Grenada Lake also has a reputation for some of the best crappie fishing in the South; its many coves and an area below the dam are favorites with anglers.

Hugh White's ten duplex cabins sit on a bluff overlooking the lake. Each of the twenty units has air conditioning, a kitchenette, a bedroom, a bath with shower, and a screened porch. A thirty-foot by fifty-foot swimming pool and a lakefront beach await cabin guests.

Grenada Landing's recently remodeled motel, near the dam, has ten rooms with two double beds and a bath and eight rooms with one double bed and a bath. A swimming area and a full-service restaurant, Lakeshore Lodge, are nearby.

Stands of pine and hardwood overlie much of this park, particularly in the cabin area. Visitors can rent fishing boats and bicycles at the park office, and four courts serve tennis enthusiasts.

Hugh White State Park is five miles east of Grenada, Mississippi, on Rte. 8. Cabins and motel open year-round. Rates: cabins, $33 per night; motel, $16 to $28 per night. Rates reduced off-season. Cash, checks, Visa, and Master-Card accepted. Reservations taken starting in January for coming year. Three-night minimum cabin reservation during peak months, two nights the rest of the year. Cabins rented for one night if not reserved.

John W. Kyle State Park rests on the western shore of vast Sardis Lake, an area of northern Mississippi once crossed by Chickasaw Indians on hunting and trading missions. When the first permanent white settlers arrived here in the 1830s, they dubbed this land Chestnut Ridge, because of the countless wild chestnut trees that blanketed the hills. The chestnuts fell victim to a blight nearly a century later, and have been replaced by dogwoods, oaks, and pines.

Kyle's ten duplex cabins (twenty units) line a peninsula, and each has a noteworthy lake view. Heated and air-conditioned, these units have kitchenettes and baths with showers, and ten of them feature wood-burning fireplaces and screened porches.

Just down the road from the cabins, Kyle's lodge houses the park office, a large ballroom with a fireplace, and a dining room suitable for family reunions, banquets, dances, or receptions. Below the lodge at Sardis Lake, fishing boats can be rented — bass, crappie, bream, and catfish are plentiful — and swimmers choose among an Olympic-size pool and two lakefront beaches. A spacious recreation building offers indoor roller-skating, basketball, volleyball, and Ping-Pong; Kyle's four lighted tennis courts are outdoors.

John W. Kyle State Park is seven miles east of Sardis, Mississippi, off Rte. 315. Cabins available year-round. Rates: $33 to $34 per night, reduced off-season. Cash, checks, Visa, and MasterCard accepted. Reservations taken starting in January for coming year. Three-night minimum reservation during peak months, two nights the rest of the year. Cabins rented for one night if not reserved.

J. P. COLEMAN STATE PARK
ROUTE 5, BOX 504
IUKA, MS 38852
(601) 423-6515

Tall, graceful trees line the banks of Indian Creek. Sweet-smelling wild plum trees lend color and fragrance to J. P. Coleman's fourteen hundred acres of parklands, while massive water oaks tower above clear springs. Visitors delight in a delicate waterfall that tumbles effortlessly over huge rocks into a small, reflecting cove. The most northern of Mississippi's state parks, J. P. Coleman embraces the Tennessee River at Pickwick Lake and Indian Creek.

Ten duplex cabins (twenty units), each sleeping up to four people, trace the water's edge along Indian Creek at its junction with the Tennessee River. Each cabin has heating, air conditioning, a kitchenette, and a screened porch, and four units feature fireplaces. There are also six modern motel rooms overlooking Pickwick Lake, one with a kitchenette.

J. P. Coleman's swimming pool competes for swimmers with a sandy beach on the Tennessee River. Launching ramps and rental fishing boats assist those who want to try their luck for striped bass, bream, catfish, and walleyed pike. For anglers who don't bring back dinner, J. P. Coleman's restaurant offers Tennessee River catfish as a house specialty. The park is also ideal for hiking.

J. P. Coleman State Park is thirteen miles north of Iuka, Mississippi, off Rte. 25. Cabins and motel rooms available year-round. Rates: cabins, $33 to $40 per night; motel rooms, $28 to $35 per night. Rates reduced off-season. Cash, checks, Visa, and MasterCard accepted. Reservations taken starting in January for coming year. Three-night minimum reservation during peak months, two nights the rest of the year. Cabins and motel rooms rented for one night if not reserved.

LAKE LOWNDES STATE PARK
P.O. BOX 2331
COLUMBUS, MS 39701
(601) 328-2110

This seven-hundred-acre, eastern Mississippi park is equipped for just about any sports activity you can imagine. From indoor basketball and tennis to jogging and fishing, Lake Lowndes State Park has it all.

The focal point of these activities is the Multi-Sports Center — a two-story structure of wood and Tishomingo fieldstone, with indoor tennis, basketball, volleyball, and badminton courts. Upstairs is a complete game room, featuring pool tables, Ping-Pong, and video games; in summer, a restaurant serves fast food and snacks. Outdoor recreational facilities include three softball fields, six lighted tennis courts, and an 880-yard jogging course.

This park surrounds Lake Lowndes, a clear-water lake stocked with crappie, bass, bream, and catfish. Swimmers and sunbathers loll on a sand beach, watching water-skiers zip by. Paddleboats and fishing boats are available for rent.

Lake Lowndes's two modern duplex cabins (four units) were built in 1983. Each has two bedrooms, a living room, a kitchen, a bath, and a balcony looking out on the lake. The cabins come with heating and air conditioning, ceiling fans, and cheerful fireplaces.

Lake Lowndes State Park is twelve miles southeast of Columbus, Mississippi, off Rte. 69. Cabins available year-round. Rates: $44 per night, reduced off-season. Cash, checks, Visa, and MasterCard accepted. Reservations taken starting in January for coming year. Three-night minimum reservation during peak months, two nights the rest of the year. Cabins rented for one night if not reserved.

LEROY PERCY STATE PARK
P.O. Box 176
HOLLANDALE, MS 38748
(601) 827-5436

Hot water from four artesian wells provides a year-round environment for Leroy Percy's alligator population. A close (but safe) look at their home is possible from a boardwalk that crosses over their pond — an ideal place from which to toss the alligators a special treat: marshmallows purchased at the park office.

Mississippi's oldest and largest state park, Leroy Percy lies in the Mississippi River delta around Alligator Lake. This natural lake, just a few miles from the mighty river, was once a section of riverbed. Cypress trees, Spanish moss hanging from huge oaks, and hot, bubbling springs accent this unspoiled refuge. A self-guided nature trail wanders across the delta lowlands, a second path leads to Black Bayou, and a third circles Alligator Lake.

Civilian Conservation Corps workers completed much of the park's development in 1935, including four cabins, fishing piers, and a picnic area. Each cabin sleeps up to four people and has heating, air conditioning, and a fireplace. A fifth unit, a modern duplex cabin that accommodates up to six people on each side, opened in 1983.

Anglers at Leroy Percy pull bream, perch, catfish, and bass from Alligator Lake, where fishing boats and paddleboats can be rented. The park also has a modern swimming pool. A comprehensive wildlife exhibit at the Interpretive Center displays mounted raccoons, deer, snapping turtles, beavers, ducks, and several species of snakes.

Leroy Percy State Park is five miles west of Hollandale, Mississippi, on Rte. 12. Cabins available year-round. Rates: $22 to $44 per night, reduced off-season. Cash, checks, Visa, and MasterCard accepted. Reservations taken starting in January for coming year. Three-night minimum reservation during peak months, two nights the rest of the year. Cabins rented for one night if not reserved.

PAUL B. JOHNSON STATE PARK
ROUTE 3, BOX 408
HATTIESBURG, MS 39401
(601) 582-7721

Paul B. Johnson State Park is set in southeastern Mississippi's Piney Woods. Its 805 rolling acres of sandy soil are covered with longleaf and loblolly pines, huge oaks, and delicate dogwoods. Nature trails penetrate the landscape around Geiger Lake, a three-hundred-acre body of water fed by two rippling creeks. From wooden lookout towers, visitors at Paul B. Johnson can enjoy a commanding view of this peaceful terrain.

Accommodations here include twelve air-conditioned and heated brick cottages that sleep up to six people apiece. Also nestled under the pines are two duplex cabins, each side of which is equipped with central heating and air conditioning and a fireplace.

Geiger Lake, which has a boat dock and launching ramps, is attractive to water-skiers, and fishing boats, canoes, and paddleboats can be rented. Lifeguards watch over a swimming beach in summer. Picnic tables and barbecue grills line the lakeshore, and fast food is available at the visitors' center.

Paul B. Johnson State Park is fifteen miles south of Hattiesburg, Mississippi, on Rte. 49. Cabins available year-round. Rates: $35 to $40 per night, reduced off-season. Cash, checks, Visa, and MasterCard accepted. Reservations taken starting in January for coming year. Three-night minimum reservation during peak months, two nights the rest of the year. Cabins rented for one night if not reserved.

PERCY QUIN STATE PARK
ROUTE 3
MCCOMB, MS 39648
(601) 684-3931

Percy Quin has the distinction of being the only Mississippi state park to contain an arboretum designated by the Garden Clubs of Mississippi. Located adjacent to the park's lodge, the arboretum displays and promotes dozens of plants, all of which are labeled for easy identification.

Another notable attraction is a small railroad museum, housed in an old Liberty White caboose.

Percy Quin State Park consists of seventeen hundred acres of fresh water and magnolia and loblolly-pine forest in southwestern Mississippi. The Civilian Conservation Corps cleared and constructed much of the original park in the 1930s, when it was named for a onetime Mississippi congressman.

Lake Tangipahoa offers plenty of room for fishing, water-skiing, swimming, or relaxing on its beaches. Boat-launching ramps and rental fishing boats, paddleboats, and canoes assist those eager to get out on the water. For those interested in exploring the countryside, a three-loop, twenty-five-mile-long trail tracks the lakeshore. Rental bicycles, miniature golf, and tennis courts are also available.

Percy Quin's twenty-two brick cabins follow the lakefront; each has a screened porch and a private pier. Ranging in size from one to three bedrooms, these cabins sleep up to twelve people and come equipped with heating, air conditioning, and full kitchens and baths. Some units feature wood-burning fireplaces. Hardwoods and pines populate the cabins' setting on Lake Tangipahoa's eastern shore.

Percy Quin State Park is six miles south of McComb, Mississippi, off Rte. 48. Cabins available year-round. Rates: $34 to $48 per night, reduced off-season. Cash, checks, Visa, and MasterCard accepted. Reservations taken starting in January for coming year. Three-night minimum reservation during peak months, two nights the rest of the year. Cabins rented for one night if not reserved.

ROOSEVELT STATE PARK
MORTON, MS 39117
(601) 732-6316

Under peaceful shade trees, eleven frame cabins dot two peninsulas on Shadow Lake's southern shore, not far from several boat-launching ramps. This park's cabins sleep up to twelve people apiece in various floor plans; four of them have fireplaces. Each cabin features a bath with shower, a kitchenette, heating and air conditioning, plus a screened porch.

Located in the geographic heart of Mississippi just off Interstate 20, Roosevelt State Park completely surrounds Shadow Lake. Heavily wooded, Roosevelt bursts to life each spring with a spectacular display of wild flowers.

Visitors can stop by the boathouse to rent a canoe, paddleboat, or fishing boat, or head for the sandy beach to sun or swim. Anglers toss in a line for the bream, crappie, largemouth bass, and catfish stocked in this manmade lake. Other recreational opportunities include two lighted tennis courts, a lighted softball field, a football field, and an eighteen-hole miniature golf course. Picnic tables and grills sprinkle the landscape.

Roosevelt State Park is two miles south of Morton, Mississippi, off Rte. 13. Cabins available year-round. Rates: $29 to $41 per night, reduced off-season. Cash, checks, Visa, and MasterCard accepted. Reservations taken starting in January for coming year. Three-night minimum reservation during peak months, two nights the rest of the year. Cabins rented for one night if not reserved.

TISHOMINGO STATE PARK
DENNIS, MS 38838
(601) 438-6914

Set in the Appalachian foothills of northeastern Mississippi, Tishomingo State Park gushes with history. Archaeological excavations have confirmed the presence of Paleo-Indians here around 5000 B.C. Much later, Chickasaws inhabited this hilly terrain, roaming over its exposed rock outcroppings, ferns, wild flowers, and rocky-bottomed canoeing creek. In the early 1800s, the famed Natchez Trace — the route between Natchez and Nashville — ran through the parkland. In the 1930s, Tishomingo State Park was one of the ten original Mississippi state parks built by the Civilian Conservation Corps. Today, Appalachian crafts, folk arts, and customs still live in Tishomingo's hillsides and hollows, and each summer they come to the fore during the annual Bear Creek Folklore Festival.

Six stone cabins, each with a fireplace and a screened porch or patio, stand within hearing distance of gurgling Bear Creek. They feature single bedrooms, baths with showers, and kitchenettes.

A country lodge atop the highest hill in the park has a dining room suitable for banquets, family reunions, and receptions. Tishomingo's park office houses a museum that features wildlife mounts, Indian artifacts, and live animals. A log cabin, believed to have been built around 1840, has been restored to its original condition.

For a splendid look at Bear Creek, take the eight-mile float trip that departs daily from mid-March to mid-October. Fishermen, some in rented fishing boats, catch stringers of bass and catfish that are stocked in the small Haynes Lake, while other visitors tour in paddleboats, or swim in a spacious pool.

Tishomingo State Park is three miles north of Dennis, Mississippi, off Rte. 25. Cabins available year-round. Rates: $32 to $34 per night, reduced off-season. Cash, checks, Visa, and MasterCard accepted. Reservations taken starting in January for coming year. Three-night minimum reservation during peak months, two nights the rest of the year. Cabins rented for one night if not reserved.

TOMBIGBEE STATE PARK
ROUTE 2, BOX 336E
TUPELO, MS 38801
(601) 842-7669

Tombigbee State Park, located in the heart of the ancient Chickasaw Indian Paradise yet only minutes from downtown Tupelo, surrounds a beautiful emerald lake full of crappie, bass, and bream. Lake Lee, which has dozens of coves and inlets, is a 120-acre, spring-fed recreation lake with a swimming beach, rental boats, and launching ramps. Waterskiing is permitted on Saturdays, Sundays, and holidays.

Three marked nature trails thread through hardwood forests, past an archery range, and along the lakeshore in this picturesque northeastern Mississippi state park. High on a hill overlooking Lake Lee, a freshly remodeled lodge houses the park office, snack bar, game room, and a spacious ballroom. Films, skits, and a wide variety of programs are presented in Tombigbee's two hillside amphitheaters.

Nestled between two wooded slopes near the water's edge are Tombigbee State Park's six cabins. Each is equipped with a stone fireplace, heating and air conditioning, and a complete kitchen.

Tombigbee State Park is five miles south of Tupelo, Mississippi, on Rte. 6. Cabins available year-round. Rates: $32 to $44 per night, reduced off-season. Cash, checks, Visa, and MasterCard accepted. Reservations taken starting in January for coming year. Three-night minimum reservation during peak months, two nights the rest of the year. Cabins rented for one night if not reserved.

WALL DOXEY STATE PARK
HOLLY SPRINGS, MS 38635
(601) 252-4231

Shaded by stately oaks and tall pines and overlooking Spring Lake, Wall Doxey's five rustic and two modern duplex cabins feature kitchenettes, heating, and air conditioning. These one- and two-bedroom cabins are equipped with fireplaces, outdoor picnic tables, and barbecue grills, and seven of them have screened porches.

Spring Lake serves as the focal point of this 855-acre park in north-central Mississippi, which has a reputation for abundant wildlife, gorgeous wild flowers, vibrant fall colors, and plentiful largemouth bass. The forty-five-acre spring fed lake offers a white-sand swimming beach, rental fishing boats and paddleboats, and a three-level diving pier.

A two-and-a-half-mile nature trail traces the perimeter of Spring Lake. A timber footbridge crosses the northern tip of the lake near a beaver dam and hut, and Wall Doxey's observation tower affords splendid views of wetlands created by hard-working beavers. Wall Doxey State Park adjoins Holly Springs National Forest, renowned for its excellent hunting.

This area is rich with Civil War history: Union soldiers once made camp here, and the nearby town of Holly

Springs, some fifty miles southeast of Memphis, served for a time as headquarters of the Union Army of Tennessee. An annual tour of antebellum homes and churches gives a glimpse into the culture and life-style of people of that era.

Wall Doxey State Park is seven miles south of Holly Springs, Mississippi, on Rte. 7. Cabins available year-round. Rates: $30 to $40 per night, reduced off-season. Cash, checks, Visa, and MasterCard accepted. Reservations taken starting in January for coming year. Three-night minimum reservation during peak months, two nights the rest of the year. Cabins rented for one night if not reserved.

Tennessee

STATE PARK INFORMATION:
TENNESSEE DEPARTMENT OF CONSERVATION
DIVISION OF PARKS AND RECREATION
701 BROADWAY
NASHVILLE, TN 37219-5237
(800) 421-6683 (calls from most eastern states)
(615) 742-6667

TOURISM INFORMATION:
TENNESSEE TOURIST DEVELOPMENT
P.O. BOX 23170
NASHVILLE, TN 37202
(615) 741-2158

STATE BIRD: *Mockingbird*
STATE MAMMAL: *Raccoon*
STATE TREE: *Tulip Poplar*
STATE FLOWER: *Iris*

GREAT SMOKY MOUNTAINS
    NATIONAL PARK
GATLINBURG, TN 37738
(615) 436-5615

LECONTE LODGE
P.O. BOX 350
GATLINBURG, TN 37738
(615) 436-4473

The Smoky Mountains are the majestic climax of the Appalachian Highlands — a wilderness sanctuary preserving the world's finest example of a temperate deciduous forest. With outlines softened by a deep wooded mantle, the mountains stretch in sweeping troughs and mighty billows toward the horizon. The name "Great Smokies" comes from a smokelike haze that envelops these peaks. Cabins and barns built by early pioneers sprinkle the slopes — tangible reminders of an isolated existence in remote mountain valleys.

Fertile soils and centuries of heavy rains have stimulated a world-renowned variety of flora here; some fourteen hundred kinds of flowering plants are found in the park. Broadleaf trees predominate within coves, while along the crest, which rises to more than six thousand feet, conifer forests similar to those in central Canada flourish.

Straddling the Tennessee–North Carolina border, Great Smoky Mountains National Park has more than eight hundred miles of trails, which skirt streams and climb through woodlands into the high country. From Cades Cove, an eleven-mile loop trail leads past open fields, pioneer homesteads, and frame churches where mountain people lived and worshipped for decades.

Wild flowers and migrating birds lure visitors here in late April and early May; June and July announce the blooming of rhododendrons. Autumn's pageant of color usually reaches its zenith in mid-October. Streams beckon anglers with abundant rainbow and brown trout, and riding stables facilitate horseback exploration of the region.

LeConte Lodge rests at an open glade just below Mount LeConte's sixty-five-hundred-foot summit, which makes it the highest guest lodge in the East. Commanding a spectacular view of the Smokies, the overnight accommodations at LeConte can only be reached by trail; the shortest hike in is almost six miles.

Once you arrive, you can choose among seven small cabins and three lodges. The cabins sleep up to five people, a two-bedroom lodge accommodates up to ten, and each three-bedroom lodge can handle thirteen guests. Kerosene lights and heaters illuminate and warm these rustic structures, and the dining room serves family-style meals. Highlights of your journey to LeConte Lodge are sure to include breathtaking sunsets at Clifftop and daybreak at Myrtle Point.

Great Smoky Mountains National Park is just west of Gatlinburg, Tennessee, on Rtes. 441 and 321. LeConte Lodge open late March to early November. Rates: $36 to $38 per adult, $25 per child age ten or under, per night, including all meals and lodging. Reservations accepted starting in October for the following year.

BIG RIDGE STATE RUSTIC PARK
ROUTE 1, HIGHWAY 61
MAYNARDVILLE, TN 37807
(800) 421-6683 *(calls from most eastern states)*
(615) 992-5523 *(all other calls)*

The northeast corner of Big Ridge, which rises to this park's highest peak at 1540 feet above sea level, is just one of half a dozen ridges jutting skyward. Most of the nineteen wood-sided cabins in this park line a smaller ridge above the lakeshore, though some edge the waterfront. Built in the 1930s, each of these cabins has a living / sleeping area with fireplace, a kitchen, bathroom, and screened porch. Dwarfed by mighty pines, the cabins accommodate four people on two double beds, and each has a portable heater.

An expansive TVA lake, Norris Reservoir (known locally as Loyston Sea), bounds this 3687-acre eastern Tennessee park on three sides. Once heavily used for agriculture and badly eroded by years of misuse, the parkland now nourishes forests of graceful pine trees. Big Ridge State Park completely hems in a smaller lake, Big Ridge Lake, site of a swimming beach and rowboats, canoes, and paddleboats for rent. Anglers who launch their craft into Norris Reservoir thrill at the bass, catfish, crappie, bluegill, muskie, and rockfish found in its waters. All forms of recreational boating flourish on the reservoir.

Big Ridge State Rustic Park is twenty-five miles north of Knoxville, Tennessee, on Rte. 61. Cabins available April through October. Rates: $33 to $43 per night, $215 per week. Cash, checks, Visa, MasterCard, and American Express accepted. Reservations taken up to one year in advance. Cabins rented only for full weeks in summer.

CEDARS OF LEBANON STATE PARK
ROUTE 6, BOX 220
LEBANON, TN 37087
(800) 421-6683 *(calls from most eastern states)*
(615) 444-9394 *(all other calls)*

Although this park bears the name of a dense cedar forest of biblical renown, the "cedar" here is not true cedar, but a close cousin, juniper. In fact, this park holds the largest juniper forest in the United States. The U.S. Department of Agriculture undertook a substantial reforestation project here in the 1930s, to replenish trees lost to the pencil industry.

Of Cedars of Lebanon's 8887 acres, 901 are devoted to intensive recreation, while the rest are preserved as a state forest. The region's open limestone glades, peculiar to juniper forests, promote a broad array of rare and splendid wild flowers, including Tennessee purple coneflowers and glade violets. In addition to the junipers, various oaks, elms, hickories, dogwoods, maples, redbuds, and sassafras trees populate these hills in Tennessee's central basin.

Nine two-story cabins at Cedars of Lebanon, built in the early 1980s of wood planks, highlight a quiet woods on the park's southeast side, directly across from a large swimming pool and deck. Each cabin has a modern range and refrigerator, and a bath with a tub / shower combination. Contemporary furnishings enhance the atmosphere, as do free-standing wood-burning stoves and hardwood floors. Each cabin sleeps up to four people on full-size beds (cots also available), and comes equipped with baseboard heat and ceiling fans. Cedars of Lebanon also maintains a group lodge, which has dormitory-style accommodations for up to eighty people.

You can rent a bicycle or horse to explore pastoral beauty, or just stroll down eight miles of trails, past wild flowers, sinkholes, and caves. The historic Trail of Tears crosses the area, a reminder of the forced resettlement of the Cherokee Nation to the Oklahoma Territory. Nearby attractions include Stones River National Historic Battlefield, site of a Civil War conflict, and the Hermitage, home of President Andrew Jackson.

Cedars of Lebanon State Park is seven miles south of Lebanon, Tennessee, on Rte. 231. Cabins available year-round. Rates: $43 to $55 per night, $275 per week. Cash, checks, Visa, MasterCard, and American Express accepted. Reservations taken up to one year in advance. Preference given to full-week reservations in summer.

CHICKASAW STATE RUSTIC PARK
ROUTE 2, HIGHWAY 100 WEST
HENDERSON, TN 38340
(800) 421-6683 (calls from most eastern states)
(901) 989-5141 (all other calls)

Chickasaw's 14,384 timbered acres once served as farmland, but the soil was washed away because of poor farming techniques. During the Great Depression, many southwest Tennessee farmers went broke, so the government set about to reclaim this land for other purposes. CCC and WPA workers created Lake Placid and Lake LaJoie in 1935, and many of the structures standing at Chickasaw — including cabin #1, a favorite with visitors — date from the New Deal.

Five of Chickasaw's twelve cabins, including old #1, trace the shore of Lake Placid, and the others are nearby. Each of these one- or two-bedroom cabins features log or wood-plank construction, and all have fireplaces and outdoor picnic tables and grills. Majestic pines create a splendid setting for these cabins, which are both heated and air-conditioned.

Bass and bluegill please fishermen at fifty-acre Lake Placid and fifty-five-acre Lake LaJoie, while rental paddleboats and rowboats ply the sparkling waters. Lighted tennis courts and a stable full of trail horses round out Chickasaw's recreational opportunities.

Nearby attractions include Pinson Indian Mounds and Casey Jones Railroad Museum. Some forty miles away is Shiloh National Military Park, where museum displays depict the Civil War engagement at Shiloh.

Chickasaw State Rustic Park is eight miles west of Henderson, Tennessee, on Rte. 100. Cabins available year-round. Rates: $33 to $43 per night, $215 per week. Cash, checks, Visa, MasterCard, and American Express accepted. Reservations taken up to one year in advance, recommended three to four months in advance for summer. Cabins rented only for full weeks in summer, two-night minimum the rest of the year.

CUMBERLAND MOUNTAIN STATE RUSTIC PARK
ROUTE 8, BOX 322
CROSSVILLE, TN 38555
(800) 421-6683 *(calls from most eastern states)*
(615) 484-6138 *(all other calls)*

Cumberland Mountain State Park has the most diverse selection of cabins in the Tennessee park system. These include ultramodern deluxe cabins, four duplex cabins, and several other styles. All have kitchens with modern appliances and — except for the duplex units — wood-burning fireplaces. Dense woods surround these cabins.

The parkland here in eastern Tennessee typifies the Cumberland Plateau, a great segment of upland extending from western New York to central Alabama — America's largest timbered plateau. The Farm Security Administration acquired this 1720-acre park in 1938 as a recreation area for 250 families that had been selected to homestead here. This was part of a drive to encourage colonization of sparsely populated sections of Tennessee.

The Civilian Conservation Corps and Works Progress Administration built most of the structures here with a local sandstone known as crab orchard stone. This was the material used for the dam and bridge, which constitute the largest masonry structure ever built by the CCC and the largest nonreinforced dam in the world. Mining and shaping crab orchard stone remains a major area industry to this day.

Popular activities at calm, forty-acre Cumberland Mountain Lake include swimming from a sandy beach and boating in rental canoes, paddleboats, and rowboats. Tennis courts, horseshoe pits, shuffleboard, and playgrounds are also available, and in summer, two-hour trail rides depart from the stables.

Cumberland Mountain State Rustic Park is four miles south of Crossville, Tennessee, on Rte. 127-S. Cabins available year-round. Rates: $22 to $55 per night, $134 to $284 per week. Cash, checks, Visa, MasterCard, and American Express accepted. Reservations taken up to one year in advance. Except for duplex units, cabins rented only for full weeks in summer.

EDGAR EVINS STATE RUSTIC PARK
ROUTE 1
SILVER POINT, TN 38582
(800) 421-6683 *(calls from most eastern states)*
(615) 858-2446, 858-2114 *(all other calls)*

With its steep-walled bluffs and narrow ridges, the eastern edge of the Highland Rim once enticed Indians as a fine hunting ground for deer, bear, and buffalo. By the early 1800s, the first settlers appeared in this central Tennessee region and established many small mills along Caney Fork River. Cornmeal and lumber became the major commercial products of surrounding towns. In 1948, the U.S. Army Corps of Engineers erected Center Hill Dam across the river, for flood control and hydroelectric power.

One of Tennessee's newest state parks, Edgar Evins opened in 1975. It was named for a former state senator, the late James Edgar Evins, who was instrumental in the development of Center Hill Dam and Reservoir. His family homestead stands near Indian Creek, on the park's south side.

The reservoir partially encircles this park, and its beaches and bathhouses attract swimming enthusiasts; so does the park pool. Fishermen slide their boats down launching ramps as they set out for smallmouth and largemouth bass and walleye pike. Along Edgar Evins's hiking trails, you might come across raccoons, foxes, opossums, red-tail hawks, and even, in winter, an occasional bald eagle.

Displaying western cedar exteriors and interiors, this park's thirty-four cabins are grouped four to six units per building. These recently completed cabins have single bedrooms downstairs, and baths, kitchenettes, and living areas on the second floor. Walk out onto a second-floor balcony to take in a delightful panorama of lake and forest. These deluxe cabins even come with color televisions.

Edgar Evins State Park is twenty-five miles west of Cookeville, Tennessee, off Rte. 141. Cabins available year-round. Rates: $43 to $55 per night, $275 per week. Cash, checks, Visa, MasterCard, and American Express accepted. Full-week reservations taken up to one year in advance. Cabins rented only for full weeks in summer.

FALL CREEK FALLS STATE RESORT PARK
ROUTE 3
PIKEVILLE, TN 37367
(800) 421-6683 (calls from most eastern states)
(615) 881-3241 (Fall Creek Falls Inn)
(615) 881-3297 (park office)

The terrain of this Cumberland Plateau park comprises steep sandstone cliffs, virgin forests, and three stunning waterfalls, including Fall Creek Falls — the highest waterfall east of the Rockies. For 256 feet, water streams down a rocky ledge like a silver ribbon, before disappearing in a shaded plunge pool. The falls can be admired from two overlooks, waded across by clutching a cable, or viewed from the bottom of the gorge by descending a rigorous trail. From Buzzards Roost, a huge granite boulder, hawks and other large birds can be seen soaring six hundred feet above the gorge.

The oak and hickory forest which overlays much of this eastern Tennessee park gives way to tulip poplar and hemlock in its valleys and hollows. In fact, the plants in the moist, protected gorges resemble those found in southern Canada.

Fall Creek Falls Inn graces a hillside on the shore of Fall Creek Lake. This brick-and-concrete, seventy-three-room structure has a charming dining room, a swimming pool, and shuffleboard courts. Each guest room has either a private patio or a balcony with a view of the 350-acre lake.

Fall Creek's twenty two-bedroom cabins, built in the early 1970s, employ contemporary designs and natural woods. Ten two-story fisherman cabins, built over the water, allow guests to cook, sunbathe, and even fish from their private porches. "Plush" accurately describes all of the cabins here, which are equipped with fireplaces and televisions. Each accommodates up to eight people, on four double beds.

Canoes, paddleboats, and fishing boats can be rented at the boat docks; hikers and horseback riders wander along miles of paths. Rental bicycles, tennis courts, and a challenging eighteen-hole golf course complete Fall Creek's facilities.

Fall Creek Falls State Resort Park is eighteen miles west of Pikeville, Tennessee, on Rte. 30. Inn and cabins available year-round. Rates: inn, $32 to $44 per night for two people; cabins, $48 to $60 per night, $310 per week. Cash, checks, Visa, MasterCard, and American Express accepted. Reservations taken up to one year in advance, recommended six months in advance for spring and fall weekends and summer. Cabins rented only for full weeks in summer, two-night minimum the rest of the year.

HENRY HORTON STATE RESORT PARK
ROUTE 31-A
CHAPEL HILL, TN 37034
(800) 421-6683 *(calls from most eastern states)*
(615) 364-2222 *(all other calls)*

Situated on the former estate of the late Henry H. Horton, Tennessee's thirty-sixth governor, the Buford Ellington eighteen-hole, par-seventy-two golf course is considered one of the finest in the Southeast. A pro shop provides rental clubs, carts, and accessories, and a practice green adjoins the shop.

After a day on the links, visitors can take a dip in an Olympic-size swimming pool, complete with three diving boards; or you might prefer a quiet walk along this park's two major hiking trails. Duck River undulates through Henry Horton's 1135 acres, and picnickers along the riverbank watch canoeists float by. Skeet and trap shooting take place at a multifield range, where rental guns and ammunition are available.

Horton's accommodations include a modern, seventy-two room lodge and four twenty-year-old frame cabins. A huge fireplace and comfortable sitting area greet the lodge's guests. Each room has two double beds, air conditioning, and a television. The two-bedroom cabins sleep up to six people, and each features a fireplace. Like the lodge rooms they have telephones and color televisions, but the cabins also include complete kitchens. The historic homes of James K. Polk and Sam Davis are not far from the park, and visitors tour the Jack Daniels and George Dickel distilleries.

Henry Horton State Resort Park is two miles south of Chapel Hill, Tennessee, on Rte. 31-A. Cabins and lodge open year-round. Rates: cabins, $43 to $55 per night, $275 per week; lodge, $32 to $44 per night for two people. Cash, checks, Visa, MasterCard, and American Express accepted. Reservations taken up to one year in advance; recommended six months to a year in advance for late spring, summer, and early fall. Cabins rented only for full weeks, May through September.

MEEMAN-SHELBY STATE PARK
ROUTE 3
MILLINGTON, TN 38053
(800) 421-6683 *(calls from most eastern states)*
(901) 876-5201 *(all other calls)*

Meeman-Shelby, located exactly in the center of the Mississippi flyway, serves as a stopover for more species of migrating birds than any other spot in North America. The grand Mississippi River forms an eight-mile western boundary of this southwest Tennessee park; but unlike most of the delta, Meeman-Shelby's fourteen thousand acres consist of bluffs, blanketed with beech, oak, hickory, and poplar. Willow and cypress trees populate its swampy lowlands, the site of nearly five hundred acres of beaver ponds. Deer, wild turkey, coyote, mink, otter, fox, and raccoons all reside here, attracted by abundant vegetation and prey.

More than fifty miles of trails crisscross the bluffs and river bottoms, to the delight of hikers and those who rent a horse at the stables. The Mississippi bottoms also host managed hunts for small game, waterfowl, deer, and turkey during specified seasons. Rental bicycles and an eight-mile paved trail offer yet another way to explore this parkland.

Once a national park, Meeman-Shelby derives half its name from the late Edward J. Meeman. A Memphis newspaper editor and avid conservationist, he was instrumental in establishing both this park and Great Smoky Mountains National Park.

Hardwoods shade the park's six cabins, which follow a peninsula on Poplar Tree Lake. Of board-and-batten construction and rich wood interiors, the cabins sleep up to six people apiece. Each has two bedrooms, a kitchen, a fireplace of native Tennessee stone, heating, and air conditioning. Outdoor picnic tables and barbecue grills accommodate family cookouts.

Fishing and boating rate highly on 125-acre Poplar Tree Lake, the larger of Meeman-Shelby's two lakes. Fishing boats can be rented, or you can launch your own boat into the lake or the Mississippi. Typical catches here include largemouth bass, bluegill, bream, channel catfish, and crappie. Swimmers enjoy a spacious pool.

Meeman-Shelby State Park is twelve miles north of Memphis, Tennessee, on Rte. 51. Cabins available year-round. Rates: $43 to $55 per night, $275 per week. Cash and checks accepted. Reservations recommended one month in advance; priority given to full-week reservations.

MONTGOMERY BELL STATE RESORT PARK
ROUTE 1, BOX 686
BURNS, TN 37029
(800) 421-6683 *(calls from most eastern states)*
(615) 797-3101 *(lodge)*
(615) 797-9051 *(park office)*

Dickson County's hills contained a treasure more precious than gold to early settlers: iron ore, which lured droves of fortune hunters to middle Tennessee. The "father of Tennessee," General James Robertson, was the first to capitalize on iron deposits here, establishing Cumberland Iron Works in 1795. Seven years later a young Pennsylvanian, Montgomery Bell, came to operate the furnace for Robertson, and in 1804 he purchased it. From this modest beginning, Bell built an industrial empire. He is perhaps best known for his "Narrows of Harpeth," a 290-foot tunnel he had cut through solid rock to supply waterpower for his iron forge. Tennessee's first industrialist and the South's greatest ironmaster, he also made the history books by forging the cannonballs used by Andrew Jackson at the Battle of New Orleans.

Though silent now for decades, the iron industry has left traces, including the remains of Laurel Furnace and old ore pits. The hardwood forest, once wantonly cut to clear farmland and to supply charcoal for blast furnaces, has slowly healed its wounds.

Seven of Montgomery Bell's nine cabins sit on a hill with a view of Acorn Lake, one of three lakes here. These twenty-five-year-old cabins feature two bedrooms, fireplaces, kitchens, color televisions, and outdoor barbecue grills.

Across a cove via a rough-hewn wooden bridge is the thirty-five-room Montgomery Bell Inn and Restaurant. Blending contemporary architecture with the warmth of Tennessee crab orchard stone, this structure rests on a tree-lined bluff overlooking Acorn Lake.

Swimming and the availability of rental rowboats and paddleboats please visitors to Acorn Lake, and fishermen wet their lines in all three lakes. Other facilities include a lighted tennis court, an eighteen-hole golf course with pro shop, and twenty miles of hiking trails.

Montgomery Bell State Resort Park is thirty-five miles west of Nashville, Tennessee, on Rte. 70. Cabins and lodge open year-round. Rates: cabins, $33 to $43 per night, $215 per week; lodge, $32 to $35 per night for two people. Cash, checks, Visa, MasterCard, and American Express accepted. Reservations taken up to one year in advance. Cabins rented only for full weeks in summer, two-night minimum the rest of the year.

NATCHEZ TRACE STATE RESORT PARK
WILDERSVILLE, TN 38388
(800) 421-6683 *(calls from most eastern states)*
(901) 968-8176 *(Pin Oak Lodge)*
(901) 968-3742 *(park office)*

This enormous, forty-two-thousand-acre state park contains a natural oddity: the world's third largest pecan tree. Pecan trees, not native to the area, typically do not grow on dry ridges such as the one where the aptly named Big Pecan Tree stands, yet there it is. Legend has it that this 106-foot giant (once thought to be the world's largest) grew from a pecan carried home by one of Andrew Jackson's troops, returning from the Battle of New Orleans in 1815.

Many miles of hiking trails drift through forest and fields, along the shores of four lakes, and past countless streams at Natchez Trace. Anglers pick from varied waters, with the likely result a line of bluegill, catfish, crappie, or largemouth, rock, and hybrid bass. Lake swimming is also popular, and rental rowboats and paddleboats are available. Privately owned craft slice the waters of three of Natchez's lakes.

Guests at a ten-year-old, motel-style lodge take advantage of a swimming pool, tennis courts, and a playground. Natchez Trace's eighteen wooden cabins, built in the mid-1930s, sleep six in two rooms. Heated and air-conditioned, these cabins sit among tall trees on Cub Lake, just across a rustic footbridge from the beach. Each cabin has a complete kitchen, a fireplace, and an outdoor table and grill.

Natchez Trace State Resort Park is six miles southeast of Lexington, Tennessee, off I-40. Cabins available year-

round, lodge open April through October. Rates: cabins, $33 to $43 per night, $215 per week; lodge, $45 per night for two people (includes two meals). Cash, checks, Visa, and MasterCard accepted. Reservations recommended a month in advance; priority given to full-week cabin reservations for summer.

NORRIS DAM STATE RESORT PARK
P.O. Box 27
NORRIS, TN 37828
(800) 421-6683 (calls from most eastern states)
(615) 494-0488, 426-7461 (all other calls)

Lodging options at Norris Dam State Resort Park include three distinct styles of cabins, all on wooded sites near a lake. The thirty-five vacation and overnight cabins have wood exteriors, knotty interiors, and hardwood floors. Built in the 1930s, these one-room cabins sleep from four to six people. Vacation cabins also have kitchenettes and fireplaces. In contrast, the nine three-bedroom deluxe cabins, built in the mid-1970s, have such modern features as central heat and air conditioning, state-of-the-art kitchens, color televisions, fireplaces, and decks with tables and chairs.

Park visitors tour Norris Dam, which dates from 1933; it was the first dam built by the Tennessee Valley Authority. Norris Dam State Resort Park consists of forty-five hundred acres on Norris Lake's west shore. Situated in eastern Tennessee's Ridge and Valley Region, this park also holds sparkling streams, caves, and a unique virgin forest.

Skiing, swimming, and fishing are popular pastimes at the lake, which teems with bass, catfish, muskie, and rockfish. Trout fishermen try their luck on the Clinch River, right below the dam.

One mile south of the old park entrance are an eighteenth-century gristmill, the Lenoir Pioneer Museum, and a threshing barn. Every day in summer, meal is ground from corn at the mill, and Tennessee pioneer crafts are demonstrated.

Norris Dam State Resort Park is five miles south of Lake City, Tennessee, on Rte. 441. Deluxe cabins available year-

round, vacation cabins rented March through November, overnight cabins available summer only. Rates: $22 to $55 per night, $130 to $275 per week. Cash, checks, Visa, MasterCard, and American Express accepted. Reservations taken up to one year in advance; recommended three to five months in advance for spring and fall weekends and summer. Deluxe and vacation cabins rented only for full weeks in summer, two-night minimum the rest of the year.

PARIS LANDING STATE RESORT PARK
ROUTE 1
BUCHANAN, TN 38222
(800) 421-6683 *(calls from most eastern states)*
(901) 642-4311 *(Paris Landing Inn)*
(901) 642-4140 *(park office)*

Like many steamboat and freight landings on the Tennessee River in the mid-1800s, Paris Landing unloaded riverboats, then shipped supplies to area towns and farms by oxcart. Today, this 841-acre park rests on the western shore of mammoth Kentucky Lake — at 200,000 acres, the world's second largest man-made lake. Located in the Eastern Gulf Coastal Plain of northwest Tennessee, Paris Landing's terrain is characterized by steep and rolling highlands forested with oak, hickory, and pine.

Yachts, sailboats, cruisers, and runabouts abound on the seemingly endless waters of the lake, and stringers of largemouth, smallmouth, and white bass, crappie, bluegill, catfish, and sauger reward fishermen. The park's marina, snug in a protected harbor, offers rental fishing boats, sailboats, and slip space, plus launching ramps.

Swimmers find relief from the heat in an Olympic-size pool or at a lakefront beach. Golf is another Paris Landing diversion, on a par-seventy-two, eighteen-hole course, while tennis enthusiasts match strokes on well-kept courts.

Each of the hundred guest rooms at Paris Landing Inn features a balcony with lounge chairs facing the lake. This modern resort includes a restaurant that specializes in southern dishes.

Paris Landing visitors often venture to the TVA's Land Between the Lakes recreation area — a 170,000-acre, 40-

mile-long strip between Kentucky Lake and Lake Barkley. Thirteen miles east of Paris Landing is Fort Donelson National Military Park, site of a museum and Civil War artifacts.

Paris Landing State Resort Park is sixteen miles northeast of Paris, Tennessee, on Rte. 79. Inn open year-round. Rates: $32 to $44 per night for two people. Cash, checks, Visa, MasterCard, and American Express accepted. Reservations recommended two to three months in advance.

PICKETT STATE RUSTIC PARK
ROCK CREEK ROUTE
BOX 174
JAMESTOWN, TN 38556
(800) 421-6683 *(calls from most eastern states)*
(615) 879-5821 *(all other calls)*

Consisting of 11,752 acres purchased from Stearnes Coal and Lumber Company in 1933, Pickett State Rustic Park nestles a remote section of the Cumberland Mountains in northeast Tennessee. Of particular interest in this wilderness preserve are unusual rock formations, natural bridges, caves, waterfalls, and sheer stone ledges. All are accessible via nearly sixty miles of hiking trails, many lined with thick rhododendron groves. Pickett adjoins the Big South Fork of the Cumberland River National Recreation Area, 150,000 acres of prime parkland.

Overnight accommodations here are in three forms: five stone cabins, built in the 1930s by the Civilian Conservation Corps; five wooden cabins; and five modern chalets. All rest under tall pines, and offer the ambience of wood-burning fireplaces. The two-story chalets have bedrooms and baths upstairs, while kitchens, living areas, and patios occupy the ground floors.

Fishing in Pickett's stocked, fifteen-acre lake — popular year-round — yields trout, bass, bluegill, and catfish, and a marina rents rowboats and canoes. A cliff-lined sandy beach hosts swimmers and sun-lovers in summer. Nearby attractions include Big South Fork Scenic Railway, one hour's drive from the park, and the birthplace, farm, and gristmill of World War I hero Sergeant Alvin C. York.

Pickett State Rustic Park is twelve miles north of James-

town, Tennessee, on Rte. 154. Chalets available year-round, stone and wood cabins rented April through November. Rates: $25 to $55 per night, $130 to $275 per week. Cash, checks, Visa, MasterCard, and American Express accepted. Reservations taken up to one year in advance, recommended three to five months in advance for fall weekends and summer. Cabins rented only for full weeks in summer; two-night minimum stay the rest of the year.

PICKWICK LANDING STATE RESORT PARK
P.O. Box 10
PICKWICK DAM, TN 38365
(800) 421-6683 (calls from most eastern states)
(901) 689-3135 (lodge)
(901) 689-3129 (park office)

When Pickwick Dam closed its floodgates for the first time in the spring of 1938, local people eagerly purchased and built boats to use on their new reservoir. Forested with hickory, oak, and yellow poplar, this 1440-acre, southwest Tennessee park provides a range of recreational opportunities on Pickwick Lake's west shore. A marina offers rental boats, slips, and a full line of marine supplies, while swimmers can enjoy three leisurely beaches. Anglers frequently boast of fine catches of bass, crappie, bluegill, sauger, and catfish.

White-tailed deer, rabbits, and turkeys inhabit Pickwick's woods, and migratory waterfowl visit each year. Tennis courts and an eighteen-hole golf course complete this park's facilities.

A modern, cedar-covered lodge houses seventy-five guest rooms, each of which has a balcony overlooking the lake, marina, or swimming pool. At the lodge's dining room, country favorites such as catfish, ham steak, and southern fried chicken are specialties.

Pine, oak, and brush separate Pickwick's ten cabins, which also are constructed of western cedar. These two-bedroom cabins have modern baths, kitchens, and living areas. Each is equipped with central heat and air conditioning, a fireplace, cable TV, and an outdoor grill and picnic table. Pickwick's cabins accommodate up to eight people each.

Pickwick Landing State Resort Park is fourteen miles south of Savannah, Tennessee, at the intersection of Rtes. 57 and 128. Cabins and lodge open year-round. Rates: cabins, $43 to $55 per night, $275 per week; lodge, $32 to $44 per night for two people. Cash, checks, Visa, Master-Card, and American Express accepted. Reservations taken up to one year in advance. Cabins rented only for full weeks in summer; two-night minimum the rest of the year.

REELFOOT LAKE STATE RESORT PARK
ROUTE 1, BOX 296
TIPTONVILLE, TN 38079
(800) 421-6683 (calls from most eastern states)
(901) 253-7756 (all other calls)

During the bitter winter of 1811–12, the New Madrid earthquakes — so severe that they knocked people to the ground — created Reelfoot Lake. Landslides swept down bluffs, large areas were uplifted, and still larger land masses sank. One of these depressions filled with water, and Reelfoot Lake was born.

Chickasaw Indian legend, on the other hand, credits the wrath of their gods for the lake's creation. It tells of Reelfoot, a chieftain denied the hand of a Choctaw princess because of his clubfoot. Reelfoot and his braves then kidnapped the maiden, the legend says, and during their celebration, the earth opened up and swallowed the entire tribe.

Reelfoot Lake State Resort Park lies in Tennessee's northwest corner, not far from the Mississippi River. It encompasses 18,725 acres, the vast majority of which are the waters of Reelfoot Lake. This park harbors most every kind of shore and wading bird, and also serves as a winter home for significant numbers of bald eagles. Cypress trees dominate the margins of the picturesque lake.

Reelfoot's ultramodern, twenty-room Airpark Inn and Restaurant juts out over the lake. The inn provides twelve rooms that sleep two people, and eight suites that accommodate up to six. Other Reelfoot lodging includes a five-unit motel at the spillway; three of those units are equipped with kitchenettes.

Crappie, bass, and bream, among other species, await anglers in the lake, and a seventy-five-slip marina rents boats and has launching ramps. Visitors swim either from lakefront beaches or at the inn's pool. Excursion boats tour Reelfoot Lake, and the park has a thirty-five-hundred-foot lighted runway.

Reelfoot Lake State Resort Park is ten miles north of Tiptonville, Tennessee, on Rte. 78. Inn and motel open year-round. Rates: $32 to $44 per night. Cash, checks, Visa, MasterCard, and American Express accepted. Reservations taken up to one year in advance, recommended a month in advance for weekends.

ROAN MOUNTAIN STATE RESORT PARK
ROUTE 1, BOX 38
ROAN MOUNTAIN, TN 37687
(800) 421-6683 *(calls from most eastern states)*
(615) 772-3303 *(all other calls)*

Roan Mountain's 6315-foot summit towers above this park in the Blue Ridge Mountains of eastern Tennessee. This 2104-acre haven of woods, waterfalls, and wildlife sustains the world's largest natural stand of rhododendron, which carpets the mountain slopes and reaches peak bloom each June. Here blackberry vines have no thorns, heather invades cracks and crannies in billion-year-old rocks, and a soft, thick cover of moss cushions the step.

Bear, bobcat, deer, and raccoon inhabit the forests and stream banks, where such wild flowers as showy orchids, trillium, and larkspur abound. One of the most popular stretches of the Appalachian Trail lies about seven miles from the park; it crosses Roan High Knob at an elevation of 6285 feet.

Visitors flock to a heated swimming pool — heated because at an average elevation of three thousand feet, nighttime temperatures in the upper forties are not uncommon in July. Three cross-country ski trails penetrate the hardwood forests, traversing a mixture of level ground and steep slopes.

Roan Mountain's modern, wooden-exterior cabins have four rooms and a sleeping loft. They accommodate up to six people apiece, and are equipped with every amenity down to coffee pots, toasters, and ice makers. In addition to electric heat, each cabin has a functional wood stove. Four rocking chairs wait for you on the porch, not far from an outdoor barbecue grill. Three of these cabins perch on a hilltop; the rest stand in a silent forest.

Roan Mountain State Resort Park is twenty miles southeast of Elizabethtown, Tennessee, on Rte. 143. Cabins available year-round. Rates: $43 to $55 per night, $275 per week. Cash, checks, Visa, and MasterCard accepted. Reservations taken up to one year in advance, recommended six months in advance for summer and fall. Cabins rented only for full weeks in summer; two-night minimum the rest of the year.

STANDING STONE STATE RUSTIC PARK
LIVINGSTON, TN 38570
(800) 421-6683 *(calls from most eastern states)*
(615) 823-6347, 823-6487 *(all other calls)*

This state park takes its name from a "standing stone" that apparently once marked the boundary line between two Indian tribes. The eight-foot-high sandstone landmark initially stood upright, on a rock ledge. After it fell, the Indians placed it on an improvised monument. The stone is preserved to this day in Monterey, Tennessee.

Standing Stone's eleven thousand acres of wooded mountains, waterfalls, cliffs, and caves are located in north-central Tennessee along the Cumberland Plateau. This great plateau extends without a break from New York to Alabama; it created a very real barrier to westward migration in the 1700s. At that time, no road crossed it, and only a few footpaths (such as Warriors' Path at Cumberland Gap) gave access to the interior lowlands beyond.

Oak furniture fills the fourteen chestnut-log cabins at Standing Stone, which date from the late 1930s. Heated by rock fireplaces, these cabins sleep up to six people. Six redwood "timber-lodge" cabins are another form of overnight accommodation. Furnished with fine maple pieces, these cabins have three bedrooms, electric heaters, and fireplaces. All Standing Stone cabins feature air conditioning and outdoor barbecue grills. Resting on a hilltop with a view of Kelly Lake, the cabins enjoy cool breezes and the shade of pines, oaks, poplars, beeches, cedars, and redwoods.

Ten miles of trails amble through this expanse of public land, past wild flowers and a variety of forest creatures. Fishing goes on year-round in sixty-nine-acre Standing Stone Lake for bass and bluegill, and rental rowboats are available. Other activities range from swimming and tennis to badminton, horseshoes, and shuffleboard.

Standing Stone State Rustic Park is ten miles west of Livingston, Tennessee, on Rte. 52. Timber-lodge cabins available year-round, smaller cabins rented April through November. Rates: $25 to $43 per night, $120 to $255 per week. Cash and checks accepted. Reservations taken up to one year in advance. Cabins rented only for full weeks in summer.

TIMS FORD STATE RUSTIC PARK
ROUTE 4
WINCHESTER, TN 37398
(800) 421-6683 (calls from most eastern states)
(615) 967-4457, 967-3230 (all other calls)

Long before the Tennessee Valley Authority (TVA) built Tims Ford Dam on the headwaters of the Elk River, Indians hunted and fished in south-central Tennessee. In fact, artifacts and other evidence indicate that ancient tribes lived here as far back as ten thousand to twelve thousand years ago. The Indians eventually relinquished their land to the United States, and by the early 1800s, white settlers had laid their claims to the Elk River valley's fertile soil. The pioneers depended on waterways for food, power, and transportation, and they built numerous mills along the river and its tributaries — mills that ground corn, wheat, and other grains, mills that cleaned cotton, mills that sawed timber.

Tims Ford's twenty two-bedroom cabins feature western cedar exteriors and interiors, as well as wood-decked patios.

Each sleeps up to ten people and is equipped with a complete kitchen, a color television, a fireplace, and central heat and air conditioning. These seven-year-old cabins line the shore of Tims Ford Lake under tall trees.

Tims Ford Lake, 10,700 acres in area, has a reputation as one of the best bass-fishing lakes in the Southeast, and rockfish, bluegill, catfish, and crappie are also plentiful. A marina rents fishing boats, or you can launch your own at the boat ramps. Tims Ford's "double L"-shaped pool has a diving tank, wading area, and a sunbathing deck. Five miles of paved trails let hikers and bikers soak up the scenery, and rental bikes are available.

Tims Ford State Rustic Park is twelve miles southeast of Tullahoma, Tennessee, off Rte. 130. Cabins available March through November. Rates: $43 to $55 per night, $275 per week. Cash, checks, Visa, MasterCard, and American Express accepted. Reservations taken up to one year in advance, recommended eight months to a year in advance for holiday weekends and summer. Cabins rented only for full weeks in summer; two-night minimum the rest of the season.

The

NORTHWEST

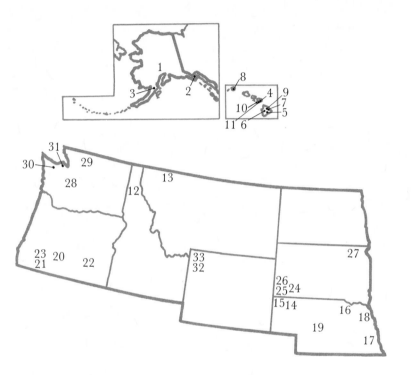

Alaska

STATE PARK INFORMATION:
ALASKA DIVISION OF STATE PARKS AND OUTDOOR
   RECREATION
225A CORDOVA STREET
ANCHORAGE, AK 99501
(907) 265-4518

TOURISM INFORMATION:
ALASKA DIVISION OF TOURISM
POUCH E
JUNEAU, AK 99811
(907) 465-2010

STATE BIRD: *Willow Ptarmigan*
STATE TREE: *Sitka Spruce*
STATE FLOWER: *Forget-me-not*
STATE FISH: *King Salmon*

DENALI NATIONAL PARK AND PRESERVE
P.O. Box 9
DENALI NATIONAL PARK, AK 99755
(907) 683-2294

DENALI NATIONAL PARK HOTEL / MCKINLEY CHALETS
ARA OUTDOOR WORLD LTD.
DENALI NATIONAL PARK, AK 99755 (MAY THROUGH
  SEPTEMBER)
(907) 278-1122, 683-2215

825 WEST EIGHTH AVENUE, #240
ANCHORAGE, AK 99501 (OCTOBER THROUGH APRIL)
(907) 278-1122

CAMP DENALI
P.O. Box 67
DENALI NATIONAL PARK, AK 99755
(907) 683-2290 *(summer)*
(907) 683-2302 *(winter)*

Athabascan natives dubbed the massive peak that is the highest point in North America "Denali," the "high one," and that is now the name of this vast, six-million-acre preserve in central Alaska. Formerly Mount McKinley National Park, this territory, larger than the state of Massachusetts, comprises rolling tundra and deep forests, lofty peaks, green valleys, enormous glaciers, and endless fields of flowers. Mount McKinley has been called the Alaskan landscape's most impressive feature, as it reigns in lofty isolation over the six-hundred-mile Alaska Range. The summit of this massif tops out at 20,320 feet. Permanent snowfields cover more than 50 percent of the mountain and feed the many glaciers that surround its base. Mount McKinley's granite and slate core is overlain, in fact, by ice hundreds of meters thick.

Dall sheep, relatives of the bighorn, graze the alpine tundra for young shoots of mountain avens. Majestic caribou travel great distances from their calving grounds south of the Alaska Range to their winter turf in the western and northern reaches of the park. Moose, grizzly bears, and wolves also roam this stunning terrain, along with such smaller mammals as fox, weasel, lynx, marten, beaver, and porcupine. Short-eared owls and marsh hawks wing low in search of rodents, while golden eagles patrol higher elevations.

An excellent way to view a portion of Denali is the six- to seven-hour Tundra Wildlife Tour, which follows the park road through breathtaking mountains and valleys. The driver / guide provides a running narration along the way, and stops at favorite photographic locations. For another angle, take a leisurely float trip or a whitewater excursion down the great Nenana River; or saddle up for one of three daily trail rides departing from the stables. "Flightseers" marvel at an aerial view of Mount McKinley.

At the park entrance, Denali National Park Hotel offers 140 guest rooms and a pleasant restaurant. For truly unique accommodations, try a compartment in a Pullman sleeper car. The newest lodging here — McKinley Chalets — overlooks the Nenana River, on Denali's eastern boundary. These chalets sleep up to five people, and a dining room, swimming pool, hot tub, sauna, and exercise room serve the chalet complex.

Hotel rooms, pullman cars, and chalets available late May to mid-September. Rates: hotel, $92 per night for two people; Pullmans, $32 per night for two; chalets, $102 per night. Reservations taken up to one year in advance.

Denali's main entrance is 240 miles north of Anchorage and 120 miles south of Fairbanks, on George Parks Highway. The Alaska Railroad also stops at the park, near the hotel.

For those looking for more rugged accommodations, Camp Denali is a wilderness vacation retreat in the heart of the park, ninety miles from the main entrance, near Wonder Lake. Some guests fish for mackinaw trout in the lake and grayling in local streams, but more often visitors hike, photograph, and just soak up the outstanding scenery. As a special treat, you can pan for gold in the brisk streams.

Camp Denali's eighteen rustic frame or log cabins sleep from two to six people, and have piped-in cold river water, propane lights, propane hot plates, and Yukon stoves. A central shower facility is nearby, as is the log lodge, site of a dining room and evening get-togethers around a warm fireplace.

Camp Denali is open early June to early September.

Rates include lodging, meals, and transportation to and from the park entrance, and range from $150 to $165 per person per day. Cash and checks accepted. Reservations taken up to two years in advance.

GLACIER BAY NATIONAL PARK AND PRESERVE
P.O. Box 1089
JUNEAU, AK 99801
(907) 697-3254

GLACIER BAY LODGE
1500 METROPOLITAN PARK BUILDING
SEATTLE, WA 98101
(800) 426-0600 *(reservations from outside state of Washington)*
(206) 624-8551 *(reservations from Washington)*
(206) 625-9600 *(lodging information)*

When Captain George Vancouver sailed the ice-choked waters of Icy Strait in 1794, Glacier Bay was little more than a dent in the shoreline. Across the head of this then-minor inlet stood a towering wall of ice, which marked the seaward outlet of an immense glacier that plugged the broad basin of what is today Glacier Bay. In many places the ice mantle was more than four thousand feet thick.

John Muir, noted naturalist and explorer, discovered that by the time of his canoe trek into the bay in 1879, the ice front had retreated almost fifty miles, and a tall spruce and hemlock forest had begun to take its place at higher elevations. Tidewaters had invaded the basin and filled the deep, narrow fjords. Nowhere else have glaciers retreated at such a rapid pace.

The fascinating natural history of Glacier Bay's more than three million acres captivates visitors, and thus exploring the glaciers in boats and by plane is a top attraction. Excursion boats depart from the docks of Bartlett Cove and head north into the bay, past icebergs, toward numerous active glaciers. Porpoises and humpback and killer whales surface along the waterways, while harbor seals choose densely packed icebergs at the face of Muir and Johns Hopkins glaciers for pupping grounds. Anglers try for running salmon from mid-July through September, and Dolly Varden and cutthroat trout thrive in the many crystal-clear lakes and streams. Halibut, a saltwater species popular with sport fishermen, inhabit Glacier Bay and Icy Strait.

Glacier Bay National Park is situated in southeastern Alaska; no roads give access to the park. By boat, Glacier Bay is about one hundred miles from Juneau, and air travel from that city takes approximately thirty minutes. Many visitors take advantage of air and cruise packages from Juneau; overnight accommodations are available on larger cruise ships. Other packages provide accommodations at Glacier Bay Lodge, which serves nonpackage guests as well.

The award-winning design of this cedar lodge enhances any stay here. Located on Bartlett Cove, the lodge holds fifty-five guest rooms that sleep up to six people apiece. This twenty-year-old structure has many windows overlooking the fish-filled cove and the spectacular Fairweather Mountain Range. Other amenities include a full-service dining room, a fireplace in the lobby, and a relaxing pub.

Glacier Bay Lodge is open late May to late September. Rates: $91 per night for two people. Cash, checks, Visa, and MasterCard accepted. Reservations recommended four months in advance.

Katmai National Monument
P.O. Box 7
King Salmon, AK 99613
(907) 246-3305

Katmailand, Inc. (Brooks Lodge, Grosvenor Lodge)
455 H Street
Anchorage, AK 99501
(907) 227-4314, 227-5149

Your first foray into four-million-acre Katami National Monument, on the Alaska Peninsula, might be through Lake Naknek, part of a system of rivers, streams, marshes, ponds, and elongated lakes in valleys eroded by glacial ice. Naknek, largest of the lakes, is bordered by mountains that rise three thousand feet above its pumice beaches. The lower slopes of these mountains hold dense stands of spruce and birch, forests that merge with tundra at higher elevations. Alaska brown bear, moose, arctic tern, beaver, and bald eagle all make their homes here, 290 miles southwest of Anchorage. Deep bays, rock shoals, wide beaches, sheer cliffs, narrow fjords, and intricate coves accent the park's hundred-mile coastline, where sea lions, sea otters, and seals frolic.

In June 1912, the violent eruption of Novarupta Volcano quickly transformed the Katmai area. Destroying all living things in its path, a blast of hot wind and gas snapped across slopes of trees, carbonizing them. Within minutes, more than forty square miles of lush, green land were buried under volcanic deposits as much as seven hundred feet deep.

As days passed, Novarupta gradually became dormant. In the Katmai valley, innumerable small holes and cracks developed, permitting gas and steam to escape. When two National Geographic Society explorers reached the area in 1915, they dubbed it the "Valley of Ten Thousand Smokes." Today, only a few active volcanic vents remain, at the head of the valley.

Fishermen flock to this parkland, lured by rainbow and lake trout, grayling, char, and northern pike. Freshwater lakes and streams at Katmai serve as spawning grounds for five salmon species: nearly a million salmon return to the Naknek system each summer.

Brooks Lodge has sixteen cedar-log cabins that sleep from two to four people apiece. Each has hot and cold running water, a bath with shower, heat, and electricity. Although the cabins do not have kitchens, meals are served at the main lodge. After dinner, you can pull up to a blazing fire in the circular fireplace.

Visitors to Brooks Lodge enjoy taking bus trips to the Valley of Ten Thousand Smokes, hiking a vast expanse of countryside, or renting a canoe to ply the rivers and lakes. Brooks River, adjacent to the lodge, holds rainbow and lake trout, grayling, and sockeye (red) salmon, with the rainbow trout running to trophy-size ten- and twelve-pounders. Sight-seeing airplane trips and drop-off camping and fishing flights from the lodge are also available. In July and August at nearby Brooks Falls, running salmon make spectacular leaps upstream to their favorite spawning areas.

Grosvenor Lodge caters to anglers and offers a more secluded setting, on the point separating Lake Grosvenor and Lake Coville. Three cabins here sleep up to six people apiece and have electric lights and heat; a bathhouse is nearby. The lodge features a lounge and a cookhouse that serves family-style meals.

Trout fishing is superb in a short section of river right in front of the lodge, the site of a salmon run from mid-July to mid-August. Boat excursions depart for numerous destinations, including the American River, famous for arctic char and rainbow trout.

Brooks Lodge is open June to mid-September; Grosvenor Lodge, June to early October. Rates: Brooks Lodge, $70 to $90 per night per person (package rates available); Grosvenor Lodge, from $700 for three nights to $1500 for seven nights per person, including meals, lodging, guide and boat service, fishing tackle, and round trip air fare from King Salmon, Alaska. Cash and checks accepted. Reservations taken up to one year in advance, recommended six months to a year in advance. Reservations must be prepaid through the Anchorage office.

Hawaii

STATE PARK INFORMATION:
HAWAII DEPARTMENT OF LAND AND NATURAL
  RESOURCES
DIVISION OF STATE PARKS
P.O. BOX 621
HONOLULU, HI 96809
(808) 548-7455

TOURISM INFORMATION:
HAWAII VISITORS BUREAU
P.O. BOX 8527
HONOLULU, HI 96830
(808) 923-1811

STATE BIRD: *Nene*
STATE MAMMAL: *Humpback Whale*
STATE TREE: *Kukui*
STATE FLOWER: *Hibiscus*

HALEAKALA NATIONAL PARK
P.O. Box 369
MAKAWAO, MAUI, HI 96768
(808) 572-9306

Streaks of red, yellow, gray, and black trace the progress of centuries of lava, ash, and cinder flows at Haleakala Crater, now a cool, cone-studded reminder of a once-tempestuous volcano. The island of Maui began when two volcanoes on the ocean floor erupted time and again, eon after eon, and thin new sheets of lava spread over the old, building and building, until the twin volcano heads emerged from the sea. Lava, windblown ash, and alluvium eventually joined the two with an isthmus, forming Maui, the "valley isle."

In contrast to the stark beauty of Haleakala Crater are the lush greenness and abundant waters in the Kipahulu section of this 28,665-acre park. A sparkling chain of placid pools, large and small, is connected by short cascades and waterfalls. But 'Ohe'o, the stream flowing between the pools, has many moods; at times it becomes a thundering torrent of white water as it churns and plunges toward the ocean. Ginger and ti form an understory in forests of kukui, mango, guava, and bamboo, while beach naupaka, false kamani, and pandanus abound along the rugged coastal cliffs. In higher elevations, a vast native koa and ohia rain forest flourishes, just as it has for thousands of years.

Haleakala's three primitive wilderness cabins rest within the crater, separated from one another by four to six miles of trails. Grassy areas amid stark, desertlike, volcanic terrain typify the scenery around Kapalaoa and Holua cabins, while Paliku cabin sits among lush ferns and forest, thanks to the heavy rainfall on the crater's eastern edge. These wooden, three-room cabins have twelve bunks apiece in their bunk rooms, kitchens with wood stoves, and a limited supply of firewood and water, but no electricity. The cabins can be reached only by hiking four to ten miles of trail.

Several stables offer trail rides and pack trips through Haleakala's intriguing terrain. Swimmers enjoy the many cool ponds along the eastern section of the park.

Haleakala National Park is eighteen miles east of Pukalani, Maui, Hawaii, on Rte. 378. Cabins available year-round. Rates: $5 per night per adult, $3 per night per child, $15 per night minimum. Cash and checks accepted. Reservations determined by monthly lotteries. Two-night maximum stay.

HAWAII VOLCANOES NATIONAL PARK
P.O. Box 52
HAWAII VOLCANOES NATIONAL PARK, HI 96718
(808) 967-7311

VOLCANO HOUSE (ACCOMMODATIONS)
P.O. Box 53
HAWAII VOLCANOES NATIONAL PARK, HI 96718
(808) 967-7321

The islands in the Hawaiian archipelago constitute only the very tops of immense mountains built up from the bottom of the sea during the last 25 million years. By far the largest island in the archipelago, Hawaii is also one of earth's most prodigious volcanic constructions.

One of the park's volcanoes, Kilauea, rises some twenty-two thousand feet above the ocean floor — slightly more than four thousand feet above sea level. Like the rest of Hawaii's volcanoes, it is active, yet remains relatively gentle. Violent outbursts — characterized by tremendous explosions, destructive earthquakes, clouds of poisonous gases, showers of hot mud, and rains of erupted rock — have occurred only twice in recorded Hawaiian history, once in about 1790, the other time in 1924. Both were at Kilauea. In general, Kilauea's eruptions are mild, taking the form of slow-moving lava flows.

Hawaii Volcanoes National Park has more than 120 miles of hiking trails, ranging from the ocean shore to Mauna Loa's 13,677-foot peak. A network of short trails at Kilauea's summit provides numerous day hikes.

The area around park headquarters on Kilauea receives in excess of one hundred inches of rain per year, stimulating tropical forests of ohia trees and tree ferns. Just three miles across the summit caldera, rainfall drops to approximately thirty inches per year, at an area known as Ka'u Desert.

Located at forty-two hundred feet above sea level, near the edge of Kilauea Crater, is the thirty-seven-room Volcano House hotel. Surrounded by a great primitive rain forest, this two-story, wooden hotel was constructed more than forty years ago. A blazing fire in the lobby fireplace burns year-round, and wood-covered walls and oversized furniture help to create a hunting-lodge atmosphere. Lodge visitors discover both a full-service dining room and a cozy lounge.

Engulfed by eucalyptus and koa trees, Na Makani Paio's ten one-room A-frames each sleep up to four people, on a double bed and a pair of bunk beds. Since no electricity is provided, all cooking takes place on outdoor barbecue grills. A nearby bathhouse has restrooms and hot showers.

Hawaii Volcanoes National Park is thirty miles south of Hilo, Hawaii, on the southeastern side of the island. Cabins and lodge open year-round. Rates: cabins, $14 per night; lodge, $37 to $48 per night for two people. Cash, checks, Visa, MasterCard, and American Express accepted. Reservations taken up to one year in advance, recommended six months in advance.

HAPUNA BEACH STATE RECREATION AREA
DIVISION OF STATE PARKS
P.O. Box 936
HILO, HI 96720
(808) 961-7200

Hapuna's six A-frame shelters — each a cross between a cabin and a tent — are actually somewhat inland from the beach, in a savannah of scrubby kiawe trees. These unique accommodations feature wooden lower walls, metal roofs, concrete foundations and floors, and screened mesh upper walls that allow ocean breezes to drift through. Each 168-square-foot A-frame has two built-in wooden sleeping platforms and a picnic table, and they sleep up to four people. A shared A-frame pavilion, with kitchen and dining areas, and bathhouses serve these six unusual structures.

Hapuna Beach stretches across the coastal plain on the

leeward (west) side of the island of Hawaii. The white sand beach, cradled between two small volcanic headlands, is more than a half mile in length and reaches a maximum width of 210 feet in summer. By early fall, however, the beach will have eroded back more than one hundred feet.

The spacious beach provides a base for swimming during calm conditions in summer, and bodysurfing during periods of shore breaks. The vegetation of this seasonally dry area consists of sparse groundcover, such as bunch grasses and herbs, and scattered kiawe trees. Shore anglers dunk and whip for ocean fishes along the coastline.

Hapuna Beach State Recreation Area is two miles south of Kawaihae on Queen Kaahumanu Highway (Rte. 19) on the island of Hawaii. A-frame shelters available year-round. Rates: $7 per night. Cash and checks accepted. Reservations taken one year in advance, recommended one year in advance for summer and holiday weekends. Five-night maximum stay.

KILAUEA STATE RECREATION AREA
DIVISION OF STATE PARKS
P.O. Box 936
HILO, HI 96720
(808) 961-7200

Set in a forest, the lone cabin at Kilauea State Recreation Area offers an opportunity for solitude, and for exploration of Kilauea Volcano at nearby Hawaii Volcanoes National Park. At an elevation of thirty-seven hundred feet above sea level, the forest has a closed canopy of ohia trees and an understory of tree ferns. The cabin and its lawn area represent the only development on this seven-acre park, which is surrounded by scattered houses on country roads.

The two-bedroom, twenty-two-year-old Niaulani cabin is a modern wooden cottage with a garage. Rainwater fills its five-thousand-gallon water tank — its only water source — and patters on its galvanized metal roof. Four twin beds and two sofas sleep a maximum of six people, and the cabin has a bath with shower. The kitchen comes complete with an electric range, refrigerator, and tables and chairs, plus all utensils and pots and pans.

Kilauea State Recreation Area is twenty-nine miles southwest of Hilo, Hawaii, on Kalanikoa Street off Rte. 11 (Mamalahoa Highway). Cabin available year-round. Rates: $14 per night for two people. Cash and checks accepted. Reservations taken up to one year in advance, recommended one year in advance for summer and holiday weekends. Five-night maximum stay.

KOKEE STATE PARK
DIVISION OF STATE PARKS
P.O. Box 1671
LIHUE, KAUAI, HI 96766
(808) 335-5871

KOKEE LODGE
P.O. Box 819
WAIMEA, KAUAI, HI 96796
(808) 335-6061

Kokee State Park, a verdant paradise of luxuriant forests and magnificent views on the northwest corner of the island of Kauai, rests at an elevation of some thirty-six hundred feet, where the air is cool, crisp, and invigorating. Kokee Lodge stands midway between Kauai's two premiere scenic attractions: Waimea Canyon and Kalalau Lookout. Often called the Grand Canyon of the Pacific, Waimea's rich valleys and tropical forests provide a striking contrast with its exposed volcanic-rock walls.

A few miles from the lodge in the other direction waits the majestic Kalalua Lookout — a four-thousand-foot-high prospect on a green-carpeted valley with the shimmering blue Pacific at its mouth. Bounded by razor-edged cliffs laced with waterfalls, the valley was once intensely cultivated.

Within this wilderness park and adjoining forest reserves are some forty-five miles of hiking and hunting trails (the latter for wild boar, black-tailed deer, goat, and various game birds), as well as freshwater streams. Some of the trails lead hikers on pleasant, gentle jaunts to scenic overlooks. Others demand· rugged climbs through the surrounding forest reserve to towering fluted precipices that drop steeply to the ocean. Alakai Swamp Trail traverses thickets of stunted growth and open bogs, concluding at a viewpoint above the beaches of Hanalei. A special feature at Kokee is its jungle fowl — wild chickens, believed to be descendants of birds carried to Hawaii in outrigger canoes by early Polynesian voyagers.

Kokee's dozen wood cabins come equipped with refrigerators, stoves, and firewood for the pleasing fireplaces. They have names like Koa, Olopua, Ohe-Ohe, and Kukui, and range in size from one large room that sleeps three to two-bedroom structures that accommodate up to seven people. The rustic, thirty-year-old lodge houses a restaurant, a cocktail lounge with fireplace and sixteen-foot koa slab bar, and a gift shop.

Kokee State Park is fifteen miles north of Kekaha, Kauai, Hawaii, on Rte. 55. Cabins available year-round. Rates: $25 per night. Cash, Visa, MasterCard, and American Express accepted. Reservations recommended three to four months in advance for July and August weekends. Five-night maximum stay.

MAUNA KEA STATE PARK
DIVISION OF STATE PARKS
P.O. Box 936
HILO, HI 96720
(808) 961-7200

This five-hundred-acre state park separates the volcanic mountains of Mauna Kea and Mauna Loa in the center of the island of Hawaii. At an elevation of some sixty-five hundred feet, the weather here is dry and clear, with cold nights. Small trees and shrubs populate the flat "saddle" area between the volcanic masses — an area that receives only fifteen inches of rainfall annually. The severity of the landscape here lends itself to out-of-the-ordinary activities: hunting for sheep, game birds, and wild pigs on nearby public grounds, and — a wintertime exception to the tropical norm — snow skiing down the summit of Mauna Kea.

Accommodations at Mauna Kea include seven cabins, and a group facility capable of sleeping up to sixty-four people. Each of the cabins, built of wood and ten to twenty years old, features two bedrooms, a bath with shower, and a combination kitchen-living area. An electric heater or fireplace warms the living area, and kitchens come equipped with refrigerators, ranges, and all cooking equipment. The group accommodations consist of two fourplex structures and a large recreation-dining hall.

Mauna Kea State Park is thirty-five miles west of Hilo, Hawaii, on Rte. 200 (Saddle Road). Cabins available year-round. Rates: $14 per night for two people. Cash and checks accepted. Reservations taken up to one year in advance, recommended one year in advance for summer and holiday weekends. Five-night maximum stay.

POLIPOLI SPRING STATE RECREATION AREA
DIVISION OF STATE PARKS
P.O. BOX 1049
WAILUKU, MAUI, HI 96793
(808) 244-4354

The expansive Kula Forest Reserve completely encircles this two-acre park on an upper slope of Haleakala Crater's southwest rift zone. At sixty-two hundred feet above sea level, the park affords sweeping views of central and western Maui and, on clear days, across the channels to the islands of Molokai and Lanai. Polipoli Spring's varied and unpredictable weather ranges from cool, rainy, even frosty nights in winter to dry summers broken by foggy afternoons.

The park has an extensive trail network in the Kula Reserve, including paths through a conifer forest reminiscent of those in the Pacific Northwest. Haleakala Ridge Trail passes through rough cinders, native scrub brush, and grassy swales, and by pines, eucalyptus, and other species of trees. This 1.6-mile trail breaks out of the last stretch of forest onto a ridge crest overlooking the rift valley and pastured slopes below. Some park visitors hunt wild pigs, wild goats, and game birds.

Polipoli's lone cabin, constructed of wood in 1960, features nearly thirteen hundred square feet of floor space, divided among three bedrooms, a bathroom, and a combined living area / kitchen. Kitchen gear includes a gas stove and a gas hot-water heater, but because of the cabin's remote location, it does not have electricity or a refrigerator. Four gas lanterns light this spacious cabin, which sleeps up to ten people.

Polipoli Spring State Recreation Area is east of the Kula Highway on Waipoli Road, off Rte. 377, on Maui, Hawaii. Cabin available year-round. Rates: $14 per night *for two people. Cash and checks accepted. Reservations taken up to one year in advance, recommended six months in advance for summer and holiday weekends. Five-night maximum stay.*

WAIANAPANAPA STATE PARK
DIVISION OF STATE PARKS
P.O. BOX 1049
WAILUKU, MAUI, HI 96793
(808) 244-4354

This remote park's 120-acre volcanic coastline offers a tranquil respite from life's humdrum routine. Situated on a slightly weathered flow of a'a lava (clinker-type lava), Waianapanapa covers gently sloping terrain, rough and broken, with many caves. The surf-pounded shore commands attention because of its natural stone formations, sea stacks, blowholes, and a small bay lined with a black sand beach. Coastal shrubs and herbs, occasionally forming dense thickets, mingle with inland stands of a thick hala (pandanus) forest.

The three-mile Hana-Waianapanapa Coastal Trail begins at Kainalimu Bay, and follows a jagged lava beach, where smooth stepping-stones have been set into rough lava and cinders. Black lava juts into the deep blue ocean, and looking inland, the trail affords a magnificent view of Hana Forest Reserve. A short, paved footpath leads to Waianapanapa Cave — site, according to legend, of a dastardly crime. An irrationally jealous warrior is said to have killed his wife and her maid in this cave, which can only be entered by swimming underwater through a cold freshwater pool. In spring, when shrimp gather in the cave's water, tinting it red, the change is supposed to indicate the casting out of the warrior's evil spirit.

Sunbathers can recline at an unusual beach here, composed of small, smooth, water-rounded pebbles. And while swimming is discouraged because of strong rip currents, anglers fish from the low cliffs at Waianapanapa.

The park's twelve wooden cabins sleep up to six people apiece, and each has a bedroom, bath with shower, kitchen including refrigerator and range, living room, and porch.

These cabins occupy a hala forest not far from the water's edge.

Waianapanapa State Park is fifty-three miles east of Kahului Airport, off Rte. 60 (Hana Highway), on Maui, Hawaii. Cabins available year-round. Rates: $14 per night for two people. Cash and checks accepted. Reservations taken up to one year in advance, recommended six months in advance for summer and holiday weekends. Five-night maximum stay.

Idaho

HEYBURN STATE PARK
ROUTE 1, BOX 139
PLUMMER, ID 83851
(208) 686-1308 (park office)
(208) 686-1380 (lodge)
(208) 245-3288 (cabins)

The Coeur d'Alene Indians lived in northern Idaho's lake country for generations, holding their annual clan gatherings on grassy meadows surrounding Lake Chatcolet. The meadows and lake provided plentiful game and fish for the Indians, as well as the edible camas root. The ridges above, now called Indian Cliffs, served as burial grounds and worship sites.

The Indians are dispersed now, but the area's natural beauty remains to be appreciated. Heyburn State Park comprises fifty-five hundred acres at the southern end of Lake Coeur d'Alene, a long, narrow body of water that once was three separate lakes: Chatcolet, Hidden, and Benewah. Heyburn's hilly terrain includes numerous rock outcroppings and exposed lava formations, and its altitude varies from 2125 feet above sea level to 3400 feet, on top of Schoeffler Butte. Clearly visible from Heyburn, the Saint Joe Mountains rise in the distance to heights of six thousand feet.

Ponderosa pines flourish in thick forests here; some large stands feature four-hundred-year-old trees with four-foot diameters. Douglas-fir, white fir, and western red cedar also thrive, as do flowering shrubs such as syringa, Idaho's state flower. The many wetlands along the lake foster large populations of wood ducks, mallards, and an occasional blue heron. Heyburn also contains the nesting area for the largest colony of osprey in North America.

Docks and launching ramps jut into the lake at several locations, assisting boaters, skiers, and anglers. Fishermen bring back fine catches of bass, trout, kokanee, and assorted panfish, and duck hunting is permitted in season. Rowboats and pontoon boats can be rented.

Heyburn's five rustic cabins sleep from two to four people, on double beds. Set close to the lake at the forest's edge, near a field of wild rice, these small cabins have stoves, iceboxes, and heating. Benewah Resort serves the cabins with three meals daily, and also makes cocktails available.

Rocky Point Lodge and Motel rests on the shores of Lake Coeur d'Alene, near the beach, boat docks, and launching ramp. The fifty-year-old lodge, constructed of logs, houses a dining room, game room, and a small grocery store. Each of its six guest rooms sleeps two people. The eight motel rooms accommodate up to six people apiece.

Heyburn State Park is five miles east of Plummer, Idaho, on Rte. 5. Cabins available from April through mid-October, lodge and motel rooms from April through September. Rates: cabins, $15 to $20 per night, $90 to $120 per week; lodge rooms, $15 per night; motel rooms, $25 to $35 per night. Cash, local checks, MasterCard, and Visa accepted. Reservations taken up to one year in advance, recommended two months in advance for July and August.

Montana

~~~~~

STATE PARK INFORMATION:
MONTANA DEPARTMENT OF FISH, WILDLIFE AND
 PARKS
1420 EAST SIXTH AVENUE
HELENA, MT 59620
(406) 444-2535

TOURISM INFORMATION:
MONTANA TRAVEL PROMOTION BUREAU
DEPARTMENT OF COMMERCE
1424 NINTH AVENUE
HELENA, MT 59620
(800) 548-3390 (out-of-state calls)
(406) 444-2654 (all other calls)

STATE BIRD: *Western Meadowlark*
STATE TREE: *Ponderosa Pine*
STATE FLOWER: *Bitterroot*
STATE FISH: *Black Spotted Cutthroat Trout*

Prince of Wales Hotel, Glacier National Park, Montana

GLACIER NATIONAL PARK
WEST GLACIER, MT 59936
(406) 888-5441

GLACIER PARK, INC. (LODGES)
   (SUMMER ADDRESS)
EAST GLACIER PARK, MT
   59434
(406) 226-5551

   (WINTER ADDRESS)
GREYHOUND TOWER
STATION 5185
PHOENIX, AZ 85077
(602) 248-6000

BELTON CHALETS, INC.
SOUTHSIDE U.S. 2, EAST
P.O. BOX 188
WEST GLACIER, MT 59936
(406) 888-5511

Lofty mountain ranges, sculptured valleys, ice-cold lakes that mirror summits and sky, wild flowers and wildlife flourishing in alpine meadows, prairie grasslands — these exquisite elements constitute Glacier National Park and adjoining Waterton Lakes National Park in Canada. Though divided by an international boundary, these parks share a common geologic heritage. Glaciers carved Upper Waterton Valley, and the Rocky Mountains connect these two nations with peaks reaching ten thousand feet.

Glacier, one of the largest parks in the continental United States at 1.4 million acres, features awesome mountaintops, brilliant lakes, and thundering waterfalls. More than 750 miles of hiking and bridle trails meander this alpine paradise, the home of fifty glaciers. The towering mountains that bisect both parks capture rainfall on their western slopes, generating a Pacific-like climate. These warm, moist conditions produce dense forests of larch, spruce, fir, and lodgepole pine.

Fishing is an excellent way to enjoy Glacier's many lakes and streams, where pike, whitefish, and rainbow, eastern brook, and cutthroat trout congregrate. These swiftly running streams are very cold, even in summer. Boat cruises tour Waterton Lake, Swiftcurrent Lake, Saint Mary Lake, and Lake McDonald, and rowboats, fishing boats, and canoes can be rented. Guided horseback trail rides commence from several park locations; some overnight trips are offered.

Hikers here are aided by unique pack animals — llamas. These gentle, surefooted creatures have proven themselves in the South American Andes, and will carry your gear while you hike the lush, forested canyons, timberline ridgetops, and glaciers. Though most trails are passable at lower elevations by mid-June, many high-country passes may not be free of snow until late July.

Glacier Park, Inc. operates a number of lodges sprinkled throughout this stunning acreage. Glacier Park Lodge, built more than a half century ago, holds 154 guest rooms. Sixty immense timbers, probably five hundred to eight hundred years old when cut, were used in the construction of this imposing edifice. Huge, Douglas-fir beams support the lobby, while cedar forms the verandas.

Many Glacier Hotel, a jewel constructed in 1914 on the shore of Swiftcurrent Lake, has more than two hundred rooms and Swiss-style decor. Perhaps the most intriguing lodging here is the magnificent three-story, gabled Prince of Wales Hotel in the Canadian section of the park. Its high lobby windows look out on a chain of lakes that stretches to the horizon.

On Glacier's west side, Lake McDonald Lodge offers

101 rooms in the atmosphere of the Old West. Built in 1913 as a private mountain retreat, its rustic lobby sports the heads of mountain goat, elk, moose, and sheep. Other Glacier Park, Inc. accommodations include motels and one- and two-bedroom cabins.

Glacier Park, Inc. lodging is available from early June through early September. Rates: $20 to $53 per night for two people. Cash, checks, Visa, and MasterCard accepted. Reservations recommended at least five months in advance.

Belton Chalets, Inc. presents two additional lodging options at Glacier National Park: Sperry Chalet and Granite Park Chalet. These native-stone structures offer alpine serenity, meals, and lodging for those willing to hike or ride horseback in.

The chalets are available from July 1 through Labor Day. Rates: $45 per night per person (includes three meals). Cash and checks accepted.

Nebraska

STATE PARK INFORMATION:
NEBRASKA GAME AND PARKS COMMISSION
2200 NORTH THIRTY-THIRD STREET
P.O. BOX 30370
LINCOLN, NE 68503
(402) 464-0641

TOURISM INFORMATION:
TRAVEL AND TOURISM DIVISION
NEBRASKA DEPARTMENT OF ECONOMIC
  DEVELOPMENT
P.O. BOX 94666
LINCOLN, NE 68509
(800) 742-7595 (in-state calls)
(800) 228-4307 (out-of-state calls)

STATE BIRD: *Western Meadowlark*
STATE MAMMAL: *White-tailed Deer*
STATE TREE: *Cottonwood*
STATE FLOWER: *Goldenrod*

This park bears the name (almost) of a French-Canadian fur trader, Louis B. Chartran, who befriended the Brule Sioux and built a trading post here in the winter of 1841–42. Chartran operated the post until the mid-1840s, then took a squaw as his wife and spent his last years traveling with the nomadic tribe.

Chadron State Park occupies 801 acres of Nebraska's Pine Ridge, an arch-shaped escarpment one hundred miles long and twenty miles wide. Intermingling prairie and stands of ponderosa pine, this rugged country features jagged ridges, towering buttes, and countless small streams. Surrounded by U.S. Forest Service acreage, this north-western Nebraska park approaches elevations of five thousand feet, which means cool evenings can follow hot summer days.

Chadron's sixteen wood cabins perch on a hilltop flanked by pines; its six brick cabins stand in a nearby meadow. All cabins have two bedrooms, baths, kitchens, heating, fans, and outdoor barbecue grills and picnic tables. Three feature fireplaces, and the rough wooden cabins show off varnished knotty-pine interiors and screened porches.

Exploring Chadron's trails, either on foot or on horseback, careful observers may spot wild turkey, deer, bobcat, raccoon, porcupine, or coyote. Predators here include turkey vultures, red-tailed and marsh hawks, and golden eagles. Swimmers take advantage of a large pool, while boating and fishing for rainbow and brown trout take place in the lagoon.

At the Trading Post, visitors appreciate demonstrations of black powder muzzle-loading, tomahawk throwing, and archery. Three miles east of Chadron is the Museum of the Fur Trade, which depicts the lives and history of traders, trappers, and Indians. South Dakota's Black Hills are seventy-five miles north of the park, and Mount Rushmore is one hundred miles away.

Chadron State Park is eight miles south of Chadron, Nebraska, on Rte. 385. Cabins available Memorial Day to Labor Day and specified hunting seasons. Rates: $22 to

$26 per night. Cash, in-state checks, Visa, and MasterCard accepted. Reservations taken starting in January; minimum reservation, two nights. Cabins rented for one night if not reserved.

FORT ROBINSON STATE PARK
P.O. Box 392
CRAWFORD, NE 69339
(308) 665-2660

Crazy Horse, Walter Reed, Chief Red Cloud, Arthur McArthur, Dull Knife, General Crook, Doc Middleton — these are just a few of the colorful characters who helped make Fort Robinson the historic "outpost on the plains." Established as an Indian Agency fort in the 1870s, Fort Robinson survived the subsequent Indian wars and remained active through World War II. Having earned its place in the history books as the site of the epic Cheyenne outbreak, of the last great gathering of the Sioux nation, and even of a prisoner of war camp, Fort Robinson today encompasses twenty-two thousand austere acres of the Pine Ridge. It's the showplace of the Nebraska park system.

To explore this spectacular countryside, saddle a horse, or hitch a ride on the stagecoach — a replica of the old Sidney-Deadwood Stage — or in an open-air Jeep. Smiley Canyon Scenic Drive rises through one of Nebraska's most stunning canyons to a breathtaking overlook, passing herds of buffalo, longhorn, wild horses, elk, and bighorn sheep. After your tour, you can slow the pace by fishing White River or Soldier Creek for brown and brook trout, or try the numerous ponds for bass, bluegill, and bullheads. In the heat of the day, a swim in the large pool refreshes; visitors unwind at night at the Chuckwagon Cookout, featuring buffalo stew and western entertainment.

Fort Robinson's historic lodging includes adobe-and-brick officers' quarters, built between 1874 and 1909, which now serve as cabins for overnight guests. Robinson's lodge is a 1909-vintage enlisted men's barracks, which now houses twenty-three guest rooms with private baths. Some of these accommodations are air-conditioned, all have heat, and the lodge also has a cafeteria-style restaurant.

Wandering the fort complex, you pass an 1884 wheelwright's shop and a harness repair shop built in 1904. The Sioux warrior Crazy Horse was mortally wounded in the guardhouse, built in 1874; he died later in the adjutant's office.

Fort Robinson State Park is three miles west of Crawford, Nebraska, on Rte. 20. Cabins and lodge open Memorial Day to Labor Day, and in turkey, deer, and antelope seasons. Rates: cabins, $26 per night; lodge rooms, $16 to $18 per night. Cash, in-state checks, Visa, and MasterCard accepted. Reservations taken starting in January; three-night minimum rental for cabins.

NIOBRARA STATE PARK
Box 226
NIOBRARA, NE 68760
(402) 857-3373

Niobrara State Park hugs the confluence of the Niobrara and Missouri rivers, in northeastern Nebraska. Located in flat bottomlands, this park has more than four hundred recreational acres, including a lagoon and a fishing pond.

Niobrara's fifteen thirty-year-old cabins are sprinkled over its territory; some are right on the water. Each of these modern one- or two-bedroom cabins has a full kitchen, a bath with shower, and air conditioning.

Western-style trail rides take place each morning and afternoon, led by a qualified wrangler. In summer, lifeguards watch over Niobrara's swimming pool. Paddleboats splash through the lagoon's peaceful waters, while anglers fish for bass, crappie, catfish, and bluegill. Playground equipment is also available. Those less ambitious can loll in the shade or soak up some sun. A dining hall can be rented for daytime group gatherings; it handles up to ninety people.

Niobrara State Park is one mile west of Niobrara, Nebraska, on Rte. 12. Cabins available late May to early September. Rates: $20 to $26 per night. Cash, checks, and Visa accepted. Reservations taken starting in January for a minimum of two nights. Cabins rented for one night if not reserved.

Tepee, Platte River State Park, Nebraska

PLATTE RIVER STATE PARK
RR, Box 161A
LOUISVILLE, NE 68037
(402) 234-2217

Platte River State Park in eastern Nebraska offers an incredibly varied selection of overnight accommodations: everything from Indian tepees to modern cabins. The eight wooden cabins contain one, two, or four bedrooms and are scattered throughout this four-hundred-acre park. Each has a full kitchen and a bath with shower, and some feature screened porches and stone fireplaces.

A new concept for Nebraska parks, Platte River's camper cabins have no indoor plumbing or cooking facilities. Instead, a central shower, restroom, and dishwashing building serves each "pod" of four or five units. Each camper cabin comes with four to six beds, electrical outlets, an indoor table and chairs, and an outdoor picnic table and fire grate.

An even more adventurous prospect awaits those who rent one of Platte River's wooden-floored tepees, which are arranged village-style. Each tepee accommodates up to six people and has a picnic table, fire grate, and pit toilet.

Once ensconced at Platte River, visitors discover activities ranging from swimming in a large pool and guided horseback riding to hiking, paddleboat rentals on Jenny Newman Lake, and bicycle rentals. If you'd like to take a shot with a bow and arrow, stop by the park's archery range.

For thousands of years, the land of the Platte belonged solely to nomadic Indians, including at various times the Plains Apache, Paducah, Sioux, Pawnee, Omaha, Missouri, and Oto. The Spanish probably were the first white explorers in the area, coming north from Santa Fe in 1662. The French brothers Pierre and Paul Mallet arrived here during their explorations in 1739.

An eighty-five-foot-high observation tower allows the Platte River valley to unfold before you, creating a breathtaking panorama. Down on the river, fisherman wet a line for the catfish and carp that lurk in deep holes. After a day of outdoor activity, you can join the Buffalo Stew Hoedown for fine stew and cornbread, followed by campfire entertainment.

Platte River State Park is three miles southwest of Louisville, Nebraska, on Rte. 13. Lodging available late May through October. Rates: cabins, $20 to $30 per night; camper cabins, $8 to $12 per night; tepees, $6 per night. Cash, in-state checks, Visa, and MasterCard accepted. Reservations taken starting in January for a minimum of two nights. Lodging rented for one night if not reserved.

PONCA STATE PARK
P.O. Box 486
PONCA, NE 68770
(402) 755-2284

Many a sun has set since 1804, when Meriwether Lewis and William Clark led their band of explorers on an epic journey up the Missouri River. Nonetheless, the mighty river that was their highway continues to churn its way along Nebraska's eastern border, edged at Ponca State Park by picturesque bluffs.

The bluffs form the western boundary of a vast eastern hardwood forest that adjoins the river. A diverse understory of vegetation follows the river: each spring, delicate wild flowers, such as Dutchman's breeches, wood violets, and phlox, bloom first; mayapple and red and orange columbines bloom shortly thereafter; and finally a leafy canopy of oaks and basswoods fills in above. The wooded terrain comes alive with songbirds; the whistle of bob-whites and the tapping of woodpeckers greet each sunrise, and whippoorwills sound off near dusk. Hundreds of thousands of snow and blue geese migrate here annually. In winter, bald and golden eagles circle overhead.

Ponca's fourteen two-bedroom cabins nestle under tall trees not far from the Missouri River. Each has two double beds, a bath with shower, and a kitchenette. These modern cabins, built in the 1960s, feature screened porches, air conditioning, and outdoor picnic tables and barbecue grills.

A refreshing dip in the large pool or a horseback ride will entertain any visitor. Anglers test their abilities on channel catfish and other catches in the "Mighty Mo."

Ponca State Park is two miles north of Ponca, Nebraska, off Rte. 12. Cabins available late May to early September. Rates: $26 per night. Cash, in-state checks, Visa, and MasterCard accepted. Reservations taken starting in January for a minimum of two nights. Cabins rented for one night if not reserved.

VICTORIA SPRINGS STATE RECREATION AREA
BOX 117, NORTHEAST STAR ROUTE
ANSELMO, NE 68813
(308) 749-2235

Established as a public recreation area in 1925, Victoria Springs, named for the mineral springs here in central Nebraska, has been described as an oasis in the Sand Hills. Custer County Judge Charles R. Matthews arrived here from Virginia in the early 1870s, and he received the first post office charter in the area, which he named New Helena.

Around the turn of the century, commercial interest in the springs accelerated: a newspaper article referred to the "peculiarity that each spring is heavily charged with a different medicinal property." A health resort company was formed, which erected a bathhouse, lunch stands, and bridges across the spring waters. A bottling works cranked out five hundred bottles per day of mineral water, ginger ale, pop, champagne, and cider.

In addition to the springs, this seventy-acre state park contains a stretch of Victoria Creek and a calm, six-acre lake. Fishing is popular in both places; the creek offers trout, northern pike, bass, and carp, while the lake has bluegill, bass, and catfish. Paddleboats can be rented, and canoes, rafts, and other nonmotorized craft are permitted.

Shaded by tall trees, Victoria Springs's two forty-year-old cabins have wood exteriors and knotty-pine interiors, and sleep up to six people apiece in two bedrooms. Set one hundred yards apart on the west side of the park, these cabins have full kitchens, heating and air conditioning, screened porches, picnic tables, barbecue grills, and lake views.

Victoria Springs State Recreation Area is seven miles east of Anselmo, Nebraska, on Rte. 21A. Cabins available Memorial Day to Labor Day. Rates: $26 per night. Cash, in-state checks, Visa, and MasterCard accepted. Reservations taken starting in January for a minimum of two nights. Cabins rented for one night if not reserved.

Oregon

STATE PARK INFORMATION:
OREGON STATE PARKS AND RECREATION DIVISION
525 TRADE STREET, SE
SALEM, OR 97310
(503) 378-6305

TOURISM INFORMATION:
TOURISM DIVISION
OREGON ECONOMIC DEVELOPMENT DEPARTMENT
595 COTTAGE STREET, NE
SALEM, OR 97310
(800) 547-7842 (out-of-state calls)
(503) 373-1200 (all other calls)

STATE BIRD: *Western Meadowlark*
STATE MAMMAL: *American Beaver*
STATE TREE: *Douglas-fir*
STATE FLOWER: *Oregon Grape*
STATE FISH: *Chinook Salmon*

CRATER LAKE NATIONAL PARK
CRATER LAKE, OR 97604
(503) 594-2211 (park office)
(503) 594-2511 (cabin and lodge reservations)

Rolling mountains, volcanic peaks, and evergreen forests form the backdrop for an enormous lake high in the Cascade Range of southwest Oregon — a lake recognized worldwide as a scenic wonder. Crater Lake fills the depression of an ancient volcano, Mount Mazama. On sunny days, neither words nor photographs can depict the water's remarkable blueness. Much of the year, a thick shroud of snow encircles Crater Lake, creating a winter wonderland that is enhanced by the crystal-clear air.

About sixty-eight hundred years ago, Mazama erupted, emptying its magma chamber; the volcano eventually collapsed, leaving a huge, bowl-shaped caldera. For the past thousand years, snow and rain have slowly filled the basin. As the lake deepened and widened, evaporation and seepage came into balance with precipitation: today Crater Lake's depth varies less than three feet per year. America's deepest lake, at 1932 feet, has reached equilibrium.

No streams run into or out of Crater Lake; it is a closed ecological system. The lack of streams kept the lake free of fish until the nineteenth century, when several species were stocked here. Three remain today: rainbow and brown trout, and kokanee salmon. Fish feed primarily at the surface, since the pure water is nearly devoid of food.

At higher elevations in Crater Lake National Park, snowpack precludes fires and insulates the roots of mountain hemlocks, which grow to massive dimensions despite the short growing season. Lodgepole pines pioneer the mountain flanks, while ponderosa pines prosper at lower elevations.

Bus and boat tours offer different Crater Lake vantage points: while boats glide by Wizard Island and a free-standing formation known as Phantom Ship, busses travel 360 degrees around the lake on Rim Drive. Trails ascend prominent peaks, and Cleetwood Trail drops to the water's edge.

At Rim Village, the four-story Crater Lake Lodge blends with the stunning terrain. This seventy-year-old lodge has seventy-eight guest rooms, many with lake views, and a stone-walled dining room with rough exposed beams. Two types of one-room cabins also shelter overnight guests — Ponderosa Cottages and Sleeping Cottages. Ponderosa Cottages, twenty years old, have hot and cold running water, electric lights, baths with showers, and electric heat. Crater Lake's forty-year-old Sleeping Cottages have electric heat, and some have private toilets. Neither type includes kitchen facilities.

Crater Lake National Park is eighty miles northeast of Medford, Oregon, on Rte. 62. Lodge open mid-June to mid-September, cottages available May through October. Rates: lodge, $27 to $73 per night; cottages, $21 to $57 per night for two people. Cash and checks accepted. Reservations taken up to one year in advance, recommended one to two months in advance for August.

OREGON CAVES NATIONAL MONUMENT 19000 CAVES HIGHWAY CAVE JUNCTION, OR 97523 (503) 592-3400	OREGON CAVES CHATEAU (LODGING) P.O. BOX 128 CAVE JUNCTION, OR 97523 (503) 592-3400

One fall day in 1874, Elijah Davidson's deer hunting was interrupted when his dog, Bruno, chased a bear into a dark, mossy-green hole high on a slope of the Siskiyou Mountains in southwest Oregon. Davidson followed the bear and dog into the mountainside. Drawn by Bruno's howls, Davidson struck a sulfur match and crept through the gray and cream-colored marble corridors, thereby discovering Oregon Caves.

During the 1890s, developers "opened" the cave, but this mountainous area near the California border was too remote to offer much commercial return. In 1909, prompted by publicity given the cave by Joaquin Miller — the "poet of the Sierra" — President Taft proclaimed it and 480 acres of Siskiyou National Forest as Oregon Caves National Monument.

Virgin woods and mountain trails surround the cave, which straddles a natural transition zone between two types of forest. At elevations below four thousand feet grows a mix of broadleaf trees and conifers. Tall Douglas-firs and scattered pines tower above tan oak, prickly-leaved canyon live oak, and orange-barked Pacific madrone, among others.

An all-conifer forest takes over above four thousand feet. Here one can admire Douglas-firs with trunks three to six feet thick, and graceful stands of white fir and incense cedar. Mosses and alumroot flourish around cave openings and on damp cliffs and rocks along the trails.

Hiking from the cave entrance toward Oregon Caves Chateau, you pass two tumbling waterfalls and may catch a glimpse of black-tailed deer. Constructed in 1934, the chateau has twenty-five guest rooms in a handsome rough-wood building that rises six stories, set against green woods and moss-covered marble ledges. Nearly every window in the chateau — in guest rooms, in the dining room, in the huge lobby with its double fireplace — features a view of the falls and pristine canyon. Just up the hill are fourteen duplex sleeping cabins, each equipped with a private bath but no kitchen facilities.

Oregon Caves National Monument is twenty miles east of Cave Junction, Oregon, on Rte. 46. Cabins and chateau open mid-June to Labor Day. Rates: cabins, $34 per night for two people; Chateau, $38 to $43 per night for two people. Cash and checks accepted. Reservations taken up to nine months in advance.

FRENCHGLEN HOTEL
FRENCHGLEN, OR 97736
(503) 493-2565

The town of Frenchglen, Oregon (population: approximately ten), appears about as it did when Frenchglen Hotel opened in 1924. In fact, the entire town, set in southeastern Oregon's high desert country, consists of the hotel, a store, and a schoolhouse. A one-time stopping place for cowboys working cattle drives, the hotel now serves as the gateway to Malheur National Wildlife Refuge and the Steens Mountains.

Frenchglen Hotel rests on a one-acre state wayside, embellished by juniper trees, sagebrush uplands, freshwater marshes, willow-bordered streams, greasewood flats, and basalt rimrock. Mule deer, antelope, beaver, coyotes, mountain lions, and bobcats flourish in this wide-open country; the Malheur Refuge also hosts migratory birds traveling the Pacific Flyway. The Jackass Mountains loom directly behind the hotel, while the Steens rise in the distance farther south. Visitors discover many lakes and creeks in the area, along with Donner und Blitzen River, a proposed Oregon Scenic Waterway. Hunting, fishing (particularly for trout), and swimming are popular pastimes nearby, but no facilities exist at the hotel.

What this white, frame, two-story hotel does provide is a charming base for discovering the countryside. Inside a screened porch, a sitting area greets weary travelers with overstuffed couches and chairs. In the dining room, be prepared for family-style meals served on large tables. Upstairs, eight guest rooms (some of whose furniture dates back to the hotel's construction) share a bath.

Typical Frenchglen guests include fishermen, hunters, photographers, and bird-watchers, all here to soak up the scenery and bask in the history of cattle country. Frenchglen bears the names of two giants of those cattle ranch days: John William "Peter" French, who owned a spread near the hotel, and Dr. Hugh James Glenn, French's financial backer.

Frenchglen Hotel is fifty-nine miles south of Burns, Oregon, on Rte. 205. Hotel open March through November. Rates: $33 to $39 per night for two people. Cash accepted. Reservations recommended one to two months in advance.

WOLF CREEK TAVERN
P.O. Box 97
WOLF CREEK, OR 97497
(503) 866-2474

Wolf Creek Tavern, an imposing relic from the stage-coach era, sprang up in southwest Oregon along the California Stage Company's Portland-to-Sacramento line in the 1860s. A well-known example of nineteenth-century

Wolf Creek Tavern, Oregon

Classical Revival architecture, this two-story structure typifies stagecoach inns and hostelries associated with early roads and trails in Oregon.

Originally an L-shaped building, the inn has a central stairs and hallway that divide the ladies' parlor from the men's sitting room, or "tap room." The tap-room fireplace still bears boot marks where men propped up their feet, warming them near the fire.

A number of notables have enjoyed the tavern's hospitality over the years, among them President Rutherford B. Hayes, who traveled through Oregon in the 1880s; author Sinclair Lewis; and movie stars Mary Pickford and Clark Gable.

Today, the ladies' parlor and men's sitting room have been restored to their original configurations and furnished with appropriate antiques and reproductions. Wolf Creek's restoration reflects various periods of its history; some guest chambers contain pieces from the early 1900s, while others have been decorated as they were in the 1870s.

In the eight guest rooms, some of which feature massive wooden headboards, kerosene lamps, marble-topped washstands, and magnificent wood floors, such modern amenities as heating, air conditioning, and private baths are welcome additions. Innkeepers Vernon and Donna Wiard serve satisfying food and drink in these historic surroundings. Nearby attractions include the breathtaking fury of the Rogue River, as seen from Hellgate viewpoint or boat cruises.

Wolf Creek Tavern is twenty miles north of Grants Pass, Oregon, off I-5. Tavern open year-round. Rates: $26 to $34 per night for two people. Cash, Visa, and Master-Card accepted. Reservations preferred, but not mandatory.

South Dakota

~~~~

STATE PARK INFORMATION:
SOUTH DAKOTA GAME, FISH AND PARKS
    DEPARTMENT
PARKS AND RECREATION DIVISION
445 EAST CAPITOL AVENUE
PIERRE, SD 57501
(800) 952-2217 (in-state calls)
(800) 843-1930 (out-of-state calls)
(605) 773-3391

TOURISM INFORMATION:
SOUTH DAKOTA DIVISION OF TOURISM
CAPITOL LAKE PLAZA
BOX 6000
PIERRE, SD 57501
(800) 952-2217 (in-state calls)
(800) 843-1930 (out-of-state calls)
(605) 773-3301

STATE BIRD: *Ring-necked Pheasant*
STATE MAMMAL: *Coyote*
STATE TREE: *Black Hills Spruce*
STATE FLOWER: *Pasqueflower*

BADLANDS NATIONAL PARK
Box 6
INTERIOR, SD 57750
(605) 433-5361 (park office)
(605) 433-5460 (Cedar Pass Lodge)

The Badlands is a southwestern South Dakota wonderland of bizarre, colorful spires and pinnacles, massive buttes, and deep gorges. The natural forces — wind, rain and frost — that carved these sharp ridges, steep-walled canyons, pyramids, and gullies not only created a unique topography; they have given a strange beauty to an almost desolate landscape. Tributaries of the White River erode soft, sedimentary layers of sandstone. Beneath the capping sandstone, a deposit of clay may suddenly fall away, leaving a shallow cave, or a bank may slump into a gulley below. Few landmarks remain unchanged here.

This barren terrain supports little life, yet some plants and animals have adapted. Swifts and cliff swallows nest on ledge faces, while rock wrens build in crevasses. Golden eagles can occasionally be spotted on high buttes. On gentle slopes, junipers patch the canyon with green; birds and other small animals seek shelter in islands of cottonwood and wild rose.

No doubt the most dramatic wildlife here is the North American bison, commonly known as buffalo. In the early 1800s, travelers to the Dakotas encountered huge herds of bison, which darkened large sections of prairie. In fact, one herd of 1839 measured thirty miles by forty-five miles, an area slightly larger than the state of Rhode Island. During their westward expansion, American settlers almost exterminated the bison, and converted much of the prairie into cropland. The once-plentiful bison, cornerstone of the elaborate and advanced culture of the Plains Indians, numbered fewer than one thousand by 1889. Today, Badlands National Park maintains a herd of some three hundred bison at Sage Creek Wilderness Area.

Cedar Pass Lodge, operated by the Oglala Sioux tribe, has nineteen one- and two-bedroom cabins. These fifty-year-old structures feature tan stucco exteriors and knotty-pine interiors, and they sleep up to eight people apiece.

Elm and cedar trees break the prairie near the two rows of cabins, and an expansive butte serves as their backdrop. These sleeping cabins have private baths, heating, and air conditioning, but no kitchens.

A Native American theme dominates the main lodge building, which is within walking distance of the cabins. Its gift shop sells Sioux handicrafts, including beadwork, pottery, and moccasins, along with a selection of items in Black Hills gold. One favorite dish at the Cedar Pass dining room is Indian tacos, made from buffalo meat. Trail rides into the Badlands countryside originate at the lodge.

Badlands National Park is nine miles south of Wall, South Dakota, on Rte. 240. Lodge open May to mid-October. Rates: $27 to $37 per night for two people. Cash, checks, Visa, MasterCard, and American Express accepted. Reservations recommended one month in advance.

ANGOSTURA STATE
  RECREATION AREA
STAR ROUTE, BOX 131A
HOT SPRINGS, SD 57747
(605) 745-6996

LONG'S RESORT
STAR ROUTE, BOX 139
HOT SPRINGS, SD 57747
(605) 745-4713

An Indian legend tells of a fierce battle here in southwestern South Dakota between the Lakota and Cheyenne tribes, long before white men came to the region. The tribes fought to control the warm-water springs, which they regarded as health-restoring.

Prehistoric man, fearing the Black Hills because of religious superstition, preferred to live near, but not in, that awesome range. The Cheyenne River valley offered village sites for many generations of these paleo-Indians. The south fork of the Cheyenne flows around the southern edge of the Black Hills, a short distance to the southeast of the mineral springs. Smithsonian Institute archaeologists have carbon-dated Indian artifacts from this area at more than ten thousand years of age.

The Teton Lakota controlled this region for a comparatively short time before the arrival of whites, who came first to explore new land, then to collect furs and buffalo hides, and later for gold. The new settlers took a long time to recognize the value of the lush grassland for grazing cattle.

The immigrants were quick, however, to realize the healthful benefits of the many warm-water, mineral-laden springs here. This gift of nature was a dependable phenomenon. Unfortunately, the flow of the Cheyenne River was not; it swung erratically from flood to drought several times a season. This condition was corrected by an earth-and-concrete dam in 1940.

Today, most of the prehistoric sites have been covered by the clear waters of the Angostura Reservoir, a five-thousand-acre lake that is popular for waterskiing, boating, sailing, and fishing. Scenic drives, campgrounds, picnic areas, hiking trails, and beaches ring the spacious reservoir. Moreover, it's just a few minutes' drive from Wind Cave National Park, Mount Rushmore National Memorial, and Custer State Park.

Overnight guests take advantage of a four-unit motel at Long's Resort. These modern rooms feature two double beds and baths with showers, but no cooking facilities. Just a stone's throw from a marina, launching ramps, and rental boats, this motel was built in the early 1970s.

Angostura State Recreation Area is ten miles southeast of Hot Springs, South Dakota, off Rte. 385. Motel open May through September. Rates: $25 per night. Cash accepted. Reservations taken up to one year in advance, recommended one month in advance.

CUSTER STATE PARK
STAR ROUTE 3, Box 70
CUSTER, SD 57730
(605) 255-4515

LEGION LAKE RESORT
STAR ROUTE 3, Box 67
CUSTER, SD 57730
(605) 255-4521

SYLVAN LAKE RESORT
Box 1000
HILL CITY, SD 57745
(605) 574-2561

BLUE BELL LODGE
STAR ROUTE 3, Box 63
CUSTER, SD 57730
(605) 255-4531

STATE GAME LODGE
STAR ROUTE 3, Box 74
CUSTER, SD 57730
(605) 255-4541

Set in the isolated Black Hills of southwestern South Dakota, Custer State Park occupies seventy-three thousand acres of one of the oldest mountain chains on earth. Elevations here range from thirty-seven hundred feet at French Creek to sixty-eight hundred feet at Cathedral Spires. These heights contribute to Custer's cool summer nights, while the Chinook winds moderate (by South Dakota standards) the winter temperatures.

Four man-made lakes and three major streams guarantee diverse recreational opportunities, including fishing, boating, and swimming. Vegetation is highlighted by ever-present ponderosa pine and, at higher elevations, white spruce. Oak, aspen, and birch also occur in substantial numbers.

Custer's northwest section intrigues visitors with its massive granite outcroppings, severe topography, and diversified forests. Bison flourish here, along with elk, mountain goats, bighorn sheep, and mule deer. Rainbow, brook, and brown trout thrive in cool streams, and each December the park hosts a buffalo hunt.

Four distinct lodging options exist at Custer State Park, each of which is under separate management. Sylvan Lake Resort encompasses log and rough wood cabins, and a forty-five-year-old lodge perched above brilliant Sylvan Lake. The resort's thirty-four cabins sleep from two to ten people. All are equipped with refrigerators and hot plates, and some have fireplaces.

In addition to twenty-one guest rooms, Sylvan Lodge —

known for its ponderosa-pine walls, natural cedar floors, and marble fireplaces — has a spacious dining lounge and a comfortable lobby with overstuffed leather furniture. A flagstone terrace faces the lake and Harney Peak, the highest point east of the Rocky Mountains.

Open mid-May to late September, Sylvan Lake Resort cabins rent for $35 to $80 per night; lodge rooms, $30 to $45 per night. Cash, Visa, MasterCard, and American Express accepted.

Rimmed by mountains that are blanketed with pine, and adjacent to Grace Coolidge Creek, State Game Lodge — the summer White House of presidents Coolidge (1927) and Eisenhower (1953) — offers forty-seven guest rooms. Listed on the National Register of Historic Places, this sixty-year-old lodge was built of native stone and wood siding. Specialties on the dining-room menu include buffalo steaks, South Dakota pheasant, and Black Hills rainbow trout. State Game Lodge's twenty-one log and frame cabins sleep up to eight people apiece in as many as three bedrooms. Horseback rides and Jeep tours depart from this facility.

Open May through September, State Game Lodge rooms rent for $32 to $50 per night; cabins range from $32 to $90 per night. Cash and checks accepted.

Legion Lake Resort's twenty-five cabins line a hilltop within walking distance of Legion Lake, a nine-acre impoundment that boasts fine fishing and swimming. This resort serves three meals daily in Legion Lake Lodge, which also houses a small grocery store. The forty-year-old cabins sleep from four to eight people in one or two bedrooms; each comes with an outdoor picnic table and fire grate.

Open mid-May through September, the cabins rent for $25 to $40 per night.

A mature stand of ponderosa pines shades Blue Bell Lodge and its seventeen log and frame cabins, near French Creek — a favorite fishing spot for rainbow and brown trout. The lodge contains a dining room decorated with antique tools and animal heads, and a cheerful lounge. Blue Bell's cabins, ten to fifty years old, sleep from four to eight people apiece in one to four rooms. All have completely equipped kitchens, and one has a fireplace.

Open May through September, Blue Bell's cabins rent for $38 to $60 per night. Cash, checks, Visa, and Master-Card accepted.

ROY LAKE STATE PARK
RR 2, Box 51
LAKE CITY, SD 57247
(605) 448-5701 (park office)
(605) 448-5498 (cabin reservations)

Once the home of prehistoric Indians, this five-hundred-acre park in northeastern South Dakota presents excellent fishing and spectacular scenery. Undulating prairie hills circle the wooded shoreline of the fifteen-hundred-acre Roy Lake — one of a chain of glacial lakes and ponds that provide a habitat for abundant white-tailed deer and an occasional antelope. Giant Canada geese flock to a nearby game refuge, along with a variety of ducks. White pelicans pass overhead, and great blue herons, egrets, and other wading birds fish the shallows. A stealthy canoeist may even come across a muskrat or beaver.

While the master angler entices largemouth bass, walleye, northern pike, and panfish from the lake, the rest of your group can take advantage of a swimming beach. Boat-launching ramps and rental boats are also available.

Roy Lake's eight vacation cabins, built in 1968, feature wood frame construction and knotty interiors. With one or two bedrooms, they each accommodate from three to six people. Six of the eight have gas heat and showers, and all come with ranges and refrigerators. Ash, elm, and oak trees shade the cabins' outdoor picnic tables and barbecue grills, on a peninsula along the park's western edge.

Roy Lake State Park is two miles southwest of Lake City, South Dakota, off Rte. 10. Cabins available April through October. Rates: $17 to $23 per night for two people, $102 to $138 per week for two people. Cash and checks accepted. Reservations taken starting in January, recommended three to four months in advance for summer.

Washington

STATE PARK INFORMATION:
WASHINGTON STATE PARKS AND RECREATION
  COMMISSION
7150 CLEANWATER LANE, KY-11
OLYMPIA, WA 98504
(206) 753-2027

TOURISM INFORMATION:
WASHINGTON STATE DEPARTMENT OF COMMERCE
  AND ECONOMIC DEVELOPMENT
TRAVEL DEVELOPMENT DIVISION
101 GENERAL ADMINISTRATION BUILDING
OLYMPIA, WA 98504
(800) 562-4570 (in-state calls)
(800) 541-9274 (out-of-state calls)

STATE BIRD: *Willow Goldfinch*
STATE TREE: *Western Hemlock*
STATE FLOWER: *Coast Rhododendron*
STATE FISH: *Steelhead Trout*

MOUNT RAINIER NATIONAL PARK
STAR ROUTE
ASHFORD, WA 98304
(206) 569-2211

MOUNT RAINIER GUEST SERVICES (PARADISE INN,
    NATIONAL PARK INN)
STAR ROUTE
ASHFORD, WA 98304
(206) 569-2275

From a distance of more than one hundred miles, its glacier-clad summit can be seen looming on the western Washington horizon. When finally the lower peaks fall behind and the great mountain comes into full view, the grandeur of Mount Rainier, eight thousand feet higher than anything nearby, speaks eloquently to all who witness it.

At 14,410 feet, Rainier reaches into the upper atmosphere and disturbs great tides of moist maritime air as they flow eastward from the Pacific. The encounter creates spectacular cloud halos and produces prodigious amounts of snow. Paradise Park, at a fifty-four-hundred-foot elevation on the mountain's south slope, typically receives enough snow to bury the three-story Paradise Inn right up to its rooftop.

Mount Rainier's classic old-growth forest of Douglas-fir, red cedar, and western hemlock soars more than two hundred feet above mossy, fern-draped valley floors. As springtime chases winter up the mountainside, wild flowers and greening meadows replace melting snow. As the open, subalpine landscape sheds its expanse of pure white, thousands of visitors roam the meadow trails, taking pictures, exploring, and hiking to the edge of the snow-field. Deer and mountain goats may be seen in the distance, while furry marmots whistle, watch, and pose beside burrows and between rocks.

Each year, more than twenty-five hundred people take on the challenge of climbing Mount Rainier's summit, a two-day excursion up glacial ice to the breathtaking peak. Rainier Mountaineering guides (206/569-2227) lead mountain-climbing trips, and teach snow- and ice-climbing seminars.

Melting snow charges the rushing streams, rivers, and lakes throughout the park, all of which tempt fishermen to try their luck. Mount Rainier also hosts one of nature's anomalies: ice caves, huge caverns whose walls and roofs of solid ice were carved by rivers flowing beneath glaciers. In winter, cross-country skiers roam the stunning countryside, invigorated by crisp mountain air.

Overlooking Rainier's south slope, Paradise Inn has 127 guest rooms and a superior view of the mountain and Nisqually Glacier. The inn, built of Alaskan cedar, is distinguished by wooden-beam construction, a lobby with two enormous stone fireplaces and parquet floors, and a grand dining room. Constructed in 1916, this classic structure features western decor and handcrafted Indian rugs. Guest rooms, which sleep up to five people, either have private baths or share a community facility.

Set in a serene forest, the sixteen-room National Park Inn offers solitude and isolation, particularly during winter months. Equipped with a cafeteria-style restaurant, the inn has some rooms with private baths.

Mount Rainier National Park is sixty-eight miles southeast of Tacoma, Washington, on Rtes. 169 and 706. Paradise Inn open June to early October; National Park Inn, year-round. Rates: $24 to $42 per night for two people. Cash, checks, Visa, and MasterCard accepted. Reservations recommended at least one month in advance.

NORTH CASCADES NATIONAL PARK COMPLEX
800 STATE STREET
SEDRO WOOLLEY, WA 98284
(206) 855-1331

DIABLO LAKE RESORT
ROCKPORT, WA 98283
Call (206) operator — ask for Newhalem 5578

ROSS LAKE RESORT
ROCKPORT, WA 98283
(206) 397-7735 *(via Everett, Washington, operator)*

NORTH CASCADES LODGE
P.O. Box W
CHELAN, WA 98816
(509) 682-4711

The segment of the Cascade range encompassed by North Cascades National Park Complex has an array of alpine scenery unmatched in the conterminous forty-eight states: deep glaciated canyons, more than three hundred glaciers, hundreds of jagged peaks, and countless mountain lakes and streams. This magnificent park conserves 1053 square miles of the Cascades in northern Washington, along the Canadian border.

Rumbling sounds frequently interrupt the subalpine stillness, as icefalls crash to the valley floor from glaciers precariously perched on steep slopes. At Cascade Pass, flower-sprinkled hillsides and meadows enhance splendid views of the Cascade and Stehekin valleys. Here, you observe rock ridges, snowfields, and cascading waterfalls against a backdrop of deep blue sky.

Fishing at two sizable lakes — Ross Lake and Lake Chelan — and at many smaller lakes and streams results in catches of rainbow, eastern brook, cutthroat, and Dolly Varden trout. Hikers and horseback riders follow 345 miles of trails throughout this vast wilderness. In winter, bald eagles fish the Skagit River for salmon.

Diablo Lake Resort's nineteen cabins have from one to three bedrooms and feature electric heat, kitchens, and baths with showers. Small boats can be rented at the resort, and meals, a snack bar, and groceries are available.

Diablo Lake Resort is open year-round. Rates: $40 per night for two people. Cash, Visa, MasterCard, and American Express accepted.

Ross Lake stretches some twenty-five miles into British Columbia, and native wild trout teem in its deep, cold waters. As a base to use while fishing this magnificent lake, you can rent a cabin at unique Ross Lake Resort, one mile from Ross Dam. The cabins, office, marina, and other structures here all float on log rafts along the steep shoreline.

The modern cabins have large picture windows framing snow-capped Colonial Peak, plus cooking stoves, refrigerators, baths with showers, wood-burning fireplaces, and hot running water. These cabins sleep up to five people apiece. The modern bunkhouses, which accommodate up to ten guests, are similarly equipped. Ross Lake's rustic cabins feature wood-burning stoves for cooking and heating, refrigerators, running water, and shared community baths.

Guests at Ross Lake tie up their rental boats right outside their cabins, ready for fishing and exploring. The resort is not accessible by automobile; it can be reached by a combination of boat and truck rides.

Ross Lake Resort is open mid-June through October. Rates: $18 to $40 per night. Cash accepted. Reservations taken up to one year in advance.

North Cascades Lodge consists of twenty-six guest rooms and three cabins, plus a cozy lounge and restaurant. The twenty-year-old cabins sleep up to six people in four rooms and have complete kitchens. In addition to a view of mountain peaks and Lake Chelan, the wooden lodge has a hot tub, and rents out mopeds, bicycles, fishing boats, and canoes. The lodge complex, in Stehekin, Washington, can only be reached by float plane from Chelan, Washington, or by the large excursion vessel *Lady of the Lake.*

North Cascades Lodge is open year-round. Rates: cabins, $58 per night; lodge, $36 to $72 per night for two people. Cash, checks, Visa, and MasterCard accepted. Reservations recommended one month in advance.

OLYMPIC NATIONAL PARK
600 EAST PARK AVENUE
PORT ANGELES, WA 98362
(206) 452-4501

LAKE CRESCENT LODGE
NATIONAL PARK
  CONCESSIONS, INC.
STAR ROUTE 1, BOX 11
PORT ANGELES, WA 98362
(206) 928-3211

LOG CABIN RESORT
6540 EAST BEACH ROAD
PORT ANGELES, WA 98362
(206) 928-3325

SOL DUC HOT SPRINGS
  RESORT
P.O. BOX 1355
PORT ANGELES, WA 98362
(206) 327-3583

KALALOCH LODGE
STAR ROUTE 1, BOX 1100
KALALOCH, WA 98331
(206) 962-2271

Olympic National Park is a gift of the sea. Clouds borne on moist sea winds, rain and snow wrung from clouds by the heights, and glaciers and rivers returning seaward mold this spectacular park's Pacific shoreline and nurture its rain forests. Comprising more than fourteen hundred square miles on the Olympic Peninsula (between Seattle and the Pacific Ocean), the park is a wild expanse of forest-clad and glacier-studded mountains above, and coniferous forests, lakes and streams, and a rocky fifty-mile seacoast below.

Olympic's strip of Pacific coastline remains one of the most primitive in the lower forty-eight states. The encroaching sea has created a fractured landscape of shoreline needles and offshore rocks and islands, all of which are favorite resting spots for harbor seals, river otters, and shorebirds. Migrating gray whales pass by each spring and fall.

Inland, the Roosevelt elks, once hunted nearly into extinction, now group together in small bands, moving to the high country during warm weather. Even higher in the mountains are nimble goats, bobcats, and cougars, but they are rarely observed by park visitors. More frequently spotted are black-tailed deer, bear, raccoon, and skunk, as well as 140 species of birds. Anglers pull salmon and steelhead trout from Olympic's waterways.

The west side of the Olympic Peninsula has the wettest winter climate in the continental United States, with annual precipitation exceeding 140 inches in some areas. An extraordinary rain forest has developed in these western valleys. Sitka spruce and western fir dominate the environment, although Douglas-fir and western red cedar are also present. Some of these magnificent trees reach heights of nearly three hundred feet.

Set against the backdrop of snow-capped Storm King Mountain on the shores of Lake Crescent, the native-fir-and-cedar Lake Crescent Lodge has six guest rooms, a dining room, and a sun porch facing the lake. Other accommodations in the lodge complex include one- and two-bedroom sleeping cottages, some of which have fireplaces, and a modern motel. All are near the brilliant blue, six-hundred-foot-deep lake, where rowboats can be rented.

Lake Crescent Lodge is twenty miles west of Port Angeles, Washington, on Rte. 101. Accommodations available late May to late September. Rates: $35 to $60 per night for two people. Cash, checks, Visa, and MasterCard accepted. Reservations taken up to a year in advance, recommended one to two months in advance.

Also along Lake Crescent is Log Cabin Resort, where cabins — some of which have kitchenettes — A-frame chalets, and motel rooms can be rented. Each chalet has a wet bar, a bed downstairs, and a second double bed up in the loft. The resort's fine restaurant overlooks the lake, and a marina with a launching ramp and rental boats adjoins the lodging.

Log Cabin Resort is eighteen miles west of Port Angeles, Washington, off Rte. 101. Lodging available year-round. Rates: $35 to $55 per night for two people. Cash, checks, Visa, and MasterCard accepted. Reservations recommended two to three months in advance.

In a lush valley adjacent to the Sol Duc River, where 150-foot trees are dwarfed by 4000-foot ridges, is Sol Duc Hot Springs Resort. Just three miles from the majestic Sol Duc Falls, one of Olympic's largest waterfalls, this resort originally catered to those visiting the local hot springs. Today, visitors soak in three man-made pools that capture the mineral spring water. A variety of motel, cabin, and cottage units can be rented at this resort; Sol Duc also has a dining room and lounge in a renovated sixty-year-old wooden lodge.

Sol Duc Hot Springs Resort is forty miles west of Port Angeles, Washington, south of Rte. 101. Lodging available late May through September. Rates: $32 to $47 per night for two people. Cash, checks, Visa, and MasterCard accepted. Reservations recommended two to six months in advance.

Kalaloch Lodge rests on a bluff overlooking the Pacific Ocean, at the mouth of Kalaloch Creek. Between five miles of beachfront and a background of forest, the lodge holds a dining room and eight guest rooms, four of which have ocean views. Other accommodations at Kalaloch include twenty-one log cabins, which sleep four and have baths with showers, wood-burning stoves, and kitchenettes; and fourteen modern cabins, most containing kitchenettes and some fireplaces. Set among wind-bent trees at the far end of the resort is Sea Crest House, a two-story motel. Four of its ten units feature fireplaces, and all have private baths and ocean views.

Kalaloch Lodge is thirty miles south of Forks, Washington, on Rte. 101. Accommodations available year-round. Rates: $32 to $78 per night for two people. Cash, checks, Visa, and MasterCard accepted. Reservations recommended six to eight weeks in advance. Two-night minimum stay on weekends.

Vacation House, Fort Worden State Park, Washington

FORT WORDEN STATE PARK
PORT TOWNSEND, WA 98368
(206) 385-4730

Toward the end of the nineteenth century, sail-powered, wooden men-of-war gave way to steam-powered battleships with iron hulls and powerful cannons. The United States, fearing attack by an armada of such vessels, constructed coastal forts at the entrance of every major harbor. Fort Worden, along with Fort Casey and Fort Flagler, formed the first line of defense for Puget Sound's cities and an important naval shipyard at Bremerton. No attack ever occurred here; no shot was ever fired at an adversary. The giant cannons of Fort Worden became obsolete with the advent of more sophisticated weapons, and the army abandoned its 338-acre installation on the Olympic Peninsula in 1953.

Today, Fort Worden State Park (listed on the National Register of Historic Places) offers high bluffs overlooking sandy beaches along the Straits de Juan de Fuca and Admiralty Inlet; hillsides wooded with western cedar, grand fir, willow, Douglas-fir, and hemlock; and lodging in Victorian houses once used as officers' quarters. Built at the turn of the century, these twenty-three two- and three-story houses have from two to six bedrooms. Most have been completely restored and furnished with period reproductions. Their high pressed-tin ceilings, slate roofs, and handsome woodwork exemplify the craftsmanship of the era. Renting one of these houses, each of which has a completely equipped kitchen, is reminiscent of house-sitting at a friend's beach home. Most of these grand old structures have fireplaces and spacious porches, and all are heated.

In addition to enjoying the beaches at Fort Worden, visitors can explore the tunnels and walkways of the old gun emplacements, and imagine the exquisite schooners that once passed by on their way to Puget Sound. Shore fishing brings catches of salmon, flounder, perch, and other bottom fish. Sailing enthusiasts appreciate Admiralty Inlet's brisk winds, and launching ramps are available.

After dinner, you can play tennis or walk along the beach to the lighthouse at Point Wilson, long a beacon for voyagers at sea. Seals and sea otters sometimes frolic near the wharf, and on rare occasions, killer whales can be spotted offshore.

Fort Worden State Park is two miles north of Port Townsend, Washington, off Rte. 20. Houses available year-round. Rates: $45 to $146 per night. Cash and checks accepted. Reservations taken starting in November for the following year.

Wyoming

State Park Information:
Wyoming Recreation Commission
Herschler Building
Cheyenne, WY 82002
(307) 777-7695

Tourism Information:
Wyoming Travel Commission
I-25 at Etchepare Circle
Cheyenne, WY 82002
(307) 777-7777

State Bird: *Western Meadowlark*
State Tree: *Cottonwood*
State Flower: *Indian Paintbrush*

GRAND TETON NATIONAL
  PARK
MOOSE, WY 83012
(307) 543-2851, 733-2880

GRAND TETON LODGE
  COMPANY
P.O. Box 250
MORAN, WY 83013
(307) 543-2811, 543-2855

SIGNAL MOUNTAIN LODGE
P.O. Box 50
MORAN, WY 83013
(307) 543-2831

TRIANGLE X RANCH
MOOSE, WY 83012
(307) 733-2183

The Grand Tetons, among the noblest creations in the American West, are a congregation of blue-gray peaks that soar more than a mile above the sagebrush flats and morainal lakes of Jackson Hole. Grand Teton itself, towering seven thousand feet above the valley floor and often veiled in clouds, clearly shows glacial sculpturing from the last ice age.

Until 1800, Indians held undisputed sway over the landscape dominated by the Tetons, often crossing its passes into the basins on hunting expeditions. Fur trappers, both British and American, frequented the area until the mid-1840s, but the second half of the nineteenth century passed with the terrain virtually deserted. In 1929, the Teton Range and the placid lakes at the mouths of its deep canyons were protected by the establishment of Grand Teton National Park.

Eternal snows and unceasing winds at the summits, water lilies and shimmering sagebrush in lowlands — the seasons at Grand Teton reflect both elevation and the calendar. Seasonal changes bring the parkland warmth and life, winter and stillness in their turn.

Wild flowers, migrating birds, and elk lure visitors in spring, despite frequent rains and cool temperatures. July and August days are warm (occasionally hot), perfect for hiking, climbing, boating and fishing on the numerous lakes, and horseback riding. Floating down the Snake River, a splendid way to view wildlife and scenery, is also popular, and commercial river-guide services are available throughout the region. Fishermen thrill at cutthroat, mackinaw, and German brown trout in the park's clear, cold lakes and streams, while nonanglers enjoy boat tours of Jenny and Jackson lakes in summer.

Grand Teton Lodge Company offers lodging at three sites: Jackson Lake Lodge, Jenny Lake Lodge, and Colter Bay Village. Jackson Lake Lodge, opened in 1955, features a sixty-foot picture window that looks out on the lake, and huge lobby fireplaces. In addition to a dining room, lounge, and heated swimming pool, the lodge holds 42 guest rooms. There are 343 additional rooms in wooden buildings on either side of the original structure.

Open from June through mid-September, Jackson Lake rooms range from $62 to $92 per night for two people.

Pines, firs, and aspens line a narrow road that trails past Jenny and Spring lakes and Jenny Lake Lodge, at the base of the Tetons. Originally a dude ranch built in the 1920s, the lodge houses an award-winning restaurant, and has thirty associated log cabins. These rough wood cabins sleep up to four people apiece. Five two-room suites feature fireplaces, but none of the accommodations are equipped with kitchens.

Open from June through early September, Jenny Lake Lodge charges $215 per day for two people, which includes a cabin, two meals daily, and bicycling and horseback riding.

Near the shores of Jackson Lake, Colter Bay's 209 log cabins stand amid lodgepole pines and aspens. Most of these rustic units were moved here from other locations around the valley; some came from local ranches, others were used by early trappers. The cabins each sleep up to six people and have baths with showers, but do not include kitchen facilities. They do offer views of Jackson Lake and Mount Moran, and are close to Colter Bay Marina, the site of rental boats and lake excursions.

Open from late May through September, Colter Bay cabins range from $21 to $54 per night for two people. Cash, checks, Visa, MasterCard, and American Express accepted for all Grand Teton Lodge Company accommodations. Reservations taken starting in November for the following year, recommended six to eight months in advance.

The elevation at Signal Mountain Lodge is sixty-seven hundred feet, providing daytime temperatures in summer that seldom exceed eighty-five degrees. The lodge incorporates a dining room and a cocktail lounge. Accommodations here — lakefront apartments, motel-type units, log cabins, and even houseboats — all afford spectacular mountain vistas.

Available year-round, these facilities rent for $38 to $102 per night. Cash, checks, Visa, MasterCard, and American Express accepted. Reservations recommended two to four months in advance for summer.

Horseback riding, river float trips, pack trips, fishing, hiking, cookouts — all await at Triangle X Ranch. A working dude ranch, Triangle X has one-, two-, and three-bedroom log cabins with private baths.

Rates are $410 to $575 per person per week for a party of two, which includes a cabin, all meals, and horseback riding. Cash and checks accepted. Open May through mid-November and January through mid-April, Triangle X Ranch takes reservations up to a year in advance, and recommends them several months in advance.

YELLOWSTONE NATIONAL PARK
YELLOWSTONE NATIONAL PARK, WY 82190
(307) 344-7381
TW SERVICES, INC. (CABINS AND LODGES)
YELLOWSTONE NATIONAL PARK, WY 82190
(307) 344-7311

Yellowstone: America's park. In 1872, Congress set aside two million magnificent acres of northwest Wyoming, creating the world's first national park. At Yellowstone National Park, the contrasting elements of fire and water have combined to produce a land of natural wonders. It is a land born in the fires of thundering volcanoes, and sculpted by glacial ice and rushing water into a fascinating landscape.

Thousands of hot springs dot the thermal basins; gigantic columns of boiling water leap hundreds of feet into the air, causing the ground to shake; hissing steam vents punctuate valley floors; and the stumps of redwood trees, buried by volcanic ash and petrified in an upright position, stand out starkly on eroded mountainsides.

Old Faithful Inn, Yellowstone National Park, Wyoming

Glaciers have reworked the land's surface, smoothing canyons and leaving myriad sparkling blue ponds and lakes. Even today, mountain streams still carve beautiful canyons and leap over resistant rock ledges in brilliant cascades and waterfalls.

Elk grace many a meadow at dawn, and coyotes hunt mice along deserted roadsides. Moose can be seen at most any time or place, especially in the wetlands; bison tend to congregate at higher elevations. Trout fishermen share their streams with grizzly bears, otters, and ospreys.

The Grand Canyon of Yellowstone leaves many breathless. You can look down at the deceptively tiny river below, at wisps of steam and pastel canyon walls; or stand on the lip of Lower Falls, and watch the bottle-green Yellowstone River break into frothy white jets as it drops more than three hundred feet into a canyon. Bus and boat tours, stagecoach outings, horseback rides, and guided fishing trips all help visitors eager to explore the splendor of Yellowstone, as do more than a thousand miles of hiking trails. Fishing boats can be rented at Bay Bridge Marina on vast Yellowstone Lake, which covers 136 square miles.

TW Services, Inc. offers diverse accommodations at nine separate lodging locations in Yellowstone (a park larger than Rhode Island and Delaware combined). These range from the imposing, 325-room Old Faithful Inn to rustic log cabins that contain wood-burning stoves and share community baths. Roosevelt Lodge and its associated cabins provide comfortable overnight stays amid rolling hills covered with fir, pine, aspen, and sage, and small lakes and streams that satisfy anglers. The inspiring, three-story Lake Yellowstone Hotel (painted yellow and trimmed in white) and contemporary Grant Village reward their guests with splendid views of the lake. Mammoth Hot Springs Hotel and its cabins adjoin one of Yellowstone's most unusual attractions, Mammoth Hot Springs, where more than 700,000 gallons of water and two tons of limestone cascade down stone terraces each day. In all, TW Services, Inc. has more than two thousand rooms and cabins dispersed throughout this popular park.

Yellowstone accommodations available May through October; some also open during winter months. Rates: lodge rooms, $28 to $52 per night for two people; cabins, $13 to $51 per night. Cash, checks, Visa, MasterCard, and American Express accepted. Reservations for summer recommended.

The SOUTHWEST

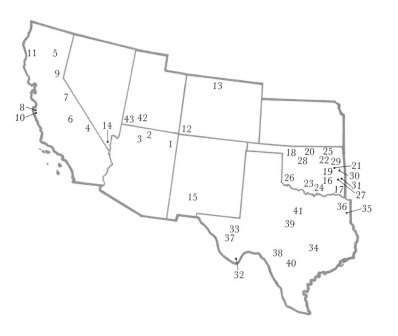

Arizona

STATE PARK INFORMATION:
ARIZONA STATE PARKS
1688 WEST ADAMS STREET, ROOM 106
PHOENIX, AZ 85007
(602) 255-4174

TOURISM INFORMATION:
ARIZONA OFFICE OF TOURISM
1480 EAST BETHANY HOME ROAD
PHOENIX, AZ 85014
(602) 255-3618

STATE BIRD: *Cactus Wren*
STATE TREE: *Paloverde*
STATE FLOWER: *Saguaro Blossom*

CANYON DE CHELLY
    NATIONAL MONUMENT
Box 588
CHINLE, AZ 86503
(602) 674-5436

JUSTIN'S THUNDERBIRD
    LODGE
P.O. Box 548
CHINLE, AZ 86503
(602) 674-5443, 674-5265

The awesome Canyon de Chelly and Canyon del Muerto sheltered prehistoric Pueblo Indians for a thousand years and served as an ancestral stronghold of the Navajos. Ruins of the ancient Indian dwellings nestle between towering cliffs and perch on high ledges, while present-day Navajos live along the canyon floors.

One of the most spectacular views in this northeast Arizona park is of Spider Rock, a spire of sandstone that rises eight hundred feet above the canyon, which can best be seen from a thousand-foot-high overlook. The most widely known cliff dwelling is called White House, after a long wall on this ruin's upper section that is covered with white plaster. Mummy Cave Ruin, in Canyon del Muerto, includes a splendid three-story tower house.

Rio de Chelly commences along the Chuska Mountains, near the Arizona–New Mexico border, and winds tortuously until it empties into Chinle Wash, just west of the monument. Until its last few miles, the river and its tributaries are hemmed in by vertical-walled cliffs of up to a thousand feet high, whose reddish hue shifts hourly.

Except for the trail to White House, visitors must employ a Navajo guide to tour the ruins and the canyon floor. Another way to see the countryside is by special sight-seeing trucks that depart from Thunderbird Lodge.

The lodge dates back to 1896, when Sam Day established an Indian trading post at this location. Rock and adobe guest rooms were added in the early 1920s. Today, twenty-two modern motel rooms supplement the twelve rooms in the lodge. All feature air conditioning, color TVs, and baths with showers; the lodge is highlighted by exposed beam ceilings. Thunderbird also houses a dining room, decorated with Indian sand paintings, and an arts-and-crafts shop loaded with authentic Navajo rugs and jewelry created by Hopi, Zuni, and Navajo craftspeople.

Canyon de Chelly National Monument is just east of

Chinle, Arizona, off Rte. 7. Lodge open year-round. Rates: $36 to $44 per night for two people. Cash, Visa, and MasterCard accepted. Reservations taken up to six months in advance.

GLEN CANYON NATIONAL RECREATION AREA
P.O. Box 1507
PAGE, AZ 86040
(602) 645-2471

DEL E. WEBB RECREATIONAL PROPERTIES, INC. (LODGING)
Box 29040
PHOENIX, AZ 85038
(800) 528-6154 *(out-of-state calls)*
(602) 278-8888 *(in-state calls)*

Wedged into a deep sandstone gorge on the Colorado River, Glen Canyon Dam backs up Lake Powell for more than 180 miles in northern Arizona and southern Utah. Where once the Colorado rushed seaward, gouging soft, sedimentary rock, broad lake waters now mirror deep blue skies. Boaters savor the sparkling lake, which twists and branches along the ancient contours of Glen Canyon between high cliffs of red sandstone, lapping at buttes and gentle sands, surrounded by vast acres of desert, rock formations, and scrub pine.

Before Glen Canyon Dam, the Colorado River ran cold and muddy; now it's cold and clear. Stocked rainbow trout thrive in Lake Powell, often reaching trophy size. Largemouth and striped bass and crappie also cruise these pristine waters, to the delight of fishing enthusiasts. Water-skiers glide through the snaking canyons, awed by each new bend and vista. Swimmers throng to sandy beaches along two thousand miles of lake shoreline; the water is a welcome relief from intense summer sun. Glen Canyon National Recreation Area, known as the "Grand Canyon with water" and encompassing more than 1 million acres, lies in the greatest concentration of national parks and national monuments in the United States: Zion, Bryce Canyon, and Grand Canyon national parks are all within 150 miles.

Del E. Webb Properties operates four marinas and

lodging facilities on Lake Powell. Wahweap Lodge, which overlooks Wahweap Bay near Page, Arizona, and Glen Canyon Dam, offers the lake's most complete resort, including 272 guest rooms, a glass-walled dining room, a lounge, and a coffee shop. Just two miles from the lodge sits the twenty-four-unit Lake Powell Motel.

Boat cruises commencing at Wahweap Marina explore turquoise waters rimmed with fire-red rocks, sheer canyon walls, ancient Indian ruins, and a premier attraction: Rainbow Bridge National Monument. This is the largest natural bridge on earth, the one Navajos call "Nonnoshoshi" or "rainbow turned to stone." Navajo influence is not surprising here, since more than 134 miles of Lake Powell's shore serve as the northern boundary of America's largest Indian reservation, the home of 140,000 Navajo.

Also available at Wahweap Marina are rental fishing boats and ski boats. For extended voyages, houseboats can be rented, ranging in length from thirty-six to fifty feet and holding berths for four to ten people.

Bullfrog and Hall's Crossing resorts and marinas, in Utah near the midpoint of the lake, and Hite Resort and Marina, further north in Utah on upper Lake Powell, provide overnight accommodations in modern house trailers, completely equipped marinas, and rental houseboats, fishing boats, and ski boats. Bullfrog Resort also offers motel accommodations.

Del E. Webb Recreational Properties also runs float and wilderness river trips down the Colorado, starting below Glen Canyon Dam. Ranging from one to twelve days, these river-running excursions slip by colorful cliffs that rise, palisade by palisade, to forested rims thousands of feet above. The river alternates turbulent rapids with stretches of calm, so that no two days are ever alike.

Del E. Webb lodging available year-round. Rates: $37 to $55 per night. Cash, checks, Visa, and American Express accepted. Reservations recommended six months to a year in advance.

GRAND CANYON NATIONAL PARK
GRAND CANYON, AZ 86023
(602) 638-7888

TW SERVICES, INC. (NORTH RIM LODGING)
P.O. Box 400
CEDAR CITY, UT 84720
(801) 586-7686

GRAND CANYON NATIONAL PARK LODGES (SOUTH RIM
  LODGING)
P.O. Box 699
GRAND CANYON, AZ 86023
(602) 638-2401

The Grand Canyon, an awesome natural spectacle, results from a colossal conflict between two powerful forces: mountain building and gravity. Though this portion of the earth's crust has been thrust upward eight thousand feet above sea level, water (in the form of the mighty Colorado River) has eroded the would-be mountains, creating multihued cliffs and a mile-deep canyon. Distinct layers of rock exposed by the river's flow record a view of geologic history that stretches back two billion years.

Northern Arizona's Grand Canyon National Park encompasses 1.2 million acres. The Colorado undulates some 280 miles through the park, dropping twenty-two hundred feet along that length and creating seventy rapids to challenge river-runners. Pastoral meadows and forests of ponderosa pine and aspen stand in contrast to the sheer chasm, abraded and polished rock, plunging waterfalls, and rushing water. The canyon's magnitude and range of altitudes result in unusual climatic variations; a storm can rage at one location while sunshine drenches other areas. Mule trips enter the canyon from both the North and South rims, and a variety of concessioners offer oar-powered and motor-powered Colorado River excursions.

TW Services, Inc. offers 173 duplex and fourplex log cabins and a forty-room motel on the North Rim. These sleeping cabins (no kitchens) date from the 1930s. The modern motel features frame construction and "ranch oak" furnishings. Meals are served at Grand Canyon Lodge, which was built of stone quarried on location and timbers from nearby Kaibab Forest. The lodge, cabins, and motel rest right on the North Rim, giving spectacular views and access to trails leading down into the canyon.

TW lodging available late May to mid-October. Rates: $38 to $52 per night. Cash, checks, Visa, MasterCard, and American Express accepted. Reservations recommended in November or December for the following season.

Grand Canyon National Park Lodges comprise 850 guest rooms in nine distinctive structures along the South Rim. When the railroad first reached the Grand Canyon, a first-class hotel was constructed of native boulders and Oregon pine. This three-story, ninety-five-room lodge — El Tovar — accommodates weary travelers as it has since 1905. In addition to the nine lodges, the South Rim hosts fifty cabins, which are nestled in pinyon pine and junipers. Some of these sleeping cabins date from the 1890s. Four of the cabins at Bright Angel are equipped with fireplaces. Horseback, airplane, helicopter, and bus tours of Grand Canyon are all available at the South Rim.

Grand Canyon National Park Lodges available year-round. Rates: cabins, $30 to $50 per night for two people; lodges, $45 to $95 per night for two people. Cash, checks, Visa, MasterCard, and American Express accepted. Reservations taken up to two years in advance, recommended two to three months in advance for April through October.

California

STATE PARK INFORMATION:
CALIFORNIA DEPARTMENT OF PARKS AND
  RECREATION
P.O. BOX 2390
SACRAMENTO, CA 95811
(916) 445-6477

TOURISM INFORMATION:
CALIFORNIA DEPARTMENT OF ECONOMIC AND
  BUSINESS DEVELOPMENT
OFFICE OF TOURISM
1121 L STREET, SUITE 103
SACRAMENTO, CA 95814
(916) 322-1396

STATE BIRD: *California Valley Quail*
STATE MAMMAL: *Grizzly Bear*
STATE TREE: *California Redwood*
STATE FLOWER: *Golden Poppy*
STATE FISH: *California Golden Trout*

DEATH VALLEY NATIONAL
    MONUMENT
DEATH VALLEY, CA 92328
(619) 786-2331

FURNACE CREEK INN AND
    RANCH RESORT
P.O. BOX 1
DEATH VALLEY, CA 92328
(800) 528-6367
(619) 786-2345

Death Valley. It is a land of stark contrast. Here in this valley, much of it below sea level, and in its surrounding mountains, you find spectacular wild-flower displays, snow-covered peaks, beautiful sand dunes, abandoned mines, and the hottest spot on the North American continent. On any given day, the valley floor shimmers silently in the heat. The air is clear — so much so that distances are telescoped — and the sky, except for a wisp of a cloud, is a rich blue. Known for *very* hot summers (the record high for the month of July is 134 degrees!), the region receives little precipitation — rain rarely gets past the guardian mountains.

Yet many forms of plant and animal life have adapted to the harsh climate, including a dozen species of birds and twenty-two flowering plants that exist nowhere else on earth. And five distinct species of fish inhabit the salt-water creeks, as they have for eons. One other intriguing attraction here — Scotty's Castle — was built in the 1920s in a remote canyon, and served as a vacation retreat for a wealthy midwesterner.

Mining and prospecting once enticed adventurers and fortune-seekers to the area, and the valley became a source of borax. During the mining heydays, the famed twenty-mule teams braved the barren environment and intense heat to pull wagon loads of borax to the railroad, some 160 miles away.

Furnace Creek offers a true oasis for visitors to the three-hundred-square-mile Death Valley National Monument, and is especially popular during cooler winter months. Furnace Creek Ranch, initially established in the 1800s to house men working on borax wagons, provided a place for them to relax after their grueling twenty-day round trip to Mojave. More than two hundred guest rooms are available at the casual ranch, along with twenty-five redwood sleeping cabins. The cabins and ranch rooms feature air conditioning and private baths, and sleep up to four people. You can saddle up for a trail ride at the ranch stable, shop in an old-fashioned general store, or tour the nearby Borax Museum. A large swimming pool draws a crowd on hot days, while the resort's eighteen-hole course challenges golfers.

Furnace Creek Inn, built of Spanish adobe, overlooks a spring-fed swimming pool, pristine valley, and lush green gardens. Initial construction of the sixty-nine-room inn began in 1926 and continued for nearly a decade. Several fine restaurants serve both the inn and ranch, as do a half-dozen lighted tennis courts. Bicycle rentals and various air and bus tours offer transportation for exploring Death Valley National Monument.

Furnace Creek Inn and Ranch Resort is 140 miles northwest of Las Vegas, Nevada, near the Nevada-California line on Rte. 190. Ranch guest rooms available year-round; Furnace Creek Inn and ranch cabins open mid-October to mid-May. Rates: cabins, $45 per night for two people; ranch guest rooms, $45 to $63 per night for two people; inn rooms (includes breakfast and dinner), $160 per night for two people. Cash, checks, Visa, Master-Card, and American Express accepted. Reservations taken up to one year in advance, recommended one month in advance.

LASSEN VOLCANIC NATIONAL PARK
MINERAL, CA 96063
(916) 595-4444

DRAKESBAD GUEST RANCH
CHESTER, CA 96020 (SUMMER ADDRESS)
Phone: Drakesbad Toll Station #2 (call Susanville operator)

2150 NORTH MAIN, #7 (WINTER ADDRESS)
RED BLUFF, CA 96080
(916) 529-1512

This 106,000-acre expanse of coniferous forest in northern California, with fifty wilderness lakes and almost as many mountains, is dominated by Lassen Peak, a plug-dome volcano of 10,457 feet at the southern tip of the Cascades. The great mass of Lassen Peak began as stiff, pasty lava forced from a vent on the north slope of a larger, now-extinct volcano known as Tehama.

Lassen Park Road winds around three sides of the peak, affording picturesque views of the volcano, woodlands and meadows, clear brooks and lakes. Some 150 miles of foot trails lead you through sparkling, radiant terrain. In the course of your hike, you encounter a variety of conifers — pines, firs, and cedars. Stands of broadleaf trees, aspens and cottonwoods, add color to the autumn landscape. Wild flowers abound from mid-June through September, and trails meander by waterfalls, thermal areas, ancient volcanoes, and lava flows.

E. R. Drake founded Drakesbad Guest Ranch more than one hundred years ago. He sold the ranch to the Sifford family in 1900, who named it Drakesbad for the spring-fed warm baths and pool on the property (*bad* is the German word for "bath"). Set in a splendid mountain valley, Drakesbad continues its traditions of fresh mountain air and old-fashioned hospitality. Fishermen savor the trout stream just a few yards from their overnight accommodations, and horseback rides and pack trips depart daily for any number of scenic destinations. After a day of hiking or horseback riding, what could be more soothing than to soak in a hundred-degree warmspring pool.

Visitors choose from thirteen one-bedroom cabins (some of them duplex units), or six guest rooms on the second floor of the lodge. The modest cabins feature pine construction and kerosene lamps, and most sleep four people. The lodge's first floor houses a registration desk and a large fireplace, where guests gather after dinner.

Drakesbad Guest Ranch is seventeen miles north of Chester, California, on Warner Valley Road. The ranch is open mid-June through mid-September. Rates: $90 to $100 per night per couple, including lodging and all meals. Cash, checks, Visa, and MasterCard accepted. Reservations taken up to one year in advance. Two-night minimum stay.

SEQUOIA AND KINGS CANYON
  NATIONAL PARKS
THREE RIVERS, CA 93271
(209) 565-3341

GUEST SERVICES, INC.
  (ACCOMMODATIONS)
SEQUOIA NATIONAL PARK,
  CA 93262
(209) 565-3373, 565-3381

The giant sequoia, having escaped the last ice age, en-
dures as a survivor of an ancient lineage of huge trees
that mantled much of the earth millions of years ago.
Today these giants grow only in scattered groves on the
western slopes of the Sierra Nevada.

In terms of volume, the giant sequoia stands alone as
the largest living thing on earth. The park's General
Sherman tree, the biggest of the great sequoias, is esti-
mated to be twenty-two hundred years old. Its trunk
weighs in at 1385 tons, its highest branch reaches a
height of 275 feet, and the circumference of the trunk at
ground level is a staggering 103 feet.

At Sequoia and Kings Canyon national parks, giant
sequoias are not alone in reaching for the sky. Mount
Whitney, elevation 14,495 feet, and several other 14,000-
foot peaks cap the Sierra Nevada — the mountains John
Muir dubbed "the range of light." Sequoia features five
hundred square miles of mountains, rushing rivers, steep
canyons, meadows, and, of course, the giant trees. Spectacular Kings Canyon consists of almost seven hundred
square miles of jagged peaks, glacial-cut canyons, waterfalls, and towering cliffs. Hikers in these adjoining parks
discover hundreds of miles of trails leading past cirques,
serrated ridges and crests, abruptly changing valley gradi-
ents, and more than a thousand glacial lakes at elevations
above ten thousand feet.

Trail rides commence at stables at several locations
in the parks, and bus tours of the mountain roads are
also available. Fine trout fishing can be found in many
high-altitude lakes and streams, and winter sports such as
downhill and cross-country skiing are popular here.

Guests Services, Inc. operates various cabin and motel
facilities at five locations in Sequoia and Kings Canyon.
Most of the 240 units consist of sleeping accommodations
only, though cabins at Lower Kaweah do have wood-
burning stoves for cooking. Some accommodations here

have indoor plumbing, while others share central rest-room and shower facilities. Cabin "H" is the only one equipped with a fireplace.

Cabins and motel rooms vary greatly in construction, amenities, and age — some fifty units were opened in 1983, while others, listed on the National Register of Historic Places, date from the 1930s — and they sleep from four to seven people. Meals are served at several park locations.

Sequoia and Kings Canyon National Parks are ninety miles east of Fresno, California, on Rte. 180. Cabins and motel rooms available year-round. Rates: $21 to $64 per night. Cash, checks, Visa, and MasterCard accepted. Reservations taken up to eleven months in advance, recommended four to six months in advance for summer and holidays.

YOSEMITE NATIONAL PARK
YOSEMITE NATIONAL PARK, CA 95389
(209) 372-4461

YOSEMITE PARK AND CURRY COMPANY (ACCOMMODATIONS)
YOSEMITE NATIONAL PARK, CA 95389
(209) 252-4848

Yosemite Valley — the "incomparable valley," as it has been called — is probably the world's best known example of a glacier-carved canyon. Its leaping waterfalls, towering cliffs, rounded domes, and massive monoliths make it a preeminent natural marvel. Wild flowers and flowering shrubs, oak woodlands, and mixed-conifer forests of ponderosa pine, incense cedar, and Douglas-fir sprinkle a mosaic of open meadows.

Yosemite National Park embraces a vast tract of wild lands set aside in 1890 to preserve the slice of the Sierra Nevadas that stretches along California's eastern flank. The park's elevation ranges from two thousand feet above sea level to thirteen-thousand-foot summits.

Glacier Point's impressive 270-degree vista overwhelms the viewer. Below your feet a sheer rock cliff, thirty-two hundred feet straight down, affords an awesome glimpse of Yosemite Valley. Across the valley you witness the

Ahwahnee Hotel, Yosemite National Park, California

dazzling drop of Yosemite Falls — foaming white water plunging more than two thousand feet down a rock mountainside.

The towering trees at Mariposa Grove, largest of the three sequoia groves in this 750,000-acre park, have endured for thousands of years. The grove's Grizzly Giant — twenty-seven hundred years old — is believed to be the oldest of all sequoias, having been here since the beginning of western civilization.

Some 200 miles of roads and 750 miles of trails unlock the wilderness to visitors, whose only real dilemma might be deciding where to start. Anglers may want to spend their first day fishing the Merced River and its tributaries for trout, while others opt for one of the many guided trail rides. Yosemite features miles of paved bicycle paths, with bike rentals available. Buses and trams also tour the park's diverse locales. In warmer months, expert rock-climbing instruction can be found at Yosemite Mountaineering School, while cross-country and downhill skiing take over during snow season.

Yosemite Park and Curry Company offers 341 sleeping cabins and 421 lodge guest rooms, at various locations in Yosemite Valley. Among the lodges is the Ahwahnee Hotel. Backed by steep granite cliffs and listed on the National Register of Historic Places, it has provided luxurious accommodations since 1927, often hosting presidents and dignitaries. Grand furnishings and thirty-foot ceilings characterize the public areas, while distinctive antiques complement each of 121 guest rooms. Continental cuisine pleases the palate in the lodge dining room.

One of California's oldest classic hotels, the Victorian-era Wawona Hotel was established in 1856. As you approach this spacious wooden structure, which is painted white, you pass a peaceful lily pond. Antiques grace the lobby and seventy-two guest rooms, and visitors relax on large verandas overlooking manicured lawns. A turn-of-the-century dining room serves exquisite meals. A heated swimming pool, tennis courts, and a golf course round out the amenities at Wawona.

Modern Yosemite Lodge, built of glass and rich woods, blends into a forest and mountain backdrop. Two restaurants provide complete meal service for the lodge's 225 guest rooms.

Yosemite's 341 sleeping cabins (no kitchens) range in age from five to fifty years and sleep up to five people. These wood-constructed units are dispersed throughout the park, including along the Merced River and at the base of Glacier Point.

Yosemite National Park is in east-central California, not far from the Nevada border. Lodging available year-round. Rates: cabins, $19 to $43 per night for two people; lodge and hotel rooms, $41 to $157 per night for two people. Cash, checks, Visa, MasterCard, and American Express accepted. Reservations taken up to one year in advance, recommended that early for summer.

ASILOMAR STATE BEACH AND CONFERENCE CENTER
800 ASILOMAR BOULEVARD
P.O. BOX 537
PACIFIC GROVE, CA 93950
(408) 372-8016

Noted California architect Julia Morgan designed the original buildings at Asilomar in the 1920s. She set the tone of this center by fashioning structures of wood and stone that fit unobtrusively in their natural surroundings.

The rustic administration building features a social hall with antique pool tables, and a large stone fireplace facing easy chairs. The historic Guest Inn — a seven-room wooden cabin built in the early 1930s — has four bedrooms, two full baths, and a living room with a fireplace and rich hardwood floors. Later architects have respected Julia Morgan's design, and newer structures blend effortlessly with the originals.

Asilomar Conference Center occupies 105 acres of forest, dune, and beach at the tip of California's Monterey Peninsula. Looking out on the surf of the Pacific Ocean, these accommodations for meetings and vacations rest among pines and cypresses. While it is primarily a facility for group gatherings, nonconference guests are also welcome at this striking resort.

Playful sea otters, harbor seals, and sea lions frolic offshore, and California gray whales pass by on their migrations between Baja California and the Bering Straits. Asilomar guests enjoy a heated swimming pool, along with volleyball and horseshoes. The famed Pebble Beach golf course is just one of ten courses within twenty minutes' drive from the Victorian community of Pacific Grove. Nearby Carmel-by-the-Sea, originally an art colony, boasts of fine restaurants, shopping, and galleries. In Monterey, Cannery Row and Fisherman's Wharf offer excellent dining and sightseeing, plus charter boat fishing, tennis, and horseback riding. The acclaimed "Seventeen-Mile Drive" starts a half mile east of Asilomar, and winds through the Del Monte Forest.

Asilomar State Beach and Conference Center is in Pacific Grove, California. Open year-round. Rates: $26 to $51 per night for two people; Guest Inn, $71 per night for up to four people. Cash and checks accepted. Nonconference reservations taken up to three months in advance.

Though it lasted less than two decades, hydraulic mining drastically changed the face of California. At Malakoff Diggins State Historic Park in northern California, you will see the largest hydraulic gold mine in the world, as well as historic remnants of this former hotbed of mining.

Hydraulic mining consisted simply of blasting a hillside with a stream of water until the soil disintegrated. The muddy stream was directed down a sluice that caught heavier, gold-bearing particles of earth and gravel; the water with the remaining mud drained into a stream or river, or wherever gravity propelled it. With a hydraulic pipe, one or two men could process hundreds of tons of earth daily, making it economical to mine gravel that yielded less than a nickel's worth of gold per cubic yard.

"Hydraulicking" required vast quantities of water, used at sufficient pressure to literally move mountains. In the California Sierra, where all of the rain falls in winter and many streams dry up entirely in summer, an extensive network of flumes, ditches, and reservoirs — many of which became part of today's water systems — was constructed to get water to the mines.

A permanent injunction in 1884 drastically restricted this method of mining, and California's free-for-all hydraulicking era was over. Today, Malakoff Diggins's museum depicts this phase of the state's gold-mining history. The Ostrom Livery Stable houses many types of wagons used when the mines were operating.

Between twenty-two hundred and forty-two hundred feet in elevation, the park's terrain varies from open meadows to tree- and chaparral-covered slopes and deep canyons. The great Malakoff pit, seven thousand feet long and three thousand feet wide, is nearly six hundred feet deep in places. Slides and erosion have partially filled it in, and the waters of the lake formed in its bottom contrast with the colorful cliffs that surround it. For anglers, the lower sections of Humbug Creek and South Yuba River offer rainbow and brown trout, while black bass, bluegill, and catfish thrive in Blair Reservoir, which is also popular for swimming and picnicking.

Malakoff's two rustic cabins, though built in 1970, approximate the homelife of a gold miner during the late nineteenth century. Each has cold running water, a wood-burning cookstove, tables and benches, two sets of bunk beds (no mattresses), and an icebox. Outside is a picnic table and barbecue grill, and a pit toilet serves each cabin. Visitors should bring a lantern, since there is no electricity.

Malakoff Diggins State Historic Park is sixteen miles north of Nevada City, California, off Rte. 49 on Tyler Foote Crossing Road. Cabins available year-round. Rates: $15 per night. Cash and in-state checks accepted. Reservations taken up to eight weeks in advance.

PFEIFFER BIG SUR STATE PARK
BIG SUR LODGE
BIG SUR, CA 93920
(408) 667-2315 (park office)
(408) 667-2171 (lodge)

About thirty miles south of Monterey, California's Route 1 leaves a spectacular view of the Pacific Ocean for a brief stretch and enters a rugged, wooded canyon. This canyon, gouged out over centuries by the Big Sur River, contains a forest of coast redwoods and Pfeiffer Big Sur State Park.

In this 810-acre park's river flats and canyons, redwoods make their home side by side with sycamores, black cottonwoods, big-leaf maples, alders, and willows. In contrast, the dry, south-facing slopes of the chaparral country sprout coast live oaks, California laurel, and numerous shrubs.

The bears that once inhabited the park have long since departed, though mountain lions and coyotes are still seen on occasion. More common are the wild boars, descendants of those introduced from Europe by wealthy ranchers decades ago. It's wise to give these animals a wide berth — an adult boar can weigh well over three hundred pounds, has sharp tusks, and will fight fearlessly when cornered.

A self-guided nature trail at Pfeiffer Big Sur, approximately one mile in length, introduces many of the trees and shrubs native to the area. Other trails lead to picturesque overlooks, to thirty-three-hundred-foot Mount Manuel, and to points of interest in Los Padres National Forest. Two public beaches on the Pacific Ocean are just four miles away.

The sixty-one cabins at Big Sur Lodge are adjoining wood-frame structures in one- and two-room configurations. Some have kitchenettes; twenty-four feature fireplaces; and all offer heating, and porches with lounge chairs. A short walk from the cabin units is the lodge office, which contains a grocery store, gift shop, and restaurant. Lodge guests can enjoy swimming in a heated outdoor pool and wading in the Big Sur River.

Pfeiffer Big Sur State Park is thirty miles south of Monterey, California, on Rte. 1. Cabins available year-round. Rates: $42 to $55 per night for two people. Cash and in-state checks accepted.

RICHARDSON GROVE STATE PARK
1600 HIGHWAY 101
GARBERVILLE, CA 95440
(707) 247-3318

Traveling north on Route 101 into Humboldt County, you enter a cool, dark, verdant forest of towering redwoods. This is Richardson Grove, named in honor of California's twenty-fifth governor, Friend W. Richardson.

The park's tranquil setting is one of shadows and semi-darkness — even at midday, only a fraction of the sun's light filters through the dense branches of closely growing redwoods. A profusion of plant life also shuts out sounds, and the tall trees temper the wind. The stillness here is not easily forgotten.

Highway 101 traverses this northern California park, following the South Fork of the Eel River. Over the past twelve hundred years, the river has deposited more than eleven feet of new soil here, making it an ideal growing location for coast redwoods.

These redwoods, which populate a five-hundred-mile-long strip of southwest Oregon and northern California that is no more than twenty to thirty miles wide, flourish in the unique mixture of moderate temperatures, summer fog, and heavy winter rainfall. These majestic giants grow rapidly, reach heights of more than 360 feet, and endure for up to two thousand years. They are the tallest trees on earth. Before the devastating effects of logging, the redwood forest extended over some two million acres.

Richardson Grove's nine hundred acres can be explored by a widely varied system of trails, ranging from short, gentle nature walks to ambitious routes that climb ridges to inspiring vantage points. One trail leads to the river and to a beach popular with sunbathers and swimmers.

Richardson Grove's seven two-room cabins, built in the late 1930s, have indoor plumbing, showers, and kitchenettes, but no beds or refrigerators. Available only in winter, these cabins are used primarily by fishermen, attracted to the area by excellent winter runs of silver and king salmon and by the steelhead trout in the Eel River.

Richardson Grove State Park is eight miles south of Garberville, California, on Rte. 101. Cabins available November through April. Rates: $12 per night. Cash accepted.

Colorado

STATE PARK INFORMATION:
COLORADO DIVISION OF PARKS AND OUTDOOR
  RECREATION
1313 SHERMAN STREET, #618
DENVER, CO 80203
(303) 866-3437

TOURISM INFORMATION:
COLORADO TOURISM BOARD
5500 SOUTH SYRACUSE CIRCLE, SUITE 267
ENGLEWOOD, CO 80111
(303) 866-2205

STATE BIRD: *Lark Bunting*
STATE MAMMAL: *Bighorn Sheep*
STATE TREE: *Blue Spruce*
STATE FLOWER: *Columbine*
STATE FISH: *Rainbow Trout*

MESA VERDE NATIONAL PARK
MESA VERDE, CO 81330
(303) 529-4461

MESA VERDE FAR VIEW
LODGE
P.O. BOX 277
109 SOUTH MAIN STREET
MANCOS, CO 81328
(303) 529-4421

Hundreds of years ago, pre-Columbian Indians constructed mesa-top villages and, later, great cities of stone in the cliffs of Mesa Verde. They fabricated sturdy, apartment-like buildings, some as high as three stories and containing more than fifty rooms. But the cliff-dwelling era lasted less than one hundred years; before the close of the thirteenth century, the cliff dwellers mysteriously abandoned Mesa Verde forever.

After the Indians' departure, the cliff structures they had meticulously crafted stood silent for centuries. The Spaniards explored this area of southwestern Colorado in the mid-1800s, but did not find the ruins. In fact, it was not until 1874 — six hundred years after the Indians abandoned the villages — that these unique stone edifices were discovered.

During the summer, park rangers now conduct guided tours through several of these intriguing dwellings. Visitors also can make self-guided explorations of a half-dozen sites during most of the year. Spruce, pine, and juniper trees dominate the four mesas here, and mule deer, coyote, chipmunk, and rabbit inhabit the rugged terrain.

Far View Lodge offers 150 guest rooms, each with a private balcony and a view of Four Corners — the junction of the Colorado, Utah, Arizona, and New Mexico state lines. The lodge's seventeen buildings perch atop Navajo Hill, four miles from the ruins. In addition to two dining areas, a lounge, and a gift shop, the lodge also houses "Anasazi" (which means "ancient ones" in Navajo), a multimedia presentation that describes the region's history.

Bicycle rentals and hiking trails are some of the touring options in this historic setting, and the Archaeological Museum at Chapin Mesa is one popular destination. Indian arts and crafts can be purchased in this fifty-two-thousand-acre national park, which adjoins the Ute Mountain Indian Reservation.

Mesa Verde National Park is ten miles east of Cortez, Colorado, on Rte. 160. Lodge open early May to late October. Rates: $42 to $49 per night for two people. Cash, checks, Visa, MasterCard, and American Express accepted. Reservations taken up to one year in advance.

COLORADO STATE FOREST
WALDEN, CO 80480
(303) 723-8366

SEVEN UTES RESORT
BOX 117
WALDEN, CO 80480
(303) 723-4335

At an average elevation of nine thousand feet, Colorado State Forest offers forty-five miles of marked cross-country ski trails and another fifty miles of packed and groomed snowmobile trails. This seventy-two-thousand-acre state forest also is a favorite for winter camping, ice fishing, and photography.

Winter recreation at the state forest begins in mid-December, and lasts through early April. The extensive trails lead past craggy peaks and down tree-shrouded slopes. At this altitude, winter temperatures average 0° Fahrenheit during the day. In January, daytime temperatures of −20° are common, and temperatures at night can fall to −50°.

Seven Utes Resort features cabin and motel accommodations, plus RV parking spaces, a ski shop with rental equipment, a restaurant, and a lounge. Six log cabins, sleeping up to six people apiece, have lush hardwood floors and wood-burning stoves. Each comes with two double beds and a pair of bunk beds, and they share a central bathhouse. The resort's seven motel rooms have private baths and sleep up to five people. A group lodge for parties of ten to twenty people is also available.

The Michigan River, a favorite with anglers, flows right behind Seven Utes's cabins. A sauna and outdoor hot tub are also popular attractions here.

Four primitive cabins can also be rented from the state forest office: two large cabins at Michigan Reservoir, each capable of sleeping fifteen people, and two smaller cabins, one at Michigan Reservoir and the other at Lake Agnes.

All four provide only minimum shelter: heat via wood stove, and no electricity or running water.

Colorado State Forest is twenty miles east of Walden, Colorado, on Rte. 14. Lodging available December through April. Rates: Seven Utes cabins, $44 per night for two people; Seven Utes motel rooms, $49 per night for two people; state forest cabins, $20 to $30 per night. Cash, Visa, and MasterCard accepted.

Nevada

STATE PARK INFORMATION:
NEVADA DIVISION OF STATE PARKS
STATE CAPITOL COMPLEX
CARSON CITY, NV 89710
(702) 885-4384

TOURISM INFORMATION:
NEVADA DEPARTMENT OF ECONOMIC DEVELOPMENT
TOURISM DIVISION
STATE CAPITOL COMPLEX
CARSON CITY, NV 89710
(702) 885-4322

STATE BIRD: *Mountain Bluebird*
STATE MAMMAL: *Desert Bighorn Sheep*
STATE TREE: *Pinyon Pine*
STATE FLOWER: *Sagebrush*
STATE FISH: *Lahontan Cutthroat Trout*

LAKE MEAD NATIONAL
RECREATION AREA
601 NEVADA HIGHWAY
BOULDER CITY, NV 89005
(702) 293-4041

ECHO BAY RESORT HOTEL
OVERTON, NV 89040
(800) 752-9669
(702) 394-4000

TEMPLE BAR RESORT
TEMPLE BAR, AZ 85443
(602) 767-3400

LAKE MOHAVE RESORT
KATHERINES LANDING
BULLHEAD CITY, AZ 86430
(602) 754-3245

LAKE MEAD LODGE
322 LAKESHORE ROAD
BOULDER CITY, NV 89005
(702) 293-2074

COTTONWOOD COVE RESORT
P.O. BOX 1000
COTTONWOOD COVE, NV
89046
(702) 297-1464

Vast expanses of clear water, stark and colorful desert landscapes, and an ideal climate welcome visitors to Lake Mead National Recreation Area, along the Nevada-Arizona border. Lake Mead stretches 105 miles up the course of the Colorado River, from Hoover Dam to Separation Canyon. Its 550-mile shoreline of wide gravel beaches, shadowed coves, and steep-walled cliffs affords endless opportunities for swimming, scuba diving, fishing, boating, and waterskiing.

Lake Mohave, a narrow reservoir created by Davis Dam, reaches northward sixty-seven miles to the base of Hoover Dam. In addition to all of the recreation area's water sports, visitors can observe intriguing geological formations and ancient Indian petroglyphs. Ducks, gulls, and grebes feed on the surface of the lakes, while largemouth bass, rainbow trout, and black crappie cruise past submerged cliffs in search of aquatic insects.

The northwest corner of Mohave Desert ranges in elevation from 517 feet above sea level at Davis Dam to 7072 feet on Shivwits Plateau. Creosote bush, Mohave yucca, Joshua tree, and a variety of cacti occupy the lower elevations, home of kit fox, kangaroo rats, and a range of reptiles and birds. Up on the plateau, Utah juniper, Colorado pinyon pine, Gambel oak, and sagebrush are found, along with mule deer, rock squirrel, and cliff chipmunk.

Once the site of Mormon gold-mining operations, Temple Bar Resort today offers eighteen lodge rooms and four cabins fifty miles east of Hoover Dam. The wooden, twenty-year-old, one-room cabins sleep up to four people apiece and share a bathhouse. Each has kitchen appliances, and three overlook Temple Basin. The concrete-block lodge rooms, heated and air-conditioned, also sleep four people, and some have kitchens. The resort's marina rents ski boats, fishing boats, and patio boats and sells fuel and supplies. At the end of the day, guests relax in the lounge and dine in Temple Bar's restaurant.

Temple Bar rooms and cabins available year-round. Rates: rooms, $38 to $64 per night for two people; cabins, $18 per night for two. Cash, Visa, and MasterCard accepted. Reservations recommended two months in advance.

Fifty-year-old Lake Mead Lodge, with its brick walls and tile roofs, has forty-four updated guest rooms, a lounge, and a restaurant. Most rooms feature views of the lake, and each has a private bath with shower. Hoover Dam is just minutes away via the tour boat *Echo*, which transports visitors through the upper end of Black Canyon. Open waters here are a favorite with sailing enthusiasts.

Lake Mead Lodge is open year-round. Rates: $35 to $42 per night. Cash, Visa, and MasterCard accepted. Reservations recommended two months in advance.

Echo Bay Resort Hotel overlooks the Overton Arm of Lake Mead fifty miles northeast of Hoover Dam. This two-story, fifty-two-room hotel has a restaurant and lounge decorated in nautical motif, a swimming pool, and a full marina, where houseboats, ski boats, and fishing boats can be rented. Echo Bay hosts the Western Bass Association's tournament on occasion, thanks to the record largemouth and striped bass caught here.

Echo Bay Resort Hotel is open year-round. Rates: $48 to $64 per night for two people. Cash, Visa, and MasterCard accepted. Reservations recommended two months in advance.

Lake Mohave Resort, on the Arizona side of the southern end of that lake, caters to visitors with fifty-one guest rooms, a lakefront dining room, and a marina. The guest rooms sleep up to four people, and the dining room serves three meals daily, year-round. Launching ramps, a swimming beach, and rental houseboats, ski boats, and fishing boats all await at the water.

Lake Mohave Resort is open year-round. Rates: $45 to $64 per night. Cash, checks, Visa, and MasterCard accepted. Reservations recommended one month in advance.

Cottonwood Cove, on the Nevada side of Lake Mohave, rents six- and twelve-bunk houseboats for exploring the lake, plus fishing boats and ski boats. The resort also offers palm-shaded motel rooms for those who prefer to spend the night ashore. The twenty-four guest rooms sleep up to four people, and some are equipped with kitchenettes. Those in rooms without cooking facilities gather for meals at the resort's restaurant.

Cottonwood Cove Resort is open year-round. Rates: $47 to $60 per night for two people. Cash, Visa, and MasterCard accepted. Reservations recommended six months in advance.

New Mexico

STATE PARK INFORMATION:
NEW MEXICO NATURAL RESOURCES DEPARTMENT
STATE PARK AND RECREATION DIVISION
141 EAST DE VARGAS
P.O. BOX 1147
SANTA FE, NM 87504
(505) 827-7465

TOURISM INFORMATION:
NEW MEXICO TOURISM AND TRAVEL DIVISION
ECONOMIC DEVELOPMENT AND TOURISM
   DEPARTMENT
BATAAN MEMORIAL BUILDING
SANTA FE, NM 87503
(800) 545-2040 (out-of-state calls)
(505) 827-6230 (in-state calls)

STATE BIRD: *Roadrunner*
STATE MAMMAL: *Black Bear*
STATE TREE: *Pinyon*
STATE FLOWER: *Yucca*
STATE FISH: *Cutthroat Trout*

ELEPHANT BUTTE STATE PARK
Box 13
ELEPHANT BUTTE, NM 87935
(505) 744-5421

DAMSITE RECREATION AREA (CABINS)
Box 77B, EAGLE STAR ROUTE
TRUTH OR CONSEQUENCES, NM 87901
(505) 894-2073, 894-2041

Elephant Butte Lake, a dammed section of the Rio Grande, is the largest man-made lake in New Mexico, at forty-five miles in length and almost two miles in width. The Fra Cristobal Mountains run along the lake's east shore, and their cliffs and buttes punctuate the high desert landscape. This southwest New Mexico park takes its name from a distinctive butte that resembles an elephant's head and back.

Warm temperatures year-round and low humidity make this state park a favorite in any season; winter days are pleasant and sunny, almost always in the fifties. In summer, highs do reach one hundred degrees, but invariably the temperature drops thirty degrees at night.

Elephant Butte Lake has earned a reputation as a fine fishing lake, thanks to abundant catfish, bass, bluegill, northern pike, crappie, and perch. In fact, the lake hosts numerous bass tournaments and other special angling events. The Rio Grande is stocked with trout below the dam each spring. Sailing, skiing, swimming, and sunbathing are all favorite activities on the lakefront, where visitors can admire the park's rolling desert terrain and such wildlife as roadrunners and jackrabbits. Three marinas in the area offer rental boats, heated and air-conditioned fishing wells, dock space, and launching ramps. Canoeing and tubing are popular on the Rio Grande.

Damsite Recreation Area offers a full-service marina, a lounge, a restaurant specializing in seafood, Mexican food, and steaks, and fifteen adobe cabins. These thirty- to forty-year-old cabins line the lakeshore, among desert vegetation. The cabins accommodate from two to four adults, and many have kitchenettes.

Nearby attractions include quaint ghost towns, hot springs with bathhouses, and abandoned gold mines.

Truth or Consequences, New Mexico, was once known as Hot Springs, but in 1950 the community changed its name to celebrate the tenth anniversary of Ralph Edwards's radio program "Truth or Consequences." Edwards is something of a local hero, and he visits each spring for an annual festival.

Elephant Butte State Park is five miles north of Truth or Consequences, New Mexico, on Rte. 52. Cabins available March through October. Rates: $20 to $34 per night. Cash, Visa, and MasterCard accepted. Reservations recommended one to four weeks in advance.

Oklahoma

STATE PARK INFORMATION:
OKLAHOMA TOURISM AND RECREATION
   DEPARTMENT
RESORTS DIVISION
500 WILL ROGERS BUILDING
OKLAHOMA CITY, OK 73105
(800) 522-8565 (in-state calls)
(800) 654-8240 (calls from neighboring states)
(405) 521-2464 (all other calls)

TOURISM INFORMATION:
OKLAHOMA TOURISM AND RECREATION
   DEPARTMENT
LITERATURE DISTRIBUTION CENTER
215 NORTHEAST TWENTY-EIGHTH STREET
OKLAHOMA CITY, OK 73105
(800) 652-6552 (calls from in-state and neighboring
   states)
(405) 521-2409 (all other calls)

STATE BIRD: *Scissor-tailed Flycatcher*
STATE MAMMAL: *American Bison*
STATE TREE: *Redbud*
STATE FLOWER: *Mistletoe*
STATE FISH: *White Bass*

ARROWHEAD STATE PARK
P.O. Box 57
CANADIAN, OK 74425
(800) 522-8565 (in-state reservations)
(800) 654-8240 (reservations from neighboring states)
(405) 521-2464 (all other reservations)
(918) 339-2204 (park office)

Most of the six-hundred-mile shoreline of Lake Eufaula
— a premier recreation lake in eastern Oklahoma — lies
within the boundaries of the old Creek and Choctaw
nations. The lake's waters now hide the Texas Road,
which carried more than a thousand wagons per week in
the 1830s as settlers headed south and west to the Lone
Star state. When the Missouri, Kansas & Texas Railroad
— the Katy — built the first rail line southward across
Indian territory in 1872, it too followed the route of the
Texas Road. Canadian, a small town at the entrance to
Arrowhead State Park, once served as a busy railhead
where cattle were loaded for shipment.

Arrowhead hugs the western shore of enormous Lake
Eufaula, at approximately midlake. Its 106-room deluxe
lodge, built of native stone and redwood, overlooks both
the lake and a refreshing swimming pool. The lodge's
lobby features an impressive free-standing fireplace, and
the dining room offers views through a wall of glass.
Flanking the lodge in two groups are Arrowhead's 104
cabins. Constructed of stone with copper roofs, these
twenty-year-old cabins accommodate up to four people.
Each has four rooms — including two bedrooms and complete kitchens — heating, and air conditioning. Half of
these duplex cabins have fireplaces.

Oak, hickory, elm, and pine cover Arrowhead's hilly
2459 acres, which are a habitat for deer, coyote, gray fox,
beaver, and rabbits. The park's marina provides rental
boats, launching ramps, and marine supplies on the
shores of Lake Eufaula, which holds abundant largemouth bass, crappie, catfish, perch, bream, carp, and
buffalo. You can swim at the lodge pool or at a lakefront
beach, or enjoy tennis and golf. Horseback riding is available at the stables from May through October, and a
thirty-five-hundred-foot runway services small aircraft.

Arrowhead State Park is twenty miles north of Mc-Alester, Oklahoma, on Rte. 69. Cabins and lodge open year-round. Rates: cabins, $45 to $55 per night; lodge, $45 to $49 per night for two people. Cash, checks, Visa, and MasterCard accepted. Reservations recommended one month in advance for summer.

BEAVERS BEND STATE PARK
P.O. Box 10
BROKEN BOW, OK 74728
(800) 522-8565 *(in-state reservations)*
(800) 654-8240 *(reservations from neighboring states)*
(405) 521-2464 *(all other reservations)*
(405) 494-6300 *(park office)*

Broken Bow Lake, one of the most picturesque settings in southeastern Oklahoma, stretches some twenty-two miles into Ouachita Mountain country, where startling beauty and scenic appeal beckons all nature enthusiasts. The mountainous terrain is densely forested by pine and hardwoods, with an undercover of holly groves, maple, dogwood, redbud, beauty bush, and a succession of flowering perennials. Many species of birds native to the region delight bird-watchers.

Broken Bow Lake covers 14,240 acres, and is contained by a 180-mile, tree-studded shoreline. A chain of islands, which once were mountaintops along Mountain Fork River, dots the lake's still blue surface. Beavers Bend State Park encompasses 3522 acres at the southern tip of the lake and along Mountain Fork River, below the dam.

In addition to swimming and boating, Broken Bow Lake offers outstanding angling for smallmouth and largemouth bass and other species. Park visitors spend leisurely days playing tennis, riding bicycles (rentals available), or tapping in shots on the miniature golf course. Horseback riding is also a favorite here.

Beavers Bend's forty-seven frame cabins are scattered throughout wooded sections of the park; some are right on the riverfront. These one- and two-bedroom cabins accommodate up to six people. Each has a completely equipped kitchen and bath, and all but five include fireplaces. The oldest of this park's cabins date from the 1930s; others were completed as recently as the late 1970s.

Be sure to sample Beavers Bend's hiking trails, including Big Oak Trail which leads to the largest white oak in Oklahoma. This three-hundred-year-old tree is more than 21 feet in circumference and 107 feet high. David Boren Hiking Trail traverses a creek bottom and an old logging road, climbs up a steep, craggy bluff, and then descends through a peaceful forest.

Beavers Bend State Park is eleven miles northeast of Broken Bow, Oklahoma, on Rte. 259A. Cabins available year-round. Rates: $35 to $50 per night for two people. Cash, checks, Visa, and MasterCard accepted. Reservations taken up to eighteen months in advance, recommended two to three months in advance for April through October.

BOILING SPRINGS STATE PARK
P.O. Box 965
WOOLWARD, OK 73802
(800) 522-8565 *(in-state reservations)*
(800) 654-8240 *(reservations from neighboring states)*
(405) 521-2464 *(all other reservations)*
(405) 256-7664 *(park office)*

Red Carpet Country is a seventeen-county area in northwestern Oklahoma that is rich in history and in contrasts of weather and terrain. From the Salt Flats near Jet, Oklahoma, to the Glass Mountains near Orienta, from the Little Sahara Desert to Foss Reservoir, the visitor will find a unique blend of sights and activities. Explore the traces of the Sante Fe Trail: much of the adventure of the Old West is intricately bound to it, and wagon-wheel ruts and watering holes still mark the time when millions of cattle were driven to northern railheads.

Boiling Springs State Park takes its name from a pressurized spring that bubbles up through the sand not far from the North Canadian River. Oaks, cottonwoods, pines, cedars, willows, and walnuts blanket the riverbanks, providing a habitat for deer, turkeys, and raccoons. Four hiking trails meander across this parkland, and a small, seven-acre lake teems with catfish, bass, and perch.

Four cabins look out on the lake; each has a bedroom, a kitchenette, a bathroom, heating, and air conditioning. The cabins sleep up to four people and are equipped with outdoor picnic tables and barbecue grills. They also feature fireplaces.

Boiling Springs State Park is six miles east of Woodward, Oklahoma, on Rte. 34C. Cabins available year-round. Rates: $35 per night. Cash, checks, Visa, and MasterCard accepted. Reservations taken up to eighteen months in advance, recommended two to three months in advance for summer.

FOUNTAINHEAD STATE PARK
WEST STAR ROUTE, BOX 185
CHECOTAH, OK 74426
(800) 522-8565 *(in-state reservations)*
(800) 654-8240 *(reservations from neighboring states)*
(405) 521-2464 *(all other reservations)*
(918) 689-5311 *(park office)*

Known for its striking architecture and gracious atmosphere, Fountainhead Resort is a sweeping five-story edifice in the shape of a gentle horseshoe. The resort offers a commanding view of vast, 102,000-acre Lake Eufaula, Oklahoma's largest man-made lake. This contemporary structure hosts 186 guest rooms, a swimming pool, a putting green, and a fine restaurant. For more private accommodations, try one of Fountainhead State Park's eleven duplex cabins (twenty-two units). These modern units have glass fronts facing the lakeshore, single bedrooms, kitchenettes, color televisions, heating, and air conditioning. Some offer fireplaces.

Water recreation thrives on Lake Eufaula, which has earned a reputation as a fine crappie, white bass, black bass, and catfish location. Nonaquatic activities at this eastern Oklahoma park include tennis, golf, horseback riding, hiking, and bicycle riding. A marina, boat-launching ramps, an enclosed fishing dock, and a three-thousand-foot lighted, paved airstrip also serve the park. The resort periodically holds special events, including lakeside terrace dining, western barbecues, and Hawaiian luaus.

To the north of Lake Eufaula is Muskogee, Oklahoma,

site of museums and other attractions. Antiques, Inc. exhibits an extensive collection of classic automobiles. At the Five Civilized Tribes Museum, you'll observe the history and artifacts of Cherokee, Chickasaw, Choctaw, Creek, and Seminole Indians. Another popular stop is the USS *Batfish*, a submarine used in World War II.

Fountainhead State Park is twelve miles southwest of Checotah, Oklahoma, on Rte. 69. Cabins and resort open year-round. Rates: cabins, $45 to $55 per night; resort, $49 to $53 per night. Cash, checks, Visa, MasterCard, and American Express accepted. Reservations taken up to one year in advance, recommended one month in advance.

GREAT SALT PLAINS STATE PARK
ROUTE 1, BOX 28
JET, OK 73749
(800) 522-8565 *(in-state reservations)*
(800) 654-8240 *(reservations from neighboring states)*
(405) 521-2464 *(all other reservations)*
(405) 626-4731 *(park office)*

The Salt Plains of north-central Oklahoma consist of a perfectly flat expanse of mud, completely devoid of vegetation, seven miles long and three miles wide. They take their name from a thin layer of salt that covers the flats, which was first used by early Indian tribes who inhabited the area. Major George C. Sibley is thought to have been the first white man to view this area, in 1811. Today, visitors flock to dig out the intriguing selenite crystals that form just below the salt-encrusted surface. (Hunting for crystals permitted April to mid-October.)

The Great Salt Plains National Wildlife Refuge, covering 32,324 acres, is one of a chain of refuges along the Continental Central Flyway from Canada to Mexico. The refuge provides a resting place for ducks and geese that travel the flyway each autumn and spring, and is the permanent home for many waterfowl.

Great Salt Plains State Park lines the shore of Great Salt Plains Lake, a ninety-three-hundred-acre recreation lake that is popular for fishing (white bass, stripers, catfish, drum, and carp), boating, and swimming, despite its salty water. Low rolling hills punctuated with chinaberry, hackberry, cottonwood, and elm trees characterize the terrain in the park. White pelicans, sandhill and whooping cranes, and golden and bald eagles can be observed here.

Six thirty-year-old cabins face the lake, not far from the water's edge. These wooden, one-room cabins sleep from four to six people and have air conditioning and heating. Each features a kitchen and bath; outdoor picnic tables, barbecue grills, and swings serve the cabin colony.

Great Salt Plains State Park is eight miles north of Jet, Oklahoma, on Rte. 38. Cabins available year-round. Rates: $35 per night for two people. Cash, checks, Visa, and MasterCard accepted. Reservations taken up to eighteen months in advance, recommended that early for April through September.

GREENLEAF STATE PARK
ROUTE 1, BOX 119
BRAGGS, OK 74423
(800) 522-8565 (in-state reservations)
(800) 654-8240 (reservations from neighboring states)
(405) 521-2464 (all other reservations)
(918) 487-5196 (park office)

Shaded by mature oaks, Greenleaf State Park's fourteen cabins rest on a hillside; five of them overlook Greenleaf Lake. Constructed of rock fifty years ago, these one-bedroom cabins provide refrigerators and electric countertop stoves, and sleep up to four people apiece. Ten come equipped with fireplaces, three have screened porches, and all include heating and air conditioning. Outdoor grills and picnic tables offer the perfect setting for a family cookout.

Beautiful Greenleaf Lake, in the verdant Cookson Hills of northeast Oklahoma, covers nine hundred acres. Although small, it hosts fine fishing for bass and crappie, and anglers can try their luck on the water or in a heated dock. Greenleaf's marina rents a variety of watercraft, and swimmers enjoy both the lake and a modern pool. During summer months, the park restaurant — an impressive structure with rough wood siding, a cathedral ceiling, and plenty of windows — serves a comprehensive menu. Nearby attractions include the Fort Gibson Stockade (an historic Indian-territory fort), trout fishing in the Illinois River, and Arkansas River barge traffic.

Greenleaf State Park is three miles south of Braggs, Oklahoma, on Rte. 10. Cabins available year-round. Rates: $35 to $40 per night for two people. Cash, checks, Visa, and MasterCard accepted. Reservations taken up to eighteen months in advance, recommended two months in advance for May through September. Two-night minimum on summer weekends.

Cabin, Keystone State Park, Oklahoma

KEYSTONE STATE PARK
P.O. BOX 147
MANNFORD, OK 74044
(800) 522-8565 *(in-state reservations)*
(800) 654-8240 *(reservations from neighboring states)*
(405) 521-2464 *(all other reservations)*
(918) 865-4991 *(park office)*

Dusk finds Keystone Lake reflecting the brilliant colors of a northeast Oklahoma sunset. The lake is peaceful at this time of day, as few boats part its waters. Gazing at this expansive reservoir — 26,300 acres, enclosed by 330 miles of shoreline — you may imagine what the setting was like before man harnessed the waters of the Cimarron and Arkansas rivers, how it looked when Creeks and Osage Indians camped here more than a century ago.

The sandy shores meld into high bluffs and grasslands, which lead in turn to the rolling Osage Hills. Among early visitors to Keystone was the noted writer Washington Irving, who accompanied a group of American Rangers on an expedition to the western prairie in 1832.

Keystone Lake is well known for having successfully introduced walleye and striped bass to its waters. Fishermen also boast of top catches of many species native to Oklahoma, including largemouth bass, white bass, channel catfish, and crappie. Hunters find the park's perimeter lands bountiful with bobwhite quail, squirrel, rabbit, dove, and waterfowl. Rental bicycles and boat-launching ramps are available here.

Keystone's twenty-one cabins perch on a hillside with a view of Keystone Lake and Dam. The cabins come in two floor plans: one bedroom with a living room / kitchenette, and two bedrooms with a living room / kitchenette. The sixteen two-bedroom duplex units have rough cedar siding and baths with showers; five of these have fireplaces. Keystone's five one-bedroom cabins were built of rough cedar on support piers (because of the steep slope) ten years ago. Each of the one-bedroom cabins has a wooden patio deck with red-cedar furniture, and a cozy fireplace. All cabins are heated and air-conditioned.

Nearby attractions include tours of Keystone Dam and of Tulsa's oil refineries. Tulsa is also the home of the Thomas Gilcrease Institute of American History and Art, the world's largest collection of art and artifacts of western history.

Keystone State Park is sixteen miles west of Tulsa, Oklahoma, on Rte. 151. Cabins available year-round. Rates: $40 to $50 per night for two people. Cash, checks, Visa, and MasterCard accepted. Reservations taken up to eighteen months in advance, recommended six months in advance for summer.

LAKE MURRAY STATE PARK
P.O. Box 1649
ARDMORE, OK 73402
(800) 522-8565 (in-state reservations)
(800) 654-8240 (reservations from neighboring states)
(405) 521-2464 (all other reservations)
(405) 223-4044 (park office)
(405) 223-6600 (resort)

On a rocky cliff high above the waters of Lake Murray, a limestone castle with a tall tower reaches into the sky. Originally designed as summer quarters for the governor of Oklahoma, this unique structure now holds the Tucker Tower Nature Center, named for Fred Tucker, a former state senator from Ardmore. The tower was constructed prior to World War II, but the advent of the war stopped work on the project before the castle's interior could be completed. It never was used as a summer home for Oklahoma governors.

The clear blue waters of Lake Murray (5728 acres) are the backdrop for a gracious resort hotel. Built in the 1950s of rock and rugged timber, the fifty-four-room lodge features a spacious lobby and dining room, a game room, a swimming pool, a lounge, and comfortable western decor.

The park's eighty-eight cabins range from Civilian Conservation Corps–era frame structures with stone fireplaces to modern, two-bedroom cabins that date from the 1950s. The modern, one- and two-bedroom villas have rock walls halfway up their exteriors, and wood frame on the top half. They have fireplaces and central heat and air conditioning, but no kitchens. The CCC-vintage "fisherman" cabins also are heated and air-conditioned; they include kitchenettes.

This south-central Oklahoma state park lies in the Cross Timbers region of the state — a savannah-type habitat composed of post-oak and blackjack forest, interspersed with pockets of tall prairie grass. Lake Murray's sparkling waters — reputed to be the clearest in the state — hold fine catches of black and sand bass, crappie, and catfish. A marina rents all types of boats, including paddleboats, sailboats, canoes, and jet skis. Other recreation facilities include a nine-hole golf course, tennis courts, and miniature golf. Two thousand acres have been set aside for motorcycles, and Lake Murray has a twenty-five-hundred-foot, paved and lighted airstrip.

Lake Murray State Park is seven miles south of Ardmore, Oklahoma, on Rte. 77. Cabins and lodge open year-round. Rates: cabins, $25 to $65 per night; lodge, $45 to $49 per night for two people. Cash, checks, Visa, MasterCard, and American Express accepted. Reservations taken up to one year in advance, recommended two months in advance for May through September.

LAKE TEXOMA STATE PARK
P.O. Box 248
KINGSTON, OK 73439
(800) 522-8565 *(in-state reservations)*
(800) 654-8240 *(reservations from neighboring states)*
(405) 521-2464 *(all other reservations)*
(405) 564-2566 *(park office)*

Lake Texoma Resort overlooks the blue-green expanse of ninety-three-thousand-acre Lake Texoma, and is surrounded by two thousand acres of parkland. This three-story hotel holds one hundred cheerful guest rooms, a cozy lobby with wood-burning fireplace, a restaurant, and a private club. The thirty-year-old facility is located near a full-service marina and an eighteen-hole golf course.

Just down the road are sixty-nine cabins, in two distinct floor plans. The duplex cabins feature combined sleeping / living areas, baths with showers, and kitchenettes. The deluxe cabins offer two bedrooms, living rooms, complete kitchens, and fireplaces. Some Texoma cabins have views of the lake; all are built of concrete block, and provide telephones and televisions.

Lake Texoma occupies the north shore of the Red River, the boundary between Texas and Oklahoma. Bass, catfish, and sunfish swarm in the lake, and anglers take advantage of the park's enclosed fishing dock. A favorite among the fishing crowd is the newly introduced striped bass. Tennis courts, rental bicycles, hiking trails, rental boats, launching ramps, a swimming pool, and horseback riding round out the recreational facilities. A lighted, paved, three-thousand-foot airstrip also serves the park.

At Tishomingo, north of Lake Texoma, stands the

Chickasaw Council House and Museum. Built in 1856, the log council house was the first capital the Chickasaws established in Oklahoma. Exhibits include artifacts that date from the Chickasaw's resettlement here in the Southwest. Also in Tishomingo is the Arrowhead Museum, which displays stone artifacts, glassware, fossils, and household items in addition to hunting points. Nearby Denison, Texas, is the birthplace of President Dwight D. Eisenhower.

Lake Texoma State Park is fifteen miles west of Durant, Oklahoma, on Rte. 70. Cabins and lodge open year-round. Rates: cabins, $55 to $75 per night; lodge, $49 to $53 per night for two people. Cash, checks, Visa, MasterCard, and American Express accepted. Reservations taken up to four years in advance, recommended one year in advance for summer. Two-night minimum rental on summer weekends.

OSAGE HILLS STATE PARK
RED EAGLE ROUTE, BOX 84
PAWHUSKA, OK 74056
(800) 522-8565 (in-state reservations)
(800) 654-8240 (reservations from neighboring states)
(405) 521-2464 (all other reservations)
(918) 336-4141 (park office)

Seven of Osage Hills State Park's eight cabins are fifty-year-old stone structures that enclose three rooms, including one bedroom. The eighth was built in the early 1980s, and has two bedrooms. The one-bedroom cabins sleep up to four people, the two-bedroom unit can handle six, and all are equipped with heating, air conditioning, kitchens, bathrooms, and fireplaces. Enjoy a family cookout at your barbecue grill and picnic table. Tall trees shade the entire cabin area.

This northeastern Oklahoma park's entertainments include an eighteen-acre lake with rental rowboats, a swimming pool and bathhouse, a tennis court, and a softball diamond. Hiking trails meander throughout the 1005-acre park, and children will enjoy the playground equipment. You can saddle a horse at the park stable for a leisurely trail ride.

Nearby attractions include the Osage Tribal Museum and Osage Country Historical Museum in Pawhuska, Oklahoma, and the Tom Mix Museum in Dewey, Oklahoma. Many points of interest await in Bartlesville, Oklahoma, such as the H.V. Foster Mansion, the Frank Phillips Home, the Phillips Exhibit Hall, and Price Tower.

Osage Hills State Park is eleven miles west of Bartlesville, Oklahoma, on Rte. 60. Cabins available year-round. Rates: $35 per night for two people. Cash, checks, Visa, and MasterCard accepted. Reservations taken up to one year in advance, recommended one month in advance for summer.

QUARTZ MOUNTAIN STATE PARK
ROUTE 1, BOX 40
LONE WOLF, OK 73655
(800) 522-8565 *(in-state reservations)*
(800) 654-8240 *(reservations from neighboring states)*
(405) 521-2464 *(all other reservations)*
(405) 563-2238 *(park office)*

Rising out of the southwest Oklahoma prairie, the granite Wichita Mountains provide unexpected and dramatic relief to the surrounding flatlands. Bordering Lake Altus Reservoir, Quartz Mountain State Park encompasses 4284 acres of this mountainous and partially wooded terrain.

Life is abundant in the mountains. As many as 260 different species of birds have been recorded; in summer, the turkey vulture is the most common, soaring high above mountain and plain. Majestic golden and southern bald eagles winter in the park.

In spring, the mountainsides and wooded lowlands explode in a profusion of color as wild flowers bloom. Bright yellow threadleaves are everywhere, but a closer inspection will reveal many others, among them red-and-yellow Indian blanket. Some of the most enchanting blooms are found on the prickly-pear and barrel cactus.

Long before Europeans set foot on the new continent, Native Americans inhabited this region. One archaeological site here, a mammoth kill, dates from ten to twenty thousand years ago. Gold, silver, zinc, and other precious metals were mined in the mountains during the nineteenth and twentieth centuries, but the mines never produced enough to be profitable.

Overnight visitors at Quartz Mountain State Park choose among fourteen cabins and a forty-two room lodge. The two-bedroom cabins, approximately fifteen years old, sleep from four to six people. Each has central heating and air conditioning and a full kitchen, and many are equipped with outdoor barbecue grills. Quartz Mountain Lodge is a natural wood structure that blends effortlessly with its surroundings. Lodge amenities include a restaurant, a private club, a pool, and a sauna indoors, plus tennis courts, another pool, and a putting green outdoors.

Recreation at Quartz Mountain focuses on the lakefront, and takes the form of swimming, boating, and fishing for catfish, bass, and walleye. Rental bicycles are available at the lodge, and a nine-hole golf course challenges enthusiasts. Trails explore craggy Quartz Mountain.

Quartz Mountain State Park is sixteen miles north of Altus, Oklahoma, on Rte. 44. Cabins and lodge open year-round. Rates: cabins, $50 to $65 per night; lodge, $44 to $48 per night for two people. Cash, checks, Visa, MasterCard, and American Express accepted. Reservations taken up to eighteen months in advance, recommended three to six months in advance for summer.

ROBBERS CAVE STATE PARK
P.O. Box 9
WILBURTON, OK 74578
(800) 522-8565 (in-state reservations)
(800) 654-8240 (reservations from neighboring states)
(405) 521-2464 (all other reservations)
(918) 465-2565 (park office)

Robbers Cave, which got its name through use by notorious outlaw gangs as a hideout, also sheltered deserters from both the Union and Confederate armies during the Civil War. After the war, guerrilla bands of robbers made it a rendezvous between raids. Stories of hidden treasure have prompted expeditions into the cave; the last, in 1931, was by three men from Texas who departed suddenly, some say with the booty.

The eighty-four-hundred-acre, eastern Oklahoma park is split by the Fourche Maline, a clear mountain stream that feeds fifty-two-acre Lake Carlton and provides excellent fishing throughout the year. The lake beach, in season, is often thronged by swimmers. Equally enticing are the picnic tables and outdoor fireplaces scattered throughout the park, which help to attract thousands of visitors annually.

Bass, catfish, and perch abound in Lake Carlton and two other small lakes in the park. Pines, oaks, and hickories dominate the landscape, along with towering sandstone formations. Rental bicycles and miniature golf also please park guests.

Robbers Cave's twenty-six cabins, including four new pine-sided structures, have one or two bedrooms and sleep four to six people. All are heated and air-conditioned, and come with complete kitchens, baths with showers, and fireplaces or wood stoves. These wooden cabins perch on a hilltop that is nestled by southern pines, blackjack oaks, and hickories, away from the bustle of the central park area. Down below shimmers Coon Creek Lake.

Robbers Cave State Park is five miles north of Wilburton, Oklahoma, on Rte. 2. Cabins available year-round. Rates: $35 to $45 per night. Cash, checks, Visa, and MasterCard accepted. Reservations taken up to eighteen months in advance, recommended twelve to eighteen months in advance for April through October.

ROMAN NOSE STATE PARK
P.O. Box 227
WATONGA, OK 73772
(800) 522-8565 *(in-state reservations)*
(800) 654-8240 *(reservations from neighboring states)*
(405) 521-2464 *(all other reservations)*
(405) 623-4215 *(park office)*
(405) 623-7281 *(resort)*

Chief Henry Roman Nose led the Cheyennes from 1897 until his death in 1917. Roman Nose's father camped in this area first, attracted by the protection its canyon offered in winter, several fine springs, good timber, and plenty of game. In 1892, this section of northwest Oklahoma was opened to white settlement, and the Cheyenne were simultaneously given allotments of land. Chief Henry Roman Nose and his family received what is today Roman Nose State Park as their allotment.

Roman Nose State Park is snuggled within a lush canyon cut into bluffs of red shale and white gypsum. Cool, fresh springs enhance the parkland; the largest, Spring of Everlasting Waters, flows at six hundred gallons per minute. Buffalo grass and yucca on the mesa tops give way to cedar and oak breaks at lower elevations, and cottonwood, hackberry, elm, chinaberry, and blackwillow decorate the bottomland.

Five duplex cabins accommodate up to four people each, along a row of evergreens overlooking Bitter Creek. Each unit has kitchen appliances, a bathroom, a living area, and a bedroom. All provide heating and air conditioning, and two have outdoor grills and picnic tables.

Roman Nose Resort Lodge offers twenty original rooms, twenty-six larger rooms with double queen beds, and one suite with a queen-size bed and a private whirlpool. Built in 1956, this rustic lodge pleases visitors with two dining rooms, a theater, numerous meeting rooms, and a game room.

Visiting swimmers can dive into crisp waters at a natural rock swimming pool, or venture to Lake Watonga or Lake Boecher. A boat-launching ramp serves Watonga, while rowboats and paddleboats can be rented at Lake Boecher. A nine-hole golf course, rental bicycles, and a lighted tennis court complete this park's faciilties.

Roman Nose State Park is seven miles north of Watonga, Oklahoma, on Rte. 8A. Cabins and lodge open year-round. Rates: cabins, $45 per night; lodge, $44 to $58 per night for two people. Cash, checks, Visa, MasterCard, and American Express accepted. Reservations taken up to two years in advance, recommended six months to a year in advance for summer.

SEQUOYAH STATE PARK
WESTERN HILLS GUEST RANCH
P.O. Box 509
WAGONER, OK 74477
(800) 522-8565 (in-state reservations)
(800) 654-8240 (reservations from neighboring states)
(405) 521-2464 (all other reservations)
(918) 772-2046 (park office)

Western Hills Guest Ranch is set on a peninsula in twenty-eight-hundred-acre Sequoyah State Park, on nineteen-thousand-acre Fort Gibson Lake. To the north and east lie the rugged foothills of the Boston Mountains; to the south, the timbered Cookson Hills. Sequoyah, the site of a state waterfowl refuge, is known for its abundance of deer, wild turkey, fox, squirrels, and other wildlife.

The lodge's ninety-nine guest rooms and twelve cabanas form a semicircle at the tip of the peninsula, enclosing a spacious swimming pool. Early American decor graces this rustic structure, which offers meeting rooms, three dining rooms, indoor games, and movies. Not far from the lodge stand forty-two cabins in duplex and fourplex formats, built of concrete block and stone. These one- and two-bedroom cabins have heating, air conditioning, full kitchens, and baths with showers.

Stagecoach rides, horseback rides, and tram rides all explore the park and lakefront, and an eighteen-hole golf course, tennis courts, and rental paddleboats and bicycles are available. Occasional campfires, hayrides, cookouts, and outdoor concerts may spice up your visit. Fishing, swimming, boating, and skiing all prevail on Fort Gibson Lake. Aviators alight at the park's thirty-three-hundred-foot, paved and lighted airstrip.

Eastern Oklahoma is where Civil War troops fought a battle that historians call the "Gettysburg of the West," which ended Confederate influence in Indian territory. East of the park is Tsa-La-Gi, an accurate reconstruction of a 1600s Cherokee village. Native Americans at Tsa-La-Gi bring their heritage to life with demonstrations of food preparation, canoe making, weaving, and basket making. Southwest of Sequoyah, the Five Civilized Tribes Museum houses exhibits and artifacts of the Cherokee,

Chickasaw, Choctaw, Creek, and Seminole tribes, plus a fine library and a gallery of traditional Indian art.

Sequoyah State Park is eight miles east of Wagoner, Oklahoma, on Rte. 51. Cabins and lodge open year-round. Rates: cabins, $45 to $70 per night, lodge, $45 to $53 per night for two people. Cash, checks, Visa, Master-Card, and American Express accepted. Reservations recommended six months in advance for summer, two-night minimum on summer weekends.

TENKILLER STATE PARK
STAR ROUTE BOX 169
VIAN, OK 74962
(800) 522-8565 *(in-state reservations)*
(800) 654-8240 *(reservations from neighboring states)*
(405) 521-2464 *(all other reservations)*
(918) 489-5643 *(park office)*

Escape from your workaday routine to the serene world of sparkling streams, wooded hills, and tufted prairies in eastern Oklahoma. Here, the world's greatest concentration of man-made lakes complements the beauty of the verdant terrain with vast expanses of water. Open the door to the rich Oklahoma Indian and western heritages, preserved in outstanding museums and such cultural celebrations as Indian powwows and rodeos.

Crystal-clear Lake Tenkiller, with its 136-mile shoreline, lies in the rolling Cookson Hills. Tenkiller boasts populations of largemouth, smallmouth, and white bass, sunfish, crappie, walleye, and catfish. Anglers take on rainbow trout in the Illinois River, below the dam on the lake. Scuba diving, skiing, boating, and swimming are other favorite activities; they are facilitated by the park's three launching ramps, marina, and swimming pool.

Thickly wooded with oak, hickory, cedar, pine, sycamore, cottonwood, dogwood, redbud, and a few tulip trees, Tenkiller State Park hosts extensive wildlife. Its hilly and rocky acreage rests along a flyway for migratory birds, making it a bird-watcher's delight.

Tenkiller's twenty duplex cabins are grouped in a semicircle; each has a private drive and is shaded by many trees. Set along the lakefront, these one- and two-bedroom cabins feature single baths and combination living / dining / kitchen areas. Most of these native-rock cabins have central heating and air conditioning; eight come with wood-burning fireplaces. Vinyl floors and paneled walls form the interiors of these twenty-five-year-old cabins. The park also has ten sleeping cabins with no kitchen facilities. The Driftwood Restaurant serves breakfast, lunch, and dinner from April through October.

Tenkiller State Park is seven miles northeast of Gore, Oklahoma, on Rte. 100. Cabins available year-round. Rates: $26 to $50 per night. Cash, checks, Visa, and MasterCard accepted. Reservations taken eighteen months in advance, recommended that early for summer. Two-night minimum on summer weekends.

WISTER STATE PARK
ROUTE 2, BOX 6B
WISTER, OK 74966
(800) 522-8565 (in-state reservations)
(800) 654-8240 (reservations from neighboring states)
(405) 521-2464 (all other reservations)
(918) 655-7756 (park office)

Two runestones, one unearthed near Heavener, the other near Poteau, have established that Norse Vikings were in this part of eastern Oklahoma in the eleventh century. Choctaw Indians discovered the Heavener runestone in the 1830s, when Oklahoma was still Indian territory. For many years, its inscription was thought to be Indian writing. It was not until 1959 that the Heavener inscription was officially recognized as rune characters. The Poteau runestone was found on a hilltop in 1967. The date inscribed on the Poteau runestone has been interpreted as November 11, 1017, or exactly five years later than the date on the Heavener runestone.

Lake Wister claims a four-thousand-acre surface and 115 miles of scenic shoreline. Fishing for largemouth and smallmouth bass, catfish, crappie, and sunfish is excellent. Swimmers choose from a lakefront pool and the lake itself, and boating and waterskiing are other favorite activities.

Half a dozen creeks and streams flow into the lake,

including Poteau River, the only Oklahoma river that flows in a northerly direction. Lining those waterways are woods of pine, oak, elm, and cedar, highlighted with dogwood, redbud, wild cherry, and northern spruce. An abundance of flowering shrubs, native grasses, and wild flowers unfold breathtaking panoramas each season. The handsome Winding Stair Mountains form a backdrop for this park's wooded hillsides and lakefront meadows.

Wister's fifteen cabins (twelve duplexes, three single cabins) have rough wood exteriors, and will accommodate up to four people apiece. Each has a single bedroom, a bathroom, and a combination living room / kitchen, plus heating and air conditioning. Two cabins include fireplaces, five have four-burner hot plates in lieu of a stove, and all are equipped with outdoor barbecue grills.

Wister State Park is two miles south of Wister, Oklahoma, on Rte. 270. Cabins available year-round. Rates: $35 to $40 per night for two people. Cash, checks, Visa, and MasterCard accepted. Reservations taken up to eighteen months in advance, recommended six months in advance for April through September.

Texas

STATE PARK INFORMATION:
TEXAS PARKS AND WILDLIFE DEPARTMENT
4200 SMITH SCHOOL ROAD
AUSTIN, TX 78744
(800) 792-1112
(512) 479-4800

TOURISM INFORMATION:
TEXAS TOURIST DEVELOPMENT AGENCY
BOX 12008
CAPITOL STATION
AUSTIN, TX 78711
(512) 475-4326

STATE BIRD: *Mockingbird*
STATE TREE: *Pecan*
STATE FLOWER: *Bluebonnet*

Cabin, Big Bend National Park, Texas

BIB BEND NATIONAL PARK
BIG BEND NATIONAL PARK,
  TX 79834
(915) 477-2251

CHISOS MOUNTAIN LODGE
BASIN RURAL STATION
BIG BEND NATIONAL PARK,
  TX 79834
(915) 477-2291

Expanses of desert sweep away to remote horizons; mountain ranges rise abruptly above arid flatlands; sheer canyons and green, ribbonlike stretches of vegetation define the course of the Rio Grande, here at the great curve of the river in southwestern Texas. Visitors to this 750,000-acre park see well-preserved remains of animals that lived millions of years ago, smell the aroma of creosote bushes, hear the calls of exotic birds, and sense the lingering echo of a Comanche war cry.

Boquillas Canyon, which was cut through the Sierra del Carmen range by the Rio Grande, is the longest of Big Bend's famous gorges. The evening sun seems to set fire to the face of Sierra del Carmen; across the river, the Mexican village of Boquillas glistens with golden light.

Hikers often climb Lost Mine Trail to a sweeping view across Juniper Canyon to the colorful South Rim. Casa Grande, a towering monolith, looms majestically two thousand feet above, while below, an incredible panorama of mountains, canyons, and desert extends beyond the Rio Grande into the purple distance of Mexico.

Rent a horse at the corral, and you can ride with skilled wranglers on a fourteen-mile journey to the spectacular South Rim. Big Bend's hiking trails vary greatly in length and difficulty, ranging from a two-mile Lost Mine Trail to desert paths many miles long that circumnavigate the Chisos Mountains. More than one hundred miles of the Rio Grande forms the park's international boundary, and fishing for catfish, and float trips are popular river pastimes.

Chisos Mountain Lodge, a modern motel, and five stone cabins all occupy a magnificent setting fifty-four hundred feet above sea level. Midsummer temperatures in the desert and down in the river valley hover above one hundred degrees during the day; at fifty-four hundred feet, the daytime highs average a comfortable eighty-five degrees, and are followed by cool nights. From the lodge dining room, guests can admire outstanding vistas while sampling everything from hamburgers to top-quality steaks. Both the lodge and the twenty-eight-room motel were built of adobe block and limestone; they feature tile roofs and "ranch-oak" furnishings. Twenty of the motel rooms have air conditioning.

Big Bend National Park is eighty miles south of Marathon, Texas, on Rte. 385. Cabins and motel open year-round. Rates: cabins, $50 per night for two people; motel, $45 per night for two people. Cash, checks, Visa, and MasterCard accepted. Reservations taken up to one year in advance, recommended two to three months in advance.

BALMORHEA STATE RECREATION AREA
P.O. BOX 15
TOYAHVALE, TX 79786
(915) 375-2370

At Balmorhea State Recreation Area, the waters of San Solomon Springs gush into the world's largest spring-fed swimming pool. The pool differs from most public pools in several respects: its size (nearly two acres), its thirty-foot depth, and its year-round temperature of seventy-two to seventy-six degrees, not to mention the variety of aquatic life found in its clear water. With a capacity of three and a half million gallons, the pool offers plenty of room for swimmers, scuba divers, and skin divers.

Discharged at a rate of twenty-two to twenty-six million gallons per day, springwater flows from the pool through canals on its way to irrigate nearby farmland. Along with minnows, perch, catfish, and crayfish, two rare and endangered species inhabit the canals: the Comanche Springs pupfish and the Pecos mosquito fish.

This "oasis of West Texas," along the foothills of the Davis Mountains, has attracted man for thousands of years; artifacts indicate that Indians used the springs long before white settlers arrived. The canals, which have been constructed since the 1850s, facilitated large-scale irrigation.

Mule deer, white-tailed deer, raccoons, javelina, porcupines, coyotes, and bobcats also savor the spring waters' relief from intense summer heat. Plant life here consists of a mixture of wetland, desert scrub, and grassland, and includes such large native shade trees as Rio Grande cottonwood, velvet ash, sycamore, hackberry, and desert willow.

Like all buildings at Balmorhea, the forty-year-old, eighteen-unit motel-type lodge features Spanish-style architecture. Each unit is heated and air-conditioned, and some have kitchenettes. An outdoor barbecue grill and a picnic table facilitate an evening cookout, on a porch that looks out on the pupfish canals.

Nearby attractions include Fort Davis National Historic Site, with its museum and reconstructed barracks. Visitors also tour the University of Texas McDonald Observatory, at Mount Locke.

Balmorhea State Recreation Area is four miles west of Balmorhea, Texas, on Rte. 290. Lodging available year-round. Rates: $20 per night for two people. Cash and in-state checks accepted. Reservations taken up to one year in advance, recommended one month in advance for summer.

Bastrop, the first settlement in Stephen F. Austin's "little colony," was founded in 1829 at the Colorado River crossing of El Camino Real (the "king's road" between San Antonio and Nacogdoches). Originally called Mina, after a martyred Spanish revolutionary, the outpost's name was changed to honor Felipe Enrique Neri, Baron de Bastrop, who was Austin's land commissioner and longtime friend.

Bastrop State Park, in central Texas, includes some of the famous Lost Pines of Texas — a loblolly-pine woodland isolated from the main body of East Texas "piney woods" by approximately one hundred miles of rolling post oak. Ten of this park's 3503 acres consist of a small fishing lake that is stocked with bass and channel catfish. Small boats are permitted on the lake, but no launching ramps are provided. Swimmers cool off in a large pool, equipped with a diving board and two wading areas.

Accommodations here encompass twelve cabins and a group lodge. Built of hand-hewn timber and native stone by Civilian Conservation Corps workers in the late 1930s, the cabins rest under pines, oaks, and cedars near the lake. They sleep up to six people apiece and have evaporative coolers, space heaters, and homey fireplaces. The group lodge accommodates up to eight people in four bedrooms, each of which opens onto a screened porch overlooking the lake. Both the cabins and the lodge have full kitchens.

Nearby Lake Bastrop offers nine hundred acres of boating, swimming, fishing, and waterskiing. Austin, the state capital, is only half an hour away. Buescher State Park, just east of Bastrop, is known for its deep forests.

Bastrop State Park is one mile east of Bastrop, Texas, on Rte. 21. Cabins and group lodge available year-round. Rates: cabins $18 per night for two people; group lodge, $40 per night. Cash and checks accepted. Reservations taken up to ninety days in advance.

CADDO LAKE STATE PARK
ROUTE 2, BOX 15
KARNACK, TX 75661
(214) 679-3351

The Caddo Indians believed that Caddo Lake, a maze of channels and bayous covering 32,700 acres, was created by their Great Spirit. According to legend, a Caddo chief who was warned in a dream of oncoming danger moved his tribe to higher ground as heavy rains began. The earth trembled and cracked, water rushed in, and the lake was formed.

Caddo Lake actually exists because of the Great Raft, a series of natural logjams that blocked the Red River in the 1800s and forced water back up its tributaries. The lake then served as part of the route for vessels coming upriver from New Orleans to Jefferson — once the largest inland port in Texas and an important agricultural trading center — and to Port Caddo. In 1873 and 1874, the Army Corp of Engineers cleared the river's channel, causing a severe drop in the lake's level and the end of commercial river traffic here in northeast Texas. Jefferson lost its former glory and much of its population, and Port Caddo disappeared entirely.

Caddo Lake State Park spreads out along the upper end of the lake. Once the South's largest natural lake, it is now reinforced with a dam. Channels or "boat roads" amble through thousands of acres of moss-draped cypress groves; in late summer, hyacinths and water lilies add to the beauty. Anglers stalk these waterways for white, yellow, black, and Florida bass, plus perch, crappie, and catfish, including spoonbills. Rental canoes and boat-launching ramps can be found at Cypress Bayou, the "road" to the main lake, and swimmers enjoy the water near the docks. Hiking Caddo's trails, you explore piney woods, hardwood bottomlands, and cypress swamps, all teeming with wildlife.

Built of wood on rock frames, the nine fifty-year-old cabins here accommodate up to six people apiece. Each has a kitchen, heating, air conditioning, attic fans, a bath, and rich hardwood floors. The cabins also offer outdoor barbecue grills and picnic tables.

Nearby points of interest include more than thirty historic buildings in Jefferson, Texas, which in recent years has undergone a meticulous restoration. Karnack, Texas, is the childhood home of Lady Bird Johnson, widow of the late president.

Caddo Lake State Park is fifteen miles north of Marshall, Texas, off Rte. 43. Cabins available year-round. Rates: $18 per night for two people. Cash and checks accepted. Reservations taken up to ninety days in advance, recommended that early for summer.

DAINGERFIELD STATE PARK
ROUTE 1, BOX 286-B
DAINGERFIELD, TX 75638
(214) 645-2921

Iron ore, a significant resource in this slice of northeast Texas, can still be extracted in a four-county area that centers on Daingerfield State Park. During the Civil War, this region developed into an iron industrial center, with factories manufacturing guns and other metal products. Sawmills, woodworking plants, and coke ovens also thrived here at one time.

Splendid East Texas pines blanket this 551-acre park, along with sweet gums, willows, and oaks. This forest of mixed pines and hardwoods has been managed as a preserve since the 1930s. A two-and-a-half-mile hiking trail circles quiet, eighty-acre Lake Daingerfield, which is popular for swimming, small-craft boating, and fishing for black bass, crappie, catfish, and pickerel. Swimmers take advantage of a grassy beach, and paddleboats, canoes, and fishing boats can be rented. A small earthen dam holds back the lake's spring-fed waters, and visitors savor a soothing waterfall just beyond the dam.

One Daingerfield hiking trail passes through a stand of dogwoods and by beds of cinnamon ferns that grow along hillside seepage. A large old chinquapin tree, once a state champion, highlights another trail. Rare, red-cockaded woodpeckers nest in pines along the lakefront, and large pileated woodpeckers can be heard hammering away at decaying pine bark.

Two of this park's three cabins have rough cedar siding;

the third was built of concrete block and clay tile. The two smaller cabins each sleep up to six people, while the larger one can handle eight. All have kitchens, baths with showers, heating, air conditioning, and outdoor grills and tables. Daingerfield also offers a group lodge, built in the late 1930s, which can accommodate up to twenty-eight people.

Daingerfield State Park is three miles east of Daingerfield, Texas, on Rte. 49. Cabins and lodge available year-round. Rates: cabins, $18 per night for two people; lodge, $65 per night for twenty people. Cash and checks accepted. Reservations taken up to ninety days in advance, recommended that early year-round.

DAVIS MOUNTAINS STATE PARK
P.O. Box 786
FORT DAVIS, TX 79734
(915) 426-3254, 426-3337

Hugging a hillside in the Davis Mountains, Texas's most extensive mountain range, Indian Lodge has white adobe walls eighteen inches thick. Constructed by the Civilian Conservation Corps in 1933, the lodge offers thirty-nine guest rooms, a dining room, a heated swimming pool, and a view of the rocky ledges and slopes that typify this park's landscape. An elevation of five thousand feet provides surprisingly cool summers here in West Texas, and winters too are mild.

Massive beams of rough-hewn timber support the lodge's lobby, which is appointed with CCC-built furniture from the 1930s. Fifteen original guest rooms also feature CCC furniture, along with charming fireplaces (no longer functional). All of the lodge's guest rooms are air-conditioned and sleep up to four people.

A four-mile trail runs parallel to Limpia Creek, which carries runoff from Keesey Canyon. The path climbs to this park's highest point — a splendid overlook of mountains and canyons. Mule deer, javelina, raccoons, and mouflon sheep roam rugged slopes populated with cacti, oak, and juniper.

Nearby attractions include McDonald Observatory, thirteen miles away on Mount Locke, and Fort Davis

National Historic Site. Fort Davis, once a Texas frontier fort, now has a museum full of military and pioneer mementos and artifacts, housed within reconstructed barracks. Established in 1854 and active until 1891, Fort Davis, which is three miles from Davis Mountains State Park, can be reached by automobile or hiking trail.

Davis Mountains State Park is three miles north of Fort Davis, Texas, on Rte. 118. Lodge open year-round. Rates: $22 to $32 per night for two people. Cash and checks accepted. Reservations taken up to one year in advance, recommended six months in advance for March through October.

GARNER STATE PARK
CONCAN, TX 78838
(512) 232-6131, 232-6132

Thousands of years ago, as the Frio River was forming, it met an impasse in the form of a massive limestone mountain. The rushing waters gradually chiseled away that mountain, leaving a towering cliff now know as Old Baldy. Its sheer face and wondrous crags rise seventeen hundred feet above sea level (six hundred feet above the Frio), affording a panorama of Garner State Park and the distant green hills of the Edwards Plateau.

The cold, spring-fed Frio (Spanish for "cold") borders this 1420-acre, south-central Texas park for almost two miles. Grassy, shaded banks lure picnickers, while swimmers and boaters take to the river on rented paddleboats and inner tubes. Many enjoy wading the shallows, where pristine water flows gently over a bed of solid rock. Anglers try their luck for catfish, bass, and perch.

Named for John Nance "Cactus Jack" Garner, vice-president under Franklin Roosevelt, Garner State Park comprises grand hills, canyons, and grassy meadows. Large bald cypress, oak, elm, and pecan trees border the sparkling Frio River, and cedar, wild cherry, persimmon, and madrone drape the hilly slopes. Ferns and mosses grow profusely in ravines; during blooming season, hikers encounter valleys blanketed with wild flowers. Stables a few miles from the park facilitate trail riding.

Garner's eighteen cabins each have a bedroom, a bath,

a living area, and a kitchen. Constructed of cypress boards and rock and topped with cedar shingles, these CCC-era cabins feature gas wall furnaces and attic fans. Oak furniture fills the cabins, and fourteen of them have delightful stone fireplaces.

Nearby attractions include Garner Memorial Museum in Uvalde, and the ruins of several missions. One of the earliest missions in this area, Mission Nuestra Señora de la Candelaria del Cañon, founded in 1762, stands on the banks of the Nueces River.

Garner State Park is seven miles north of Concan, Texas, on Rte. 83. Cabins available year-round. Rates: $18 per night for two people. Cash and in-state checks accepted. Reservations taken up to ninety days in advance; recommended that early for May through September, and all holidays and weekends.

LAKE BROWNWOOD STATE RECREATION AREA
ROUTE 5, BOX 160
BROWNWOOD, TX 76801
(915) 784-5223

Once known as Thirty-sixth Division State Park, in honor of World War II troops who trained at nearby Camp Bowie, Lake Brownwood's seventy-three hundred acres blend aquatic recreation with scenic rock bluffs and picturesque hills in central Texas. Pecan Bayou and Jim Ned Creek feed the expansive lake, which has ninety-three miles of shoreline, numerous bays and peninsulas, and several islands worth exploring.

Civilian Conservation Corps workers built many of the structures here in the 1930s, utilizing native timber and rock. Because of Lake Brownwood's proximity to several physiographic regions of Texas, flora and fauna in the park reflect the Cross Timbers and North Central prairies as well as those of the Edwards Plateau. Apache and Comanche Indians hunted deer, quail, turkey, and squirrel here long before white settlers arrived in the mid-1850s.

Oak and mesquite trees separate Lake Brownwood's seventeen stone cabins, which trace the lakefront along the park's southern boundary. These fifty-year-old cabins range in size from a combination living room / bedroom to two-bedroom models. Each has a stone fireplace. They also come equipped with a complete kitchen, a bath with shower, heating, and air conditioning. These cabins sleep up to six people apiece. Lake Brownwood's two group lodges accommodate ten and twenty-six people, respectively.

Not surprisingly, park activities center on Lake Brownwood; swimming, waterskiing, and fishing are favorites. A swimming beach, launching ramps, boat docks, a lighted fishing pier, and fish-cleaning facilities aid these pursuits, along with rental canoes and paddleboats.

Lake Brownwood State Recreation Area is twenty-two miles northwest of Brownwood, Texas, off Rte. 279. Cabins and lodges available year-round. Rates: cabins, $18 per night for two people; lodges, $50 to $80 per night basic charge. Cash and checks accepted. Reservations taken up to ninety days in advance, recommended that early for May through September and all weekends.

LANDMARK INN STATE HISTORIC SITE
P.O. Box 577
CASTROVILLE, TX 78009
(512) 538-2133

Landmark Inn, on the Medina River in historic Castroville, has reinvigorated weary travelers through south-central Texas for more than a century. Henri Castro, a French entrepreneur, acquired a colonization contract from the newly formed Republic of Texas in 1842; his followers founded Castroville in September, 1844. These colonists, most of whom came from the French-German provinces of Alsace and Lorraine, suffered Indian attacks, drought, and sickness, but they persevered and eventually prospered.

About 1849, Cesar Monod constructed what is now the first floor of the Landmark Inn, using the building as his home and as a general store. The property changed hands in 1853; the new owner, Irish immigrant John Vance, added second-story rooms, which he rented to travelers on the heavily trafficked road between San Antonio and El Paso. Vance also built a story-and-a-half residence between the Vance Hotel and the river, and a two-story bathhouse. Later owners constructed a stone gristmill behind the hotel that still exists today.

Furnishings in the inn's eight guest rooms represent various periods in Landmark's history; it's not uncommon to find an 1870 bed next to a 1930s washstand. Period floor coverings and curtains also distinguish the rooms, two of which occupy the bathhouse of stagecoach days. Five second-floor rooms open onto a quaint balcony, and eighteen-inch-thick walls and ceiling fans help cool the inn, which is heated but not air-conditioned.

A small orchard of apple, peach, and plum trees delights visitors here, as do the many large pecan trees, some more than three hundred years old. Located just half an hour west of San Antonio, the town of Castroville boasts numerous buildings that display Alsatian-style design of the mid-1800s. Visitors enjoy the natural swimming hole in the Medina River, or simply roam this delightful community, sampling Alsatian cooking and marveling at residents speaking Alsatian French.

Landmark Inn is at the corner of Florence and Florella streets, just off Rte. 90, in Castroville, Texas. Inn open year-round. Rates: $24 per night for two people. Cash and checks accepted. Reservations taken up to ninety days in advance, recommended that early for spring and fall.

POSSUM KINGDOM STATE RECREATION AREA
P.O. Box 36
CADDO, TX 76029
(817) 549-1803

Some thirty Texas longhorns graze in this sixteen-hundred-acre, north-central Texas park; they serve as a reminder of the history of the Palo Pinto Mountains and Brazos River Valley. In addition to longhorns, deer, jackrabbits, cottontail rabbits, bobcats, and (of course) possums inhabit the hilly terrain around Possum Kingdom Lake, along with less popular skunks and rattlesnakes. Formed by a dam on the Brazos River, the lake undulates up the valley, abruptly changing direction as it follows the riverbed. Renowned for its clear waters and more than three hundred miles of shoreline, Possum Kingdom Lake hosts boaters, skiers, scuba divers, and fishermen, who reel in bass, catfish, and crappie.

Boat-launching ramps assist those who have brought their own craft, while rental canoes allow visitors to explore the lake's many coves and inlets and to get a close-up look at the fascinating limestone formations here. One of the most popular formations is Hell's Gate — two towering, hundred-foot cliffs separated by a fifty-foot-wide canyon.

Shaded by cedars, oaks, and elms, and within walking distance of a swimming beach and a lighted fishing pier stand Possum Kingdom's six cabins. Built in the 1950s, these two-room cabins sleep up to four people on two double beds. Each is heated and air-conditioned, and has a kitchenette and a bath with shower. Five of the six feature wood-burning fireplaces, and all have outdoor barbecue grills.

Possum Kingdom State Recreation Area is seventeen miles north of Caddo, Texas, on Park Road 33. Cabins available year-round. Rates: $18 per night for two people. Cash and checks accepted. Reservations taken up to ninety days in advance, recommended that early year-round.

Utah

~~~~

STATE PARK INFORMATION:
Utah Division of Parks and Recreation
1636 West North Temple
Salt Lake City, UT 84116
(801) 533-6012

TOURISM INFORMATION:
Utah Travel Council
Council Hall, Capitol Hill
Salt Lake City, UT 84114
(801) 533-5681

STATE BIRD: *California Gull*
STATE MAMMAL: *Rocky Mountain Elk*
STATE TREE: *Blue Spruce*
STATE FLOWER: *Sego Lily*
STATE FISH: *Rainbow Trout*

BRYCE CANYON NATIONAL
   PARK
BRYCE CANYON, UT 84717
(801) 834-5322

TW SERVICES, INC.
   (LODGING)
P.O. Box 400
CEDAR CITY, UT 84720
(801) 586-7686

"The surface breaks off almost perpendicularly to a depth of several hundred feet . . . seems indeed as though the bottom dropped out and left rocks standing in all shapes and forms. There are thousands of red, white, purple and vermillion colored rocks resembling sentinels on the walls of castles . . . presenting the wildest and most wonderful scene that the eye of man ever beheld." Standing at Sunset Point, that's how T. C. Baily, a U.S. deputy surveyor, described the wonder of Bryce Canyon in 1876.

Its many bizarre stone shapes have conjured up all sorts of images: walls and windows, minarets, gables, pagodas and pedestals, temples, even platoons of Turkish soldiers in pantaloons! The Paiute Indians gave a name to Bryce Canyon that translates as: "red rocks standing like men in a bowl-shaped canyon."

Southwestern Utah's Bryce Canyon is not a canyon at all, but a spectacular amphitheater carved in the fifty- to sixty-million-year-old rock of the Pink Cliffs. The enormous, free-standing stone formations are the product of erosion by rain, snow, and ice. From sunrise to sunset, a changing tableau of color passes before you: vivid reds and yellows created by iron oxides in the rock, majestic purples and lavenders by manganese. Dazzling light plays upon the rock, creating an immense and breathtaking light show.

A second world can be found at higher elevations — the world of Bryce's forests. Toward Rainbow Point, Douglas-fir, white fir, blue spruce, and aspen shadow shrubs such as waxleaf current and common juniper. A pygmy forest composed of Utah juniper, pinyon pine, Fremont barberry, Gambel oak, and sagebrush struggles on the lower hills.

Hikers and horseback riders admire the delicately formed standing spires peculiar to Bryce Canyon. After a day on the trails, they settle down at Bryce Canyon Lodge, built by the Union Pacific Railroad in the late 1920s.

Listed on the National Register of Historic Places because of its unique architectural style, the lodge was built of native stone and timber at an elevation of eighty-five hundred feet above sea level. Inside is a delightful lobby with a huge stone fireplace, a post office, a gift shop, and a dining room.

Within walking distance of the lodge stand forty sleeping cabins, built in the 1930s. These adjoining units offer single bedrooms in two floor plans, but no kitchens. These log cabins each accommodate up to five people and contain private porches, fireplaces, and baths with showers. Seventy motel units, built of wood and native stone and open for the first time in 1985, complete the lodging options here.

Bryce Canyon National Park is twenty-five miles southeast of Panguitch, Utah, on Rte. 12. Cabins available mid-May to late September. Rates: $62 per night for two people. Cash, checks, Visa, MasterCard, and American Express accepted. Reservations recommended six to nine months in advance for summer.

ZION NATIONAL PARK
SPRINGDALE, UT 84767
(801) 772-3256

TW SERVICES, INC.
(LODGING)
P.O. BOX 400
CEDAR CITY, UT 84720
(801) 586-7686

Splashed with color, Zion's colossal mountains and ridges loom in contrast to the deep blue southwestern Utah sky. Meanwhile the Virgin River, deceptively tranquil at times, gouges deeper canyons and taller cliffs. From the canyon floor at four thousand feet elevation, monoliths ascend to eight thousand feet — exposed and fractured Navajo sandstone that takes on subtle hues of red, pink, yellow, and brown. Zion's rock layers reveal successive visitations of vast inland seas, tremendous earth upheavals, and the constant erosion here.

In Finger Canyons, the forces of deformation have folded the strata, and great blocks of bedrock have been thrust up and over themselves. Here towering "fingers" of sandstone resemble the bows of ships riding up on a beach.

The Virgin River, which runs along the floor of Zion Canyon, supports a narrow corridor of stream-bank woodland where broadleaf trees, birds, and small mammals abound. Deer inhabit the park's thickets of short evergreens and oaks, which are interrupted by open flats covered with low shrubs. High-country vegetation consists predominantly of ponderosa pine, quaking aspen, white fir, and Douglas-fir.

Zion's stark, mountainous, picturesque terrain pleases photographers, hikers, and horseback riders. The park's most popular trail snakes along the canyon's east wall, past cliffs trickling with streams. The Virgin River's quick waters funnel through the Narrows, echoing against the centuries-old sculpture in 160-million-year-old sandstone.

Open-air tram tours start at Zion Lodge, on the canyon floor near the river. Diners can enjoy a view of the canyon from the lodge's second-floor restaurant, which serves three meals daily during the season.

Nearby are Zion's forty duplex and fourplex sleeping cabins (no kitchens). These cabins, built in the 1930s, have porches and full baths and are heated and air-conditioned. Eighty new motel units, constructed of timber and stone, also accommodate park guests.

Zion National Park is three miles north of Springdale, Utah, on Rte. 9. Cabins available early May to early October. Rates: $54 per night for two people. Cash, checks, Visa, MasterCard, and American Express accepted. Reservations recommended in November or December for the following season.

INDEX